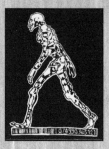

WHILE WORKING ON THIS
SERIES, I'VE BEEN LIVING
IN FEAR OF SHINIGAMI. AND
EVEN NOW THAT MY WORK
IS COMPLETE, I STILL CAN'T
BE SURE I'M SAFE. SO I
INTEND TO BE WARY OF
THEM FROM NOW ON.
– TAKESHI OBATA

Tsugumi Ohba
Born in Tokyo.
Hobby: Collecting teacups.
Day and night, develops manga plots
while holding knees on a chair.

Takeshi Obata was born in 1969 in Niigata, Japan, and
is the artist of the wildly popular SHONEN JUMP title
Hikaru no Go, which won the 2003 Tezuka Shinsei
"New Hope" award and the Shogakukan Manga award.
Obata is also the artist of **Arabian Majin Bokentan
Lamp Lamp**, **Ayatsuri Sakon**, and **Cyborg Jichan G.**

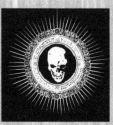

DEATH NOTE VOL 12
SHONEN JUMP ADVANCED Manga Edition

STORY BY TSUGUMI OHBA
ART BY TAKESHI OBATA

Translation & Adaptation/Tetsuichiro Miyaki
Touch-up Art & Lettering/Gia Cam Luc
Design/Sean Lee
Editor/Pancha Diaz

Printed in the U.S.A.

Published by VIZ Media, LLC
P.O. Box 77010
San Francisco, CA 94107

16
First printing, July 2007
Sixteenth printing, November 2015

www.viz.com

THE WORLD'S MOST
CUTTING-EDGE MANGA
SHONEN JUMP
ADVANCED
www.shonenjump.com

SHONEN JUMP ADVANCED MANGA

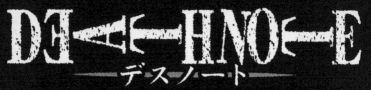

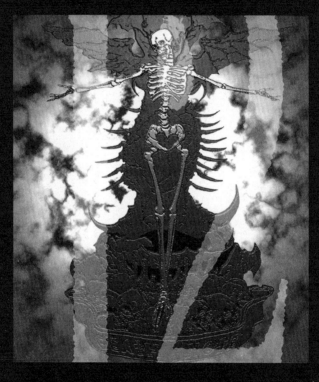

Vol. 12
Finis

Story by Tsugumi Ohba
Art by Takeshi Obata

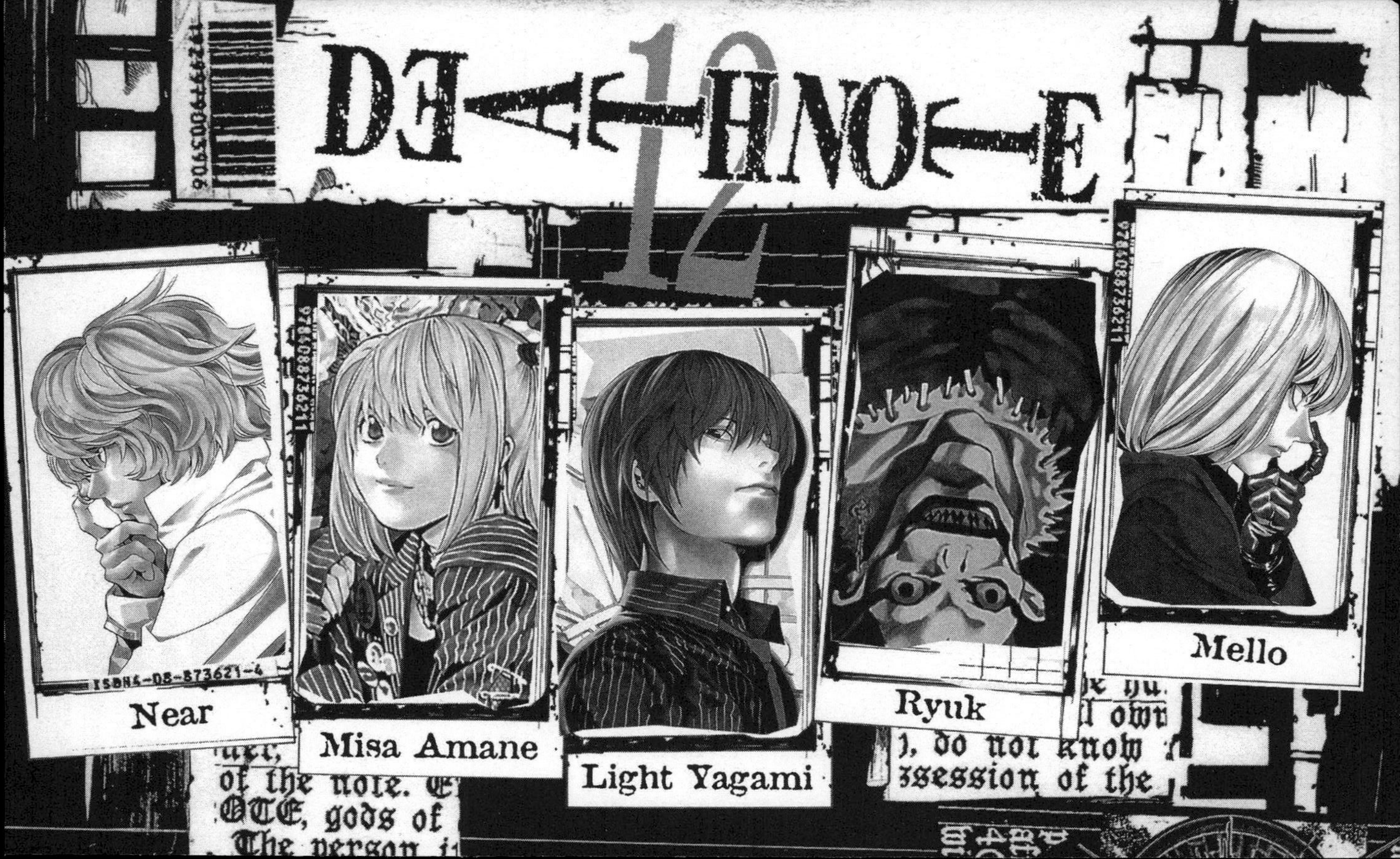
DEATH NOTE
12
Near
ISBN4-08-873621-4
Misa Amane
Light Yagami
Ryuk
Mello
of the note.
gods of
The person
do not know
ssession of the
l own

Lidner
Gevanni
Rester
Sayu Yagami
Sachiko Yagami
Soichiro Yagami
Kiyomi Takada
Teru Mikami
Matsuda
Ide
Aizawa
Mogi

"THE HUMAN WHOSE NAME IS WRITTEN IN THIS NOTE SHALL DIE"... LIGHT YAGAMI, A STRAIGHT-A HIGH SCHOOL HONORS STUDENT, PICKS UP THE "DEATH NOTE" DROPPED BY THE SHINIGAMI RYUK INTO THE HUMAN WORLD. INITIALLY HORRIFIED BY THE NOTEBOOK'S POWERS, LIGHT EVENTUALLY DECIDES TO USE THE DEATH NOTE TO PURGE THE WORLD OF VIOLENT CRIMINALS AND CREATE AN IDEAL SOCIETY. L, A SECRETIVE GENIUS WHO SPECIALIZES IN SOLVING UNSOLVED CASES, STRIVES TO TRACK DOWN KIRA, SETTING OFF AN ALMIGHTY BATTLE OF THE WITS BETWEEN LIGHT AND HIMSELF. BUT LIGHT FINALLY MANAGES TO GET RID OF L, LEAVING KIRA SEEMINGLY UNOPPOSED.

FOUR YEARS HAVE PASSED, AND LIGHT HAS TAKEN THE ROLE OF "THE SECOND L" WHILE CONTINUING TO SHAPE THE WORLD AS KIRA. BUT L'S TWO PROTÉGÉS HAVE BEGUN TO MAKE THEIR MOVE. AFTER DISCOVERING THE EXISTENCE OF THE DEATH NOTE, THEY BOTH CONCLUDE THAT ACQUIRING THE NOTEBOOK IS THE QUICKEST WAY TO GET KIRA, AND A SCRAMBLE FOR THE DEATH NOTE BEGINS.

MELLO'S INGENIOUS PLAN TO GET THE NOTEBOOK SUCCEEDS, AND HE LEARNS ABOUT THE FAKE "13 DAY RULE," BUT THE JAPANESE INVESTIGATION TEAM MANAGES TO REGAIN THE NOTEBOOK AND MELLO IS FORCED INTO HIDING. BUT RETRIEVING THE DEATH NOTE IS NOT WITHOUT COST, AND SOICHIRO YAGAMI IS FATALLY WOUNDED. AFTER A SERIES OF FURTHER INCIDENTS IN THE U.S., MELLO AND NEAR EXCHANGE INFORMATION. AFTER LEARNING OF THE FAKE "13 DAY RULE," NEAR BEGINS TO SUSPECT THAT THE NEW L IS KIRA, AND STARTS TO STIR THINGS UP IN THE JAPANESE TASKFORCE.

MEANWHILE, LIGHT HAS MISA ABANDON OWNERSHIP OF HER DEATH NOTE TO MAKE SURE NO EVIDENCE CAN BE LINKED TO HER, AND CHOOSES MIKAMI, A KIRA FOLLOWER, AS THE NEXT KIRA. BUT LIGHT IS UNDER SURVEILLANCE AND UNABLE TO GIVE DIRECT ORDERS TO HIS NEW PROTÉGÉ. BY COINCIDENCE, MIKAMI CHOOSES TAKADA, A NHN ANNOUNCER AND LIGHT'S COLLEGE GIRLFRIEND, AS THE NEW SPOKESPERSON FOR KIRA. LIGHT SEIZES THE OPPORTUNITY, AND SUCCEEDS IN CONTACTING MIKAMI THROUGH TAKADA.

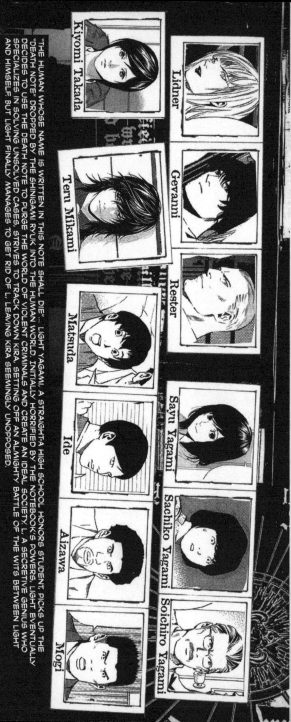

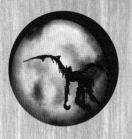

DEATH NOTE
Vol. 12

CONTENTS

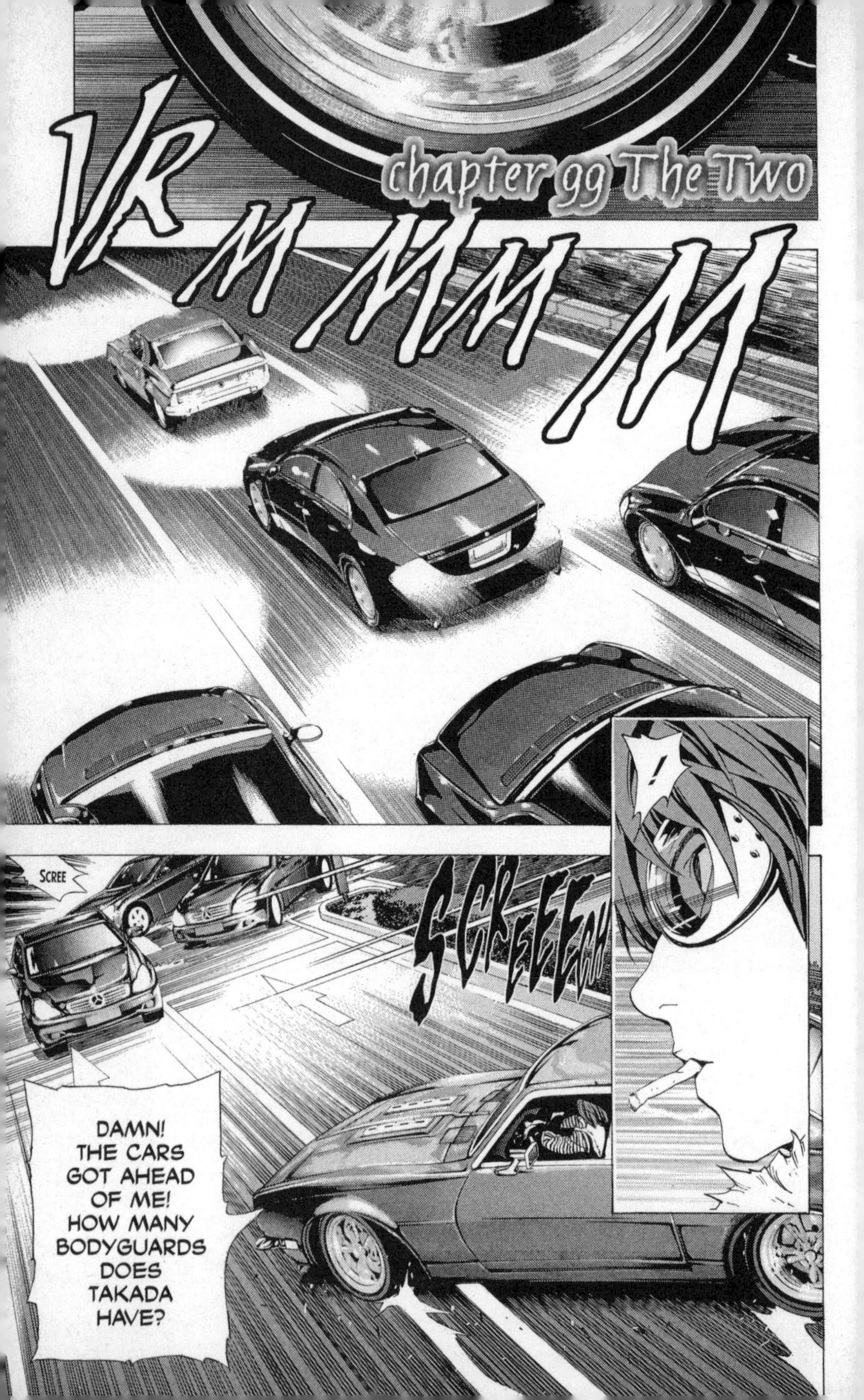
chapter 99 The Two
VRMMMMM
!
SCREEECH
SCREE
DAMN! THE CARS GOT AHEAD OF ME! HOW MANY BODYGUARDS DOES TAKADA HAVE?

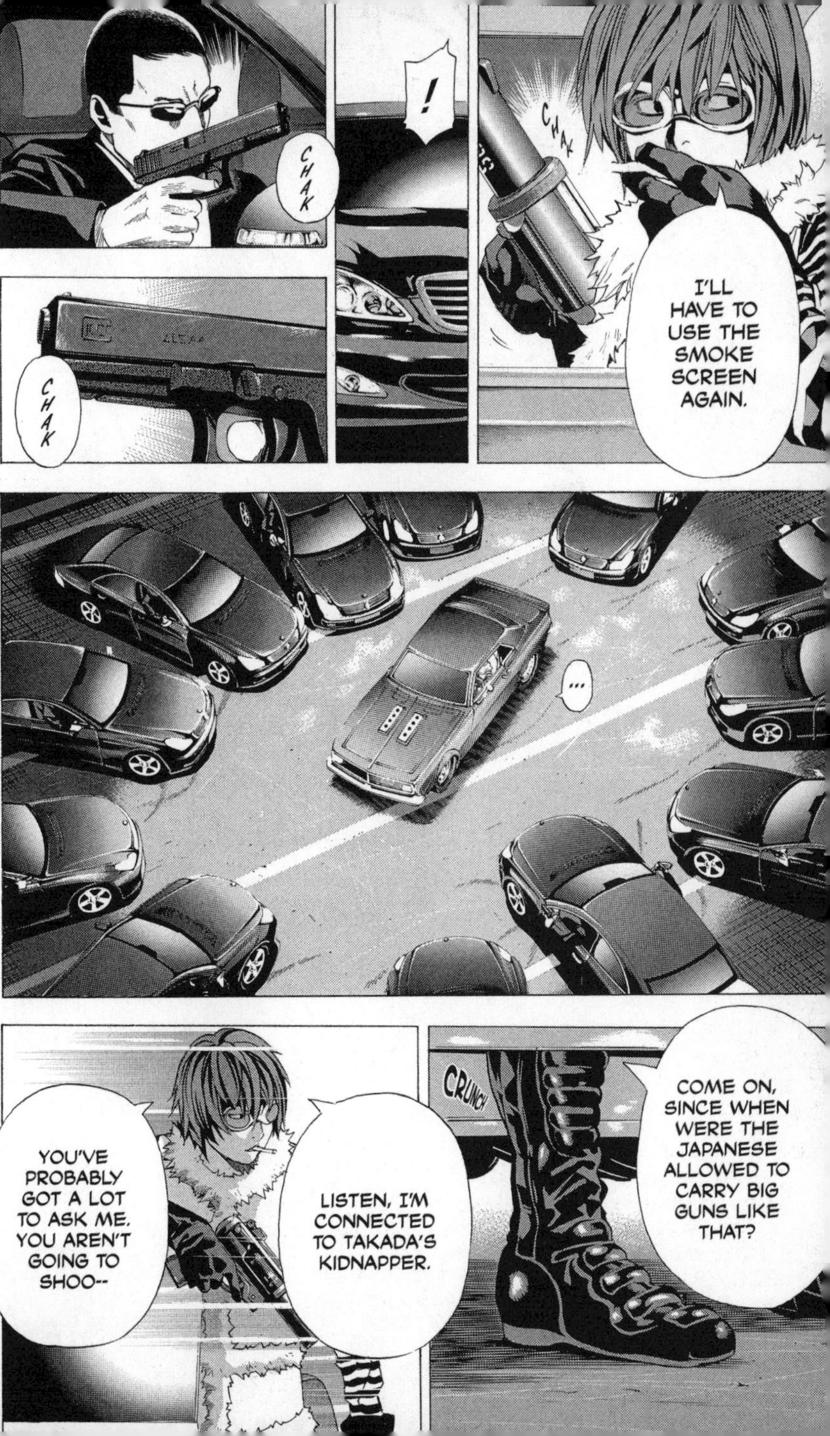
CHAK
I'LL HAVE TO USE THE SMOKE SCREEN AGAIN.
!
CHAK
CHAK
...
CRUNCH
COME ON, SINCE WHEN WERE THE JAPANESE ALLOWED TO CARRY BIG GUNS LIKE THAT?
LISTEN, I'M CONNECTED TO TAKADA'S KIDNAPPER.
YOU'VE PROBABLY GOT A LOT TO ASK ME. YOU AREN'T GOING TO SHOO--

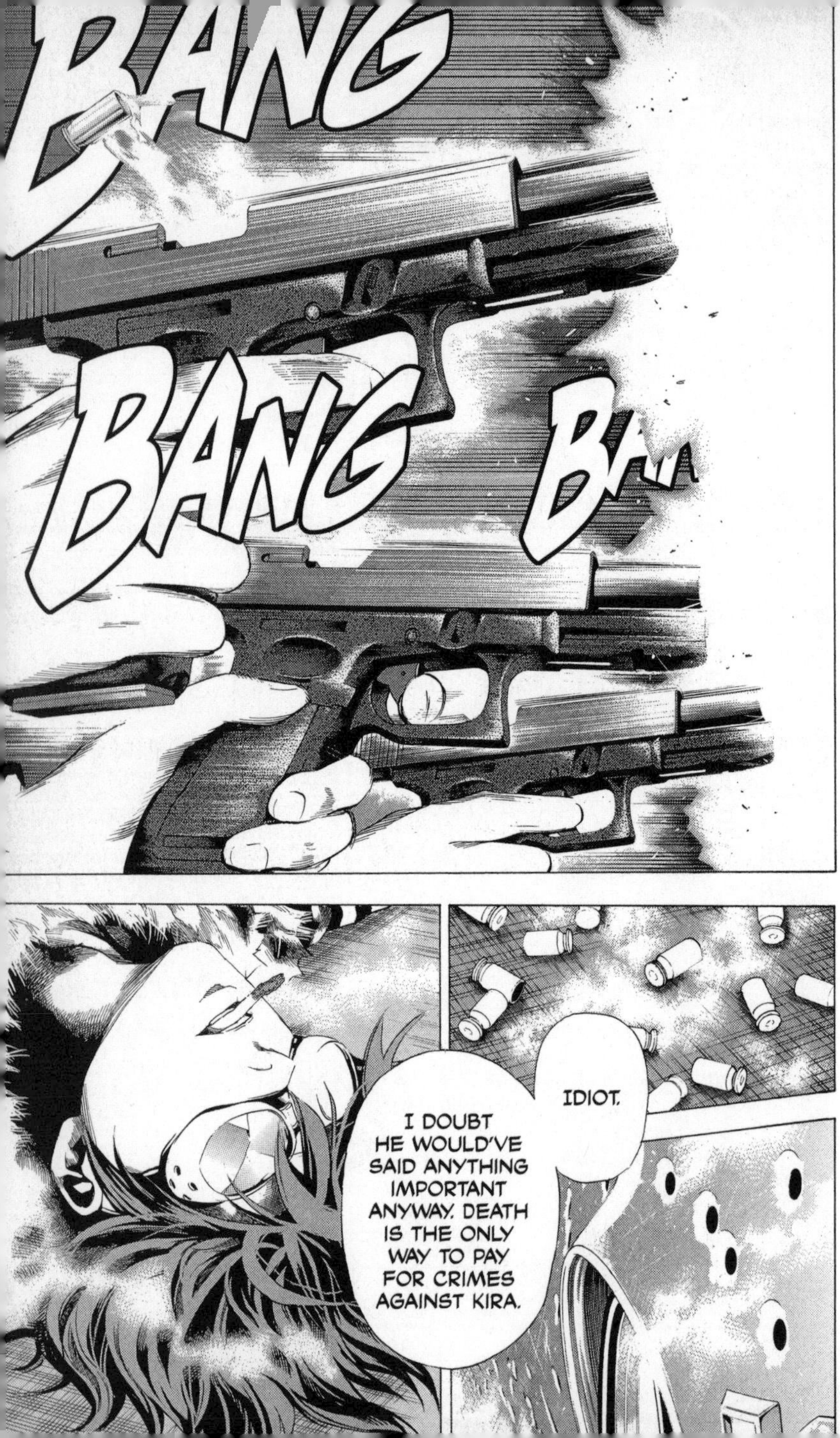
BANG
BANG
BA
IDIOT.
I DOUBT HE WOULD'VE SAID ANYTHING IMPORTANT ANYWAY. DEATH IS THE ONLY WAY TO PAY FOR CRIMES AGAINST KIRA.

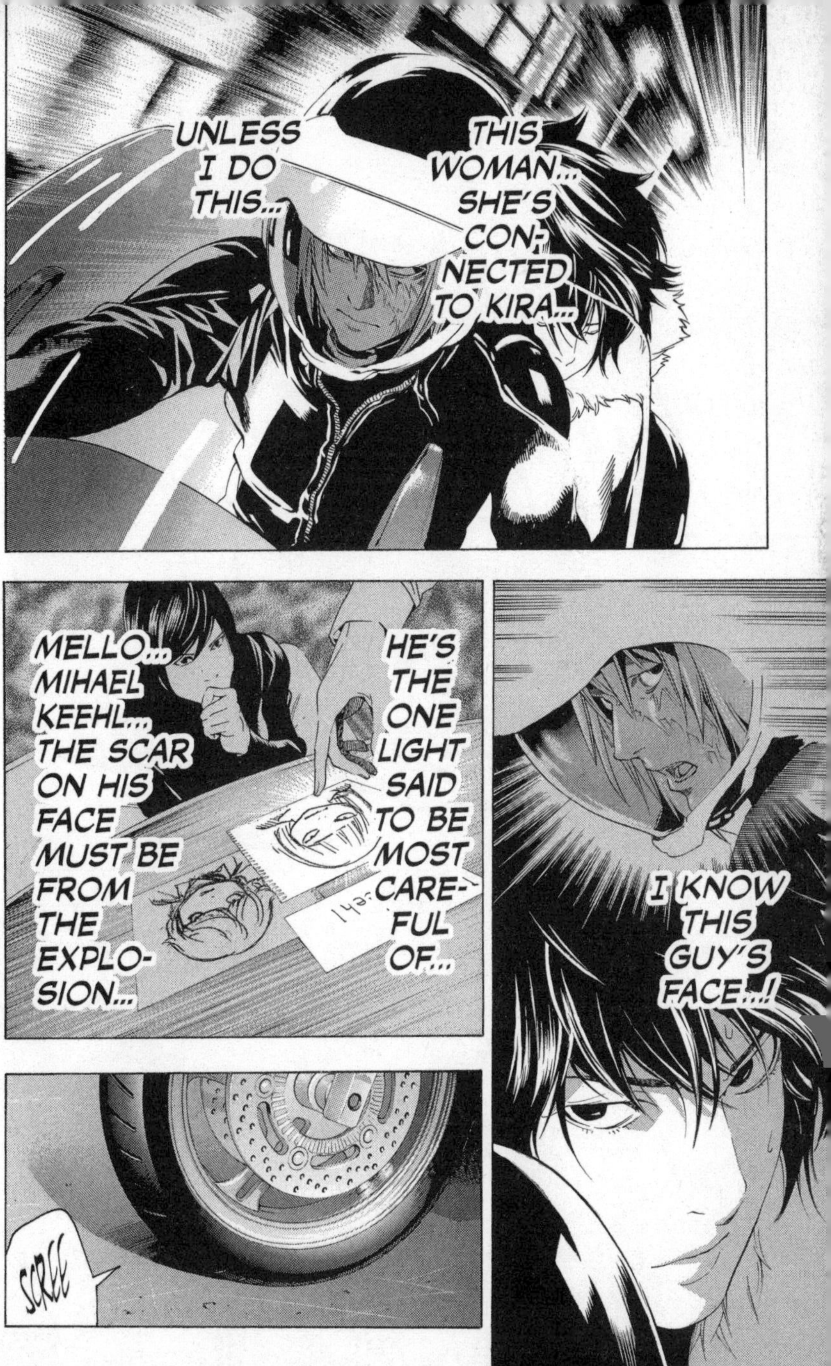
THIS WOMAN... SHE'S CON-NECTED TO KIRA...
UNLESS I DO THIS...
I KNOW THIS GUY'S FACE...!
HE'S THE ONE LIGHT SAID TO BE MOST CARE-FUL OF...
MELLO... MIHAEL KEEHL... THE SCAR ON HIS FACE MUST BE FROM THE EXPLO-SION...
SCREE

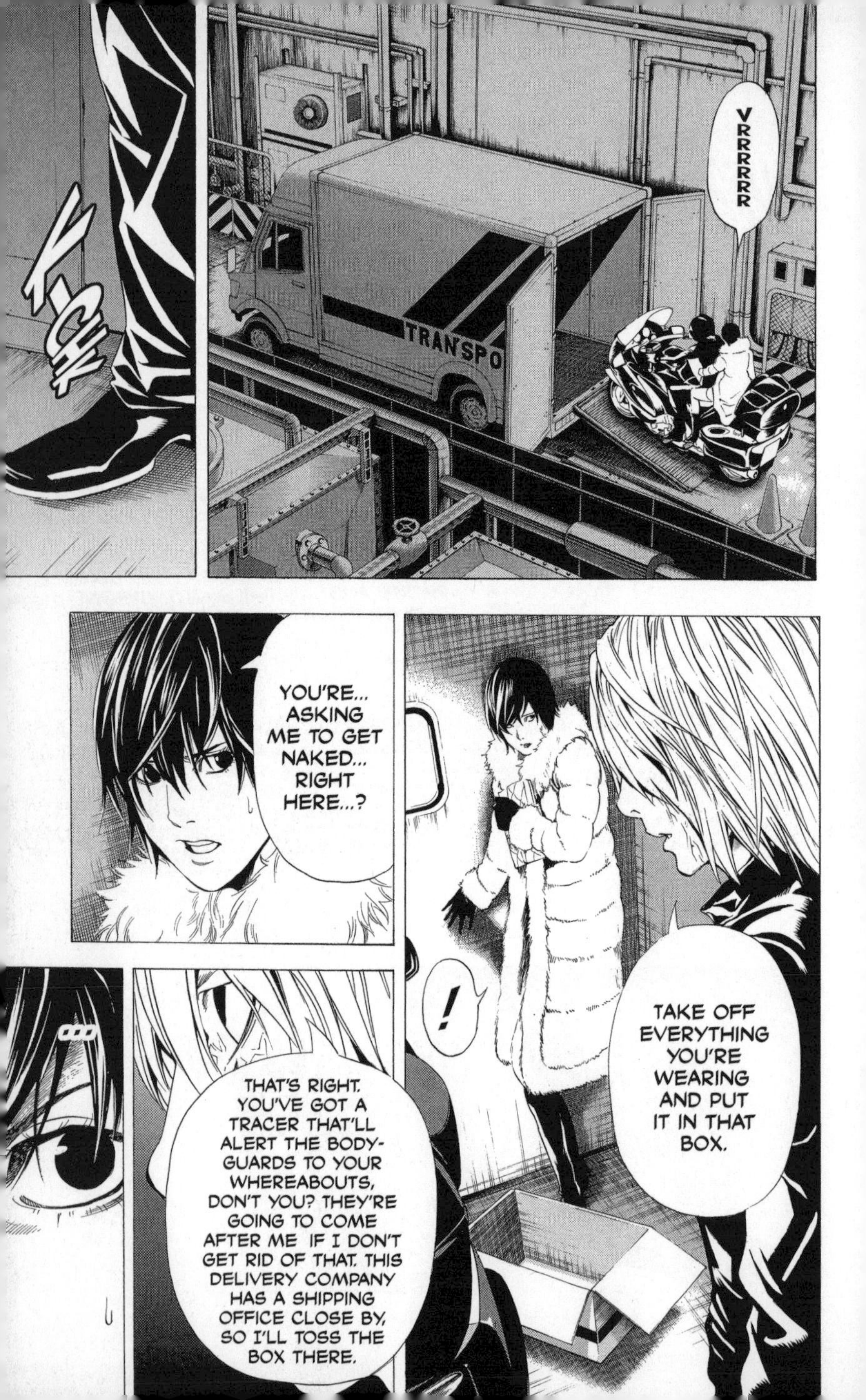

VRRRRR
TRANSPO
K-CHK
TAKE OFF EVERYTHING YOU'RE WEARING AND PUT IT IN THAT BOX.
!
YOU'RE... ASKING ME TO GET NAKED... RIGHT HERE...?
THAT'S RIGHT. YOU'VE GOT A TRACER THAT'LL ALERT THE BODY-GUARDS TO YOUR WHEREABOUTS, DON'T YOU? THEY'RE GOING TO COME AFTER ME IF I DON'T GET RID OF THAT. THIS DELIVERY COMPANY HAS A SHIPPING OFFICE CLOSE BY, SO I'LL TOSS THE BOX THERE.
...

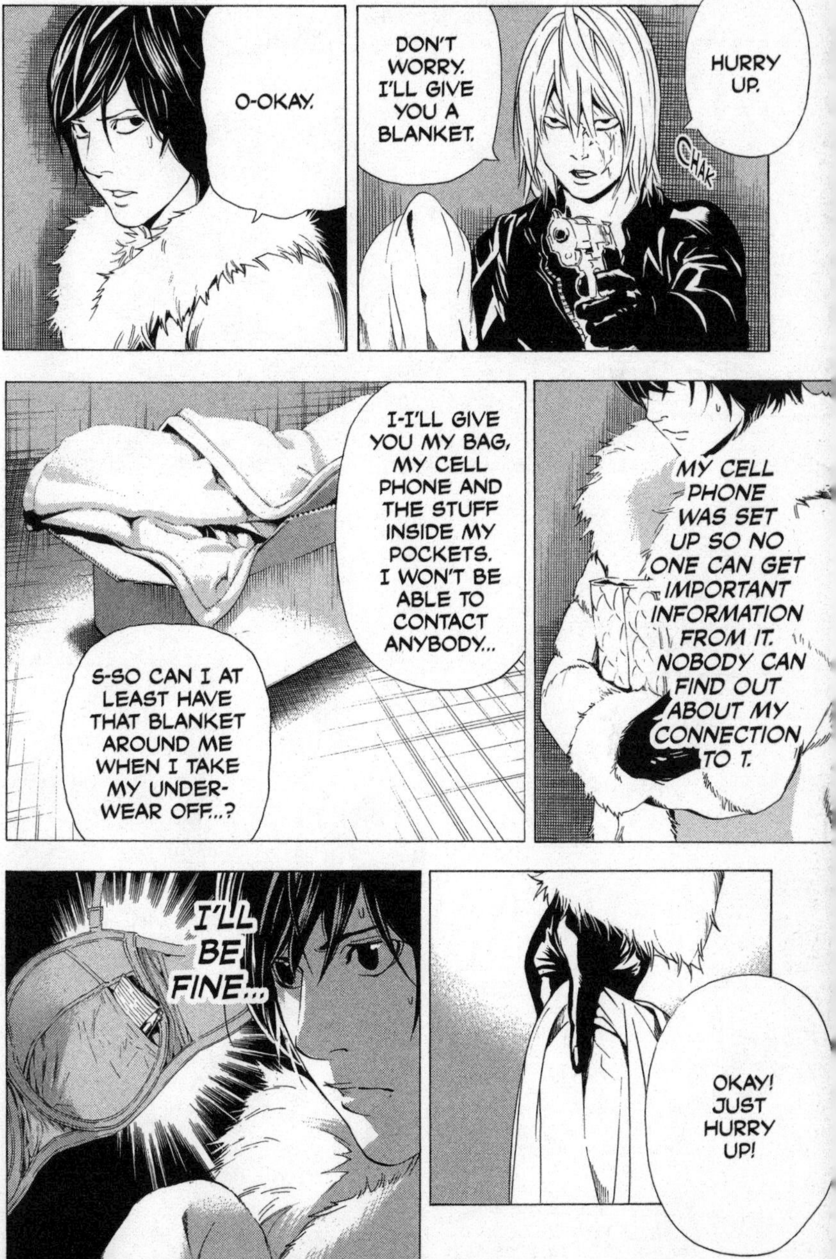
HURRY UP.
CHAK
DON'T WORRY. I'LL GIVE YOU A BLANKET.
O-OKAY.
MY CELL PHONE WAS SET UP SO NO ONE CAN GET IMPORTANT INFORMATION FROM IT. NOBODY CAN FIND OUT ABOUT MY CONNECTION TO T.
I-I'LL GIVE YOU MY BAG, MY CELL PHONE AND THE STUFF INSIDE MY POCKETS. I WON'T BE ABLE TO CONTACT ANYBODY...
S-SO CAN I AT LEAST HAVE THAT BLANKET AROUND ME WHEN I TAKE MY UNDER-WEAR OFF...?
OKAY! JUST HURRY UP!
I'LL BE FINE...

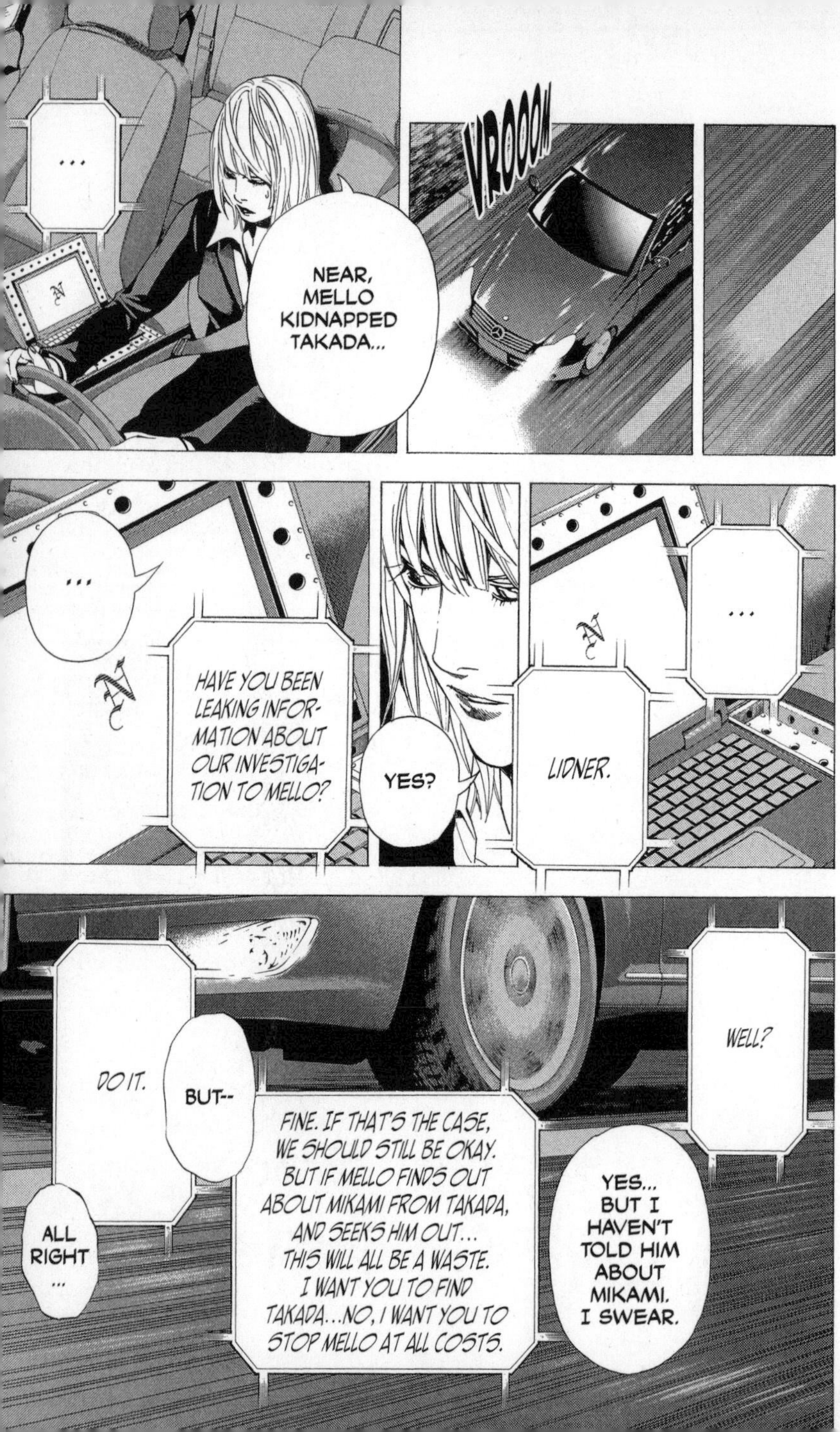
VROOOM
NEAR, MELLO KIDNAPPED TAKADA...
...
...
LIDNER.
YES?
HAVE YOU BEEN LEAKING INFORMATION ABOUT OUR INVESTIGATION TO MELLO?
...
WELL?
YES... BUT I HAVEN'T TOLD HIM ABOUT MIKAMI. I SWEAR.
FINE. IF THAT'S THE CASE, WE SHOULD STILL BE OKAY. BUT IF MELLO FINDS OUT ABOUT MIKAMI FROM TAKADA, AND SEEKS HIM OUT... THIS WILL ALL BE A WASTE. I WANT YOU TO FIND TAKADA...NO, I WANT YOU TO STOP MELLO AT ALL COSTS.
BUT--
DO IT.
ALL RIGHT...

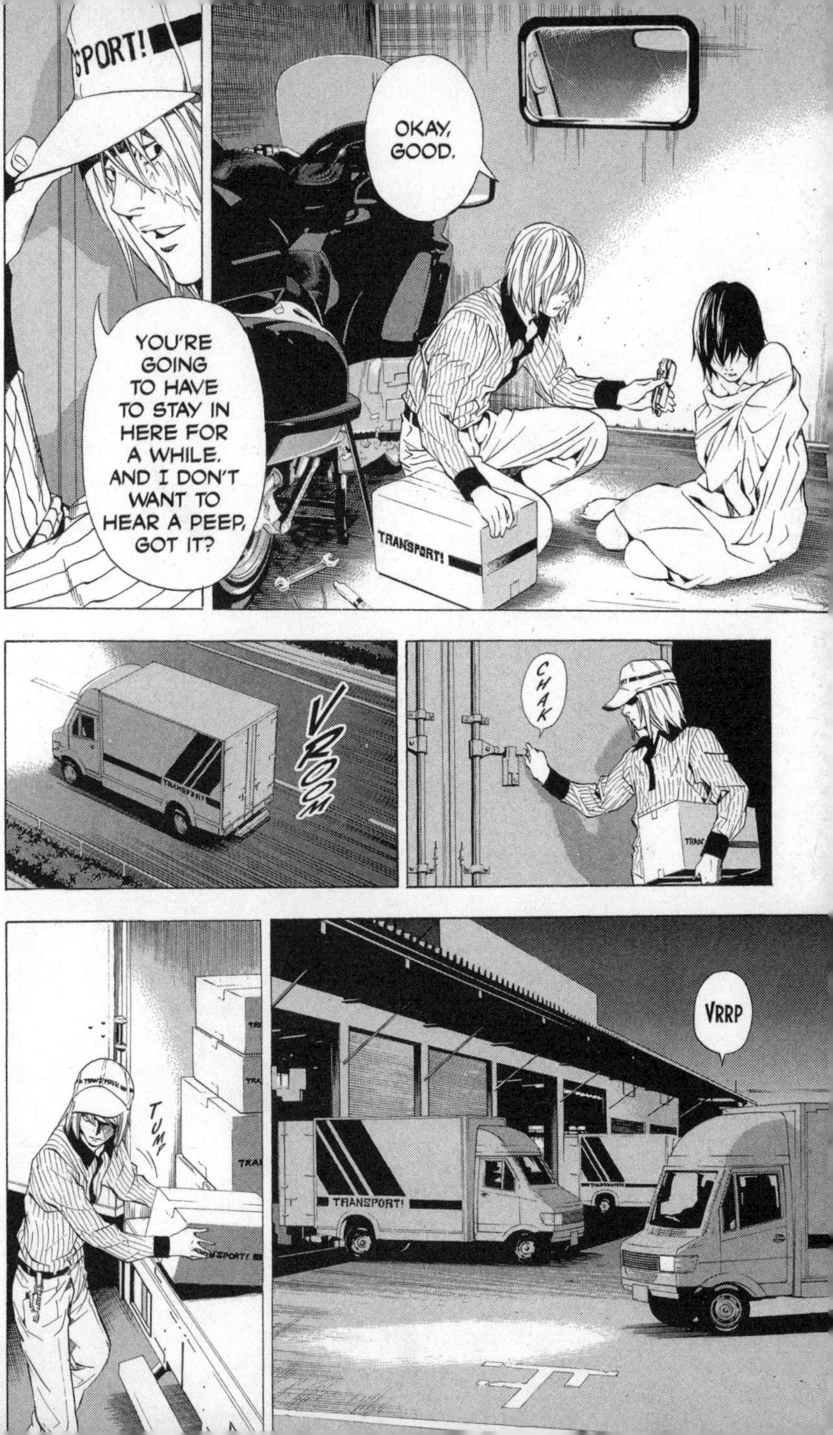
OKAY, GOOD.
YOU'RE GOING TO HAVE TO STAY IN HERE FOR A WHILE. AND I DON'T WANT TO HEAR A PEEP, GOT IT?
CHAK
VROOM
VRRP
TUMP

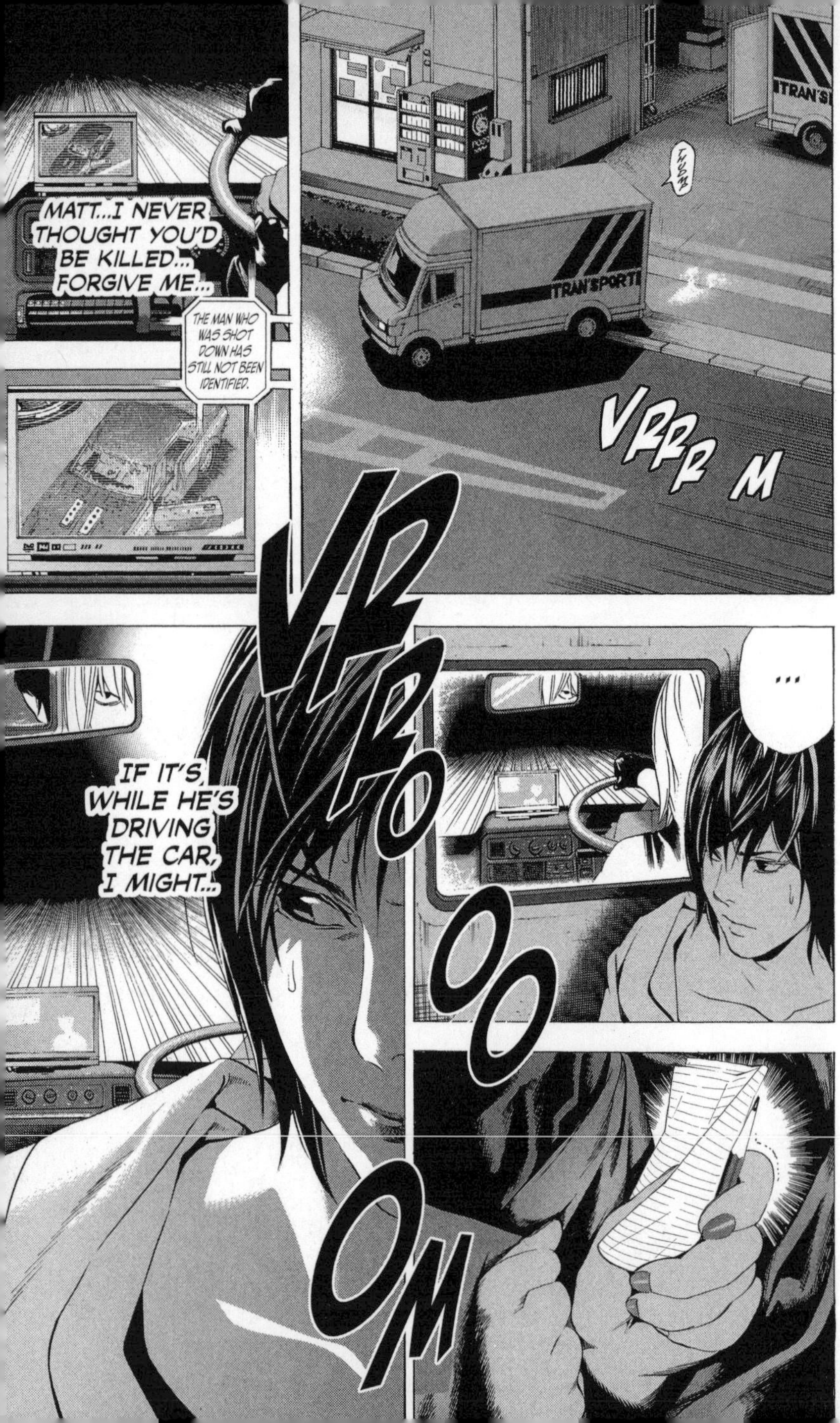
TRAN'S
THUMP
TRAN'SPORT
VRRRR M
MATT...I NEVER THOUGHT YOU'D BE KILLED... FORGIVE ME...
THE MAN WHO WAS SHOT DOWN HAS STILL NOT BEEN IDENTIFIED.
...
IF IT'S WHILE HE'S DRIVING THE CAR, I MIGHT...
VROOOOOM

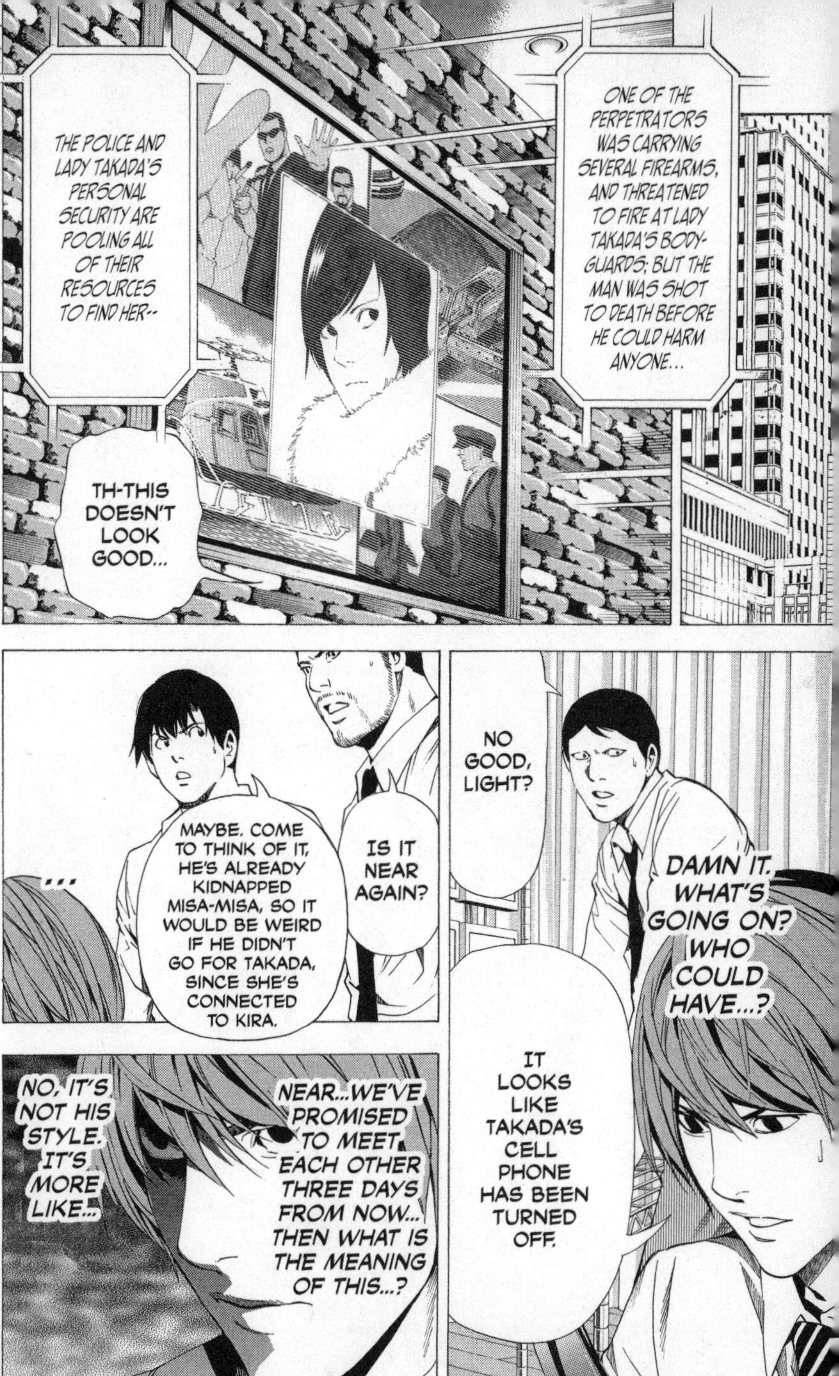
ONE OF THE PERPETRATORS WAS CARRYING SEVERAL FIREARMS, AND THREATENED TO FIRE AT LADY TAKADA'S BODY-GUARDS; BUT THE MAN WAS SHOT TO DEATH BEFORE HE COULD HARM ANYONE...
THE POLICE AND LADY TAKADA'S PERSONAL SECURITY ARE POOLING ALL OF THEIR RESOURCES TO FIND HER--
TH-THIS DOESN'T LOOK GOOD...
NO GOOD, LIGHT?
DAMN IT. WHAT'S GOING ON? WHO COULD HAVE...?
IT LOOKS LIKE TAKADA'S CELL PHONE HAS BEEN TURNED OFF.
IS IT NEAR AGAIN?
MAYBE. COME TO THINK OF IT, HE'S ALREADY KIDNAPPED MISA-MISA, SO IT WOULD BE WEIRD IF HE DIDN'T GO FOR TAKADA, SINCE SHE'S CONNECTED TO KIRA.
...
NEAR...WE'VE PROMISED TO MEET EACH OTHER THREE DAYS FROM NOW... THEN WHAT IS THE MEANING OF THIS...?
NO, IT'S NOT HIS STYLE. IT'S MORE LIKE...

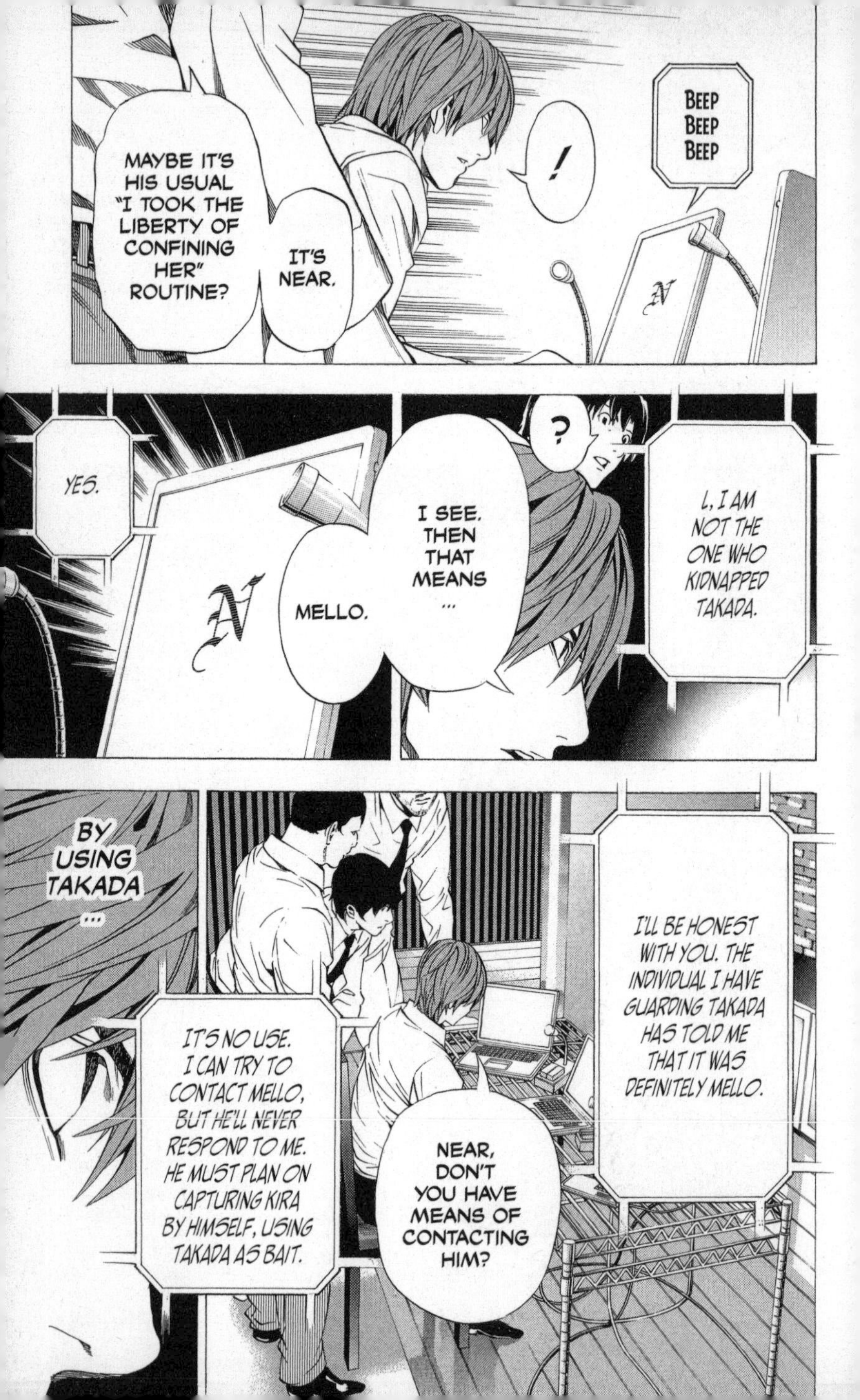
BEEP
BEEP
BEEP
!
IT'S NEAR.
MAYBE IT'S HIS USUAL "I TOOK THE LIBERTY OF CONFINING HER" ROUTINE?
L, I AM NOT THE ONE WHO KIDNAPPED TAKADA.
?
I SEE. THEN THAT MEANS ...
MELLO.
YES.
I'LL BE HONEST WITH YOU. THE INDIVIDUAL I HAVE GUARDING TAKADA HAS TOLD ME THAT IT WAS DEFINITELY MELLO.
NEAR, DON'T YOU HAVE MEANS OF CONTACTING HIM?
IT'S NO USE. I CAN TRY TO CONTACT MELLO, BUT HE'LL NEVER RESPOND TO ME. HE MUST PLAN ON CAPTURING KIRA BY HIMSELF, USING TAKADA AS BAIT.
BY USING TAKADA ...

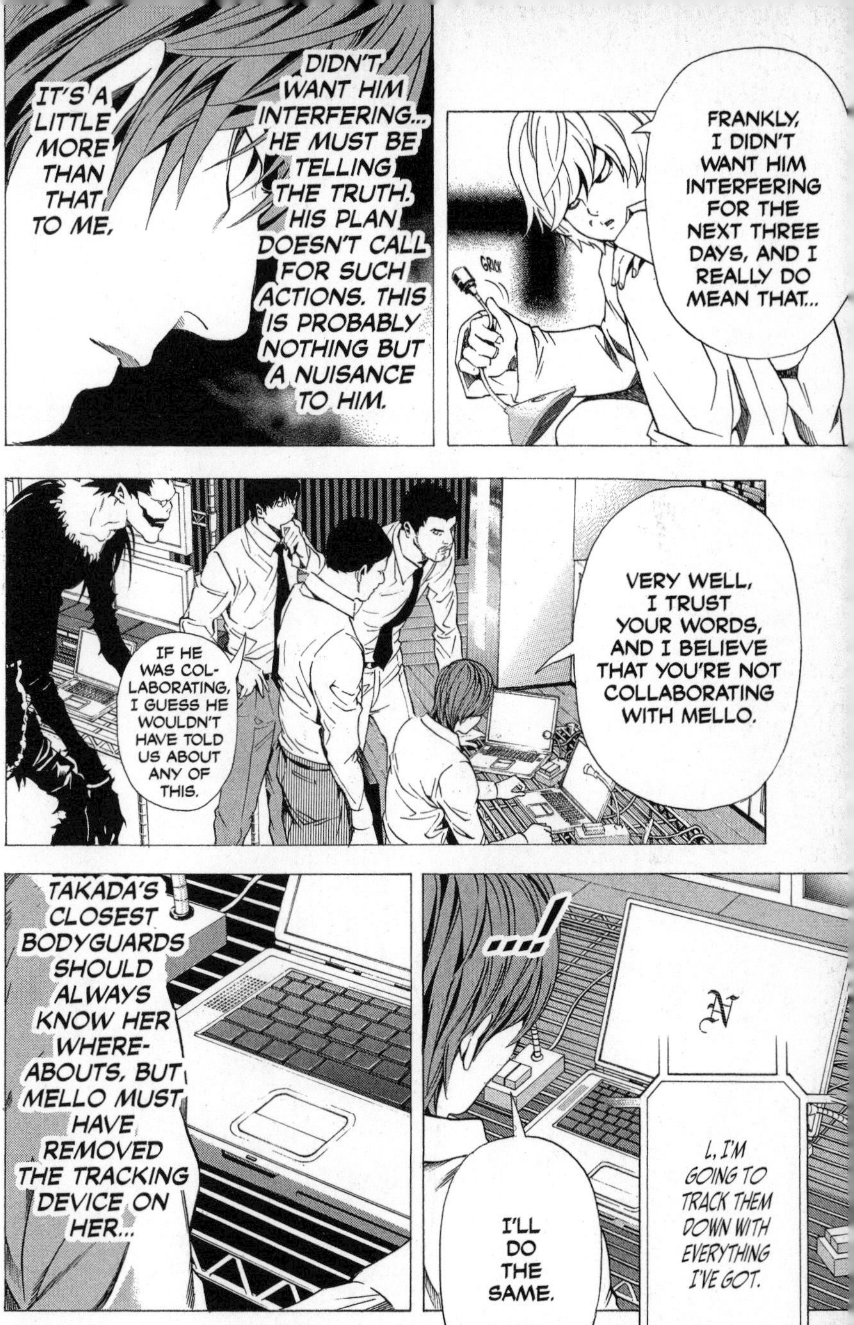

FRANKLY, I DIDN'T WANT HIM INTERFERING FOR THE NEXT THREE DAYS, AND I REALLY DO MEAN THAT...
GRICK
DIDN'T WANT HIM INTERFERING... HE MUST BE TELLING THE TRUTH. HIS PLAN DOESN'T CALL FOR SUCH ACTIONS. THIS IS PROBABLY NOTHING BUT A NUISANCE TO HIM.
IT'S A LITTLE MORE THAN THAT TO ME,
VERY WELL, I TRUST YOUR WORDS, AND I BELIEVE THAT YOU'RE NOT COLLABORATING WITH MELLO.
IF HE WAS COL-LABORATING, I GUESS HE WOULDN'T HAVE TOLD US ABOUT ANY OF THIS.
...!
N
L, I'M GOING TO TRACK THEM DOWN WITH EVERYTHING I'VE GOT.
I'LL DO THE SAME.
TAKADA'S CLOSEST BODYGUARDS SHOULD ALWAYS KNOW HER WHERE-ABOUTS, BUT MELLO MUST HAVE REMOVED THE TRACKING DEVICE ON HER...

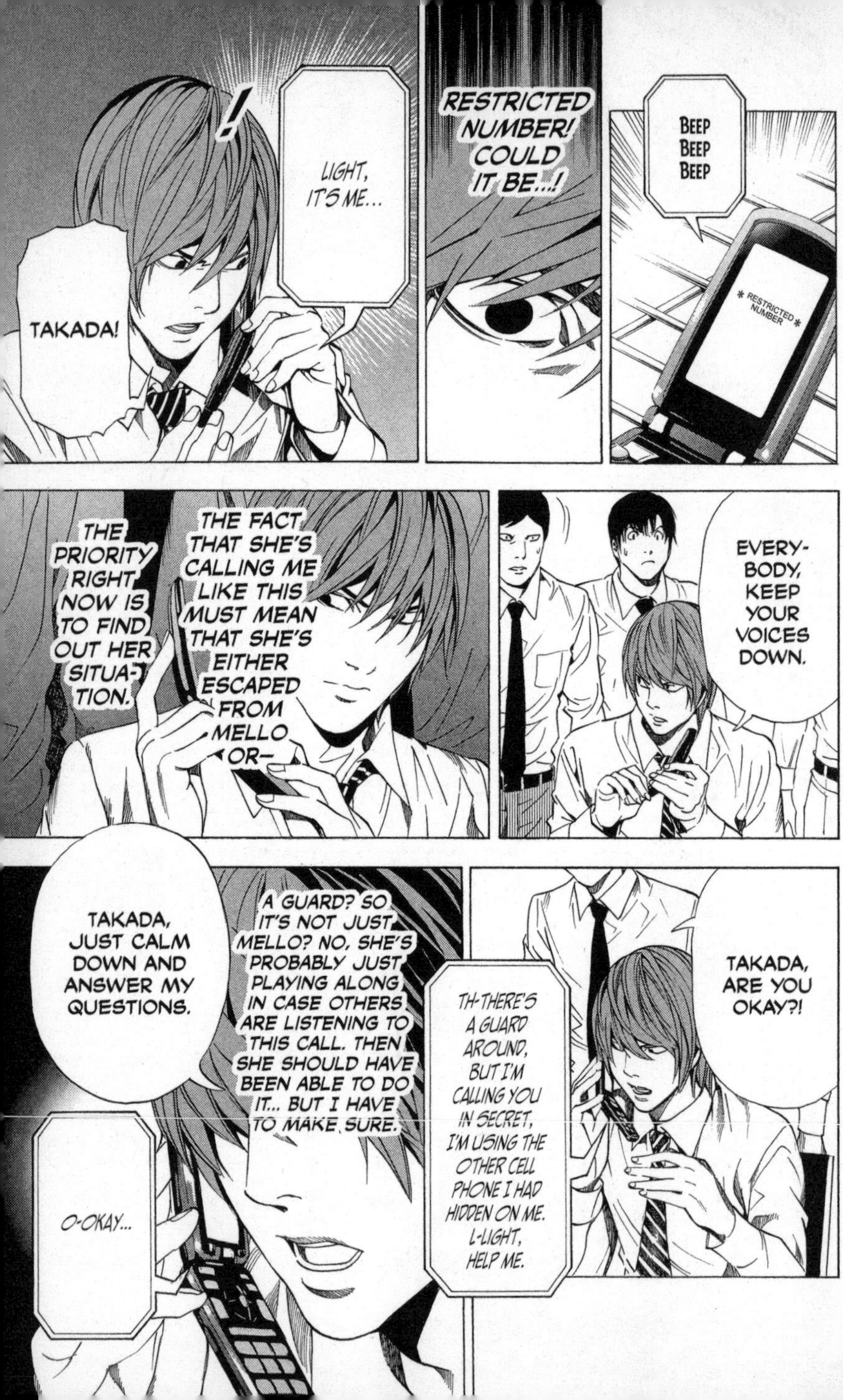
BEEP BEEP BEEP
* RESTRICTED NUMBER *
RESTRICTED NUMBER! COULD IT BE...!
LIGHT, IT'S ME...
!
TAKADA!
EVERY-BODY, KEEP YOUR VOICES DOWN.
THE FACT THAT SHE'S CALLING ME LIKE THIS MUST MEAN THAT SHE'S EITHER ESCAPED FROM MELLO OR—
THE PRIORITY RIGHT NOW IS TO FIND OUT HER SITUA-TION.
TAKADA, ARE YOU OKAY?!
TH-THERE'S A GUARD AROUND, BUT I'M CALLING YOU IN SECRET, I'M USING THE OTHER CELL PHONE I HAD HIDDEN ON ME. L-LIGHT, HELP ME.
A GUARD? SO IT'S NOT JUST MELLO? NO, SHE'S PROBABLY JUST PLAYING ALONG IN CASE OTHERS ARE LISTENING TO THIS CALL. THEN SHE SHOULD HAVE BEEN ABLE TO DO IT... BUT I HAVE TO MAKE SURE.
TAKADA, JUST CALM DOWN AND ANSWER MY QUESTIONS.
O-OKAY...

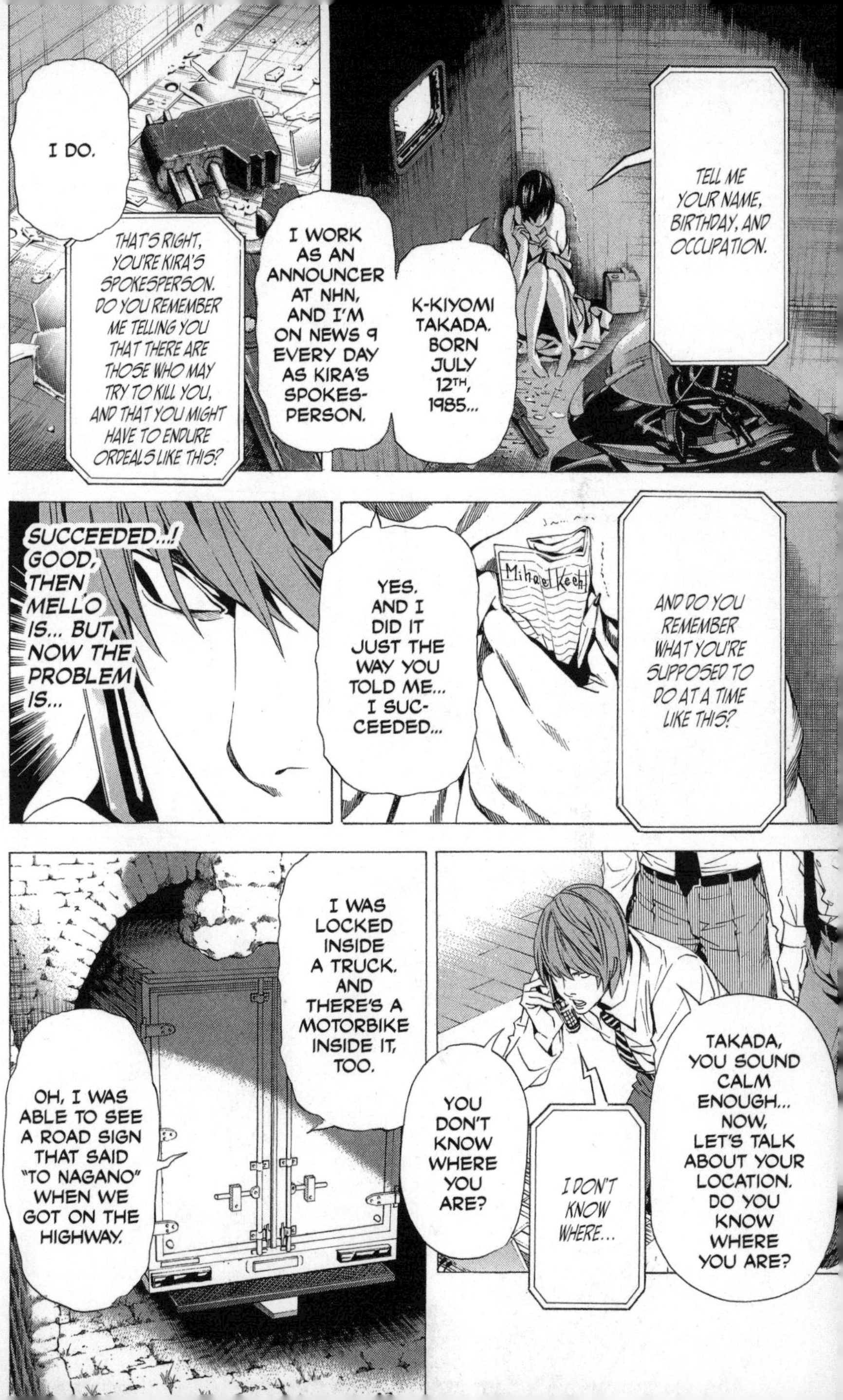
TELL ME YOUR NAME, BIRTHDAY, AND OCCUPATION.
K-KIYOMI TAKADA. BORN JULY 12TH, 1985...
I WORK AS AN ANNOUNCER AT NHN, AND I'M ON NEWS 9 EVERY DAY AS KIRA'S SPOKES-PERSON.
THAT'S RIGHT, YOU'RE KIRA'S SPOKESPERSON. DO YOU REMEMBER ME TELLING YOU THAT THERE ARE THOSE WHO MAY TRY TO KILL YOU, AND THAT YOU MIGHT HAVE TO ENDURE ORDEALS LIKE THIS?
I DO.
AND DO YOU REMEMBER WHAT YOU'RE SUPPOSED TO DO AT A TIME LIKE THIS?
Mihael Keehl
YES. AND I DID IT JUST THE WAY YOU TOLD ME... I SUC-CEEDED...
SUCCEEDED...! GOOD, THEN MELLO IS... BUT, NOW THE PROBLEM IS...
TAKADA, YOU SOUND CALM ENOUGH... NOW, LET'S TALK ABOUT YOUR LOCATION. DO YOU KNOW WHERE YOU ARE?
I DON'T KNOW WHERE...
YOU DON'T KNOW WHERE YOU ARE?
I WAS LOCKED INSIDE A TRUCK. AND THERE'S A MOTORBIKE INSIDE IT, TOO.
OH, I WAS ABLE TO SEE A ROAD SIGN THAT SAID "TO NAGANO" WHEN WE GOT ON THE HIGHWAY.

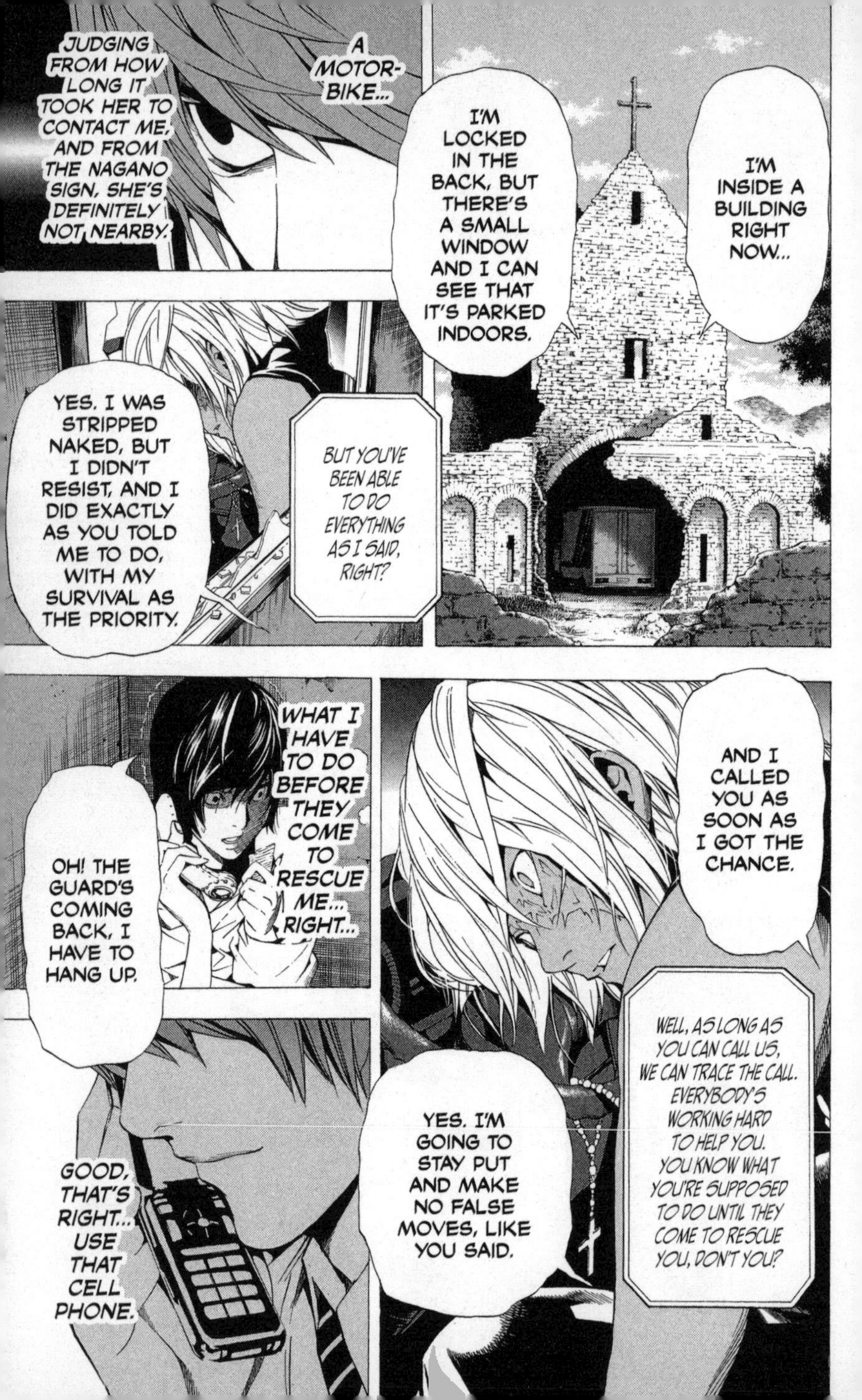
I'M INSIDE A BUILDING RIGHT NOW...
I'M LOCKED IN THE BACK, BUT THERE'S A SMALL WINDOW AND I CAN SEE THAT IT'S PARKED INDOORS.
A MOTOR-BIKE...
JUDGING FROM HOW LONG IT TOOK HER TO CONTACT ME, AND FROM THE NAGANO SIGN, SHE'S DEFINITELY NOT NEARBY.
BUT YOU'VE BEEN ABLE TO DO EVERYTHING AS I SAID, RIGHT?
YES. I WAS STRIPPED NAKED, BUT I DIDN'T RESIST, AND I DID EXACTLY AS YOU TOLD ME TO DO, WITH MY SURVIVAL AS THE PRIORITY.
AND I CALLED YOU AS SOON AS I GOT THE CHANCE.
WELL, AS LONG AS YOU CAN CALL US, WE CAN TRACE THE CALL. EVERYBODY'S WORKING HARD TO HELP YOU. YOU KNOW WHAT YOU'RE SUPPOSED TO DO UNTIL THEY COME TO RESCUE YOU, DON'T YOU?
YES. I'M GOING TO STAY PUT AND MAKE NO FALSE MOVES, LIKE YOU SAID.
WHAT I HAVE TO DO BEFORE THEY COME TO RESCUE ME... RIGHT...
OH! THE GUARD'S COMING BACK, I HAVE TO HANG UP.
GOOD, THAT'S RIGHT... USE THAT CELL PHONE.

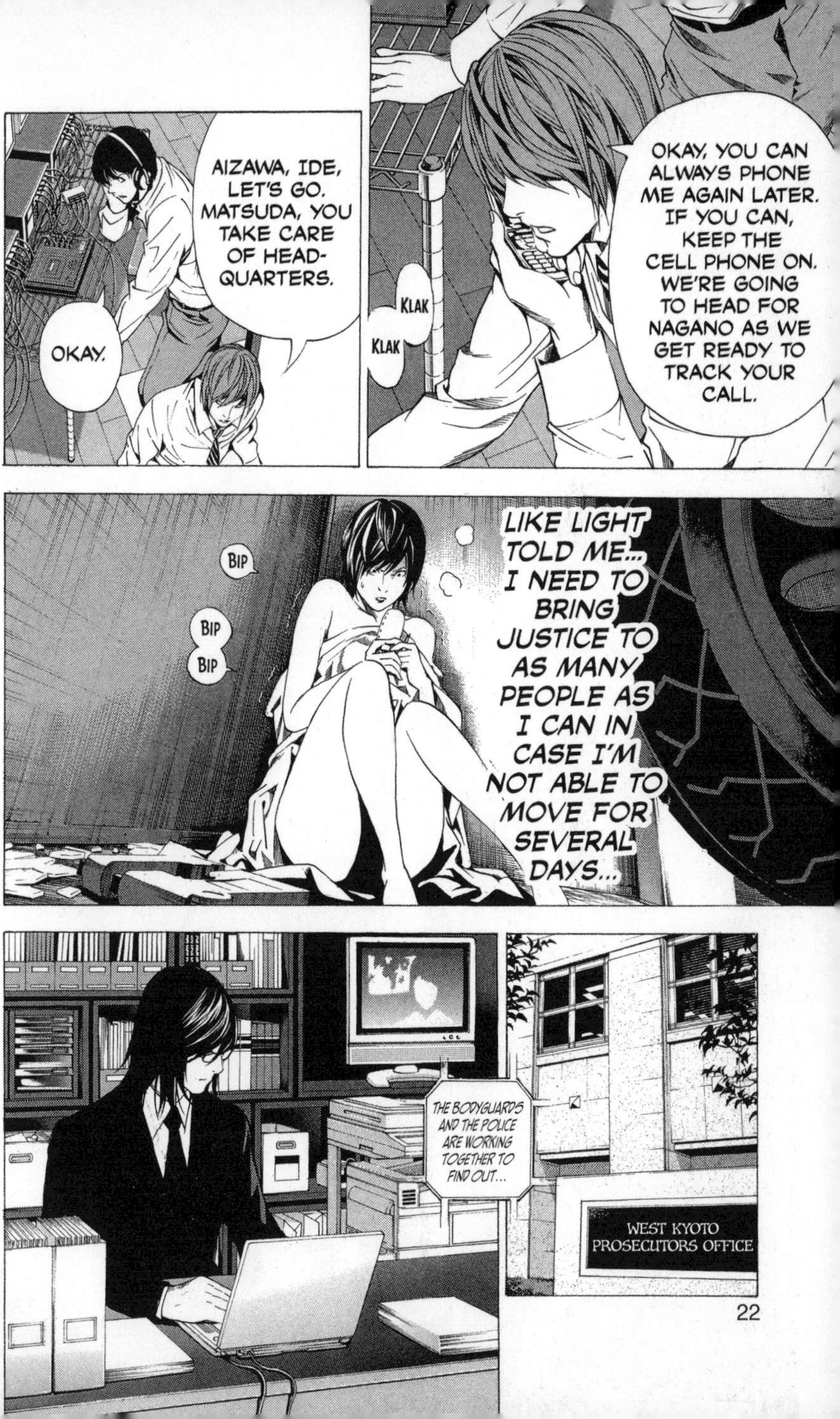
OKAY, YOU CAN ALWAYS PHONE ME AGAIN LATER. IF YOU CAN, KEEP THE CELL PHONE ON. WE'RE GOING TO HEAD FOR NAGANO AS WE GET READY TO TRACK YOUR CALL.
KLAK
KLAK
AIZAWA, IDE, LET'S GO. MATSUDA, YOU TAKE CARE OF HEAD-QUARTERS.
OKAY.
LIKE LIGHT TOLD ME... I NEED TO BRING JUSTICE TO AS MANY PEOPLE AS I CAN IN CASE I'M NOT ABLE TO MOVE FOR SEVERAL DAYS...
BIP
BIP
BIP
WEST KYOTO PROSECUTORS OFFICE
THE BODYGUARDS AND THE POLICE ARE WORKING TOGETHER TO FIND OUT...

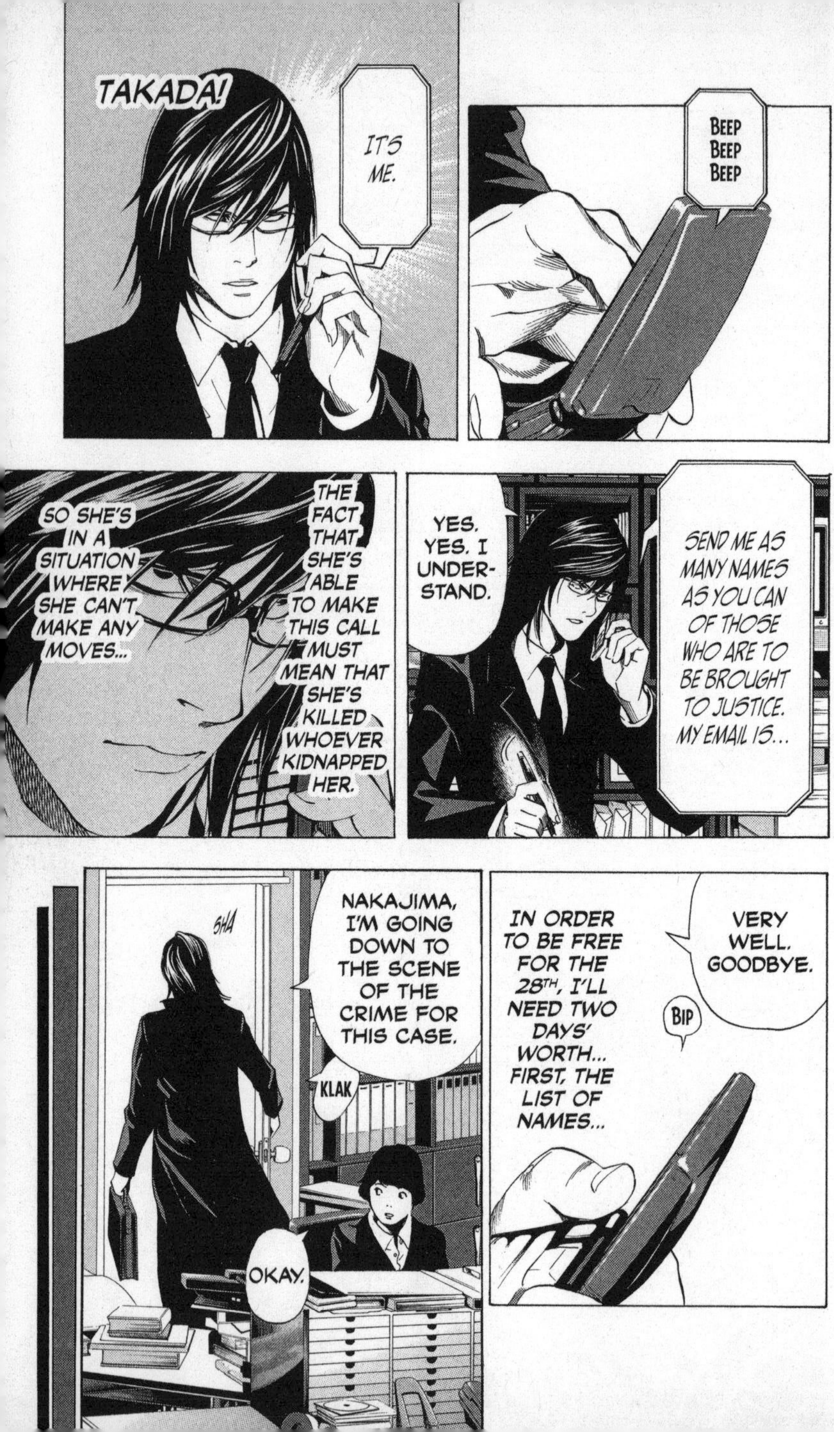
BEEP BEEP BEEP
IT'S ME.
TAKADA!
SEND ME AS MANY NAMES AS YOU CAN OF THOSE WHO ARE TO BE BROUGHT TO JUSTICE. MY EMAIL IS...
YES. YES. I UNDER-STAND.
THE FACT THAT SHE'S ABLE TO MAKE THIS CALL MUST MEAN THAT SHE'S KILLED WHOEVER KIDNAPPED HER.
SO SHE'S IN A SITUATION WHERE SHE CAN'T MAKE ANY MOVES...
VERY WELL. GOODBYE.
IN ORDER TO BE FREE FOR THE 28TH, I'LL NEED TWO DAYS' WORTH... FIRST, THE LIST OF NAMES...
BIP
NAKAJIMA, I'M GOING DOWN TO THE SCENE OF THE CRIME FOR THIS CASE.
SHA
KLAK
OKAY.

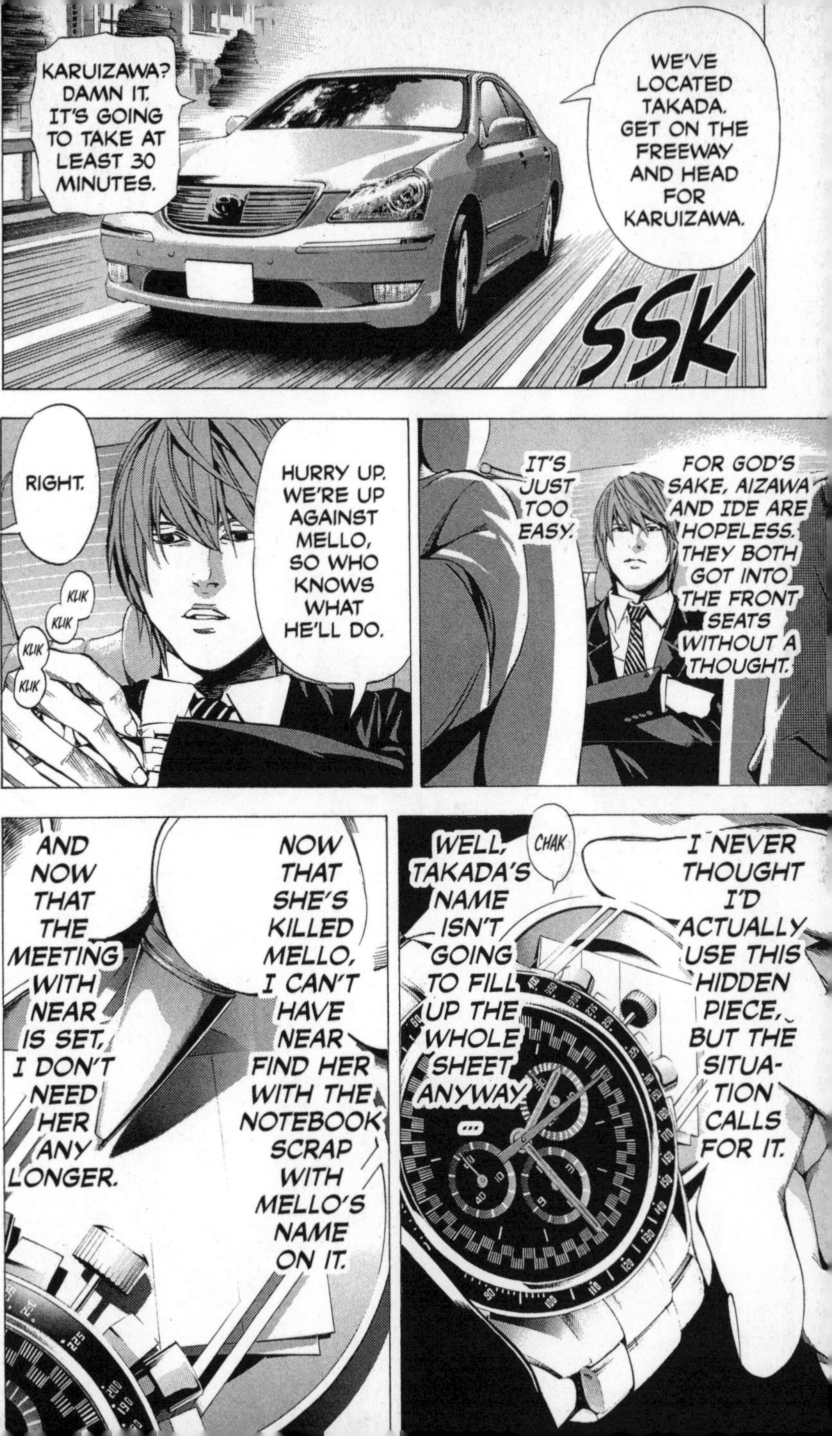
WE'VE LOCATED TAKADA. GET ON THE FREEWAY AND HEAD FOR KARUIZAWA.
KARUIZAWA? DAMN IT. IT'S GOING TO TAKE AT LEAST 30 MINUTES.
SSK
FOR GOD'S SAKE, AIZAWA AND IDE ARE HOPELESS. THEY BOTH GOT INTO THE FRONT SEATS WITHOUT A THOUGHT.
IT'S JUST TOO EASY.
HURRY UP. WE'RE UP AGAINST MELLO, SO WHO KNOWS WHAT HE'LL DO.
RIGHT.
KLIK
KLIK
KLIK
KLIK
I NEVER THOUGHT I'D ACTUALLY USE THIS HIDDEN PIECE, BUT THE SITUATION CALLS FOR IT.
CHAK
WELL, TAKADA'S NAME ISN'T GOING TO FILL UP THE WHOLE SHEET ANYWAY.
...
NOW THAT SHE'S KILLED MELLO, I CAN'T HAVE NEAR FIND HER WITH THE NOTEBOOK SCRAP WITH MELLO'S NAME ON IT.
AND NOW THAT THE MEETING WITH NEAR IS SET, I DON'T NEED HER ANY LONGER.

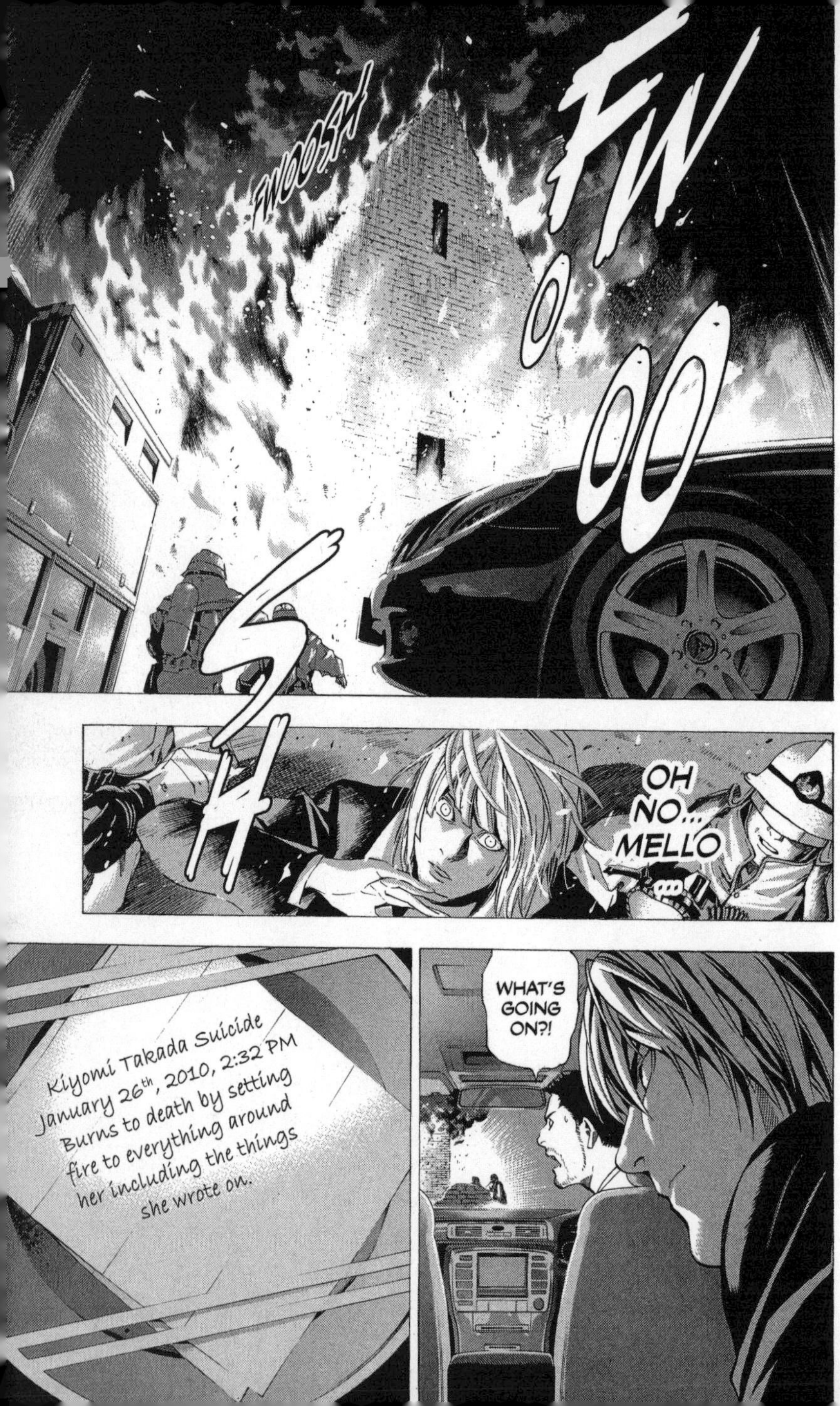
FWOOOSH
FWOOSH!
OH NO... MELLO
WHAT'S GOING ON?!
Kiyomi Takada Suicide
January 26th, 2010, 2:32 PM
Burns to death by setting
fire to everything around
her including the things
she wrote on.

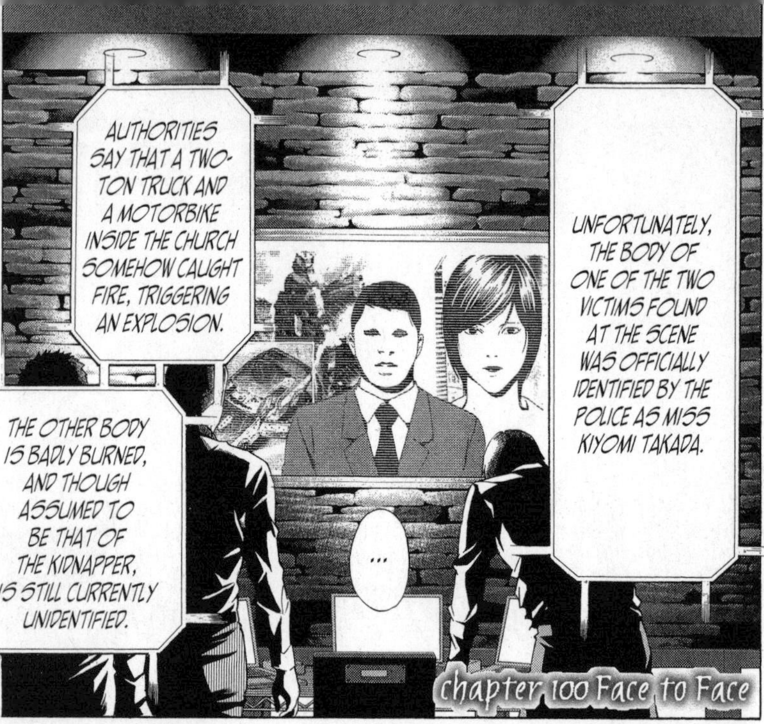
AUTHORITIES SAY THAT A TWO-TON TRUCK AND A MOTORBIKE INSIDE THE CHURCH SOMEHOW CAUGHT FIRE, TRIGGERING AN EXPLOSION.
UNFORTUNATELY, THE BODY OF ONE OF THE TWO VICTIMS FOUND AT THE SCENE WAS OFFICIALLY IDENTIFIED BY THE POLICE AS MISS KIYOMI TAKADA.
THE OTHER BODY IS BADLY BURNED, AND THOUGH ASSUMED TO BE THAT OF THE KIDNAPPER, IS STILL CURRENTLY UNIDENTIFIED.
...
chapter 100 Face to Face

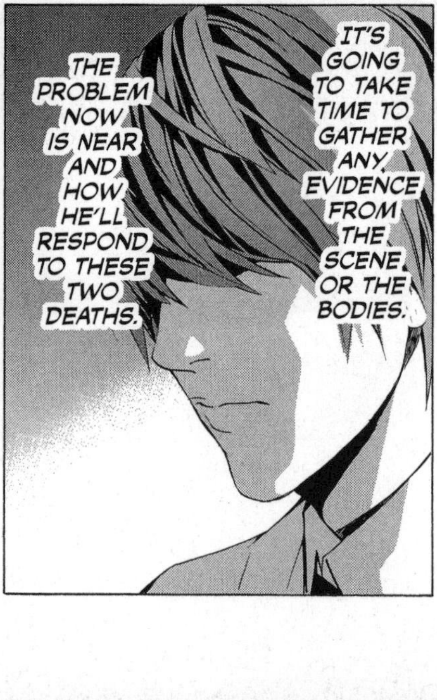
IT'S GOING TO TAKE TIME TO GATHER ANY EVIDENCE FROM THE SCENE OR THE BODIES.
THE PROBLEM NOW IS NEAR AND HOW HE'LL RESPOND TO THESE TWO DEATHS.

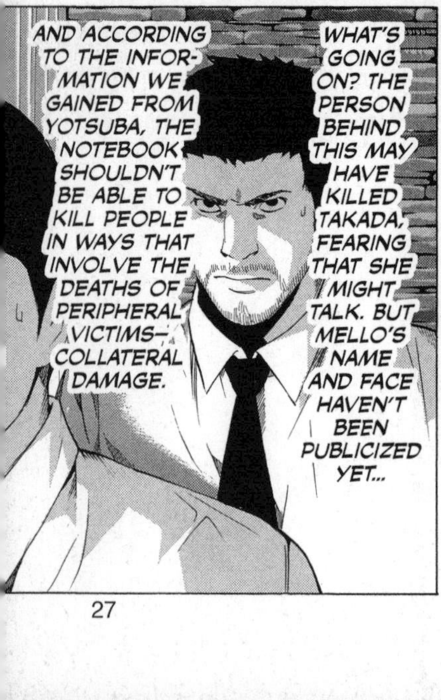
WHAT'S GOING ON? THE PERSON BEHIND THIS MAY HAVE KILLED TAKADA, FEARING THAT SHE MIGHT TALK. BUT MELLO'S NAME AND FACE HAVEN'T BEEN PUBLICIZED YET...
AND ACCORDING TO THE INFORMATION WE GAINED FROM YOTSUBA, THE NOTEBOOK SHOULDN'T BE ABLE TO KILL PEOPLE IN WAYS THAT INVOLVE THE DEATHS OF PERIPHERAL VICTIMS— COLLATERAL DAMAGE.

chapter 100 Face to Face

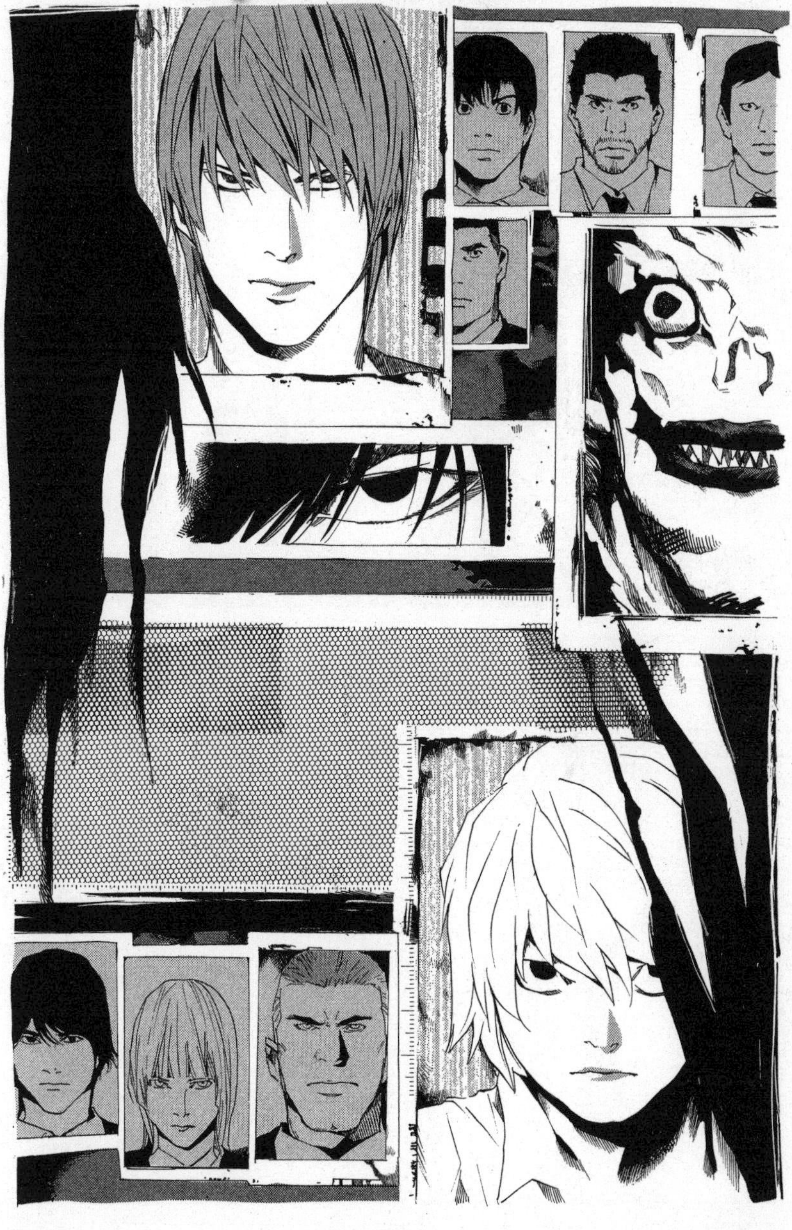

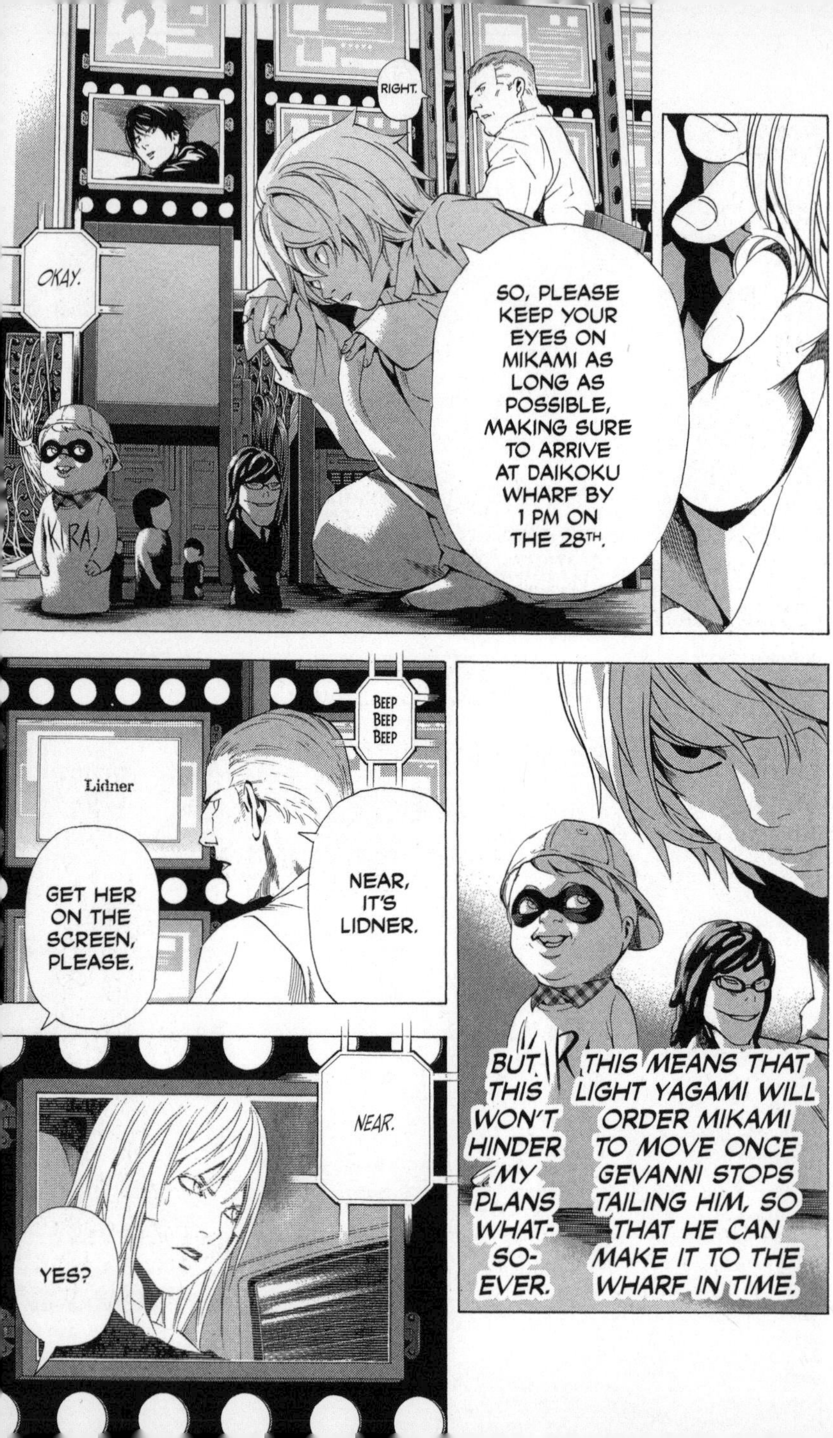
RIGHT.
SO, PLEASE KEEP YOUR EYES ON MIKAMI AS LONG AS POSSIBLE, MAKING SURE TO ARRIVE AT DAIKOKU WHARF BY 1 PM ON THE 28TH.
OKAY.
KIRA
THIS MEANS THAT LIGHT YAGAMI WILL ORDER MIKAMI TO MOVE ONCE GEVANNI STOPS TAILING HIM, SO THAT HE CAN MAKE IT TO THE WHARF IN TIME.
BUT THIS WON'T HINDER MY PLANS WHAT-SO-EVER.
BEEP BEEP BEEP
Lidner
NEAR, IT'S LIDNER.
GET HER ON THE SCREEN, PLEASE.
NEAR.
YES?

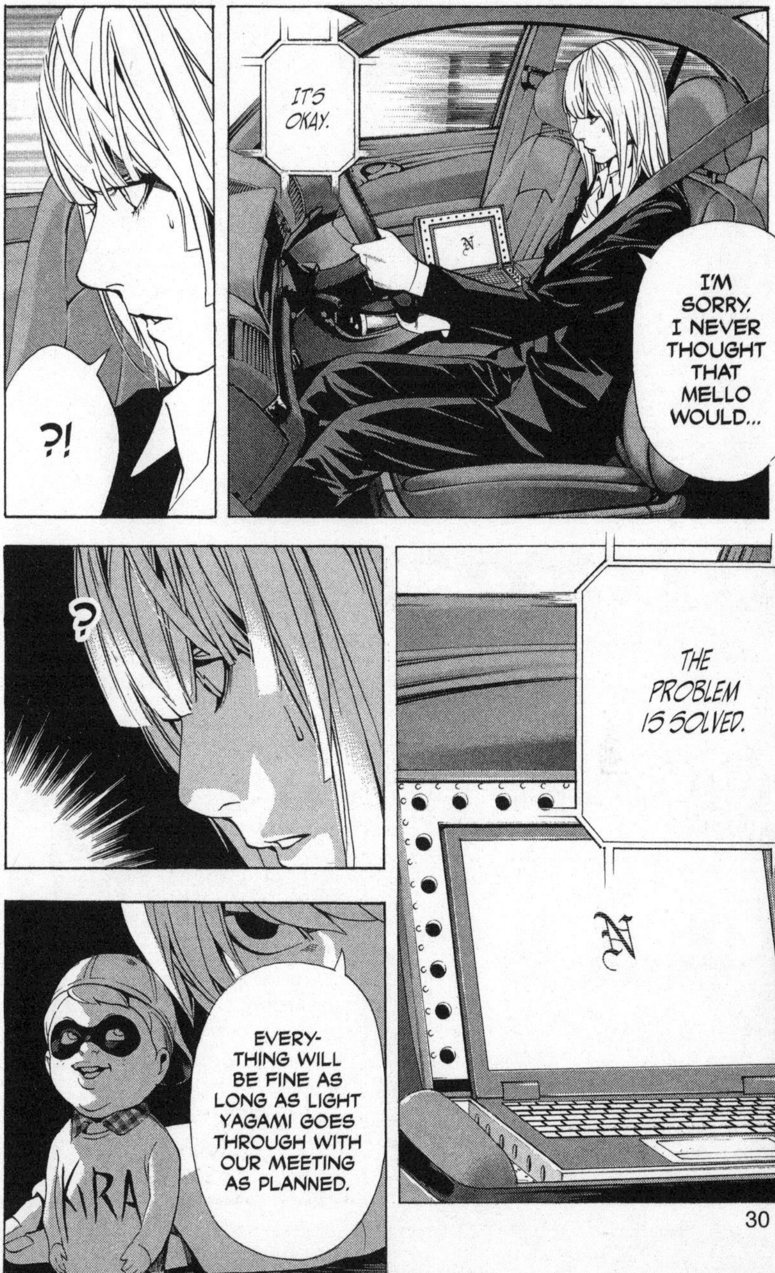
I'M SORRY. I NEVER THOUGHT THAT MELLO WOULD...
IT'S OKAY.
?!
THE PROBLEM IS SOLVED.
?
EVERY-THING WILL BE FINE AS LONG AS LIGHT YAGAMI GOES THROUGH WITH OUR MEETING AS PLANNED.
KIRA

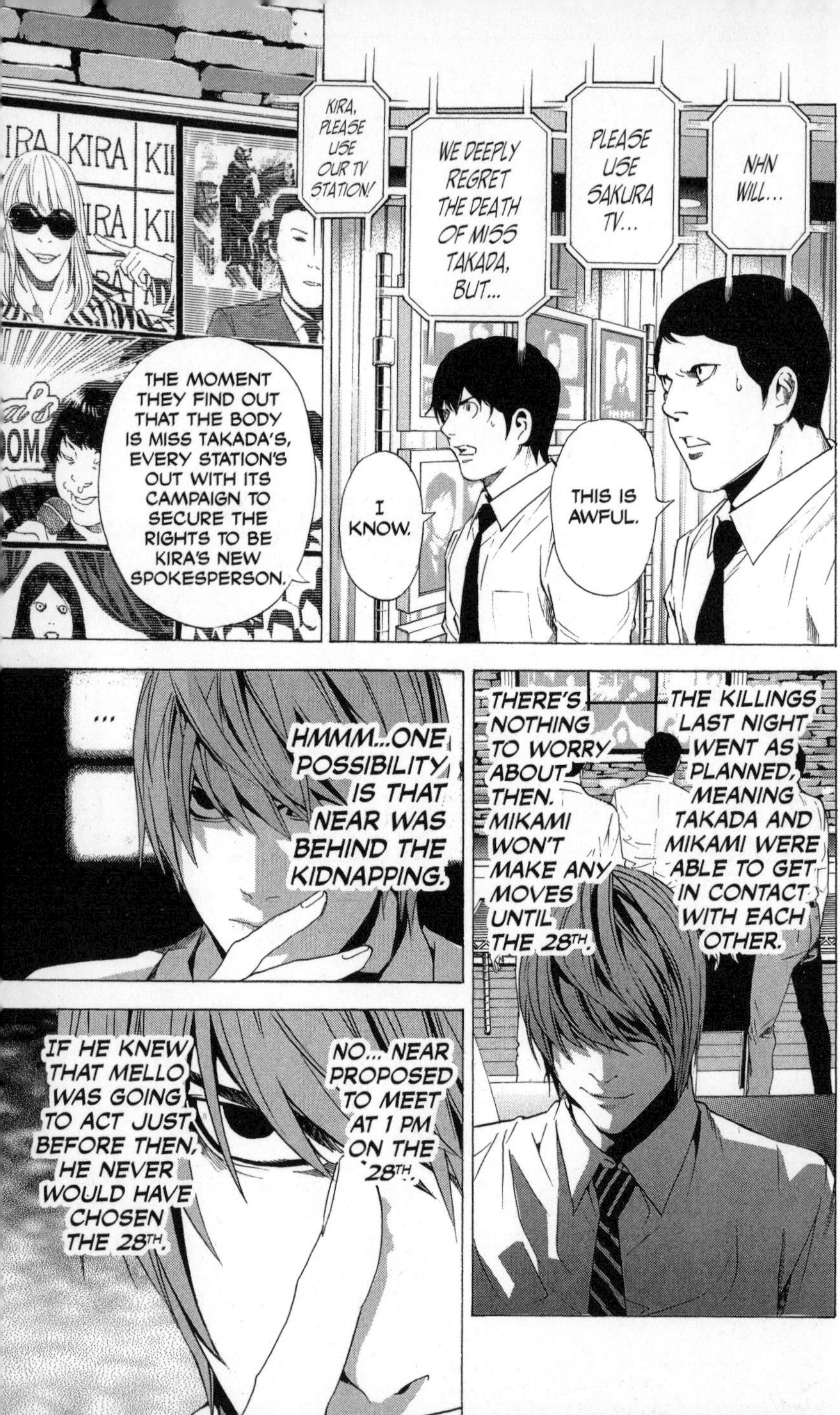
NHN WILL...
PLEASE USE SAKURA TV...
WE DEEPLY REGRET THE DEATH OF MISS TAKADA, BUT...
KIRA, PLEASE USE OUR TV STATION!
THIS IS AWFUL.
I KNOW.
THE MOMENT THEY FIND OUT THAT THE BODY IS MISS TAKADA'S, EVERY STATION'S OUT WITH ITS CAMPAIGN TO SECURE THE RIGHTS TO BE KIRA'S NEW SPOKESPERSON.
THE KILLINGS LAST NIGHT WENT AS PLANNED, MEANING TAKADA AND MIKAMI WERE ABLE TO GET IN CONTACT WITH EACH OTHER.
THERE'S NOTHING TO WORRY ABOUT THEN. MIKAMI WON'T MAKE ANY MOVES UNTIL THE 28TH.
HMMM...ONE POSSIBILITY IS THAT NEAR WAS BEHIND THE KIDNAPPING.
...
NO... NEAR PROPOSED TO MEET AT 1 PM ON THE 28TH...
IF HE KNEW THAT MELLO WAS GOING TO ACT JUST BEFORE THEN, HE NEVER WOULD HAVE CHOSEN THE 28TH.

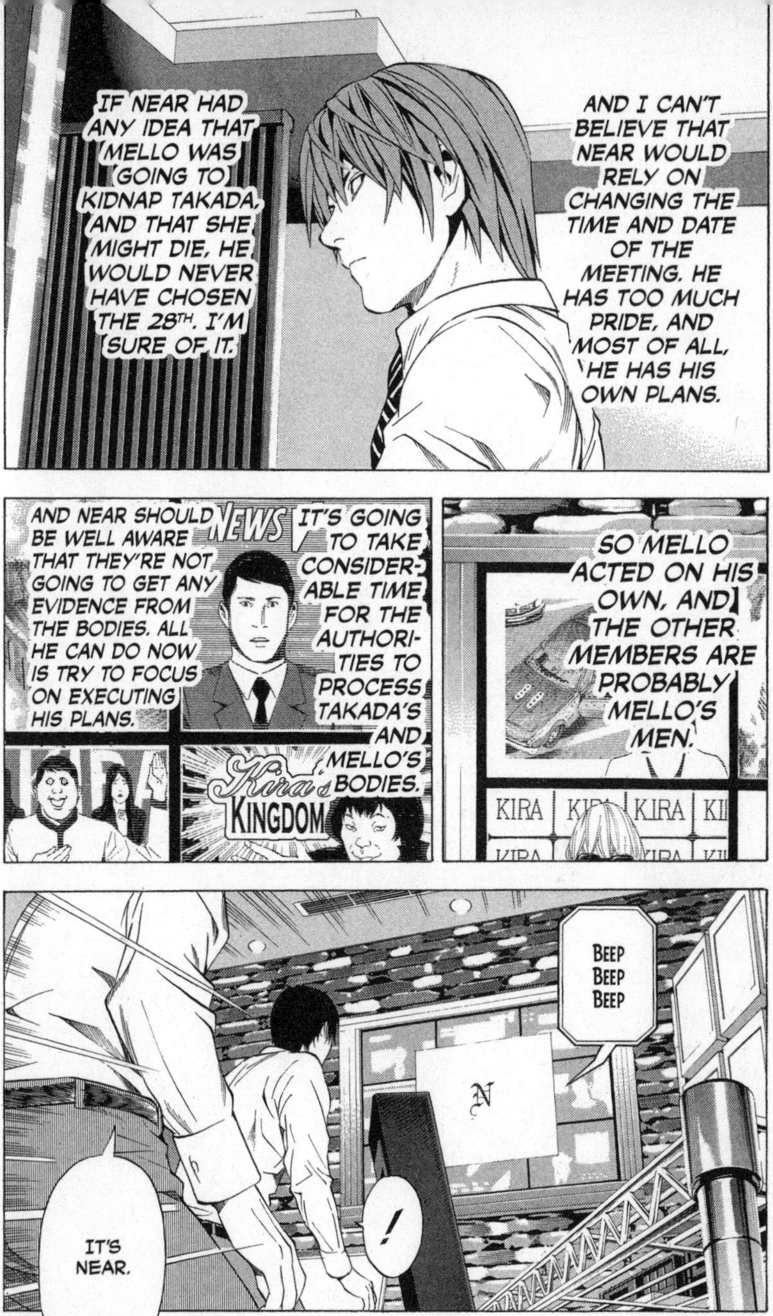
AND I CAN'T BELIEVE THAT NEAR WOULD RELY ON CHANGING THE TIME AND DATE OF THE MEETING. HE HAS TOO MUCH PRIDE, AND MOST OF ALL, HE HAS HIS OWN PLANS.
IF NEAR HAD ANY IDEA THAT MELLO WAS GOING TO KIDNAP TAKADA, AND THAT SHE MIGHT DIE, HE WOULD NEVER HAVE CHOSEN THE 28TH. I'M SURE OF IT.
SO MELLO ACTED ON HIS OWN, AND THE OTHER MEMBERS ARE PROBABLY MELLO'S MEN.
KIRA KIRA KIRA
NEWS
IT'S GOING TO TAKE CONSIDERABLE TIME FOR THE AUTHORITIES TO PROCESS TAKADA'S AND MELLO'S BODIES.
AND NEAR SHOULD BE WELL AWARE THAT THEY'RE NOT GOING TO GET ANY EVIDENCE FROM THE BODIES. ALL HE CAN DO NOW IS TRY TO FOCUS ON EXECUTING HIS PLANS.
Kira's KINGDOM
BEEP BEEP BEEP
N
!
IT'S NEAR.

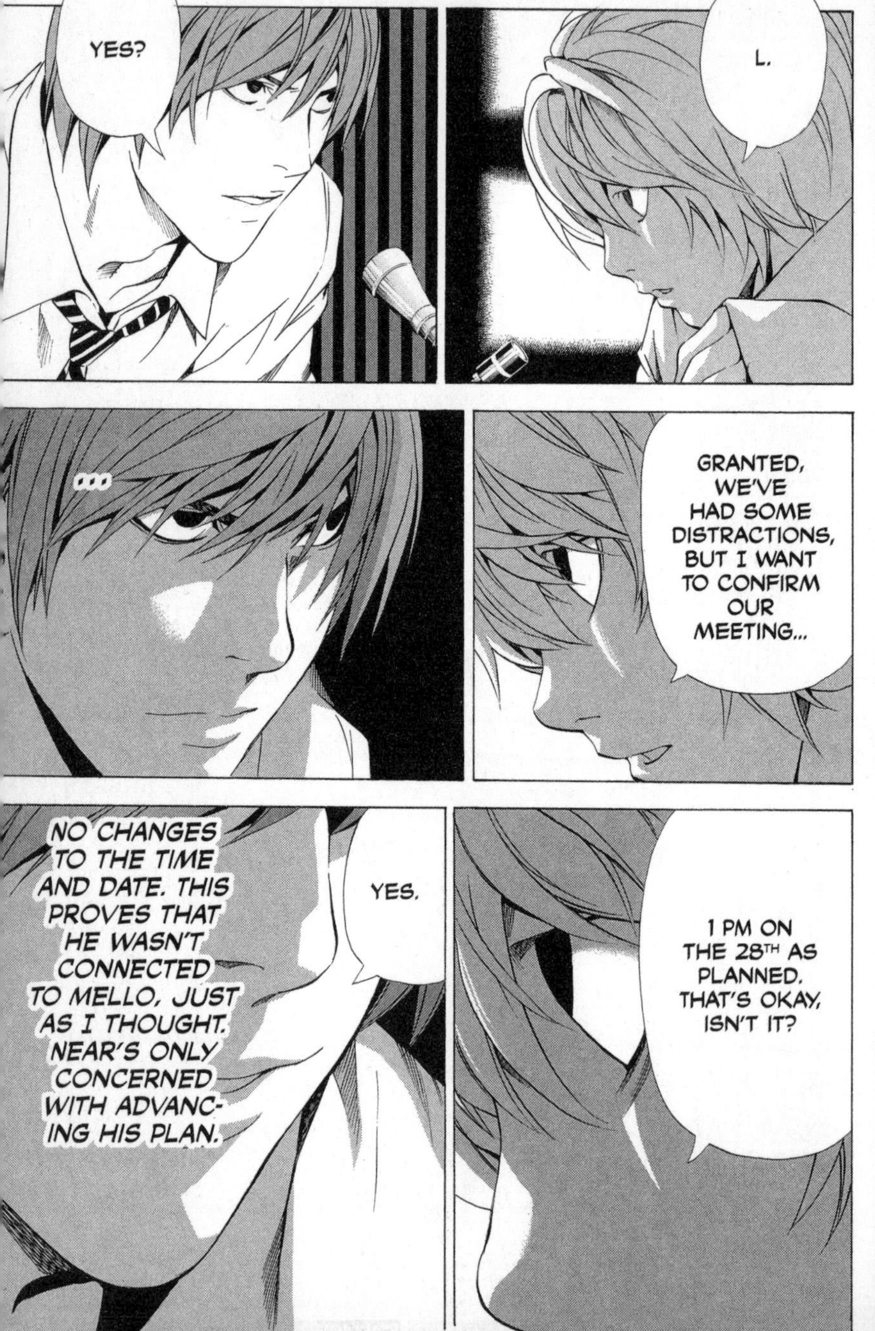
L.
YES?
GRANTED, WE'VE HAD SOME DISTRACTIONS, BUT I WANT TO CONFIRM OUR MEETING...
...
1 PM ON THE 28TH AS PLANNED. THAT'S OKAY, ISN'T IT?
YES.
NO CHANGES TO THE TIME AND DATE. THIS PROVES THAT HE WASN'T CONNECTED TO MELLO, JUST AS I THOUGHT. NEAR'S ONLY CONCERNED WITH ADVANC-ING HIS PLAN.

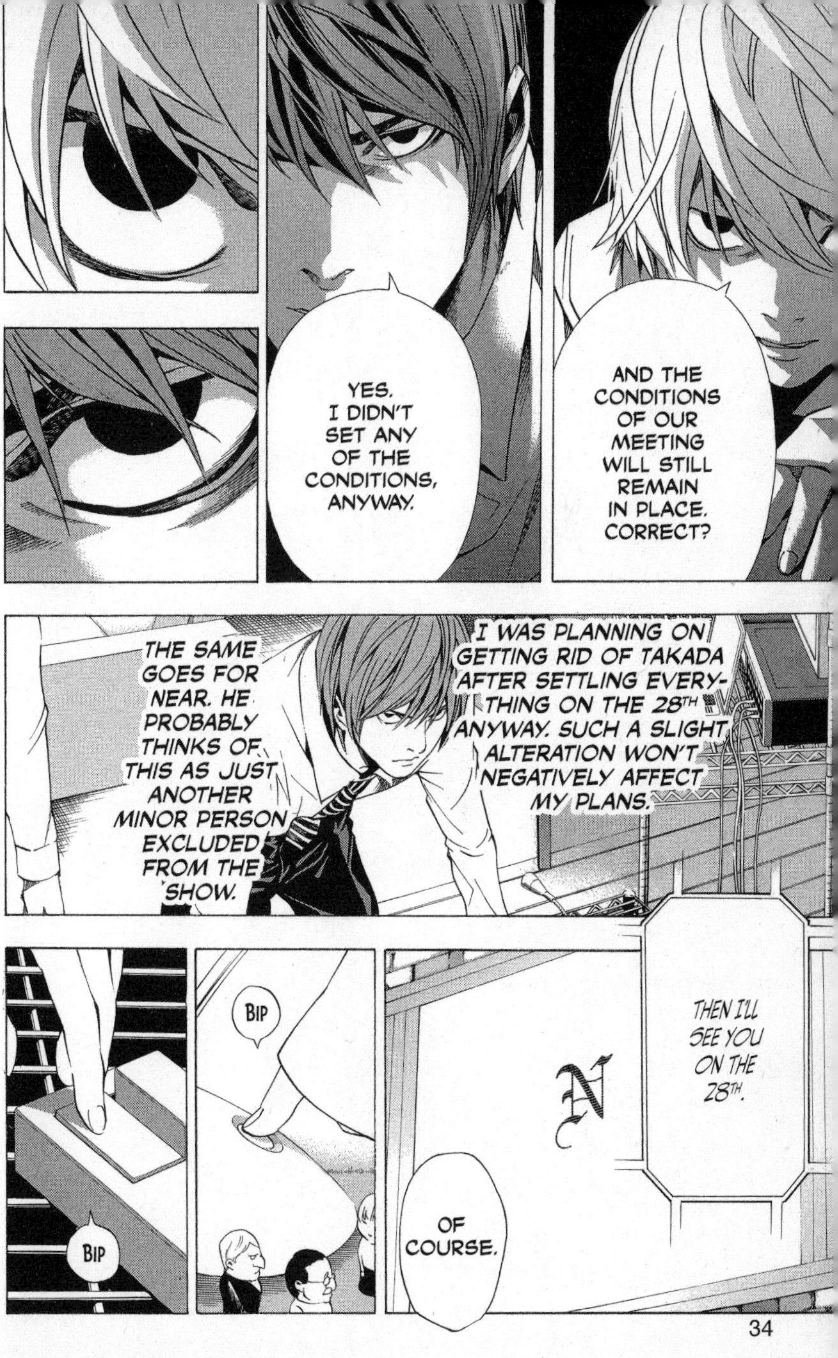
AND THE CONDITIONS OF OUR MEETING WILL STILL REMAIN IN PLACE. CORRECT?
YES. I DIDN'T SET ANY OF THE CONDITIONS, ANYWAY.
I WAS PLANNING ON GETTING RID OF TAKADA AFTER SETTLING EVERY-THING ON THE 28TH ANYWAY. SUCH A SLIGHT ALTERATION WON'T NEGATIVELY AFFECT MY PLANS.
THE SAME GOES FOR NEAR. HE PROBABLY THINKS OF THIS AS JUST ANOTHER MINOR PERSON EXCLUDED FROM THE SHOW.
THEN I'LL SEE YOU ON THE 28TH.
N
OF COURSE.
BIP
BIP

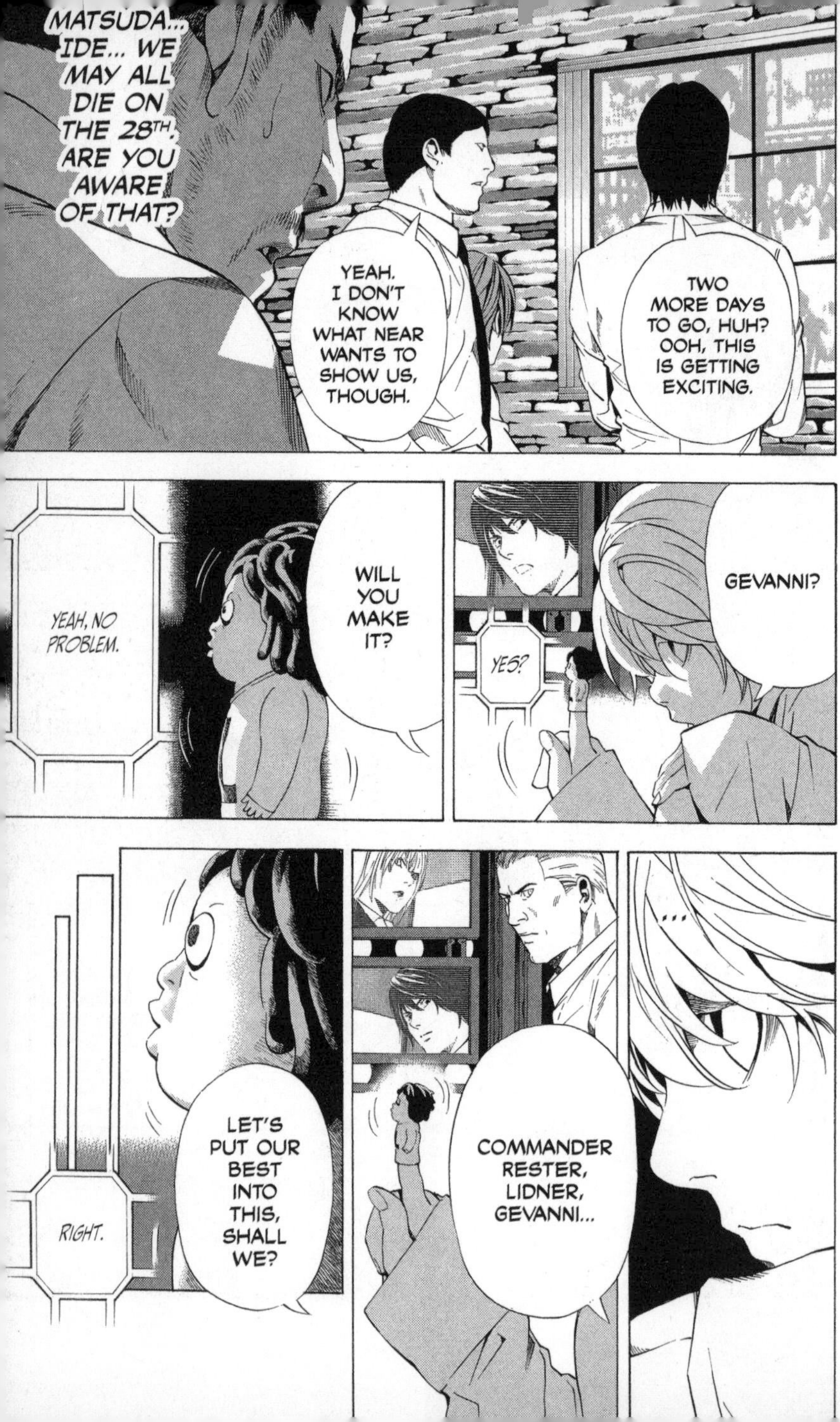
MATSUDA... IDE... WE MAY ALL DIE ON THE 28TH. ARE YOU AWARE OF THAT?
TWO MORE DAYS TO GO, HUH? OOH, THIS IS GETTING EXCITING.
YEAH. I DON'T KNOW WHAT NEAR WANTS TO SHOW US, THOUGH.
GEVANNI?
YES?
WILL YOU MAKE IT?
YEAH, NO PROBLEM.
...
COMMANDER RESTER, LIDNER, GEVANNI...
LET'S PUT OUR BEST INTO THIS, SHALL WE?
RIGHT.

January 28th, 2010

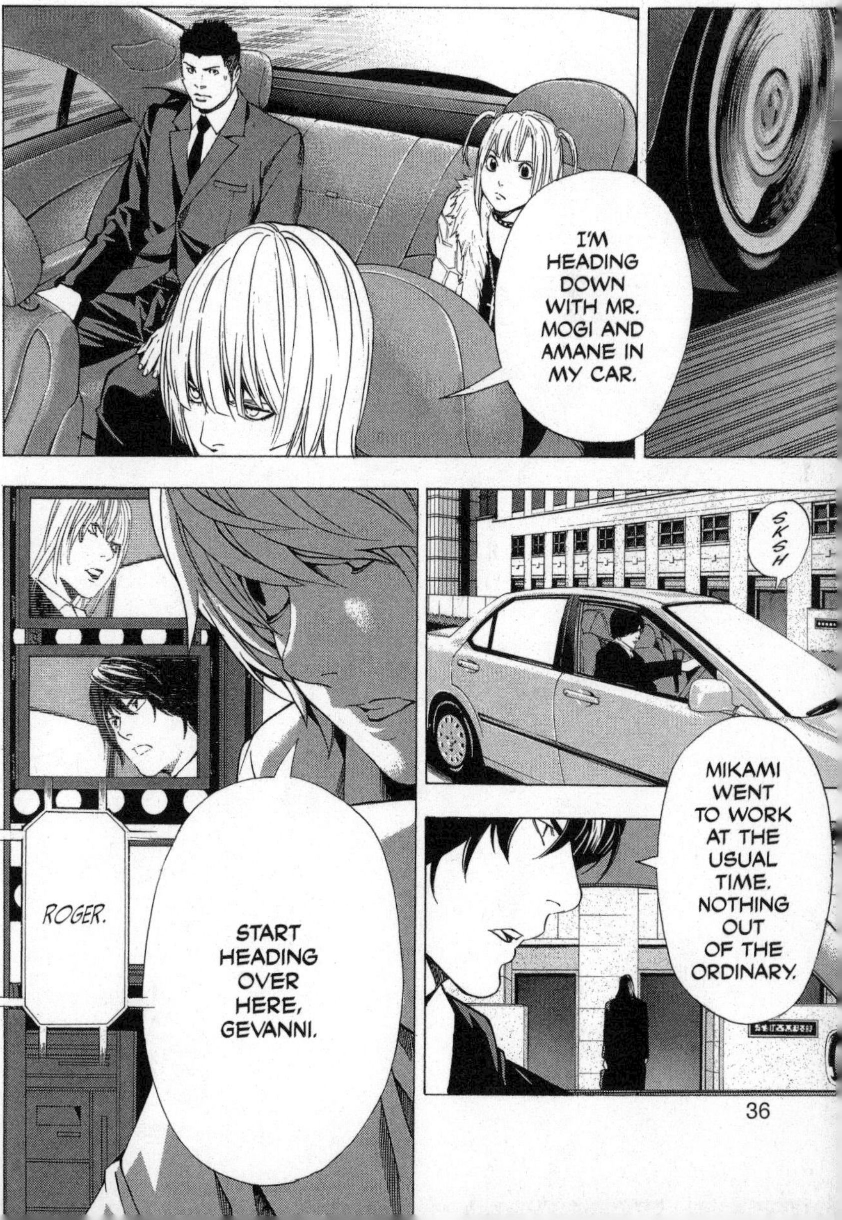
I'M HEADING DOWN WITH MR. MOGI AND AMANE IN MY CAR.
SKSH
MIKAMI WENT TO WORK AT THE USUAL TIME. NOTHING OUT OF THE ORDINARY.
START HEADING OVER HERE, GEVANNI.
ROGER.

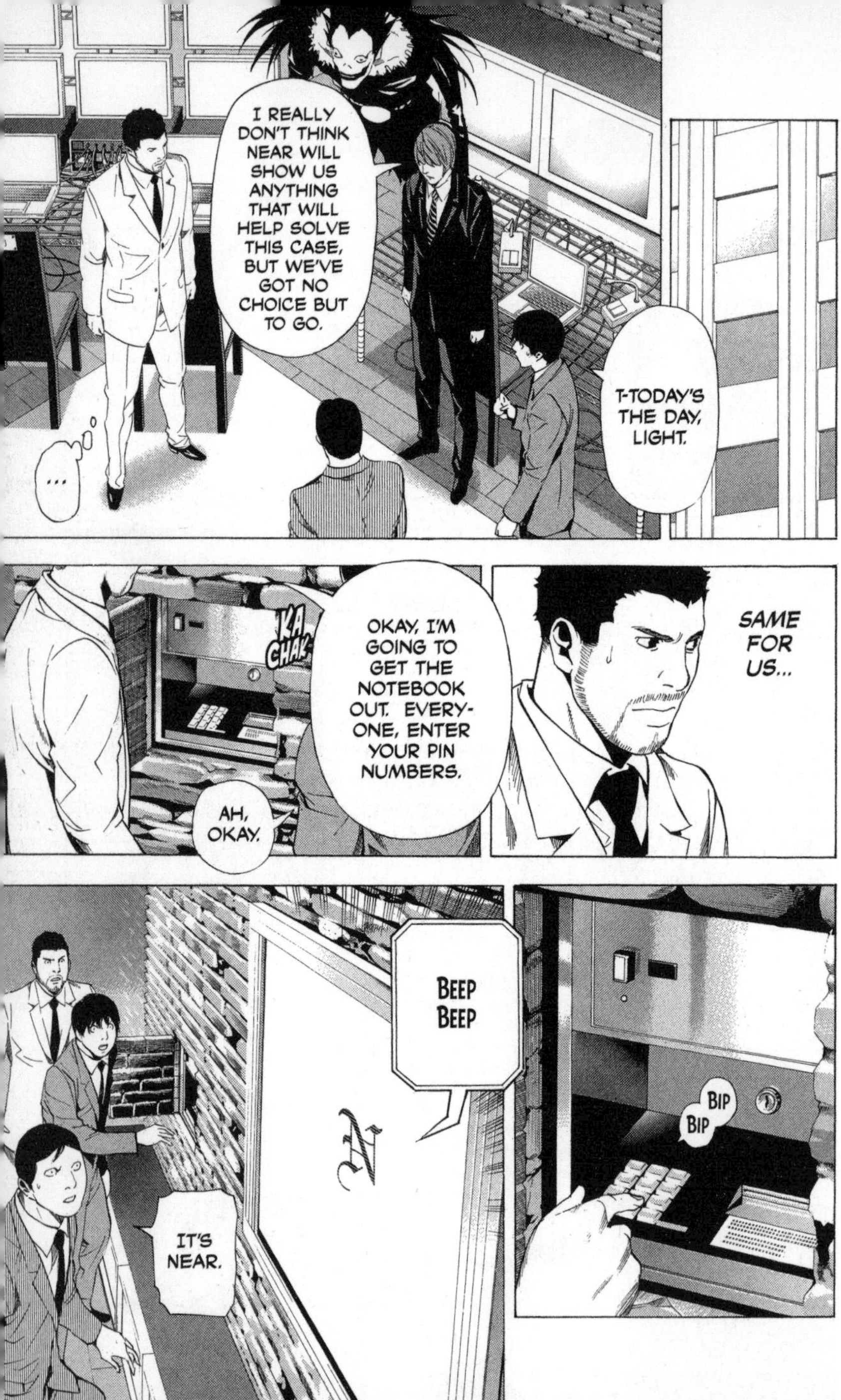
T-TODAY'S THE DAY, LIGHT.
I REALLY DON'T THINK NEAR WILL SHOW US ANYTHING THAT WILL HELP SOLVE THIS CASE, BUT WE'VE GOT NO CHOICE BUT TO GO.
...
SAME FOR US...
OKAY, I'M GOING TO GET THE NOTEBOOK OUT. EVERY-ONE, ENTER YOUR PIN NUMBERS.
KA CHAK
AH, OKAY.
BIP BIP
BEEP BEEP
IT'S NEAR.

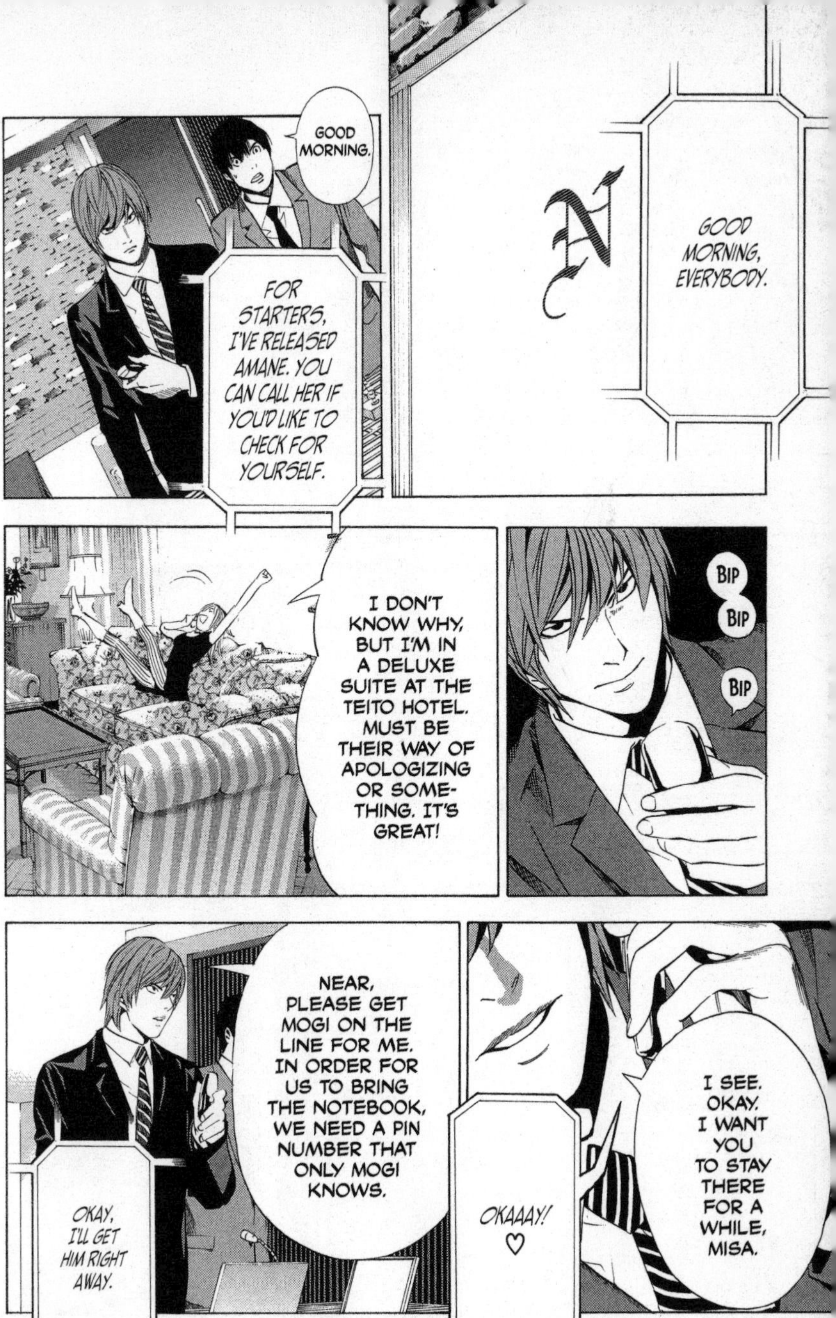
GOOD MORNING, EVERYBODY.
GOOD MORNING.
FOR STARTERS, I'VE RELEASED AMANE. YOU CAN CALL HER IF YOU'D LIKE TO CHECK FOR YOURSELF.
BIP
BIP
BIP
I DON'T KNOW WHY, BUT I'M IN A DELUXE SUITE AT THE TEITO HOTEL. MUST BE THEIR WAY OF APOLOGIZING OR SOMETHING. IT'S GREAT!
I SEE. OKAY. I WANT YOU TO STAY THERE FOR A WHILE, MISA.
OKAAAY! ♡
NEAR, PLEASE GET MOGI ON THE LINE FOR ME. IN ORDER FOR US TO BRING THE NOTEBOOK, WE NEED A PIN NUMBER THAT ONLY MOGI KNOWS.
OKAY, I'LL GET HIM RIGHT AWAY.

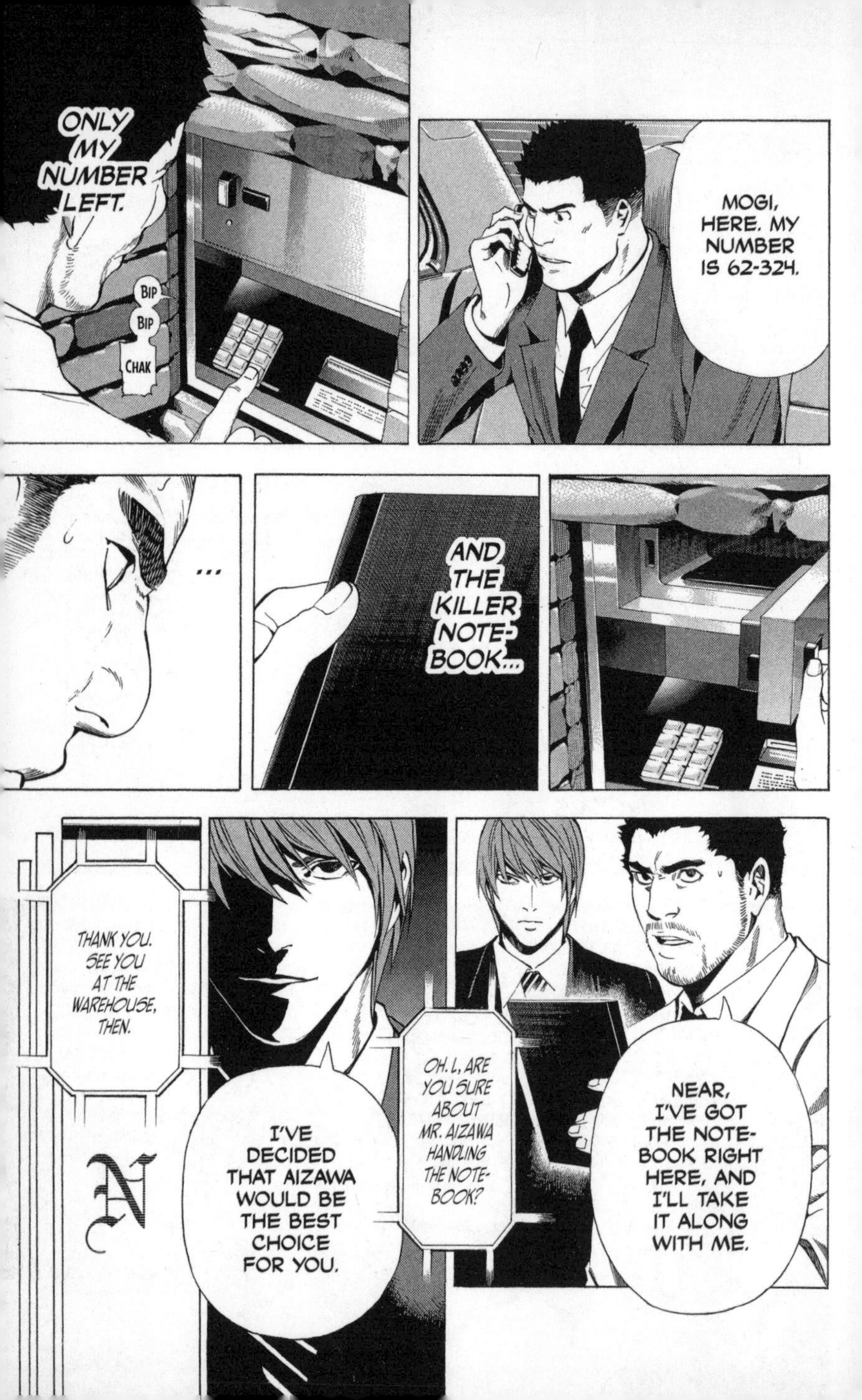
MOGI, HERE. MY NUMBER IS 62-324.
ONLY MY NUMBER LEFT.
BIP
BIP
CHAK
AND THE KILLER NOTE-BOOK...
...
NEAR, I'VE GOT THE NOTE-BOOK RIGHT HERE, AND I'LL TAKE IT ALONG WITH ME.
OH. L, ARE YOU SURE ABOUT MR. AIZAWA HANDLING THE NOTE-BOOK?
I'VE DECIDED THAT AIZAWA WOULD BE THE BEST CHOICE FOR YOU.
THANK YOU. SEE YOU AT THE WAREHOUSE, THEN.
N

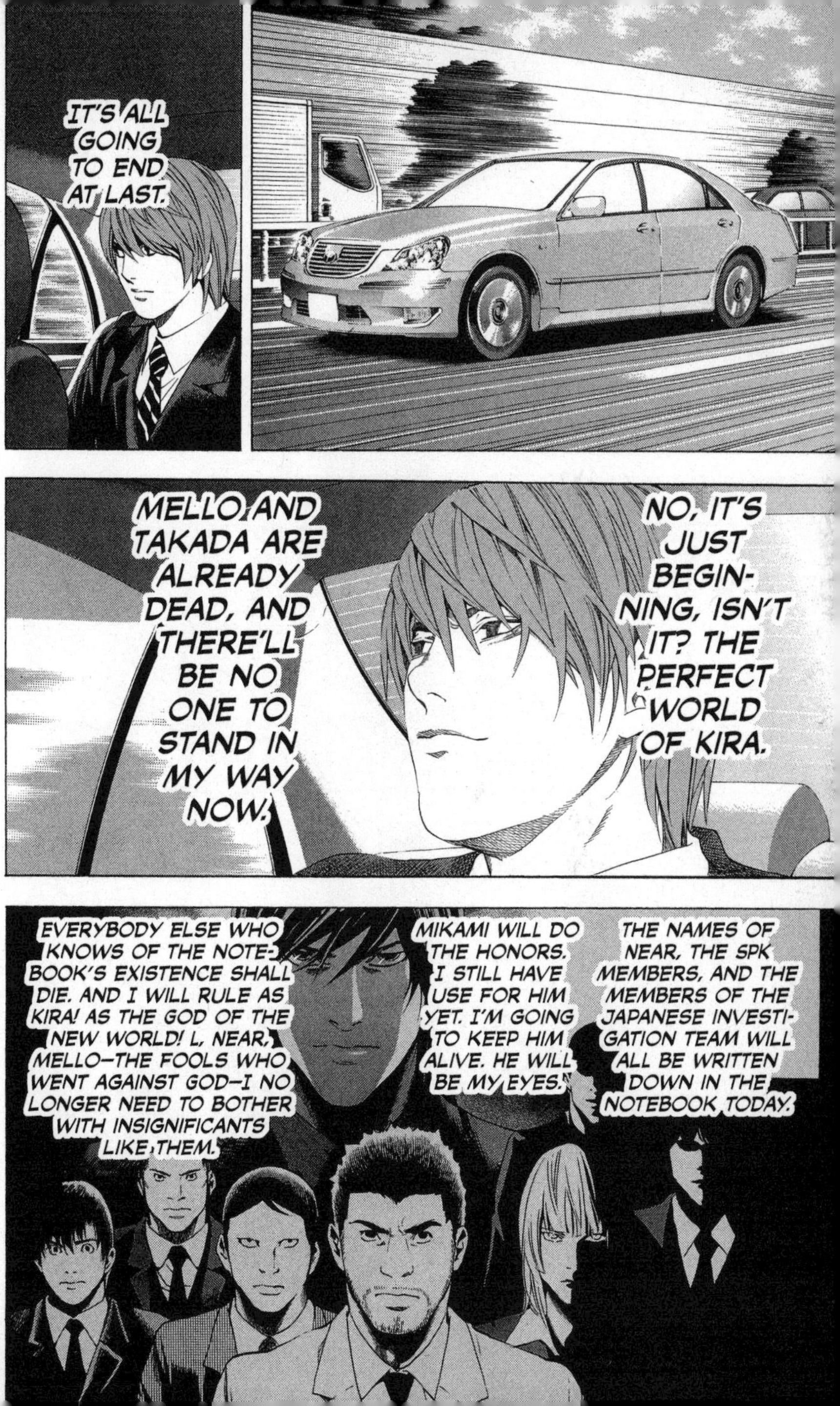
IT'S ALL GOING TO END AT LAST.
NO, IT'S JUST BEGINNING, ISN'T IT? THE PERFECT WORLD OF KIRA.
MELLO AND TAKADA ARE ALREADY DEAD, AND THERE'LL BE NO ONE TO STAND IN MY WAY NOW.
THE NAMES OF NEAR, THE SPK MEMBERS, AND THE MEMBERS OF THE JAPANESE INVESTIGATION TEAM WILL ALL BE WRITTEN DOWN IN THE NOTEBOOK TODAY.
MIKAMI WILL DO THE HONORS. I STILL HAVE USE FOR HIM YET. I'M GOING TO KEEP HIM ALIVE. HE WILL BE MY EYES.
EVERYBODY ELSE WHO KNOWS OF THE NOTEBOOK'S EXISTENCE SHALL DIE. AND I WILL RULE AS KIRA! AS THE GOD OF THE NEW WORLD! L, NEAR, MELLO—THE FOOLS WHO WENT AGAINST GOD—I NO LONGER NEED TO BOTHER WITH INSIGNIFICANTS LIKE THEM.

READ THIS WAY

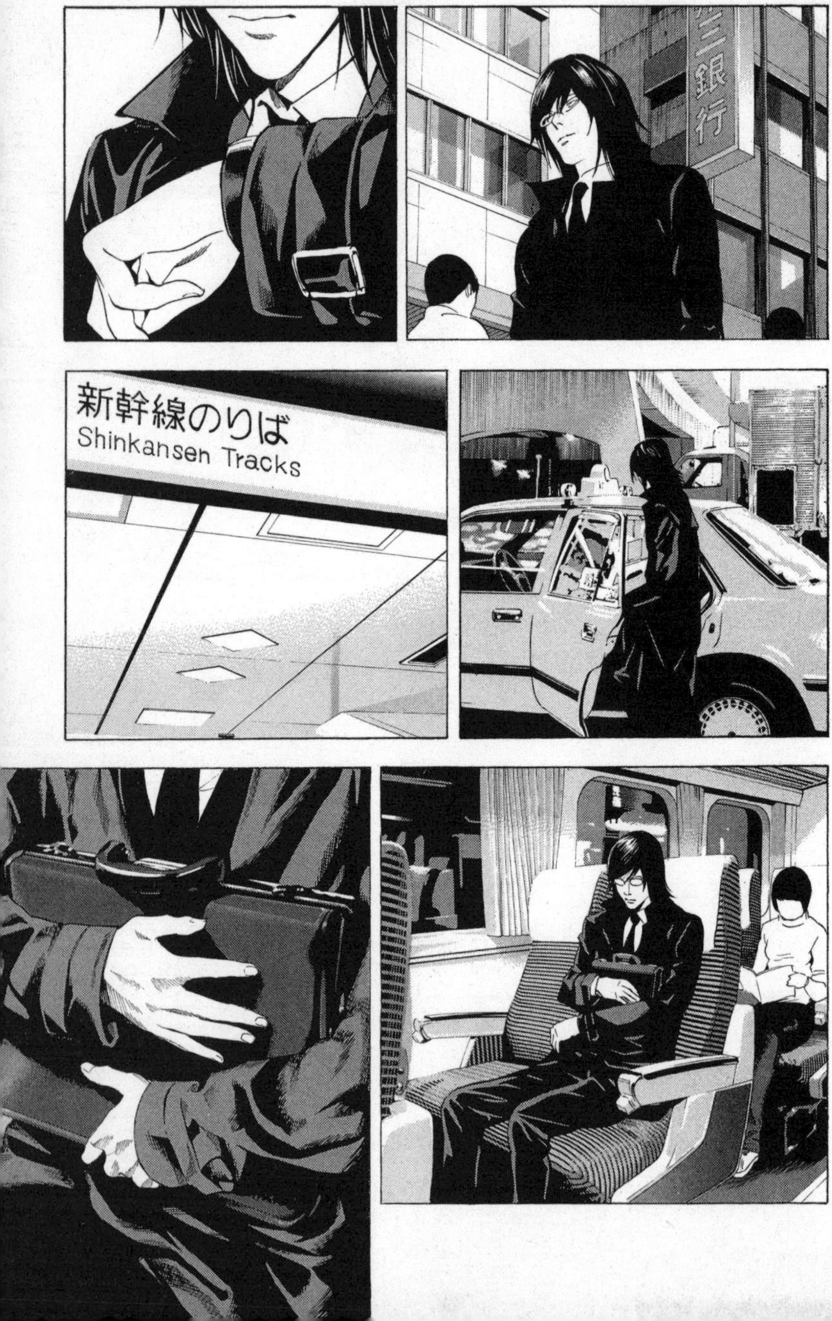
新幹線のりば
Shinkansen Tracks

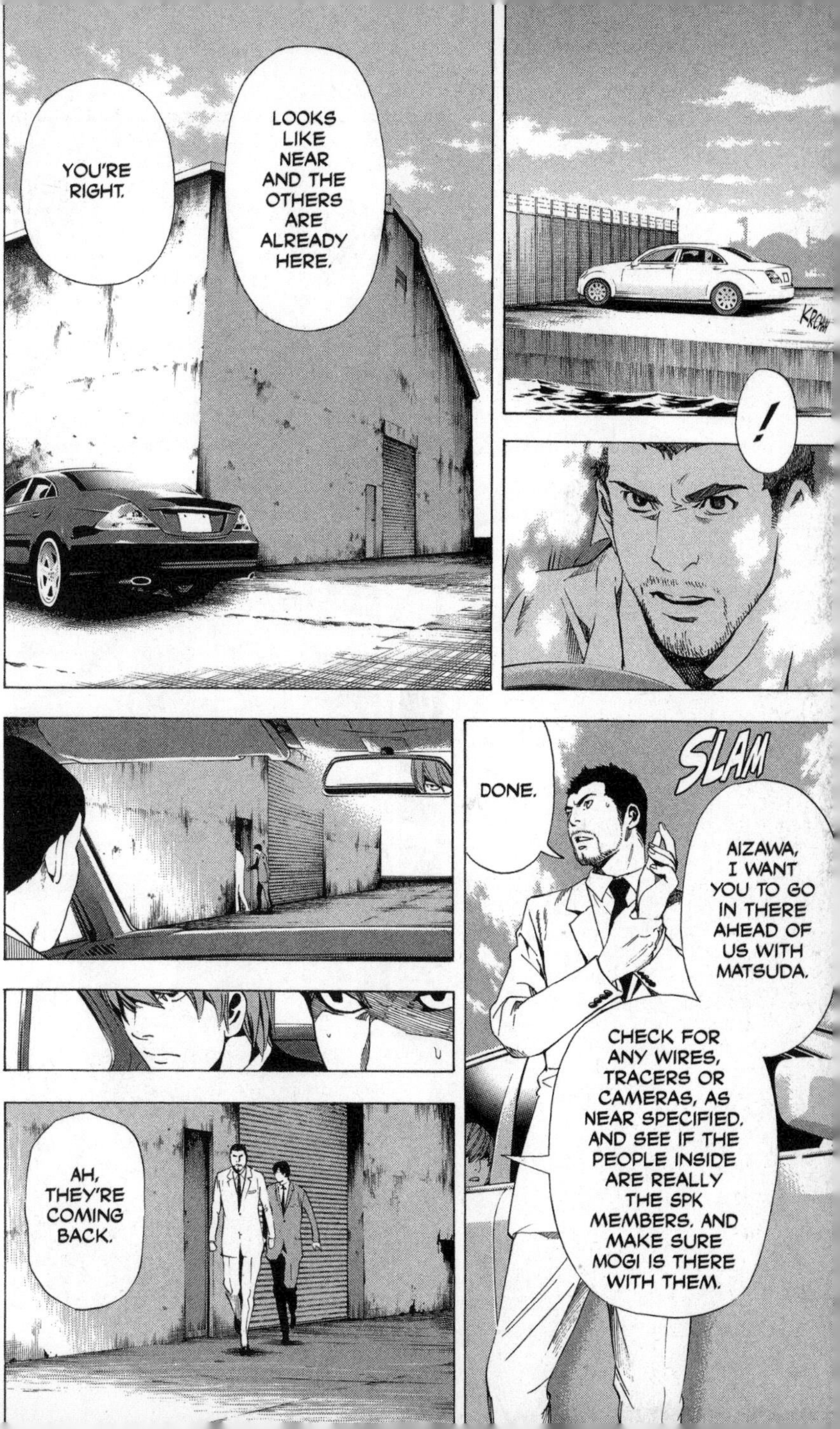
KRCHAK
!
LOOKS LIKE NEAR AND THE OTHERS ARE ALREADY HERE.
YOU'RE RIGHT.
SLAM
DONE.
AIZAWA, I WANT YOU TO GO IN THERE AHEAD OF US WITH MATSUDA.
CHECK FOR ANY WIRES, TRACERS OR CAMERAS, AS NEAR SPECIFIED, AND SEE IF THE PEOPLE INSIDE ARE REALLY THE SPK MEMBERS. AND MAKE SURE MOGI IS THERE WITH THEM.
AH, THEY'RE COMING BACK.

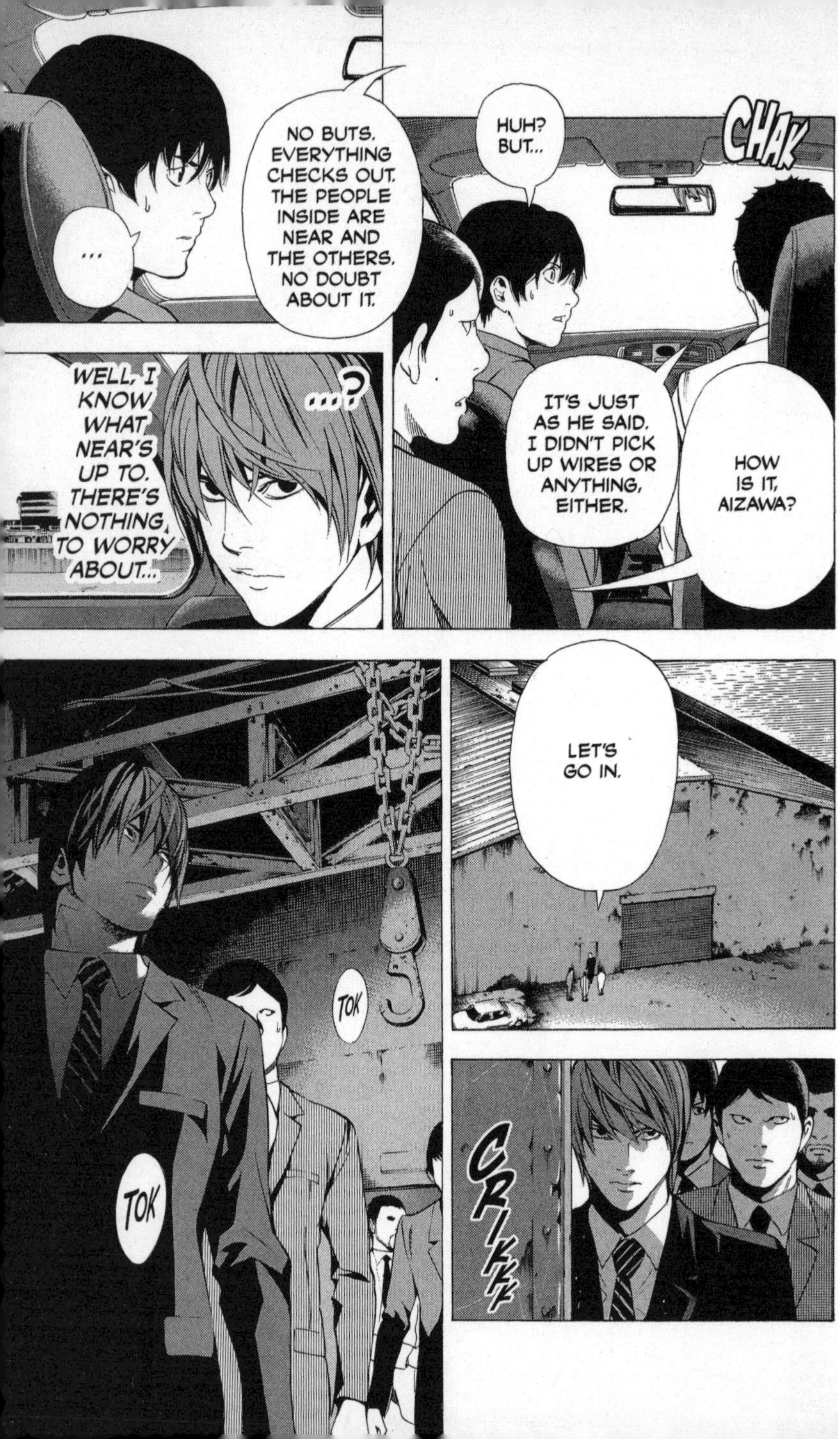

CHAK
HOW IS IT, AIZAWA?
IT'S JUST AS HE SAID. I DIDN'T PICK UP WIRES OR ANYTHING, EITHER.
HUH? BUT...
NO BUTS. EVERYTHING CHECKS OUT. THE PEOPLE INSIDE ARE NEAR AND THE OTHERS. NO DOUBT ABOUT IT.
...
...?
WELL, I KNOW WHAT NEAR'S UP TO. THERE'S NOTHING TO WORRY ABOUT...
LET'S GO IN.
CRIKKK
TOK
TOK

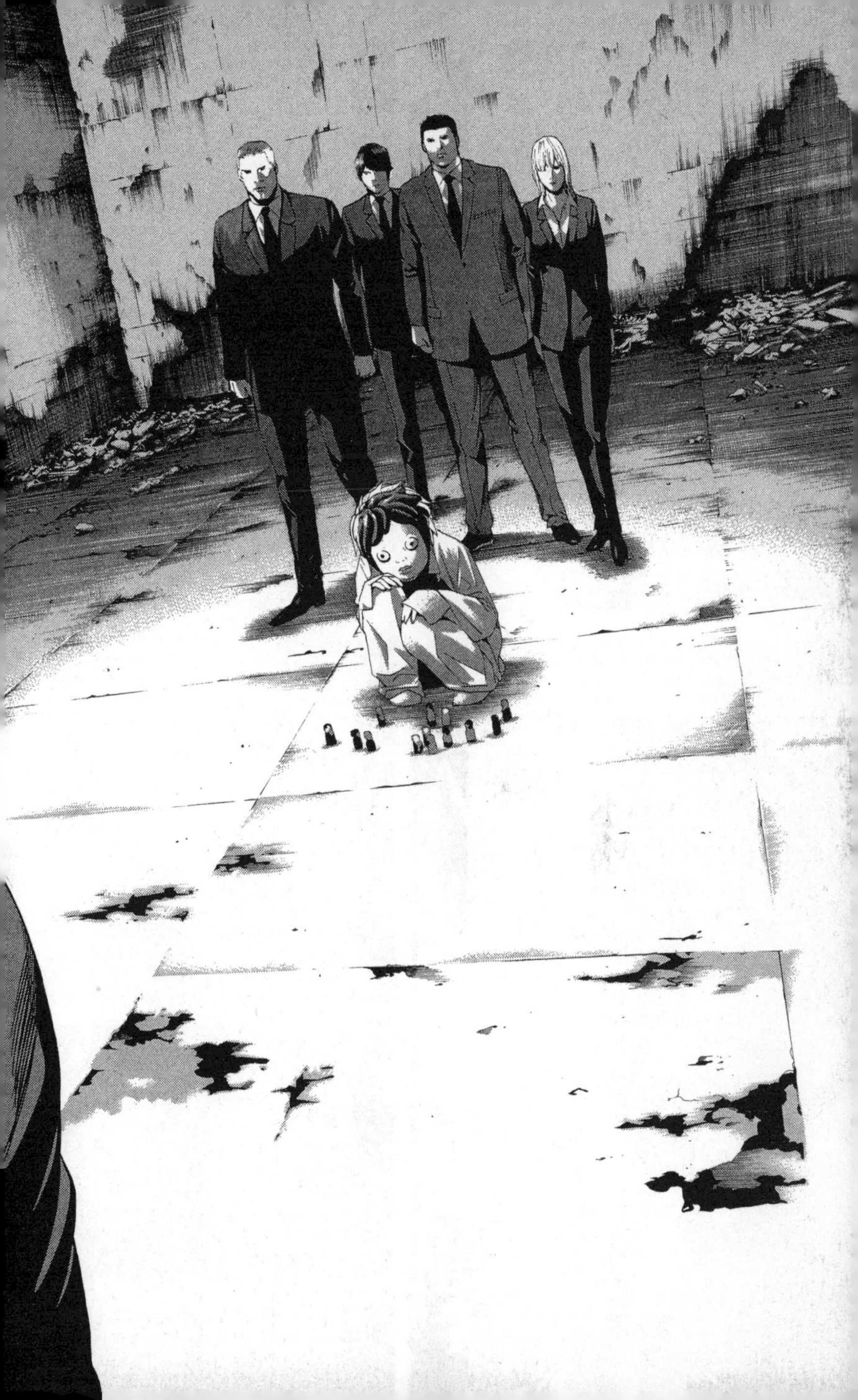

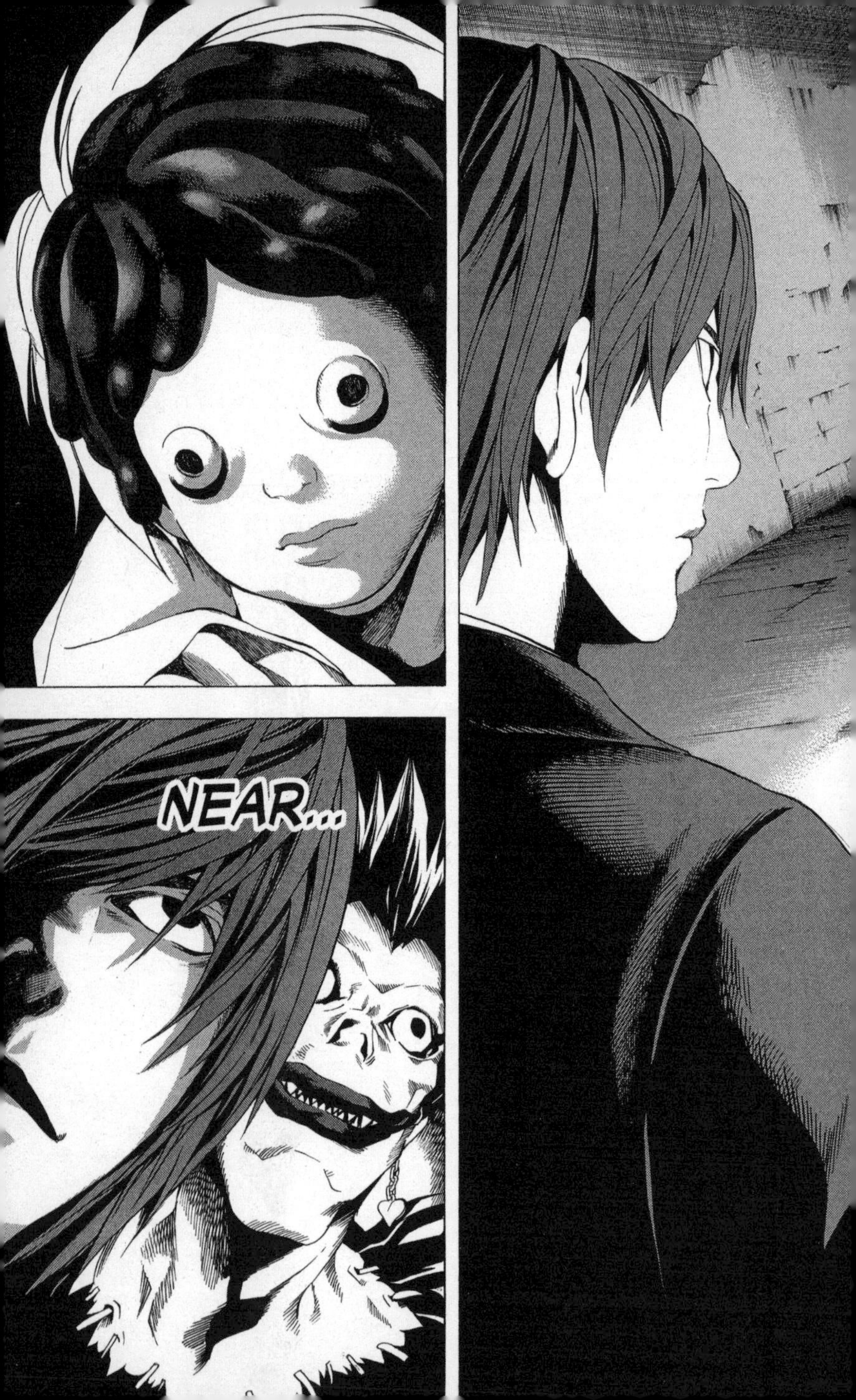
NEAR...

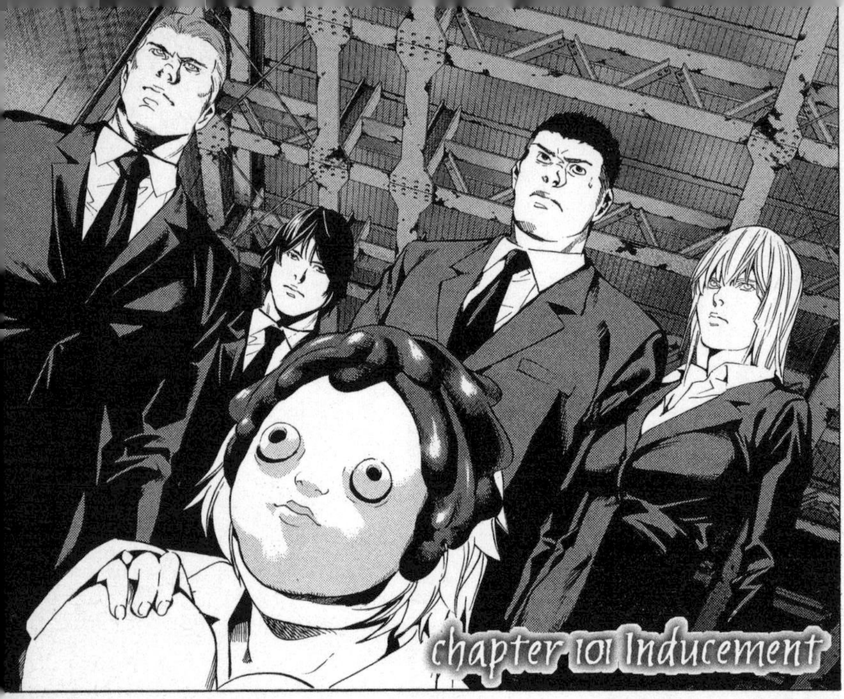
chapter 101 Inducement

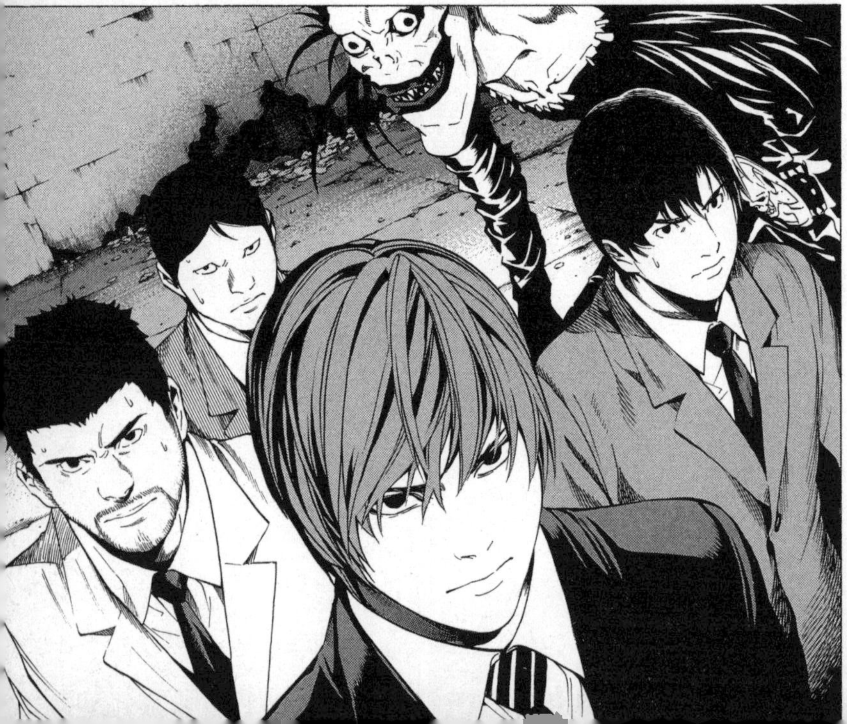

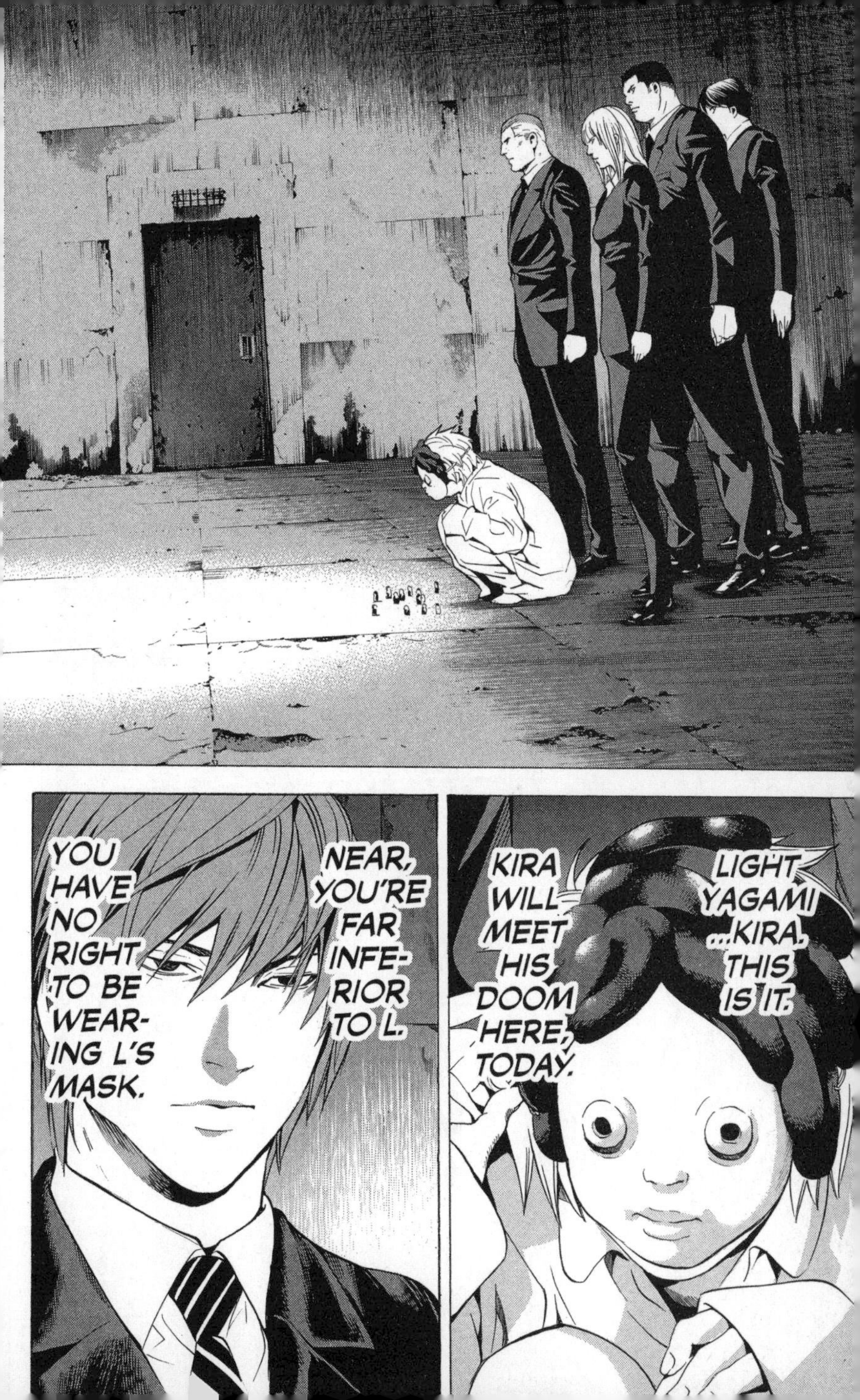
LIGHT YAGAMI ...KIRA. THIS IS IT.
KIRA WILL MEET HIS DOOM HERE, TODAY.
NEAR, YOU'RE FAR INFERIOR TO L.
YOU HAVE NO RIGHT TO BE WEARING L'S MASK.

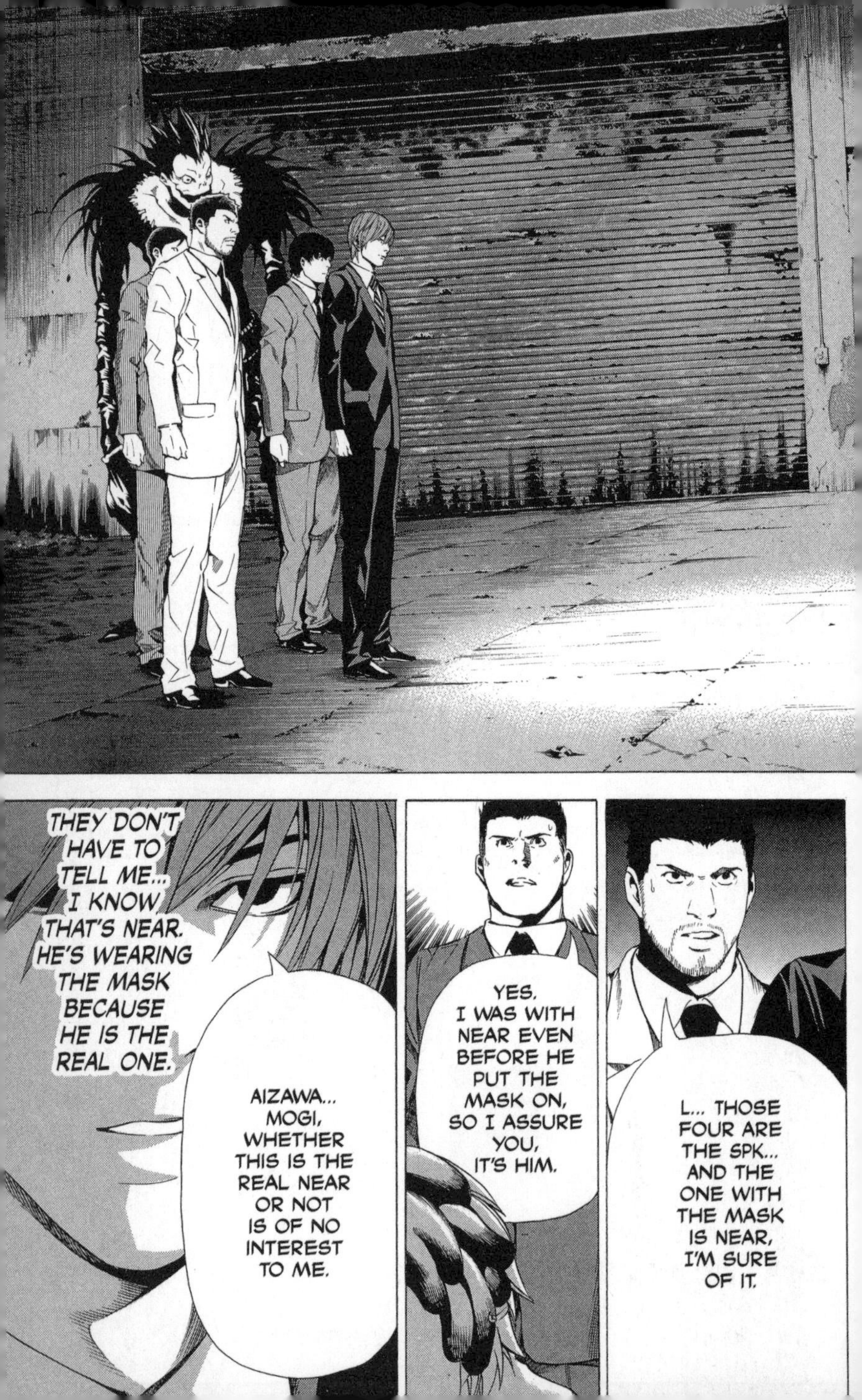
L... THOSE FOUR ARE THE SPK... AND THE ONE WITH THE MASK IS NEAR, I'M SURE OF IT.
YES. I WAS WITH NEAR EVEN BEFORE HE PUT THE MASK ON, SO I ASSURE YOU, IT'S HIM.
AIZAWA... MOGI, WHETHER THIS IS THE REAL NEAR OR NOT IS OF NO INTEREST TO ME.
THEY DON'T HAVE TO TELL ME... I KNOW THAT'S NEAR. HE'S WEARING THE MASK BECAUSE HE IS THE REAL ONE.

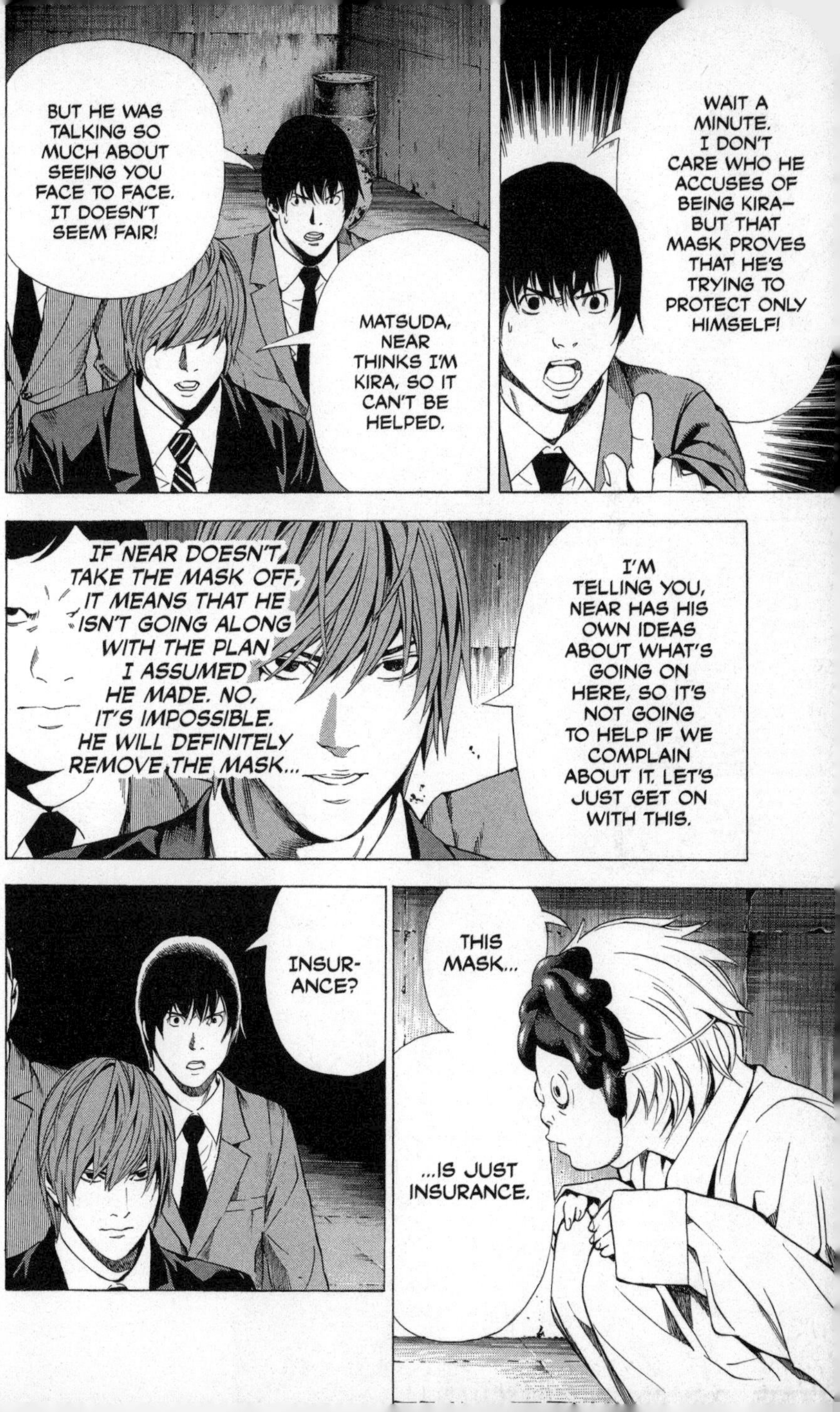
WAIT A MINUTE. I DON'T CARE WHO HE ACCUSES OF BEING KIRA– BUT THAT MASK PROVES THAT HE'S TRYING TO PROTECT ONLY HIMSELF!
BUT HE WAS TALKING SO MUCH ABOUT SEEING YOU FACE TO FACE. IT DOESN'T SEEM FAIR!
MATSUDA, NEAR THINKS I'M KIRA, SO IT CAN'T BE HELPED.
I'M TELLING YOU, NEAR HAS HIS OWN IDEAS ABOUT WHAT'S GOING ON HERE, SO IT'S NOT GOING TO HELP IF WE COMPLAIN ABOUT IT. LET'S JUST GET ON WITH THIS.
IF NEAR DOESN'T TAKE THE MASK OFF, IT MEANS THAT HE ISN'T GOING ALONG WITH THE PLAN I ASSUMED HE MADE. NO, IT'S IMPOSSIBLE. HE WILL DEFINITELY REMOVE THE MASK...
THIS MASK...
...IS JUST INSURANCE.
INSUR-ANCE?

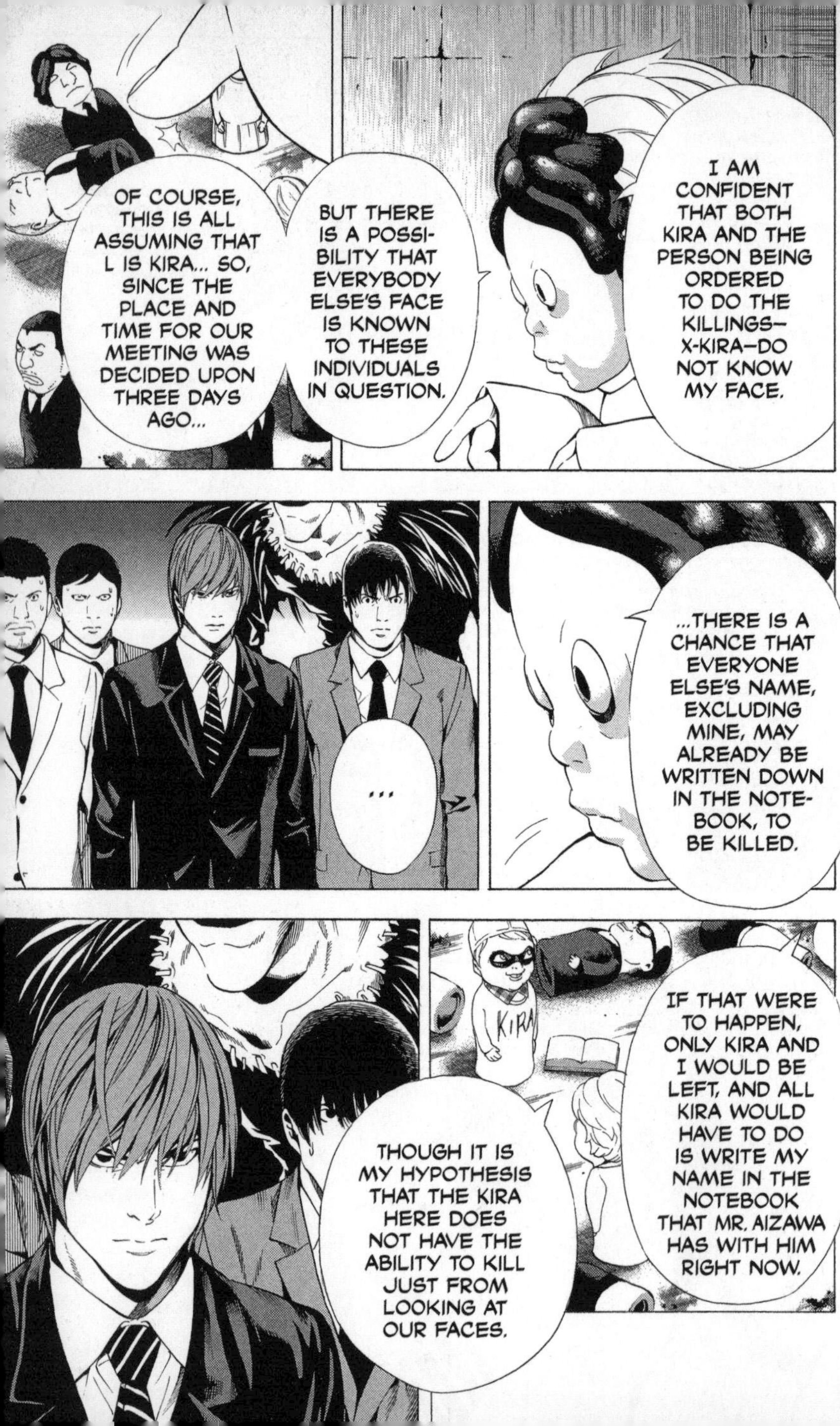
I AM CONFIDENT THAT BOTH KIRA AND THE PERSON BEING ORDERED TO DO THE KILLINGS—X-KIRA—DO NOT KNOW MY FACE.
BUT THERE IS A POSSIBILITY THAT EVERYBODY ELSE'S FACE IS KNOWN TO THESE INDIVIDUALS IN QUESTION.
OF COURSE, THIS IS ALL ASSUMING THAT L IS KIRA... SO, SINCE THE PLACE AND TIME FOR OUR MEETING WAS DECIDED UPON THREE DAYS AGO...
...THERE IS A CHANCE THAT EVERYONE ELSE'S NAME, EXCLUDING MINE, MAY ALREADY BE WRITTEN DOWN IN THE NOTEBOOK, TO BE KILLED.
...
IF THAT WERE TO HAPPEN, ONLY KIRA AND I WOULD BE LEFT, AND ALL KIRA WOULD HAVE TO DO IS WRITE MY NAME IN THE NOTEBOOK THAT MR. AIZAWA HAS WITH HIM RIGHT NOW.
KIRA
THOUGH IT IS MY HYPOTHESIS THAT THE KIRA HERE DOES NOT HAVE THE ABILITY TO KILL JUST FROM LOOKING AT OUR FACES.

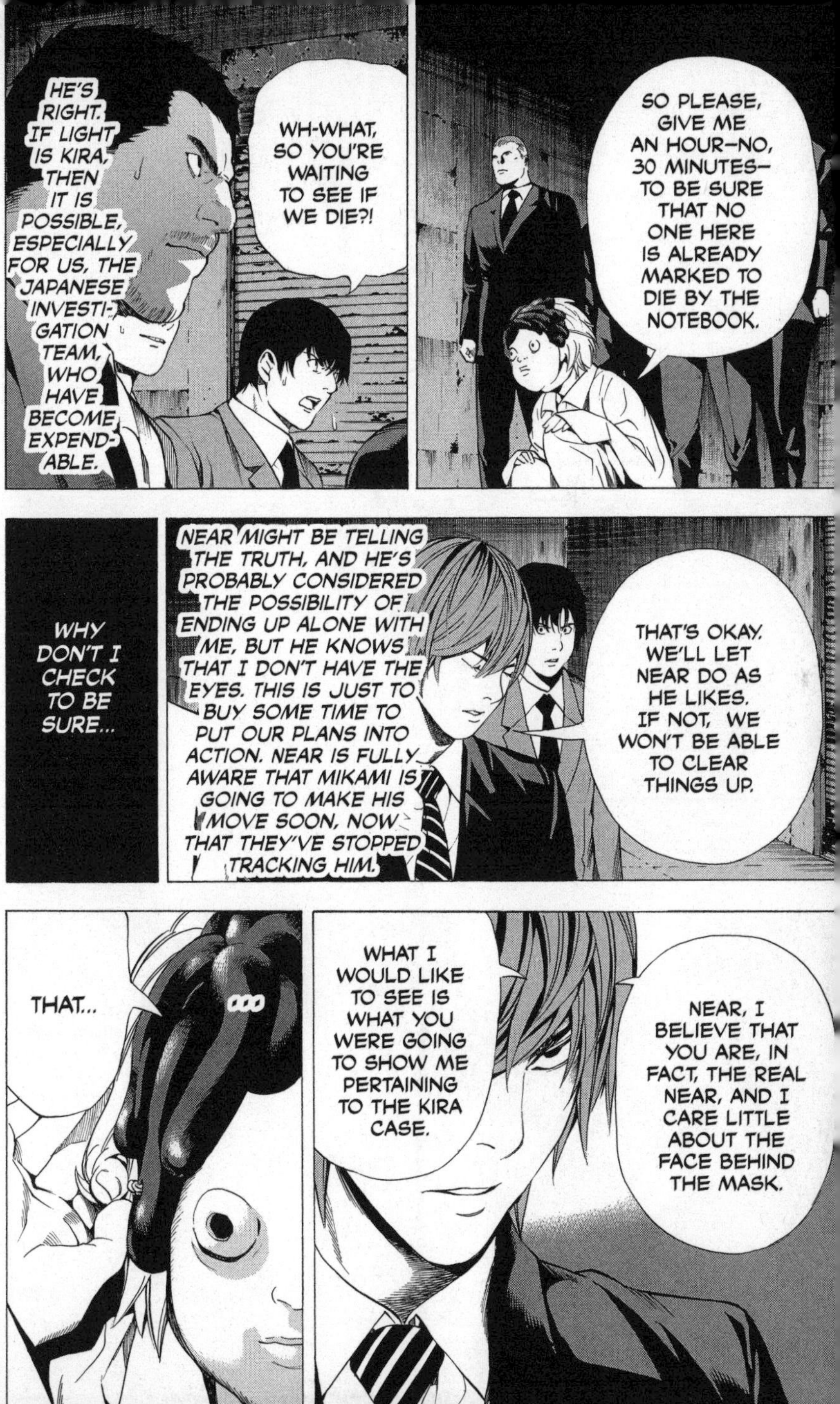
SO PLEASE, GIVE ME AN HOUR—NO, 30 MINUTES—TO BE SURE THAT NO ONE HERE IS ALREADY MARKED TO DIE BY THE NOTEBOOK.
WH-WHAT, SO YOU'RE WAITING TO SEE IF WE DIE?!
HE'S RIGHT. IF LIGHT IS KIRA, THEN IT IS POSSIBLE, ESPECIALLY FOR US, THE JAPANESE INVESTIGATION TEAM, WHO HAVE BECOME EXPENDABLE.
THAT'S OKAY. WE'LL LET NEAR DO AS HE LIKES. IF NOT, WE WON'T BE ABLE TO CLEAR THINGS UP.
NEAR MIGHT BE TELLING THE TRUTH, AND HE'S PROBABLY CONSIDERED THE POSSIBILITY OF ENDING UP ALONE WITH ME, BUT HE KNOWS THAT I DON'T HAVE THE EYES. THIS IS JUST TO BUY SOME TIME TO PUT OUR PLANS INTO ACTION. NEAR IS FULLY AWARE THAT MIKAMI IS GOING TO MAKE HIS MOVE SOON, NOW THAT THEY'VE STOPPED TRACKING HIM.
WHY DON'T I CHECK TO BE SURE...
NEAR, I BELIEVE THAT YOU ARE, IN FACT, THE REAL NEAR, AND I CARE LITTLE ABOUT THE FACE BEHIND THE MASK.
WHAT I WOULD LIKE TO SEE IS WHAT YOU WERE GOING TO SHOW ME PERTAINING TO THE KIRA CASE.
...
THAT...

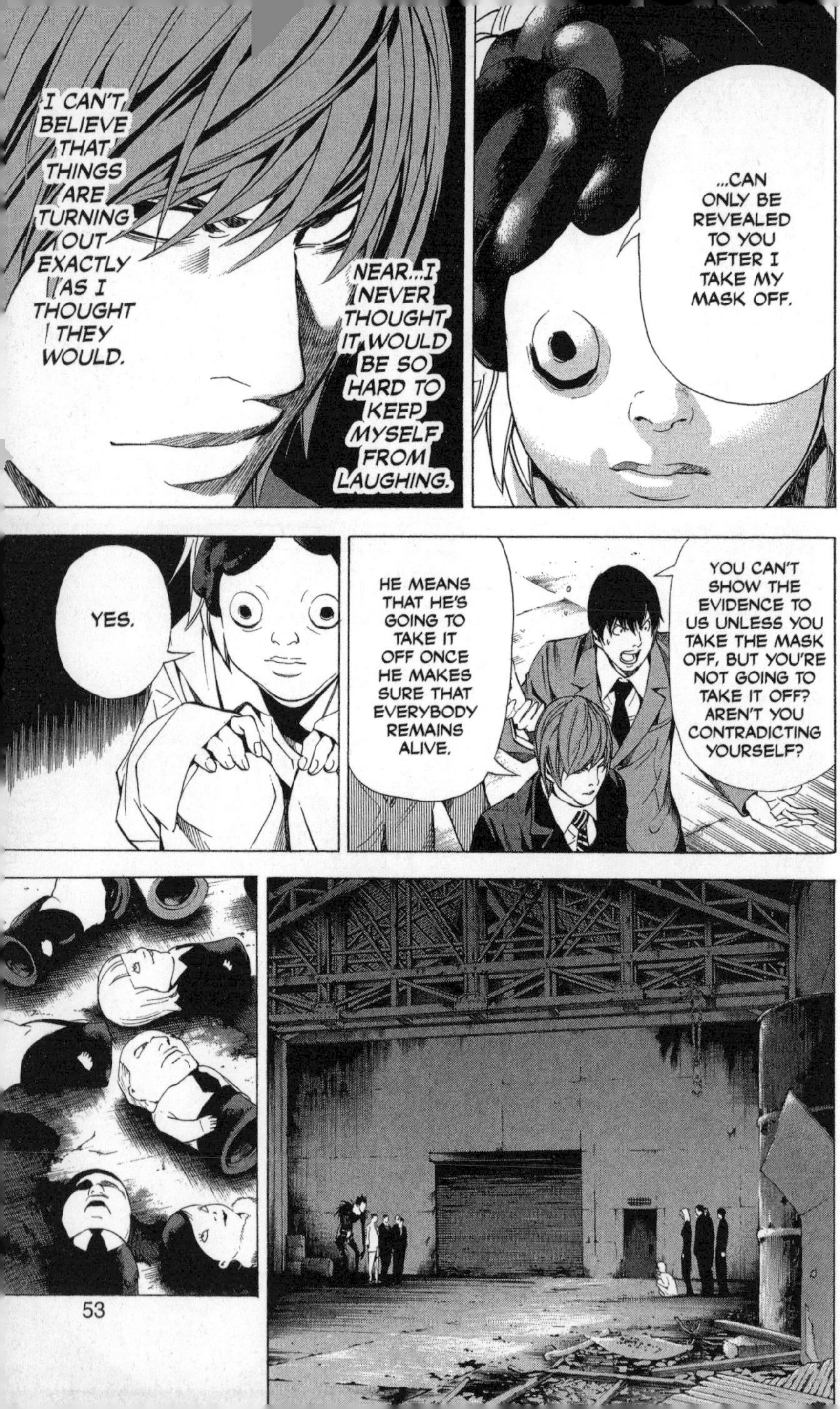
...CAN ONLY BE REVEALED TO YOU AFTER I TAKE MY MASK OFF.
I CAN'T BELIEVE THAT THINGS ARE TURNING OUT EXACTLY AS I THOUGHT THEY WOULD.
NEAR...I NEVER THOUGHT IT WOULD BE SO HARD TO KEEP MYSELF FROM LAUGHING.
YOU CAN'T SHOW THE EVIDENCE TO US UNLESS YOU TAKE THE MASK OFF, BUT YOU'RE NOT GOING TO TAKE IT OFF? AREN'T YOU CONTRADICTING YOURSELF?
HE MEANS THAT HE'S GOING TO TAKE IT OFF ONCE HE MAKES SURE THAT EVERYBODY REMAINS ALIVE.
YES.

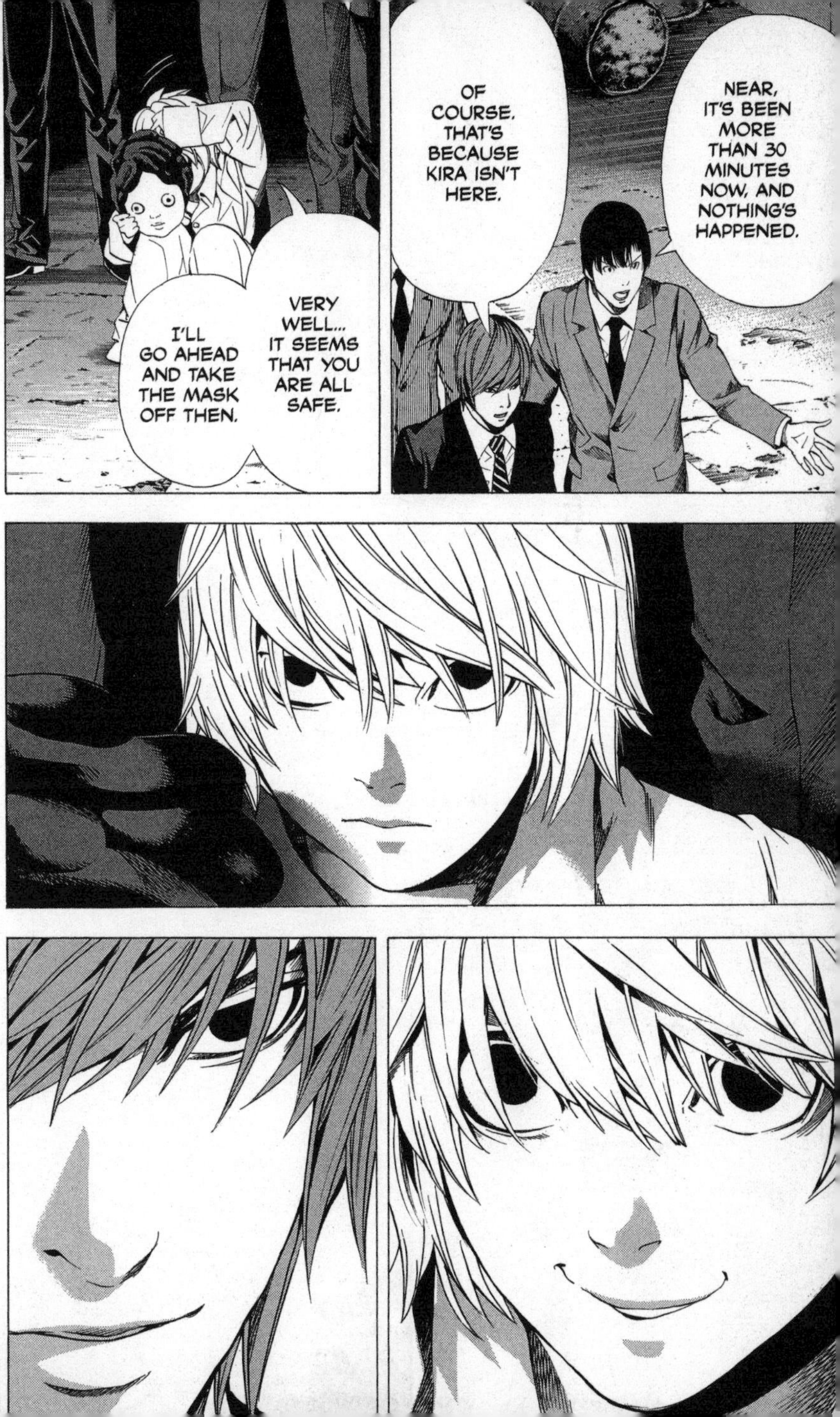
NEAR, IT'S BEEN MORE THAN 30 MINUTES NOW, AND NOTHING'S HAPPENED.
OF COURSE. THAT'S BECAUSE KIRA ISN'T HERE.
VERY WELL... IT SEEMS THAT YOU ARE ALL SAFE.
I'LL GO AHEAD AND TAKE THE MASK OFF THEN.

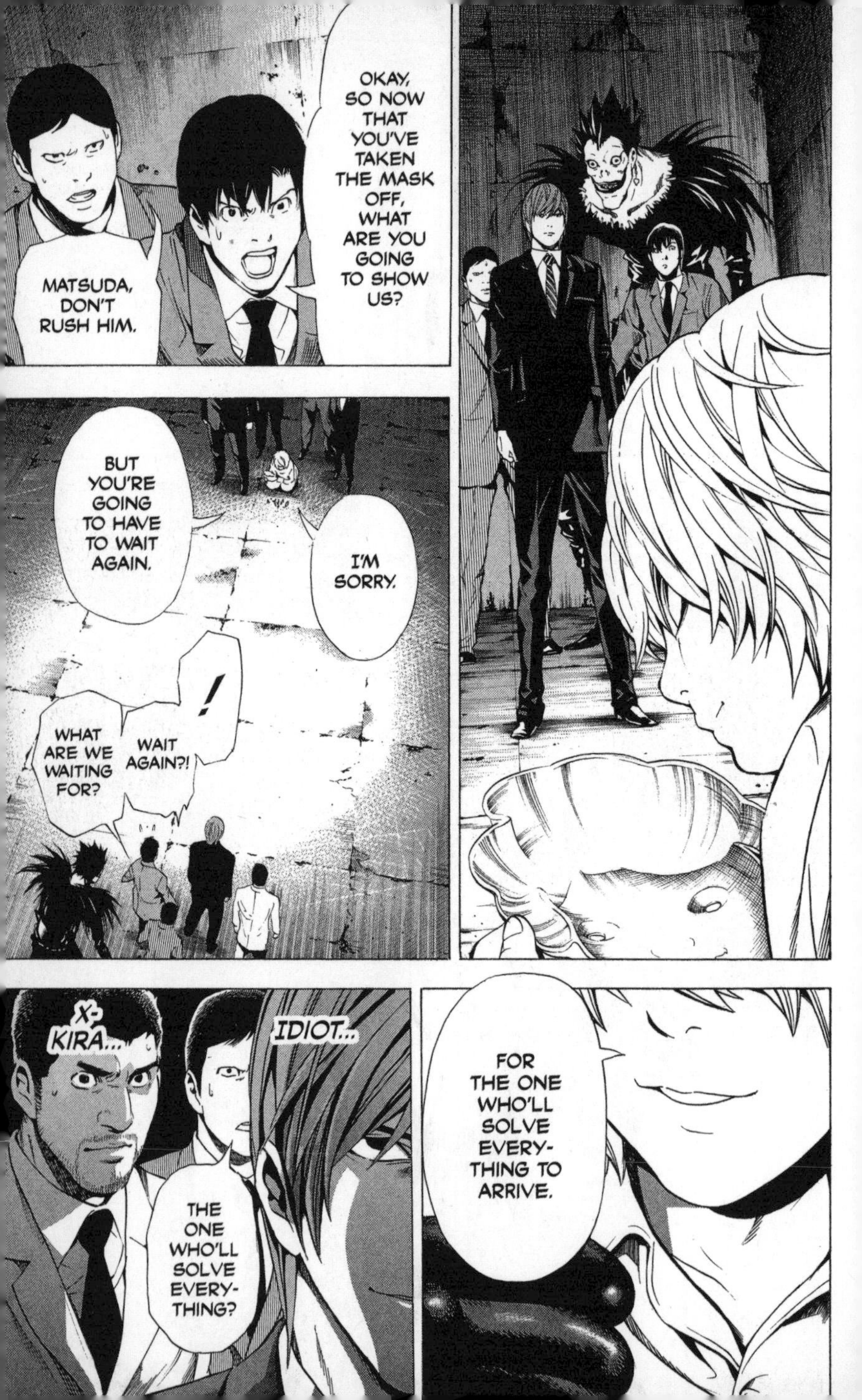
OKAY, SO NOW THAT YOU'VE TAKEN THE MASK OFF, WHAT ARE YOU GOING TO SHOW US?
MATSUDA, DON'T RUSH HIM.
I'M SORRY.
BUT YOU'RE GOING TO HAVE TO WAIT AGAIN.
!
WAIT AGAIN?!
WHAT ARE WE WAITING FOR?
FOR THE ONE WHO'LL SOLVE EVERYTHING TO ARRIVE.
IDIOT...
X-KIRA...
THE ONE WHO'LL SOLVE EVERYTHING?

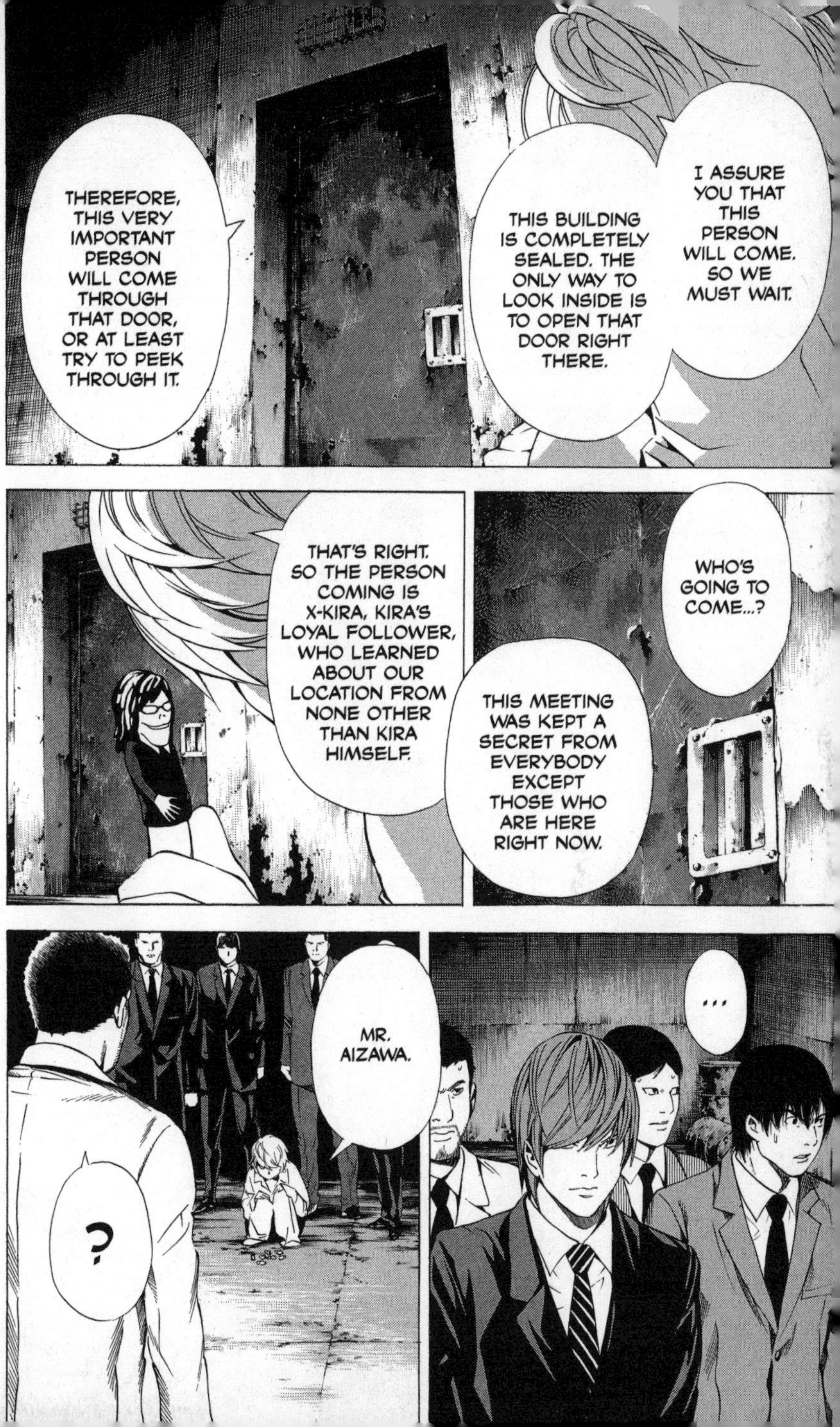
I ASSURE YOU THAT THIS PERSON WILL COME. SO WE MUST WAIT.
THIS BUILDING IS COMPLETELY SEALED. THE ONLY WAY TO LOOK INSIDE IS TO OPEN THAT DOOR RIGHT THERE.
THEREFORE, THIS VERY IMPORTANT PERSON WILL COME THROUGH THAT DOOR, OR AT LEAST TRY TO PEEK THROUGH IT.
WHO'S GOING TO COME...?
THIS MEETING WAS KEPT A SECRET FROM EVERYBODY EXCEPT THOSE WHO ARE HERE RIGHT NOW.
THAT'S RIGHT. SO THE PERSON COMING IS X-KIRA, KIRA'S LOYAL FOLLOWER, WHO LEARNED ABOUT OUR LOCATION FROM NONE OTHER THAN KIRA HIMSELF.
...
MR. AIZAWA.
?

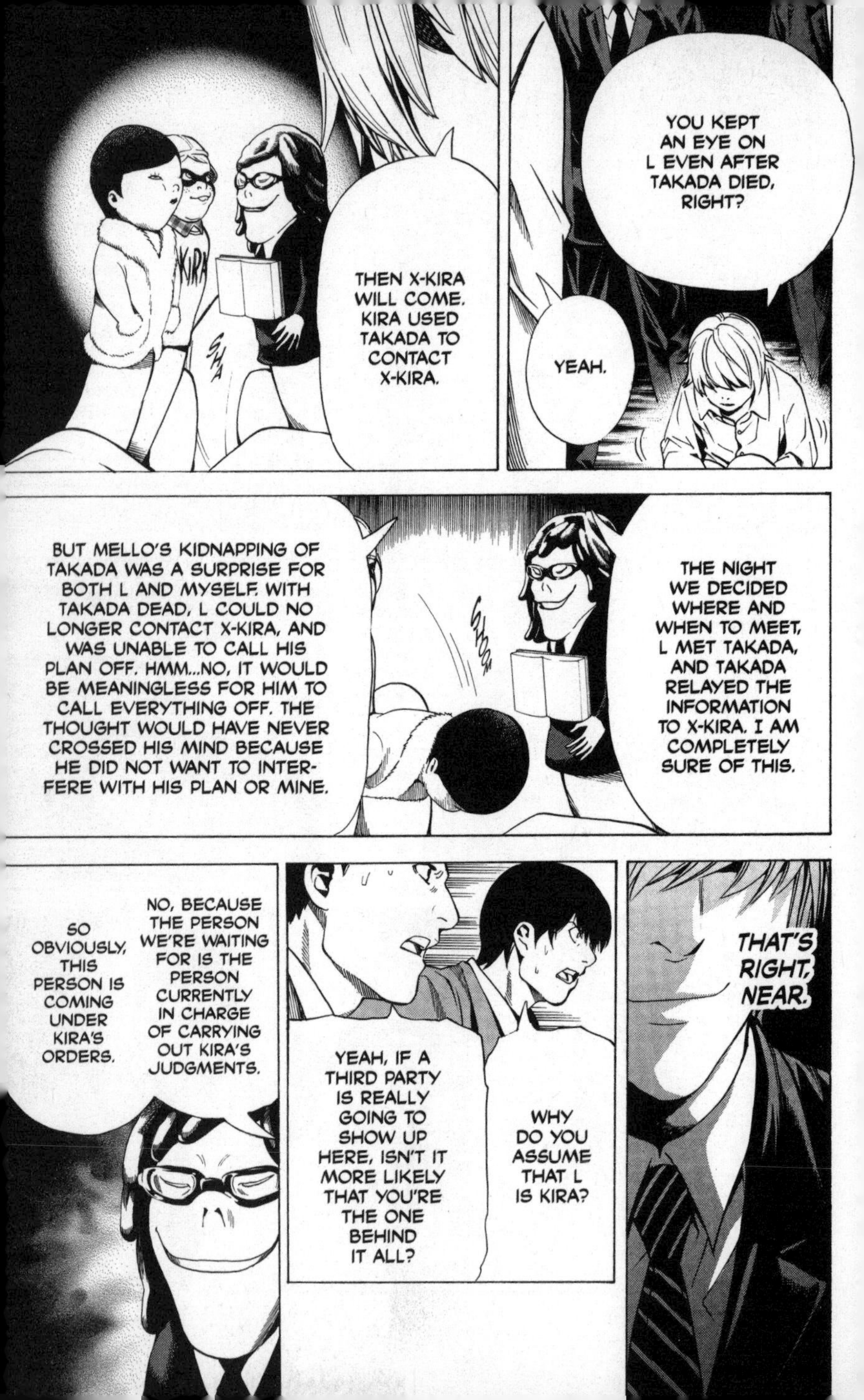
YOU KEPT AN EYE ON L EVEN AFTER TAKADA DIED, RIGHT?
YEAH.
THEN X-KIRA WILL COME. KIRA USED TAKADA TO CONTACT X-KIRA.
THE NIGHT WE DECIDED WHERE AND WHEN TO MEET, L MET TAKADA, AND TAKADA RELAYED THE INFORMATION TO X-KIRA. I AM COMPLETELY SURE OF THIS.
BUT MELLO'S KIDNAPPING OF TAKADA WAS A SURPRISE FOR BOTH L AND MYSELF. WITH TAKADA DEAD, L COULD NO LONGER CONTACT X-KIRA, AND WAS UNABLE TO CALL HIS PLAN OFF. HMM...NO, IT WOULD BE MEANINGLESS FOR HIM TO CALL EVERYTHING OFF. THE THOUGHT WOULD HAVE NEVER CROSSED HIS MIND BECAUSE HE DID NOT WANT TO INTER-FERE WITH HIS PLAN OR MINE.
THAT'S RIGHT, NEAR.
WHY DO YOU ASSUME THAT L IS KIRA?
YEAH, IF A THIRD PARTY IS REALLY GOING TO SHOW UP HERE, ISN'T IT MORE LIKELY THAT YOU'RE THE ONE BEHIND IT ALL?
NO, BECAUSE THE PERSON WE'RE WAITING FOR IS THE PERSON CURRENTLY IN CHARGE OF CARRYING OUT KIRA'S JUDGMENTS.
SO OBVIOUSLY, THIS PERSON IS COMING UNDER KIRA'S ORDERS.

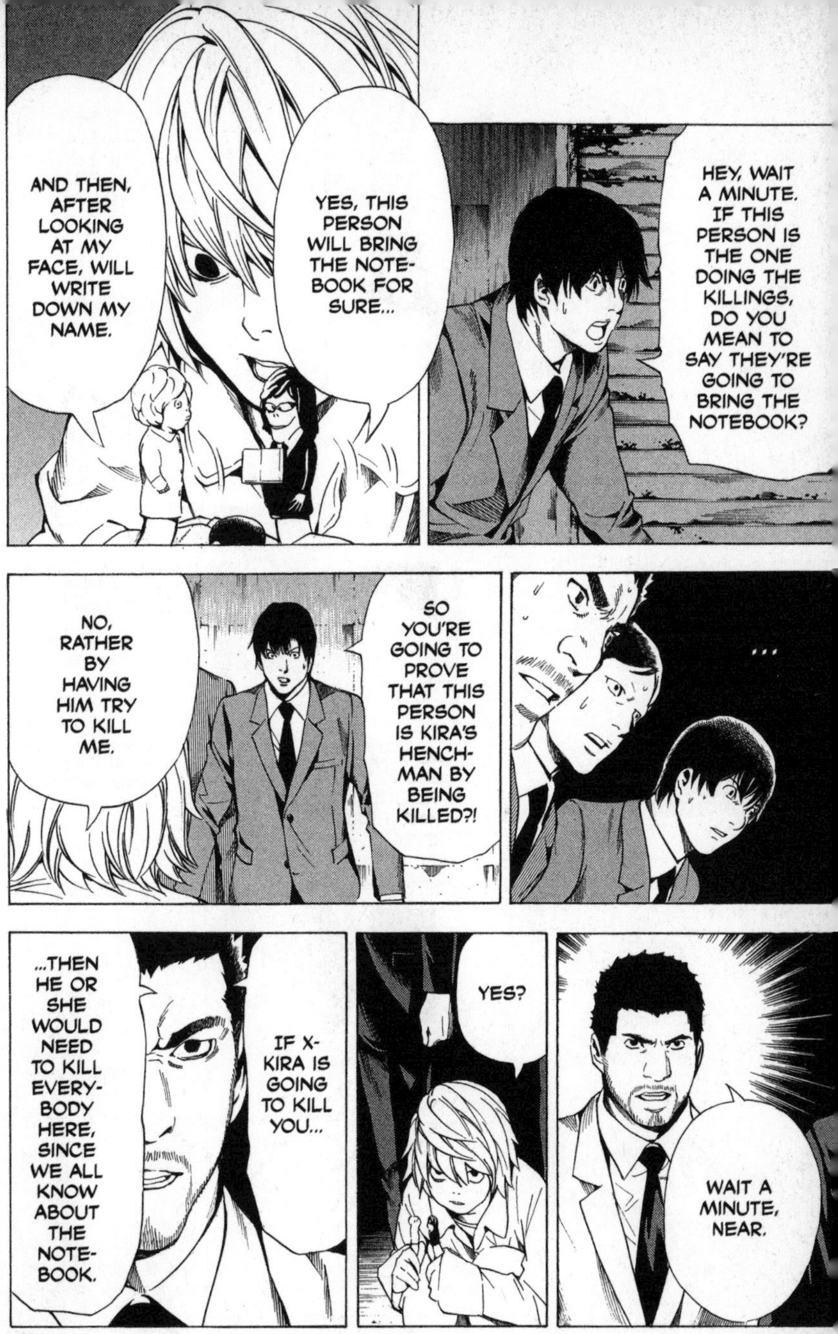
HEY, WAIT A MINUTE. IF THIS PERSON IS THE ONE DOING THE KILLINGS, DO YOU MEAN TO SAY THEY'RE GOING TO BRING THE NOTEBOOK?
YES, THIS PERSON WILL BRING THE NOTE-BOOK FOR SURE...
AND THEN, AFTER LOOKING AT MY FACE, WILL WRITE DOWN MY NAME.
...
SO YOU'RE GOING TO PROVE THAT THIS PERSON IS KIRA'S HENCH-MAN BY BEING KILLED?!
NO, RATHER BY HAVING HIM TRY TO KILL ME.
WAIT A MINUTE, NEAR.
YES?
IF X-KIRA IS GOING TO KILL YOU...
...THEN HE OR SHE WOULD NEED TO KILL EVERY-BODY HERE, SINCE WE ALL KNOW ABOUT THE NOTE-BOOK.

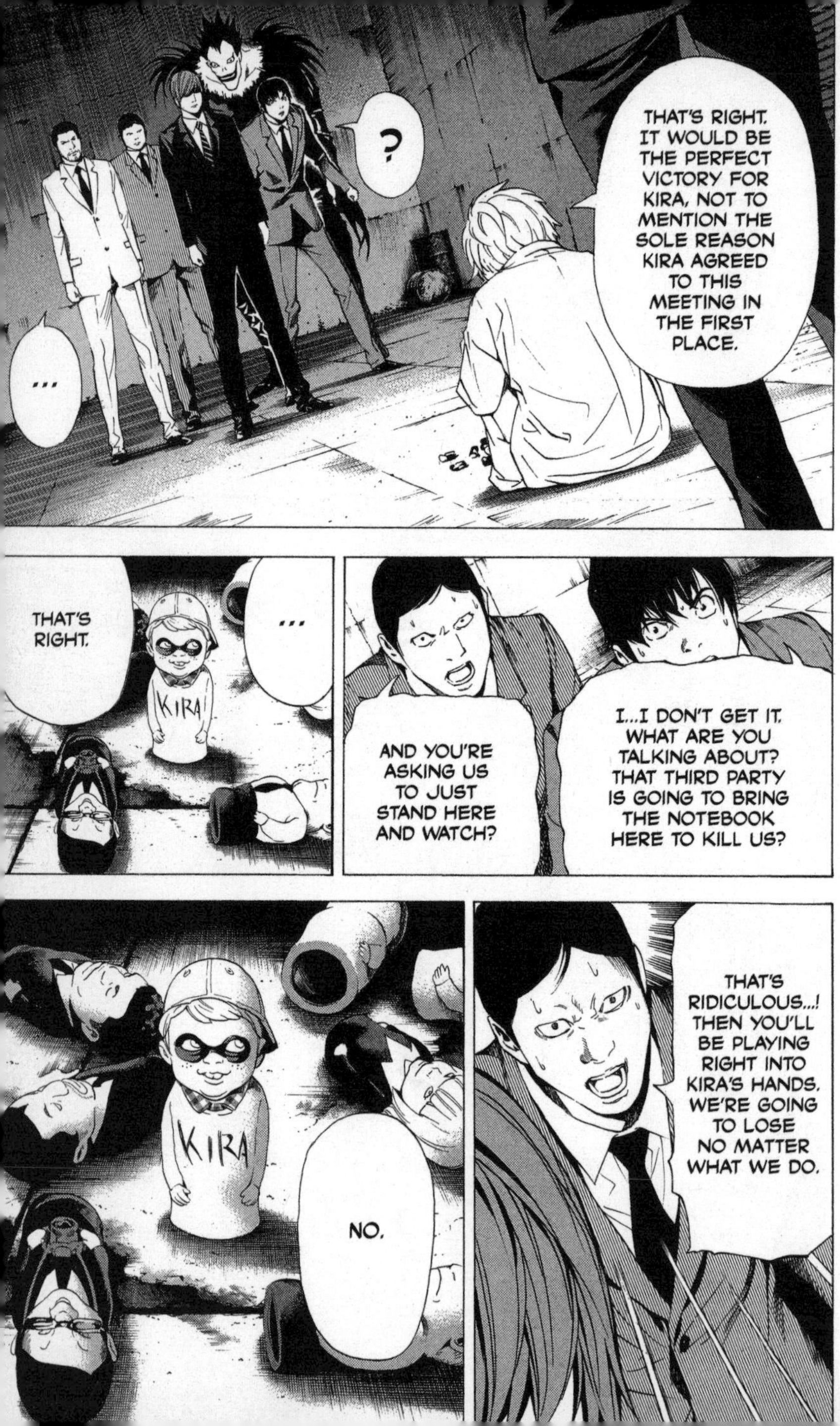
THAT'S RIGHT. IT WOULD BE THE PERFECT VICTORY FOR KIRA, NOT TO MENTION THE SOLE REASON KIRA AGREED TO THIS MEETING IN THE FIRST PLACE.
?
...
I...I DON'T GET IT. WHAT ARE YOU TALKING ABOUT? THAT THIRD PARTY IS GOING TO BRING THE NOTEBOOK HERE TO KILL US?
AND YOU'RE ASKING US TO JUST STAND HERE AND WATCH?
...
THAT'S RIGHT.
KIRA
THAT'S RIDICULOUS...! THEN YOU'LL BE PLAYING RIGHT INTO KIRA'S HANDS. WE'RE GOING TO LOSE NO MATTER WHAT WE DO.
KIRA
NO.

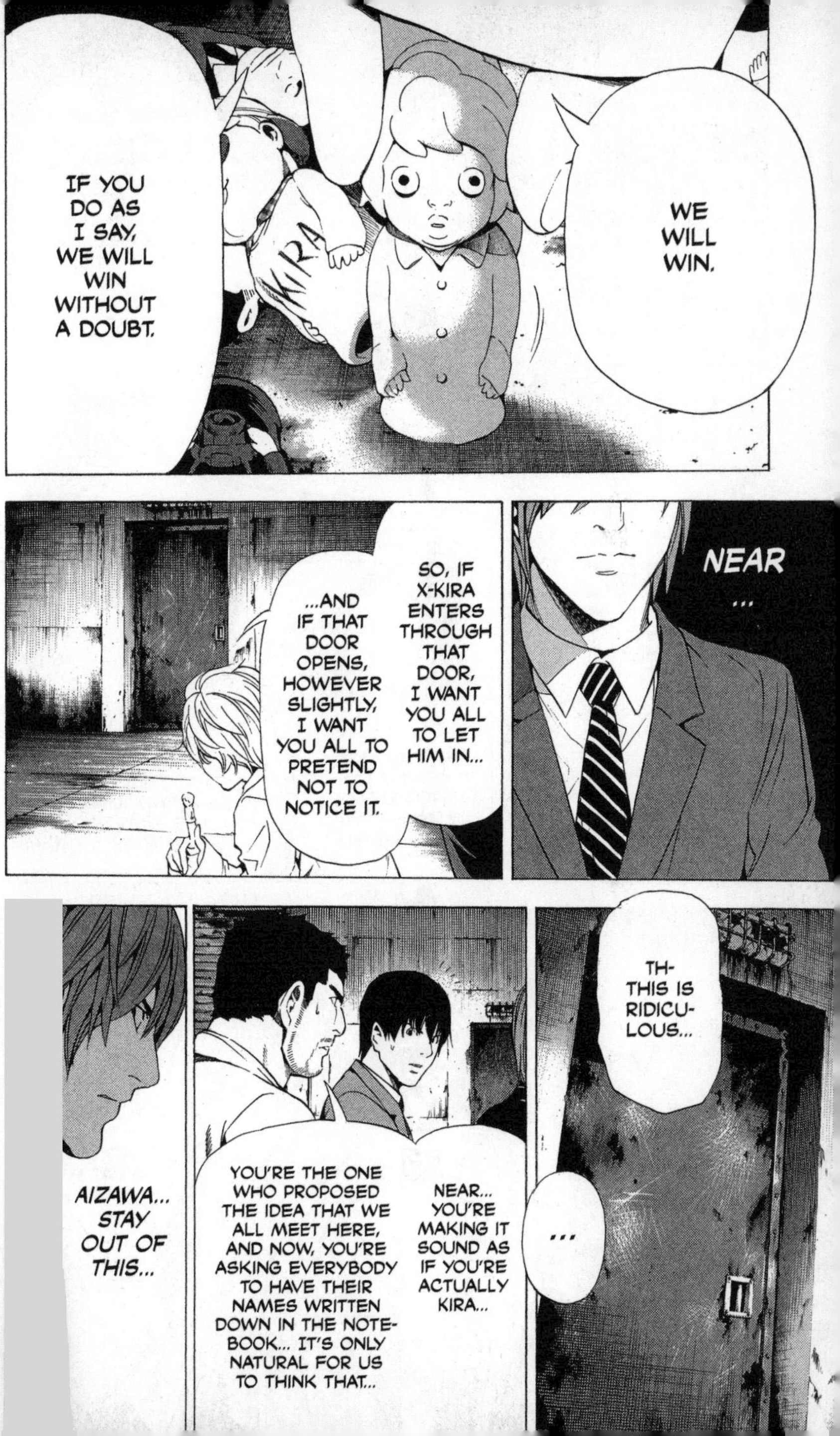
WE WILL WIN.
IF YOU DO AS I SAY, WE WILL WIN WITHOUT A DOUBT.
NEAR...
SO, IF X-KIRA ENTERS THROUGH THAT DOOR, I WANT YOU ALL TO LET HIM IN...
...AND IF THAT DOOR OPENS, HOWEVER SLIGHTLY, I WANT YOU ALL TO PRETEND NOT TO NOTICE IT.
TH- THIS IS RIDICU- LOUS...
...
NEAR... YOU'RE MAKING IT SOUND AS IF YOU'RE ACTUALLY KIRA...
YOU'RE THE ONE WHO PROPOSED THE IDEA THAT WE ALL MEET HERE, AND NOW, YOU'RE ASKING EVERYBODY TO HAVE THEIR NAMES WRITTEN DOWN IN THE NOTE- BOOK... IT'S ONLY NATURAL FOR US TO THINK THAT...
AIZAWA... STAY OUT OF THIS...

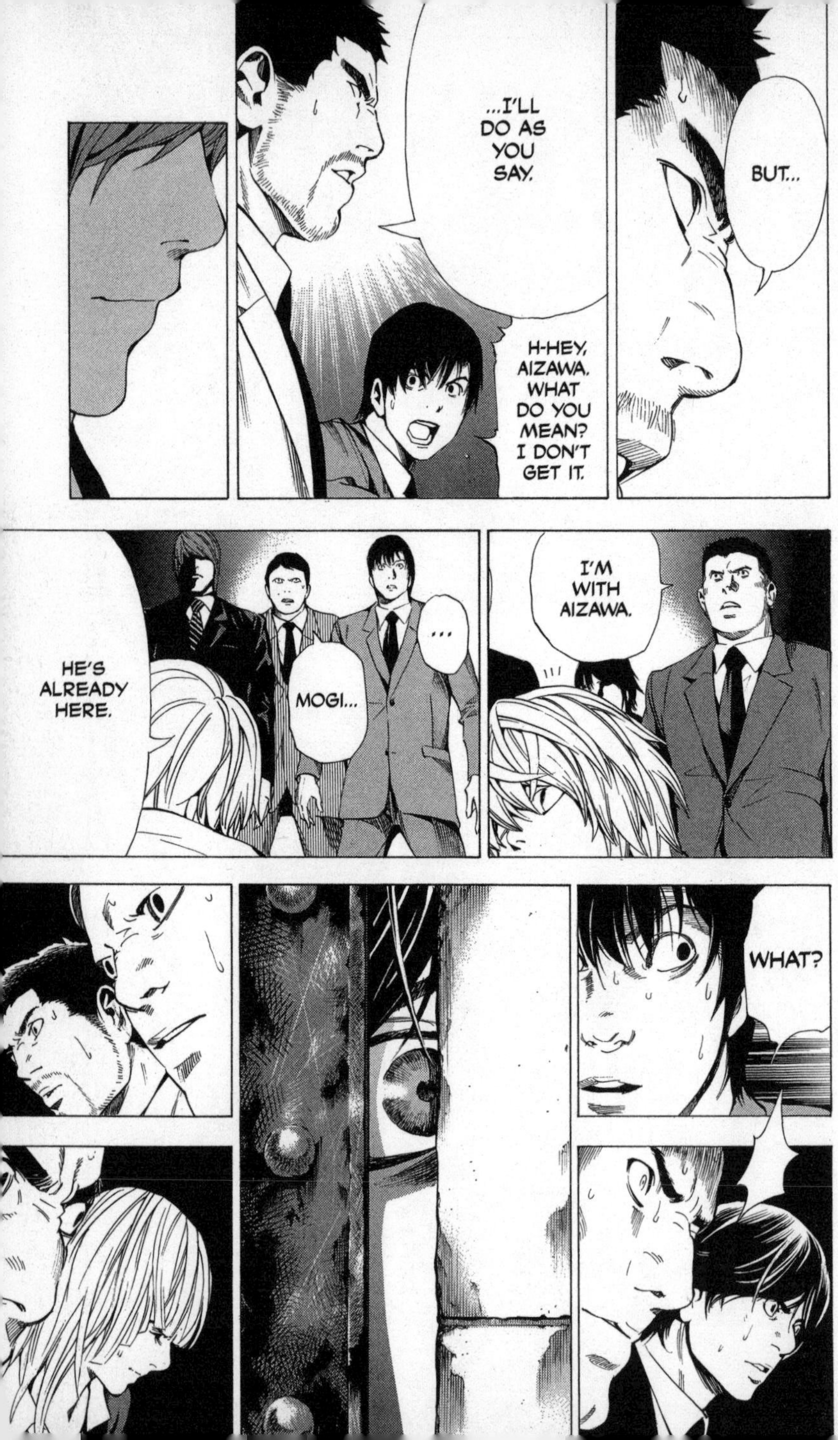
BUT...
...I'LL DO AS YOU SAY.
H-HEY, AIZAWA. WHAT DO YOU MEAN? I DON'T GET IT.
I'M WITH AIZAWA.
...
MOGI...
HE'S ALREADY HERE.
WHAT?

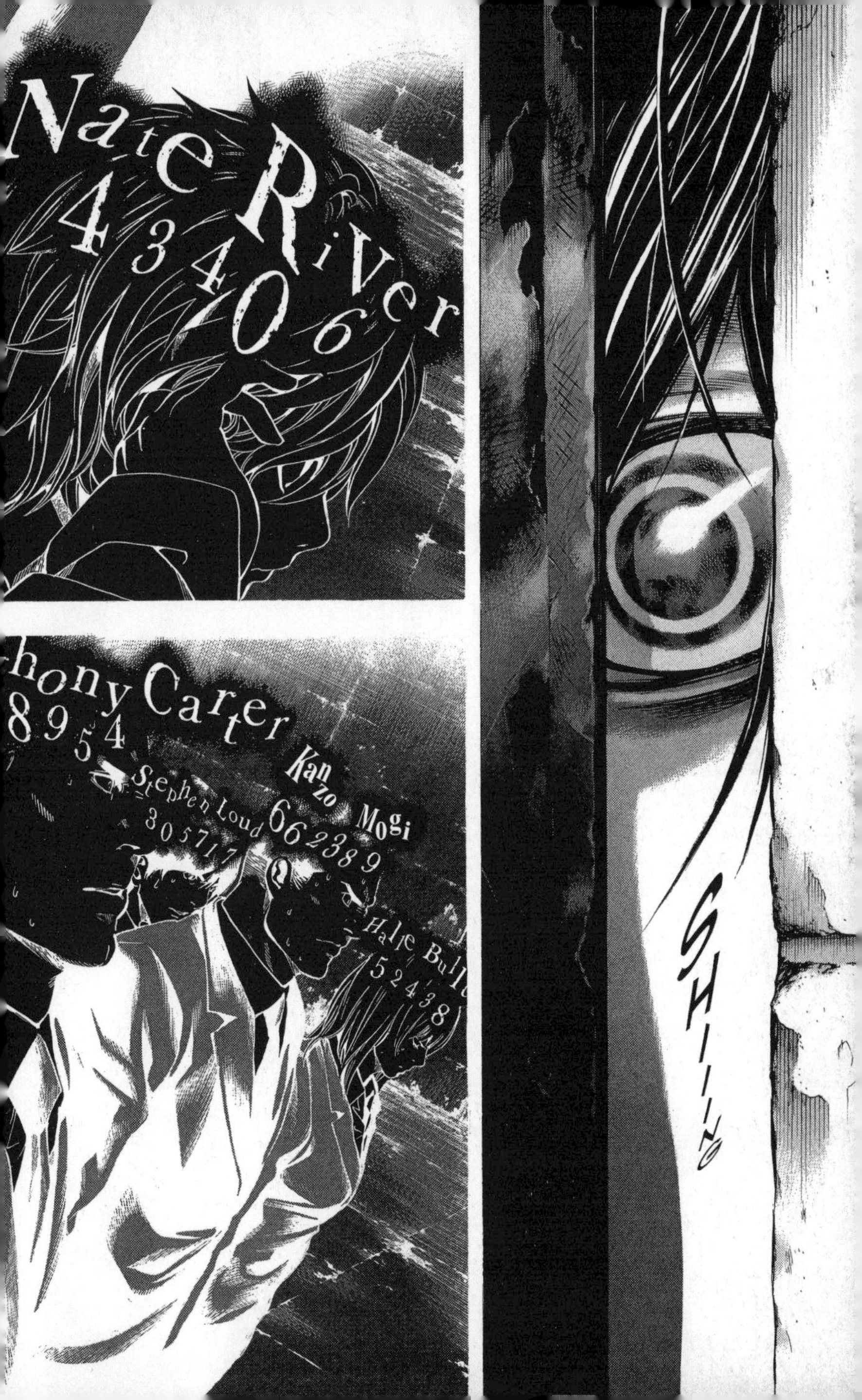
SHIIIN
Nate River
434006
hony Carter
8954
Stephen Loud
305717
Kanzo Mogi
662389
Halle Bull
52438

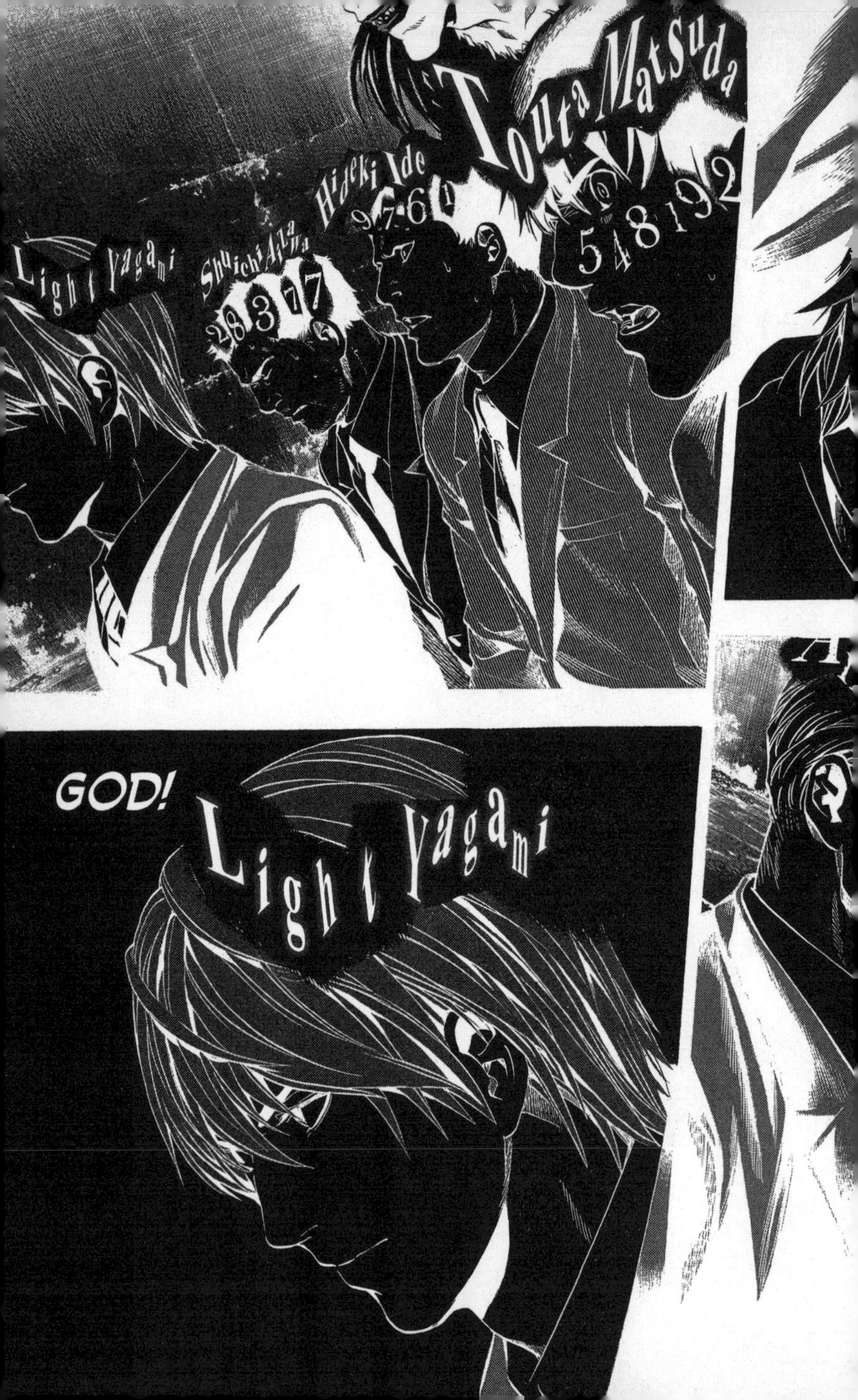

Touta Matsuda
Hideki Ide
Shuichi Aizawa
Light Yagami
GOD!
Light Yagami

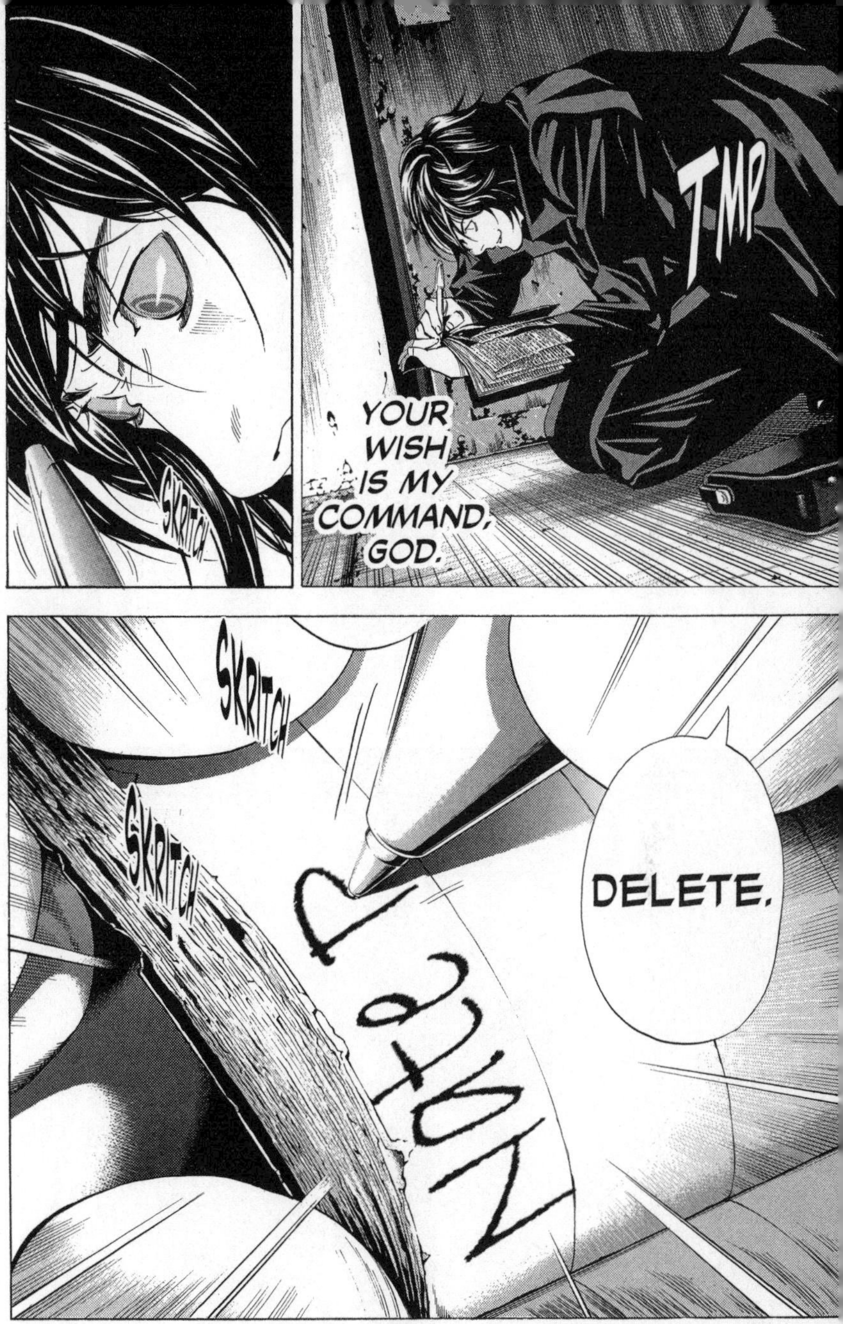
TMP
YOUR WISH IS MY COMMAND, GOD.
SKRITCH
DELETE.
SKRITCH
SKRITCH

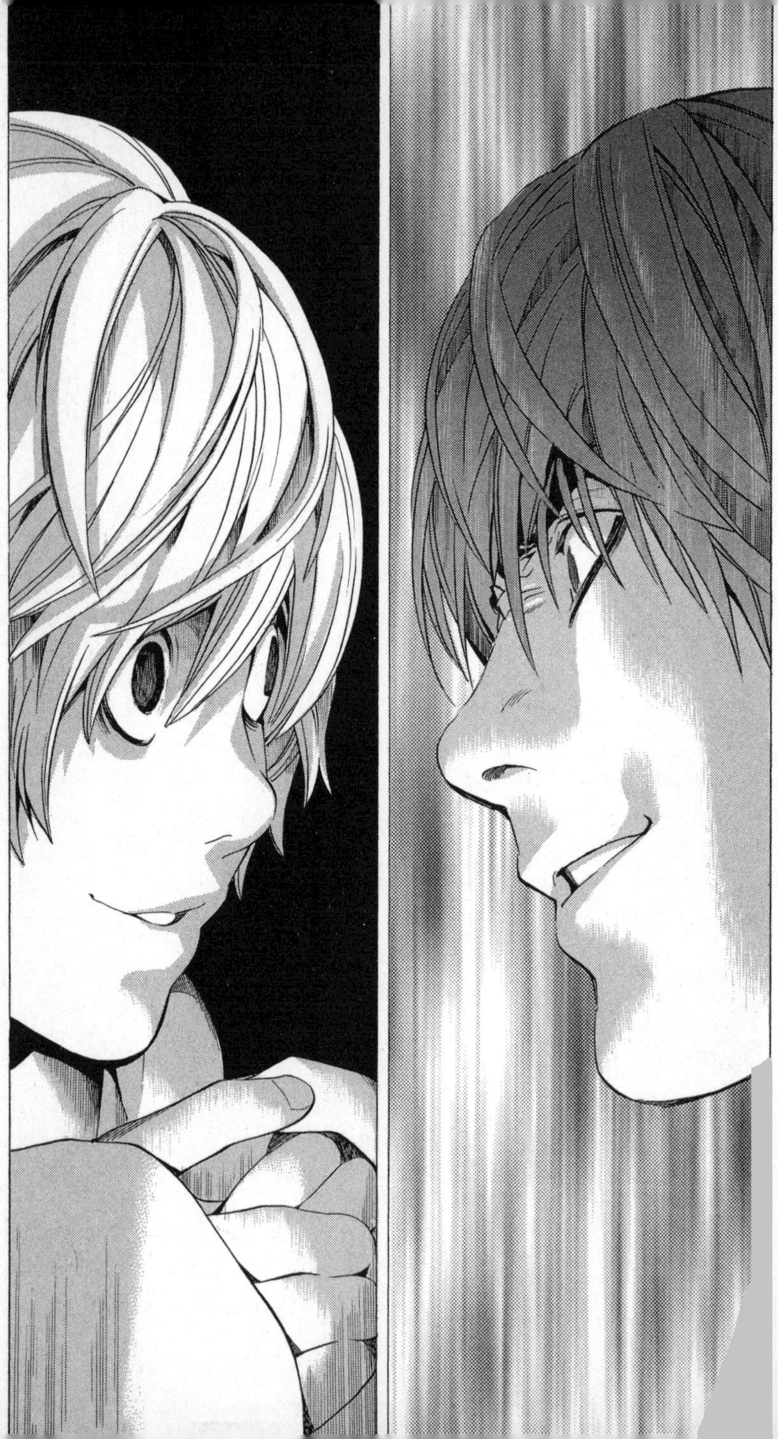

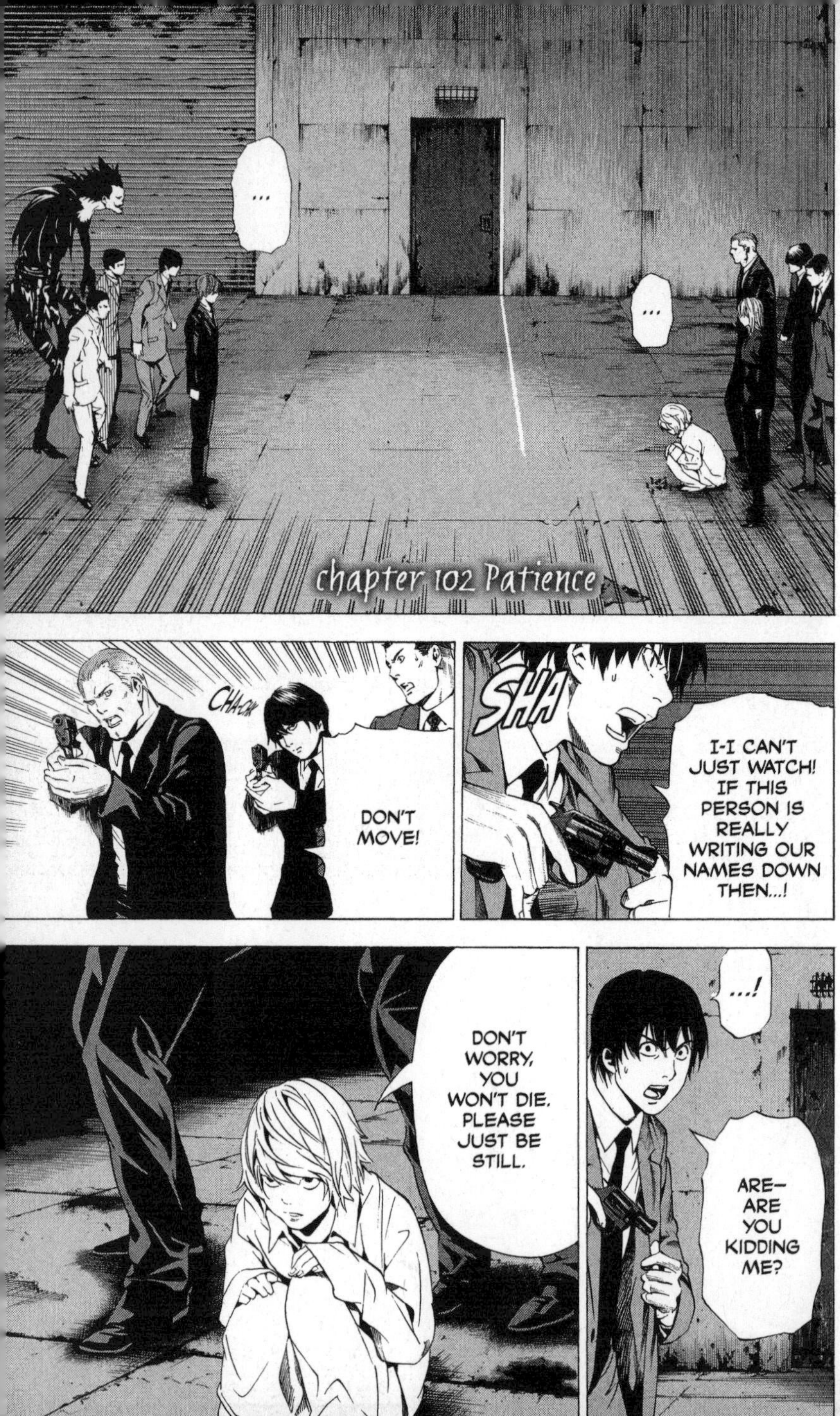
chapter 102 Patience
...
...
SHA
I-I CAN'T JUST WATCH! IF THIS PERSON IS REALLY WRITING OUR NAMES DOWN THEN...!
CHA-CHK
DON'T MOVE!
...!
ARE— ARE YOU KIDDING ME?
DON'T WORRY, YOU WON'T DIE. PLEASE JUST BE STILL.

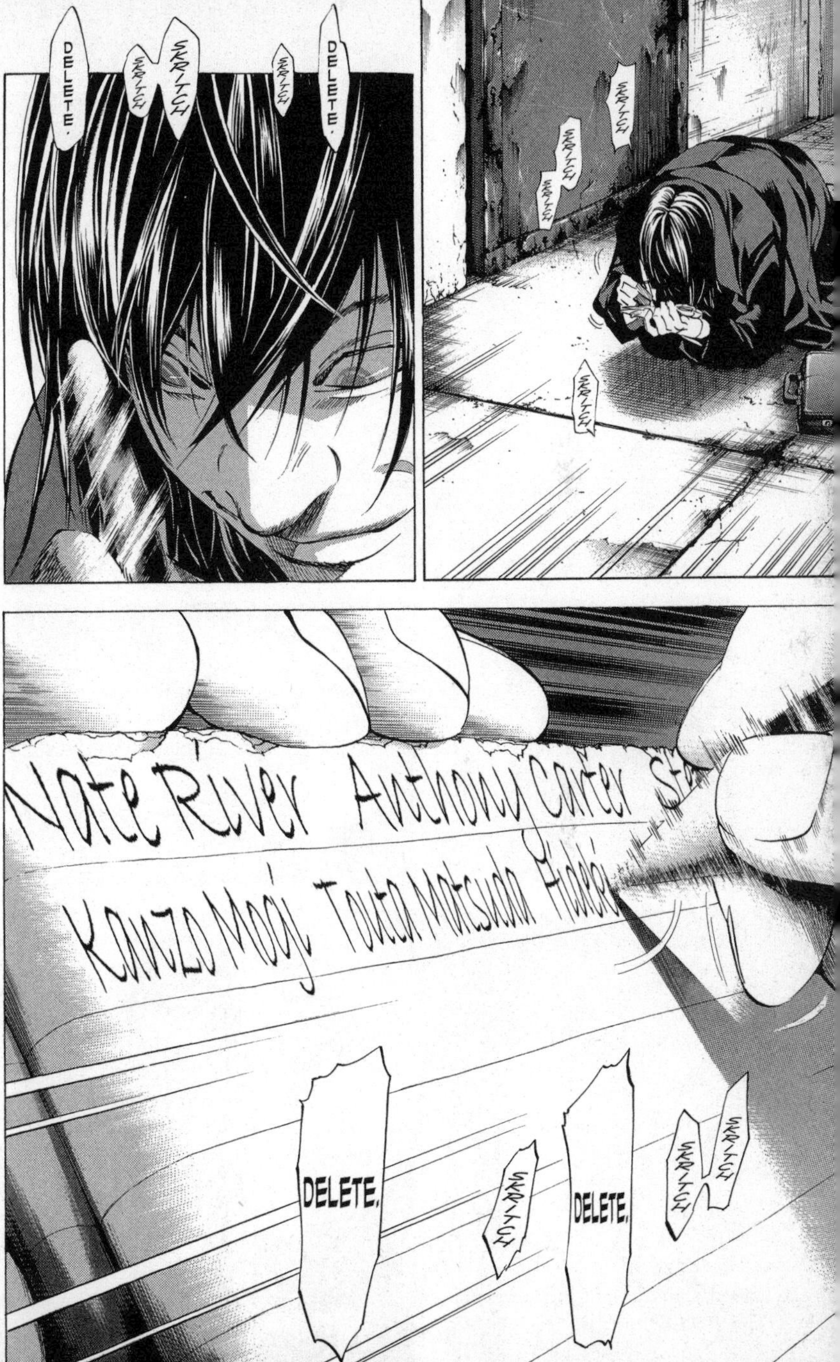
SKRITCH
SKRITCH
SKRITCH
SKRITCH
DELETE.
SKRITCH
SKRITCH
SKRITCH
DELETE.
Note River Anthony Carter Ste
Kanzo Mogi Touta Matsuda Hideki
SKRITCH
SKRITCH
DELETE.
SKRITCH
DELETE.

chapter 102 Patience

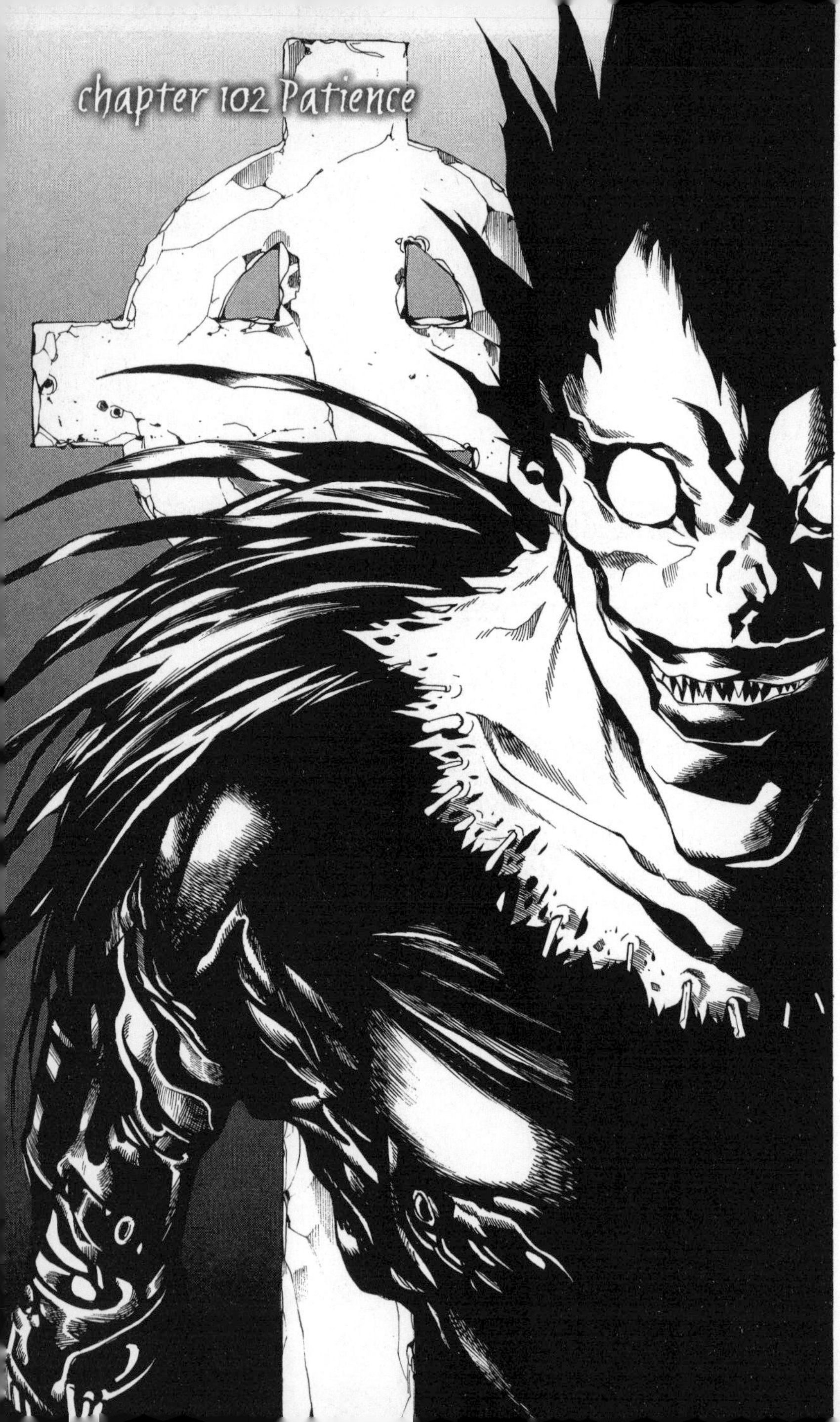

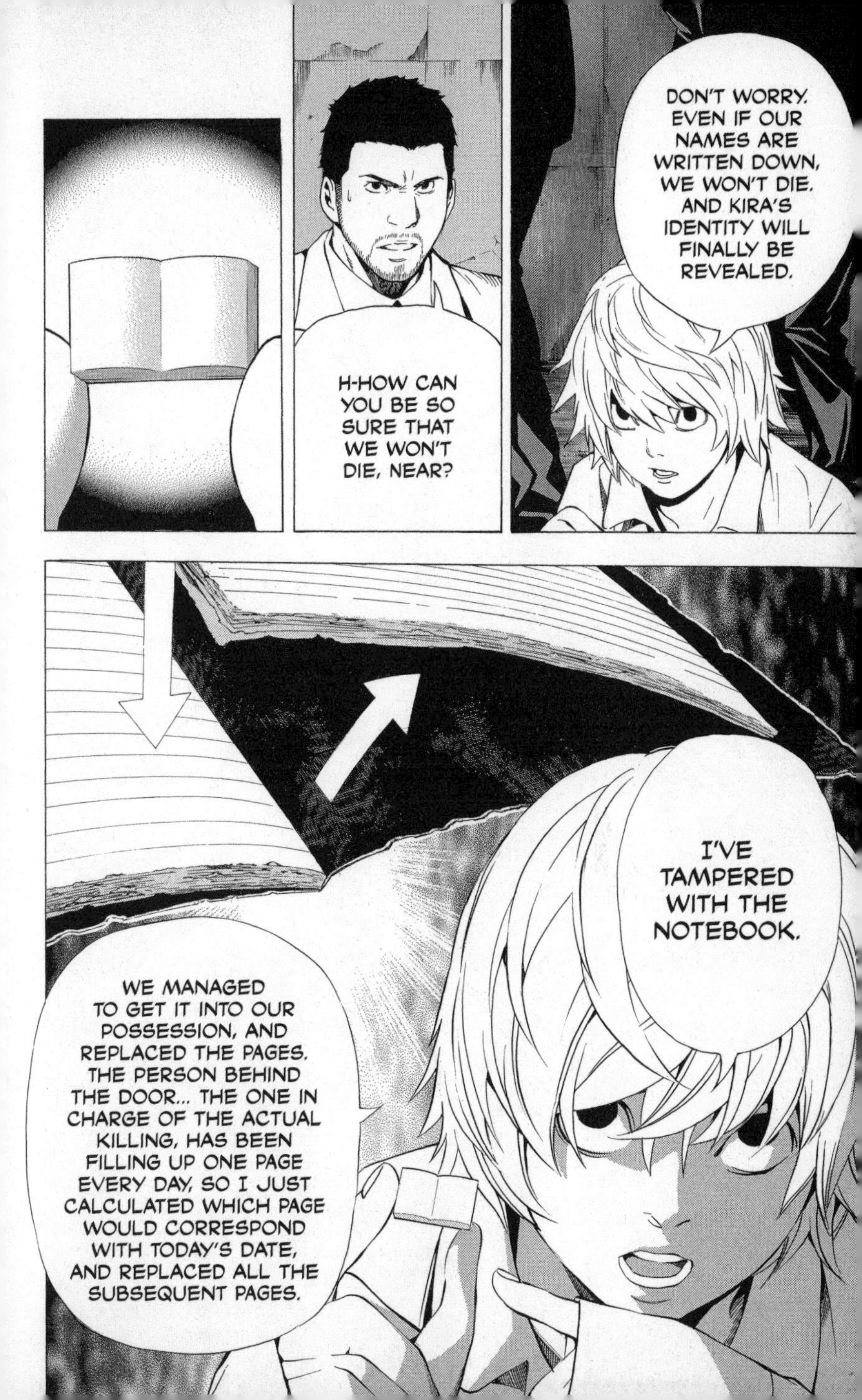
DON'T WORRY. EVEN IF OUR NAMES ARE WRITTEN DOWN, WE WON'T DIE. AND KIRA'S IDENTITY WILL FINALLY BE REVEALED.
H-HOW CAN YOU BE SO SURE THAT WE WON'T DIE, NEAR?
I'VE TAMPERED WITH THE NOTEBOOK.
WE MANAGED TO GET IT INTO OUR POSSESSION, AND REPLACED THE PAGES. THE PERSON BEHIND THE DOOR... THE ONE IN CHARGE OF THE ACTUAL KILLING, HAS BEEN FILLING UP ONE PAGE EVERY DAY, SO I JUST CALCULATED WHICH PAGE WOULD CORRESPOND WITH TODAY'S DATE, AND REPLACED ALL THE SUBSEQUENT PAGES.

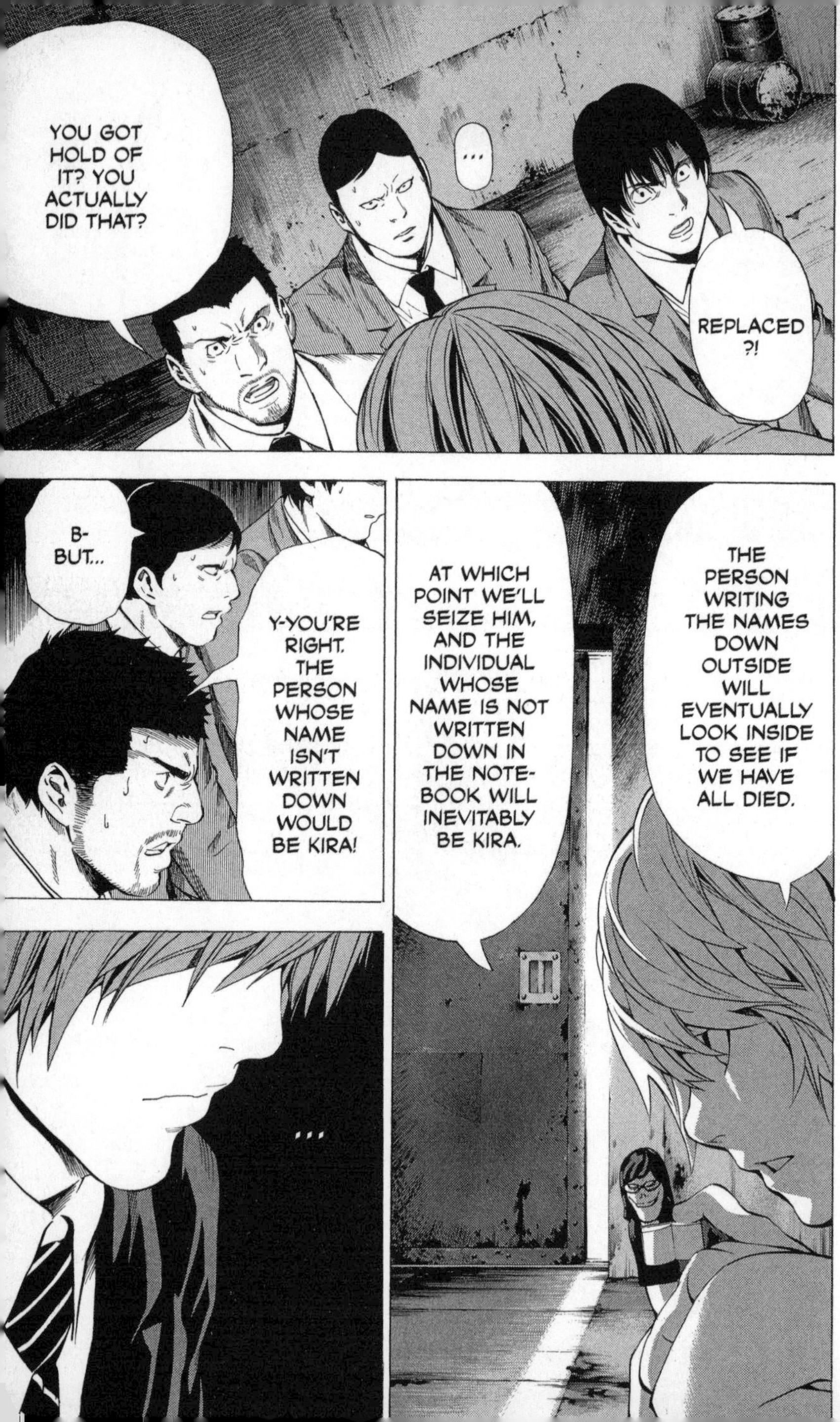
REPLACED?!
...
YOU GOT HOLD OF IT? YOU ACTUALLY DID THAT?
THE PERSON WRITING THE NAMES DOWN OUTSIDE WILL EVENTUALLY LOOK INSIDE TO SEE IF WE HAVE ALL DIED.
AT WHICH POINT WE'LL SEIZE HIM, AND THE INDIVIDUAL WHOSE NAME IS NOT WRITTEN DOWN IN THE NOTE-BOOK WILL INEVITABLY BE KIRA.
Y-YOU'RE RIGHT. THE PERSON WHOSE NAME ISN'T WRITTEN DOWN WOULD BE KIRA!
B-BUT...
...

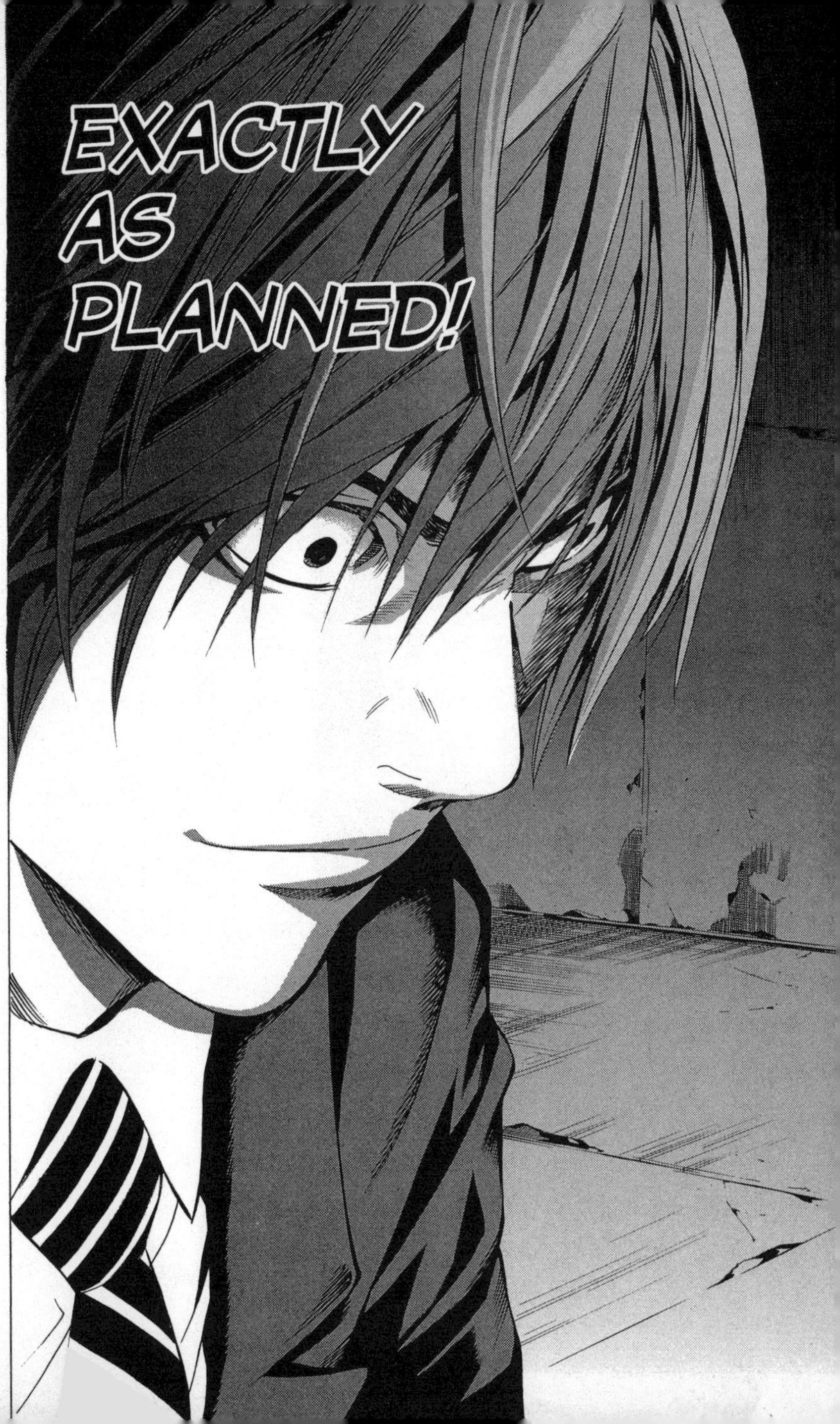
EXACTLY AS PLANNED!

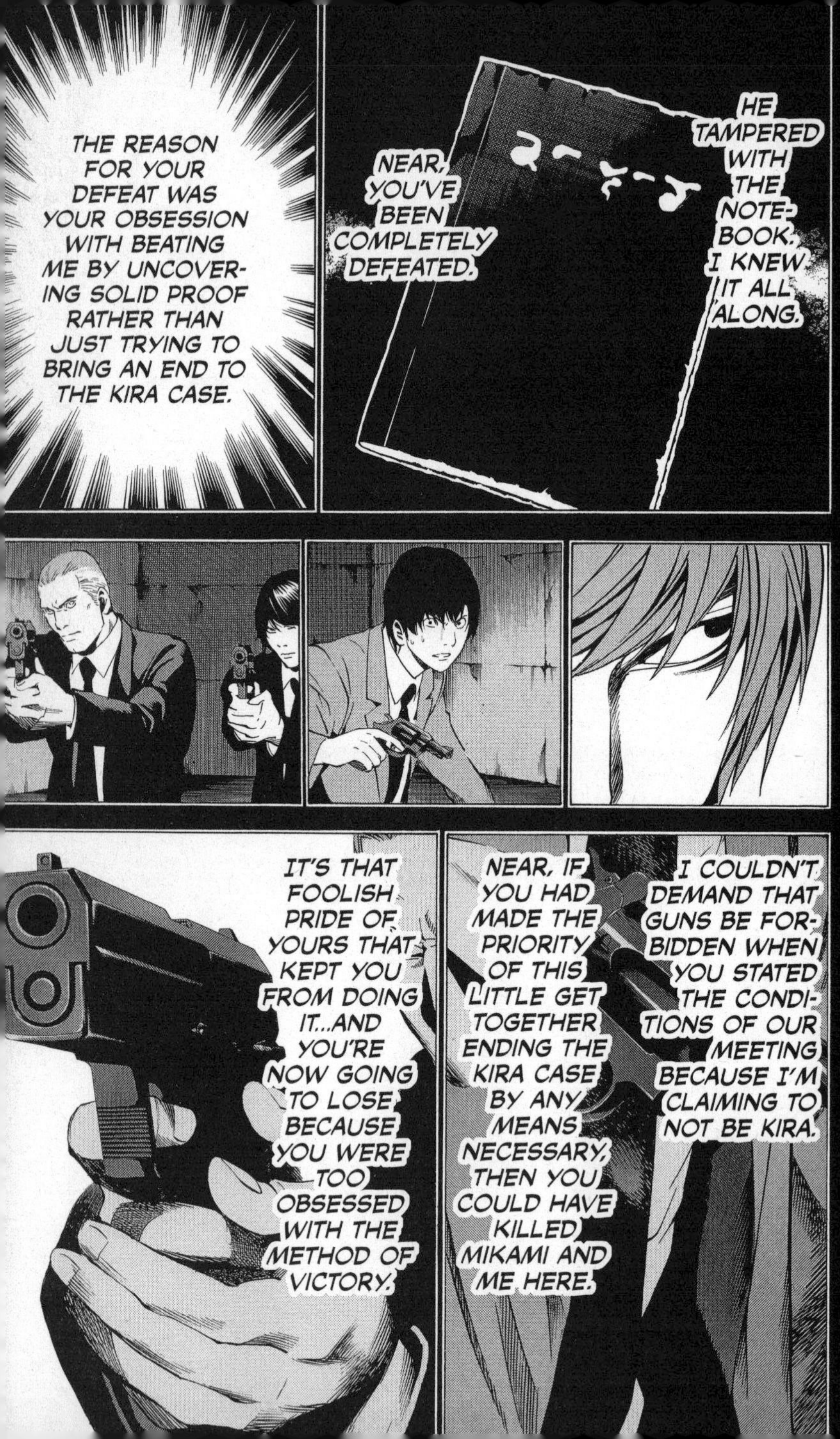
HE TAMPERED WITH THE NOTE-BOOK. I KNEW IT ALL ALONG.
NEAR, YOU'VE BEEN COMPLETELY DEFEATED.
THE REASON FOR YOUR DEFEAT WAS YOUR OBSESSION WITH BEATING ME BY UNCOVER-ING SOLID PROOF RATHER THAN JUST TRYING TO BRING AN END TO THE KIRA CASE.
I COULDN'T DEMAND THAT GUNS BE FOR-BIDDEN WHEN YOU STATED THE CONDI-TIONS OF OUR MEETING BECAUSE I'M CLAIMING TO NOT BE KIRA.
NEAR, IF YOU HAD MADE THE PRIORITY OF THIS LITTLE GET TOGETHER ENDING THE KIRA CASE BY ANY MEANS NECESSARY, THEN YOU COULD HAVE KILLED MIKAMI AND ME HERE.
IT'S THAT FOOLISH PRIDE OF YOURS THAT KEPT YOU FROM DOING IT...AND YOU'RE NOW GOING TO LOSE BECAUSE YOU WERE TOO OBSESSED WITH THE METHOD OF VICTORY.

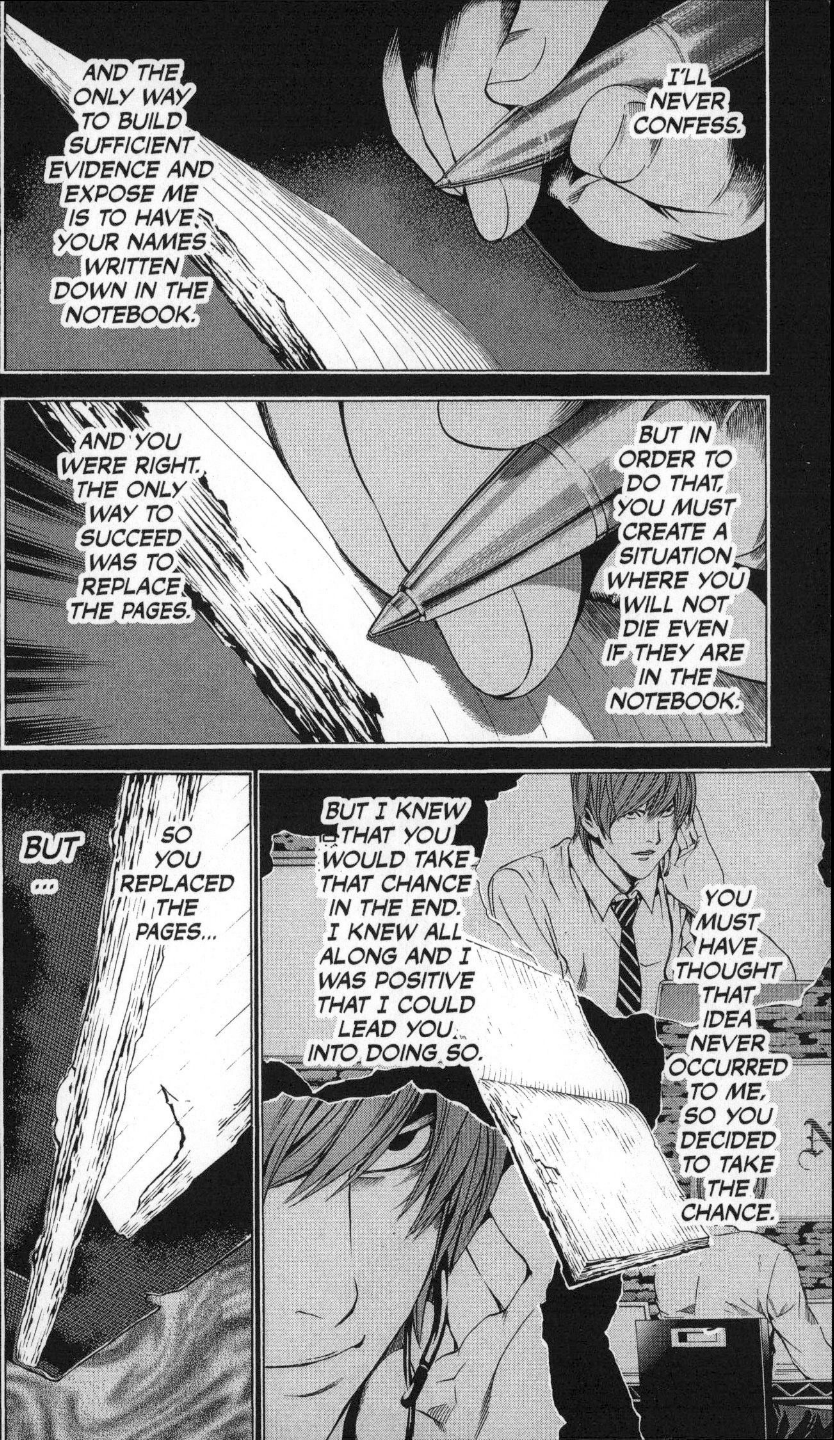

I'LL NEVER CONFESS.
AND THE ONLY WAY TO BUILD SUFFICIENT EVIDENCE AND EXPOSE ME IS TO HAVE YOUR NAMES WRITTEN DOWN IN THE NOTEBOOK.
BUT IN ORDER TO DO THAT, YOU MUST CREATE A SITUATION WHERE YOU WILL NOT DIE EVEN IF THEY ARE IN THE NOTEBOOK.
AND YOU WERE RIGHT. THE ONLY WAY TO SUCCEED WAS TO REPLACE THE PAGES.
YOU MUST HAVE THOUGHT THAT IDEA NEVER OCCURRED TO ME, SO YOU DECIDED TO TAKE THE CHANCE.
BUT I KNEW THAT YOU WOULD TAKE THAT CHANCE IN THE END. I KNEW ALL ALONG AND I WAS POSITIVE THAT I COULD LEAD YOU INTO DOING SO.
SO YOU REPLACED THE PAGES...
BUT ...

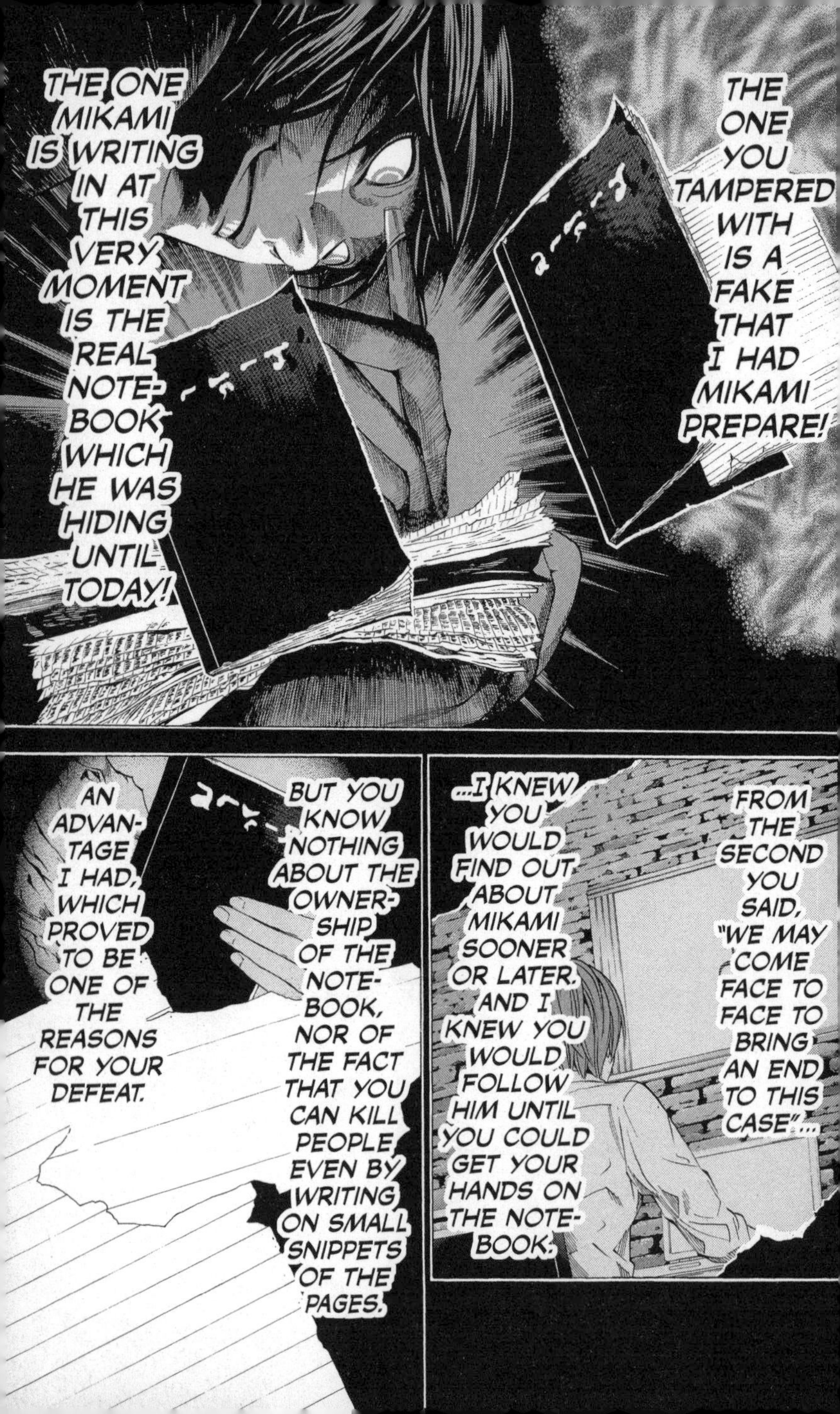
THE ONE YOU TAMPERED WITH IS A FAKE THAT I HAD MIKAMI PREPARE!
THE ONE MIKAMI IS WRITING IN AT THIS VERY MOMENT IS THE REAL NOTE-BOOK WHICH HE WAS HIDING UNTIL TODAY!
FROM THE SECOND YOU SAID, "WE MAY COME FACE TO FACE TO BRING AN END TO THIS CASE"...
...I KNEW YOU WOULD FIND OUT ABOUT MIKAMI SOONER OR LATER. AND I KNEW YOU WOULD FOLLOW HIM UNTIL YOU COULD GET YOUR HANDS ON THE NOTE-BOOK.
BUT YOU KNOW NOTHING ABOUT THE OWNER-SHIP OF THE NOTE-BOOK, NOR OF THE FACT THAT YOU CAN KILL PEOPLE EVEN BY WRITING ON SMALL SNIPPETS OF THE PAGES.
AN ADVAN-TAGE I HAD, WHICH PROVED TO BE ONE OF THE REASONS FOR YOUR DEFEAT.

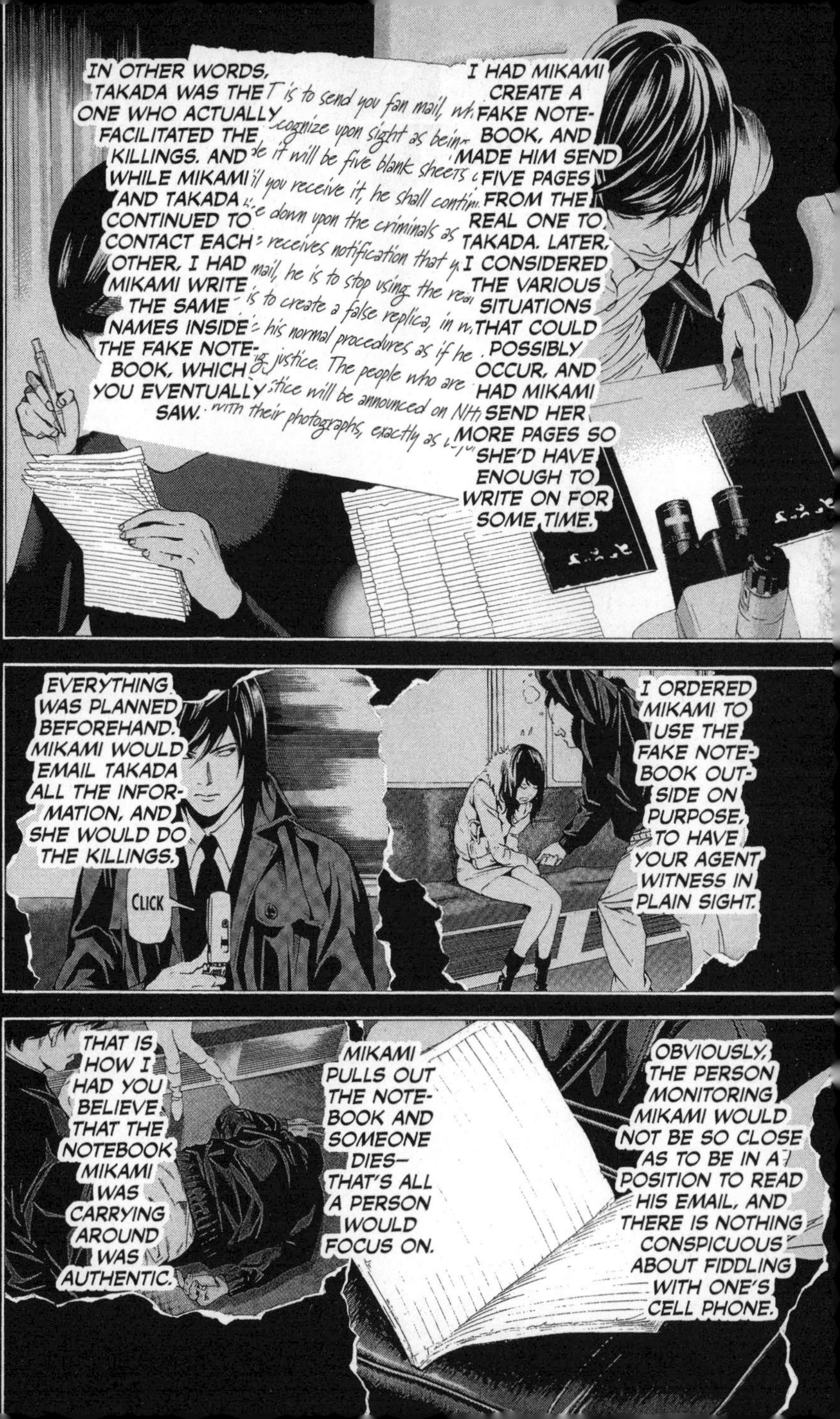
I HAD MIKAMI CREATE A FAKE NOTEBOOK, AND MADE HIM SEND FIVE PAGES FROM THE REAL ONE TO TAKADA. LATER, I CONSIDERED THE VARIOUS SITUATIONS THAT COULD POSSIBLY OCCUR, AND HAD MIKAMI SEND HER MORE PAGES SO SHE'D HAVE ENOUGH TO WRITE ON FOR SOME TIME.
IN OTHER WORDS, TAKADA WAS THE ONE WHO ACTUALLY FACILITATED THE KILLINGS. AND WHILE MIKAMI AND TAKADA CONTINUED TO CONTACT EACH OTHER, I HAD MIKAMI WRITE THE SAME NAMES INSIDE THE FAKE NOTEBOOK, WHICH YOU EVENTUALLY SAW.
I ORDERED MIKAMI TO USE THE FAKE NOTEBOOK OUTSIDE ON PURPOSE, TO HAVE YOUR AGENT WITNESS IN PLAIN SIGHT.
EVERYTHING WAS PLANNED BEFOREHAND. MIKAMI WOULD EMAIL TAKADA ALL THE INFORMATION, AND SHE WOULD DO THE KILLINGS.
CLICK
OBVIOUSLY, THE PERSON MONITORING MIKAMI WOULD NOT BE SO CLOSE AS TO BE IN A POSITION TO READ HIS EMAIL, AND THERE IS NOTHING CONSPICUOUS ABOUT FIDDLING WITH ONE'S CELL PHONE.
MIKAMI PULLS OUT THE NOTEBOOK AND SOMEONE DIES— THAT'S ALL A PERSON WOULD FOCUS ON.
THAT IS HOW I HAD YOU BELIEVE THAT THE NOTEBOOK MIKAMI WAS CARRYING AROUND WAS AUTHENTIC.

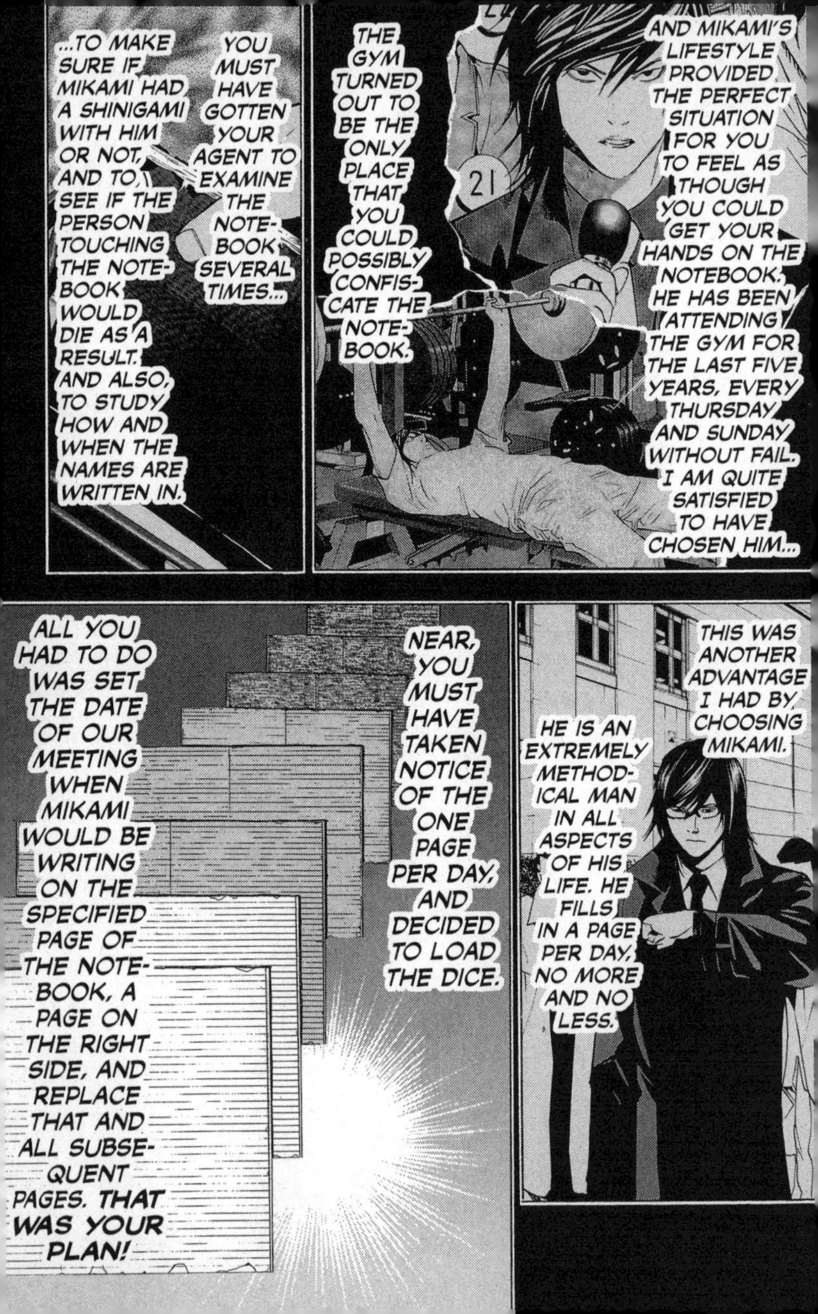
AND MIKAMI'S LIFESTYLE PROVIDED THE PERFECT SITUATION FOR YOU TO FEEL AS THOUGH YOU COULD GET YOUR HANDS ON THE NOTEBOOK. HE HAS BEEN ATTENDING THE GYM FOR THE LAST FIVE YEARS, EVERY THURSDAY AND SUNDAY WITHOUT FAIL. I AM QUITE SATISFIED TO HAVE CHOSEN HIM...
THE GYM TURNED OUT TO BE THE ONLY PLACE THAT YOU COULD POSSIBLY CONFISCATE THE NOTEBOOK.
YOU MUST HAVE GOTTEN YOUR AGENT TO EXAMINE THE NOTEBOOK SEVERAL TIMES...
...TO MAKE SURE IF MIKAMI HAD A SHINIGAMI WITH HIM OR NOT, AND TO SEE IF THE PERSON TOUCHING THE NOTEBOOK WOULD DIE AS A RESULT. AND ALSO, TO STUDY HOW AND WHEN THE NAMES ARE WRITTEN IN.
THIS WAS ANOTHER ADVANTAGE I HAD BY CHOOSING MIKAMI.
HE IS AN EXTREMELY METHODICAL MAN IN ALL ASPECTS OF HIS LIFE. HE FILLS IN A PAGE PER DAY, NO MORE AND NO LESS.
NEAR, YOU MUST HAVE TAKEN NOTICE OF THE ONE PAGE PER DAY, AND DECIDED TO LOAD THE DICE.
ALL YOU HAD TO DO WAS SET THE DATE OF OUR MEETING WHEN MIKAMI WOULD BE WRITING ON THE SPECIFIED PAGE OF THE NOTEBOOK, A PAGE ON THE RIGHT SIDE, AND REPLACE THAT AND ALL SUBSEQUENT PAGES. THAT WAS YOUR PLAN!

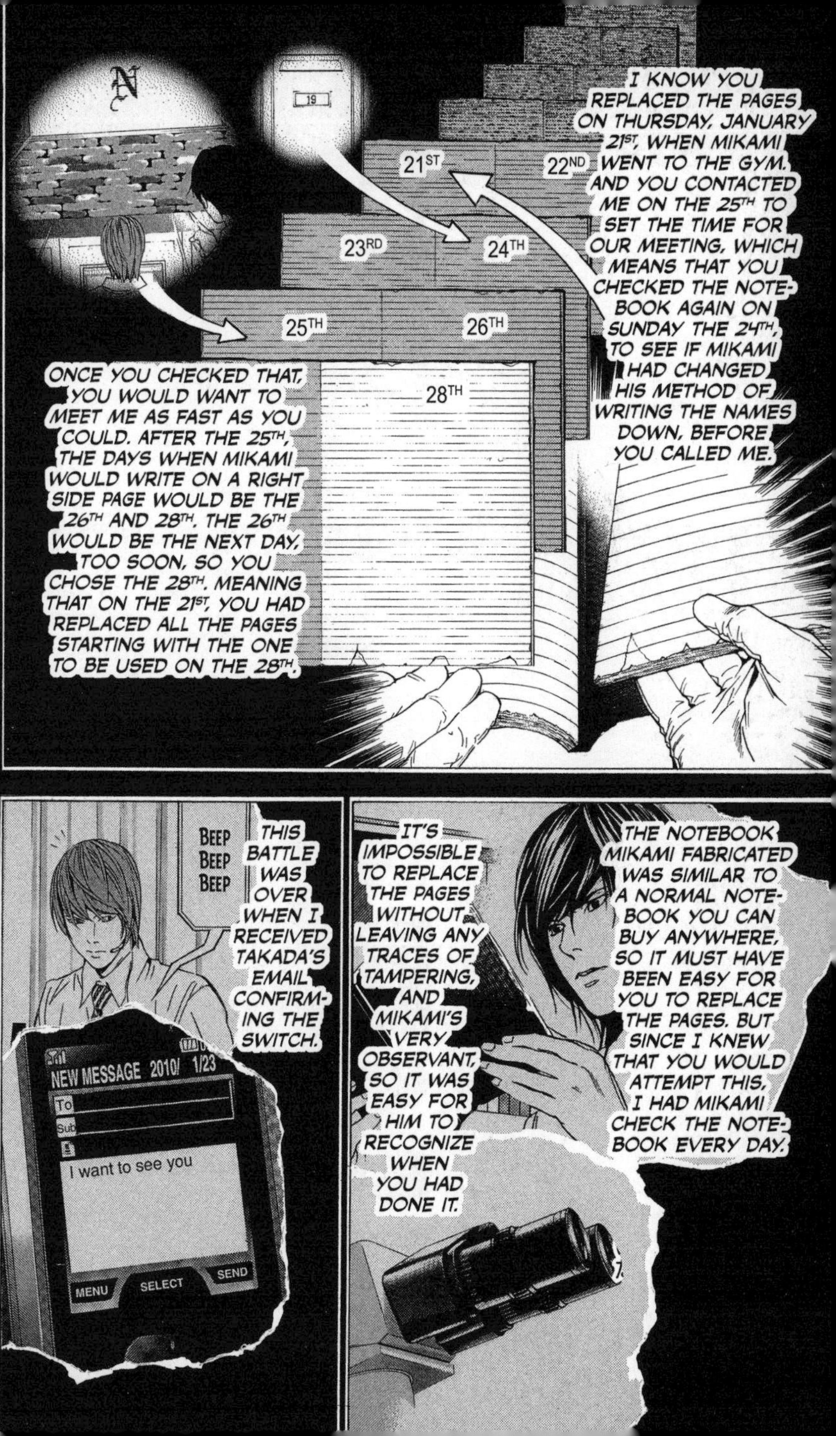
I KNOW YOU REPLACED THE PAGES ON THURSDAY, JANUARY 21ST, WHEN MIKAMI WENT TO THE GYM. AND YOU CONTACTED ME ON THE 25TH TO SET THE TIME FOR OUR MEETING, WHICH MEANS THAT YOU CHECKED THE NOTE-BOOK AGAIN ON SUNDAY THE 24TH, TO SEE IF MIKAMI HAD CHANGED HIS METHOD OF WRITING THE NAMES DOWN, BEFORE YOU CALLED ME.
19
22ND
21ST
24TH
23RD
26TH
25TH
28TH
ONCE YOU CHECKED THAT, YOU WOULD WANT TO MEET ME AS FAST AS YOU COULD. AFTER THE 25TH, THE DAYS WHEN MIKAMI WOULD WRITE ON A RIGHT SIDE PAGE WOULD BE THE 26TH AND 28TH. THE 26TH WOULD BE THE NEXT DAY, TOO SOON, SO YOU CHOSE THE 28TH. MEANING THAT ON THE 21ST, YOU HAD REPLACED ALL THE PAGES STARTING WITH THE ONE TO BE USED ON THE 28TH.
THE NOTEBOOK MIKAMI FABRICATED WAS SIMILAR TO A NORMAL NOTE-BOOK YOU CAN BUY ANYWHERE, SO IT MUST HAVE BEEN EASY FOR YOU TO REPLACE THE PAGES. BUT SINCE I KNEW THAT YOU WOULD ATTEMPT THIS, I HAD MIKAMI CHECK THE NOTE-BOOK EVERY DAY.
IT'S IMPOSSIBLE TO REPLACE THE PAGES WITHOUT LEAVING ANY TRACES OF TAMPERING, AND MIKAMI'S VERY OBSERVANT, SO IT WAS EASY FOR HIM TO RECOGNIZE WHEN YOU HAD DONE IT.
THIS BATTLE WAS OVER WHEN I RECEIVED TAKADA'S EMAIL CONFIRMING THE SWITCH.
BEEP BEEP BEEP
NEW MESSAGE 2010/ 1/23
To
Sub
I want to see you
MENU
SELECT
SEND

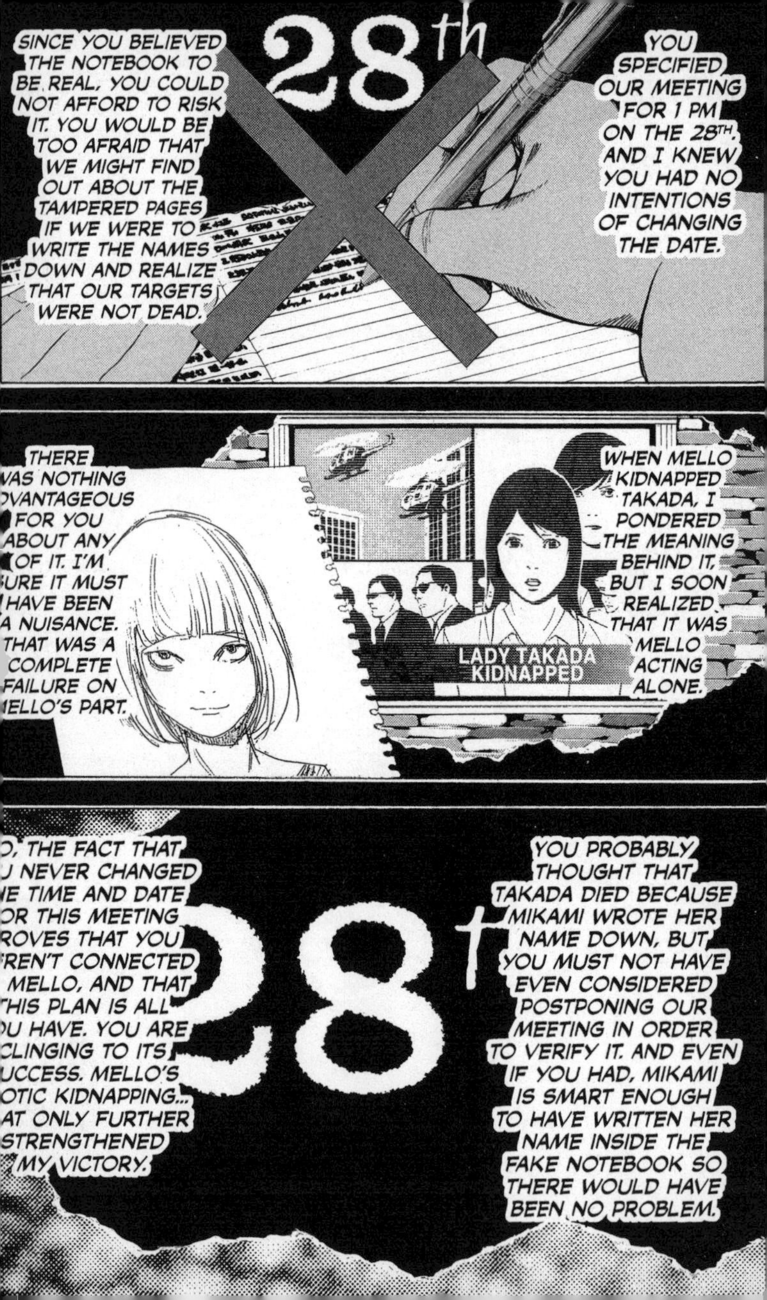

28th
YOU SPECIFIED OUR MEETING FOR 1 PM ON THE 28TH, AND I KNEW YOU HAD NO INTENTIONS OF CHANGING THE DATE.
SINCE YOU BELIEVED THE NOTEBOOK TO BE REAL, YOU COULD NOT AFFORD TO RISK IT. YOU WOULD BE TOO AFRAID THAT WE MIGHT FIND OUT ABOUT THE TAMPERED PAGES IF WE WERE TO WRITE THE NAMES DOWN AND REALIZE THAT OUR TARGETS WERE NOT DEAD.
WHEN MELLO KIDNAPPED TAKADA, I PONDERED THE MEANING BEHIND IT, BUT I SOON REALIZED THAT IT WAS MELLO ACTING ALONE.
LADY TAKADA KIDNAPPED
THERE VAS NOTHING DVANTAGEOUS FOR YOU ABOUT ANY OF IT. I'M URE IT MUST HAVE BEEN A NUISANCE. THAT WAS A COMPLETE FAILURE ON ELLO'S PART.
YOU PROBABLY THOUGHT THAT TAKADA DIED BECAUSE MIKAMI WROTE HER NAME DOWN, BUT YOU MUST NOT HAVE EVEN CONSIDERED POSTPONING OUR MEETING IN ORDER TO VERIFY IT. AND EVEN IF YOU HAD, MIKAMI IS SMART ENOUGH TO HAVE WRITTEN HER NAME INSIDE THE FAKE NOTEBOOK SO THERE WOULD HAVE BEEN NO PROBLEM.
28t
D, THE FACT THAT J NEVER CHANGED E TIME AND DATE OR THIS MEETING ROVES THAT YOU REN'T CONNECTED MELLO, AND THAT THIS PLAN IS ALL U HAVE. YOU ARE CLINGING TO ITS UCCESS. MELLO'S OTIC KIDNAPPING... AT ONLY FURTHER STRENGTHENED MY VICTORY.

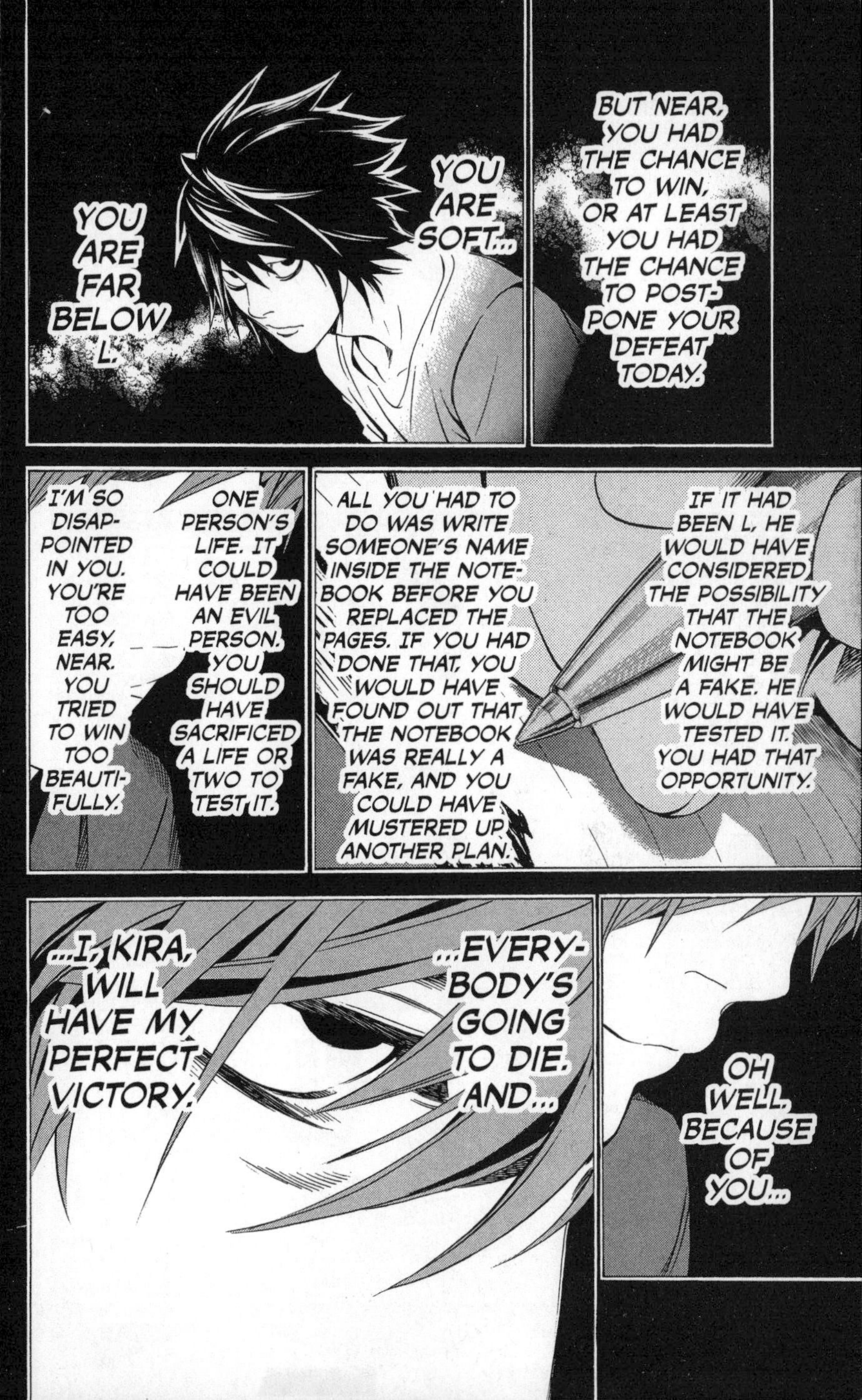
BUT NEAR, YOU HAD THE CHANCE TO WIN, OR AT LEAST YOU HAD THE CHANCE TO POSTPONE YOUR DEFEAT TODAY.
YOU ARE SOFT...
YOU ARE FAR BELOW L.
IF IT HAD BEEN L, HE WOULD HAVE CONSIDERED THE POSSIBILITY THAT THE NOTEBOOK MIGHT BE A FAKE. HE WOULD HAVE TESTED IT. YOU HAD THAT OPPORTUNITY.
ALL YOU HAD TO DO WAS WRITE SOMEONE'S NAME INSIDE THE NOTEBOOK BEFORE YOU REPLACED THE PAGES. IF YOU HAD DONE THAT, YOU WOULD HAVE FOUND OUT THAT THE NOTEBOOK WAS REALLY A FAKE, AND YOU COULD HAVE MUSTERED UP ANOTHER PLAN.
ONE PERSON'S LIFE. IT COULD HAVE BEEN AN EVIL PERSON. YOU SHOULD HAVE SACRIFICED A LIFE OR TWO TO TEST IT.
I'M SO DISAPPOINTED IN YOU. YOU'RE TOO EASY, NEAR. YOU TRIED TO WIN TOO BEAUTIFULLY.
OH WELL, BECAUSE OF YOU...
...EVERYBODY'S GOING TO DIE. AND...
...I, KIRA, WILL HAVE MY PERFECT VICTORY.

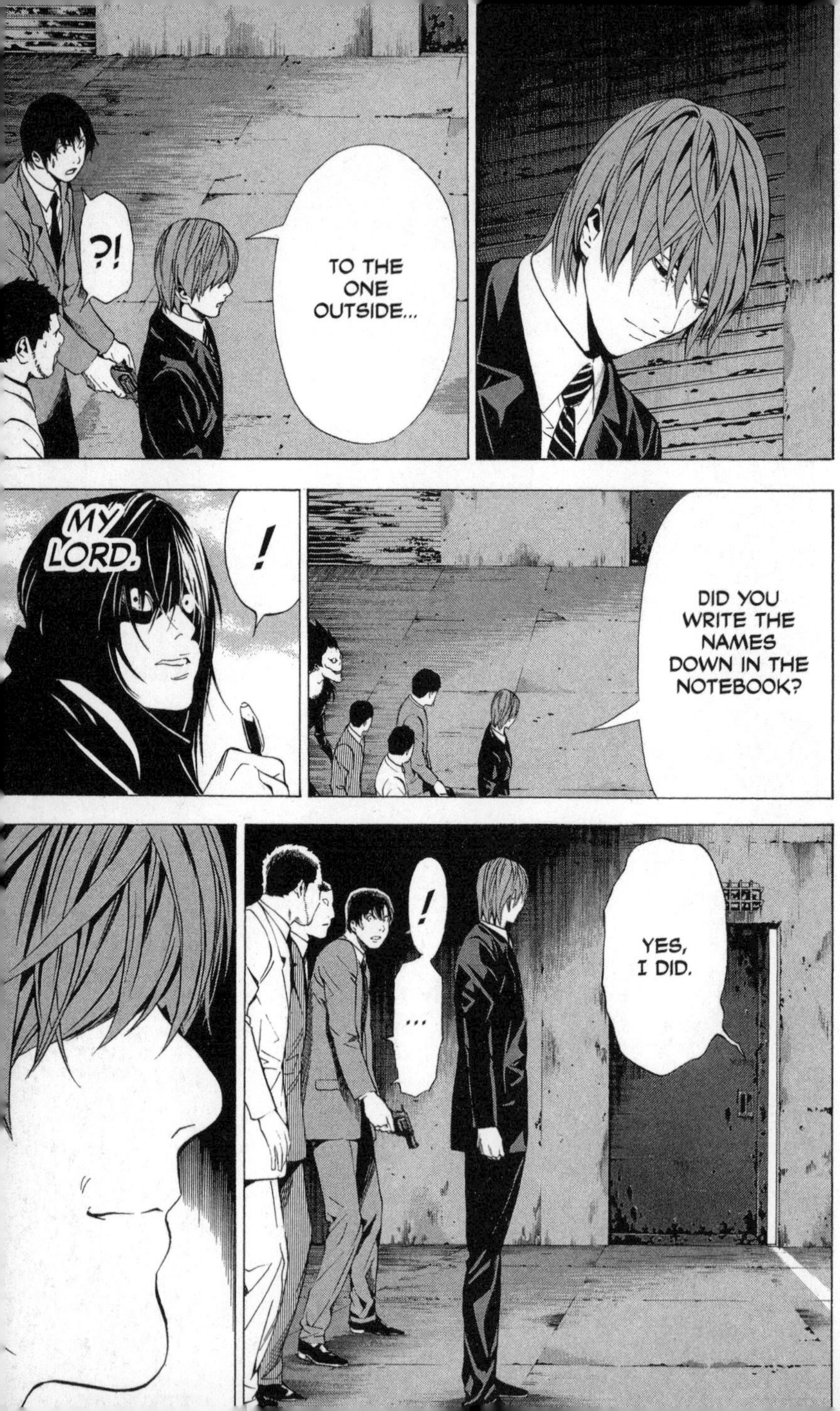
TO THE ONE OUTSIDE...
?!
DID YOU WRITE THE NAMES DOWN IN THE NOTEBOOK?
!
MY LORD.
YES, I DID.
!
...

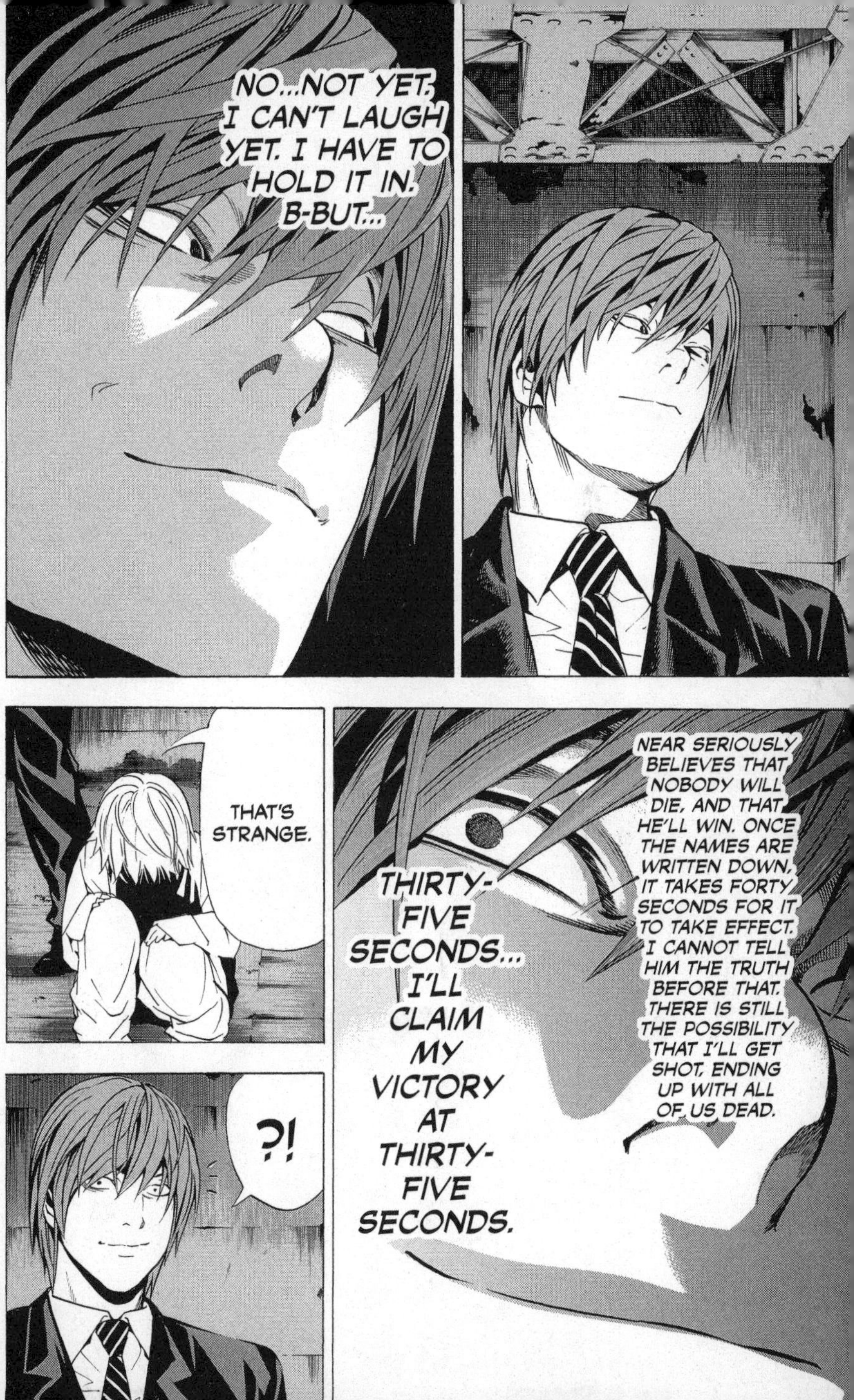
NO...NOT YET. I CAN'T LAUGH YET. I HAVE TO HOLD IT IN. B-BUT...
NEAR SERIOUSLY BELIEVES THAT NOBODY WILL DIE, AND THAT HE'LL WIN. ONCE THE NAMES ARE WRITTEN DOWN, IT TAKES FORTY SECONDS FOR IT TO TAKE EFFECT. I CANNOT TELL HIM THE TRUTH BEFORE THAT. THERE IS STILL THE POSSIBILITY THAT I'LL GET SHOT, ENDING UP WITH ALL OF US DEAD.
THIRTY-FIVE SECONDS... I'LL CLAIM MY VICTORY AT THIRTY-FIVE SECONDS.
THAT'S STRANGE.
?!

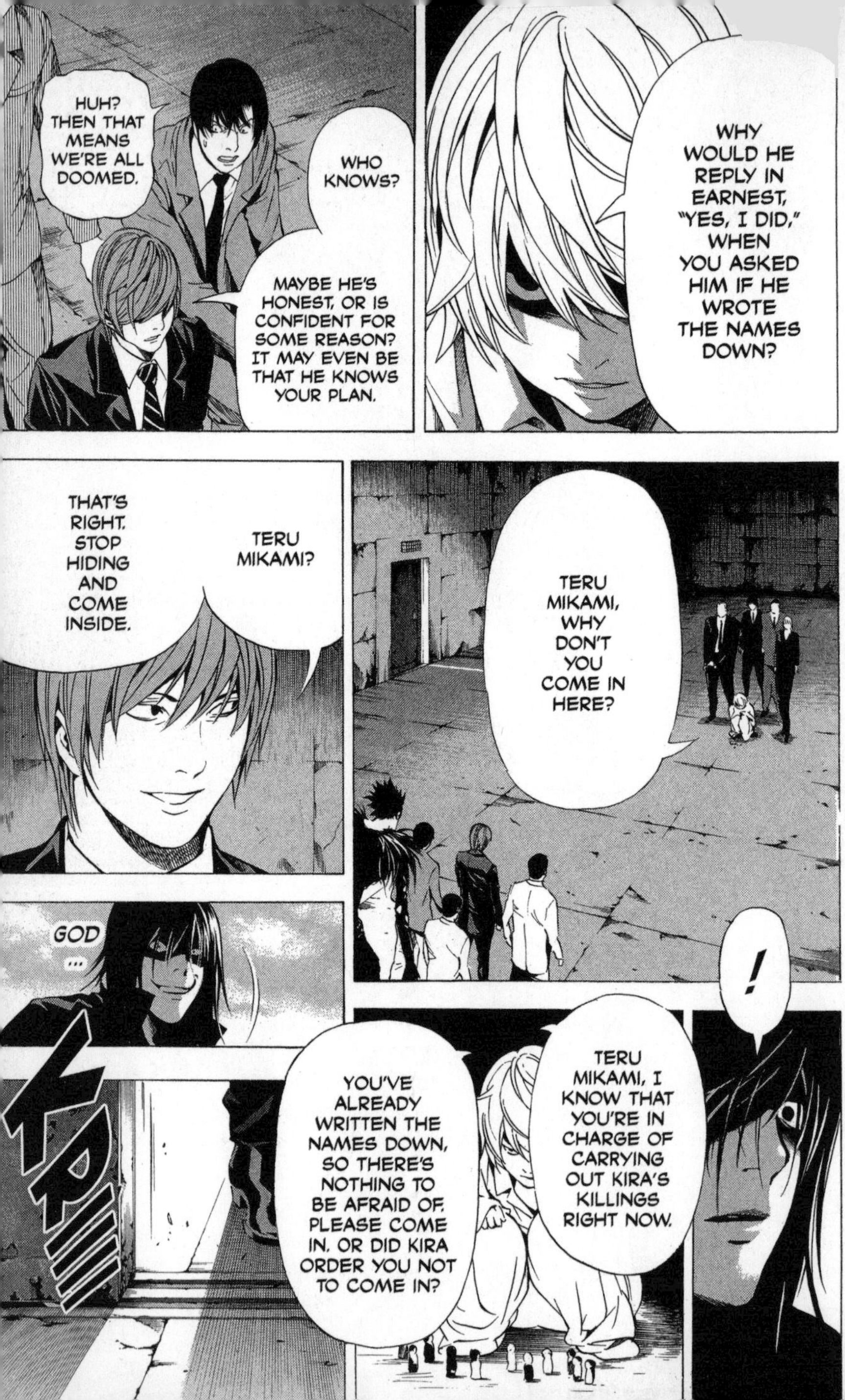
WHY WOULD HE REPLY IN EARNEST, "YES, I DID," WHEN YOU ASKED HIM IF HE WROTE THE NAMES DOWN?
WHO KNOWS?
MAYBE HE'S HONEST, OR IS CONFIDENT FOR SOME REASON? IT MAY EVEN BE THAT HE KNOWS YOUR PLAN.
HUH? THEN THAT MEANS WE'RE ALL DOOMED.
TERU MIKAMI, WHY DON'T YOU COME IN HERE?
TERU MIKAMI?
THAT'S RIGHT. STOP HIDING AND COME INSIDE.
!
TERU MIKAMI, I KNOW THAT YOU'RE IN CHARGE OF CARRYING OUT KIRA'S KILLINGS RIGHT NOW.
YOU'VE ALREADY WRITTEN THE NAMES DOWN, SO THERE'S NOTHING TO BE AFRAID OF. PLEASE COME IN. OR DID KIRA ORDER YOU NOT TO COME IN?
GOD ...
KRIIII

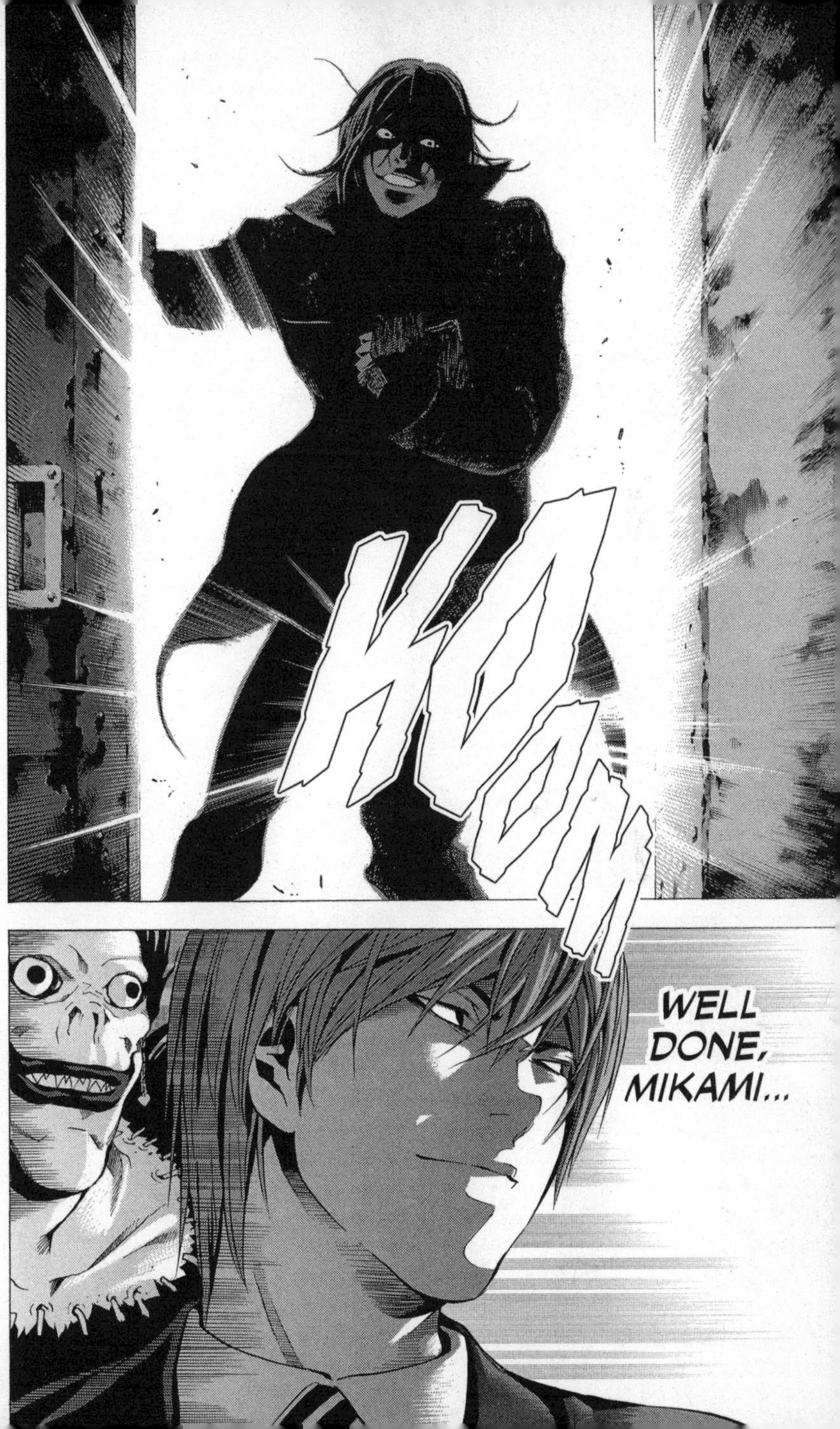
KA-CHAK
WELL DONE, MIKAMI...

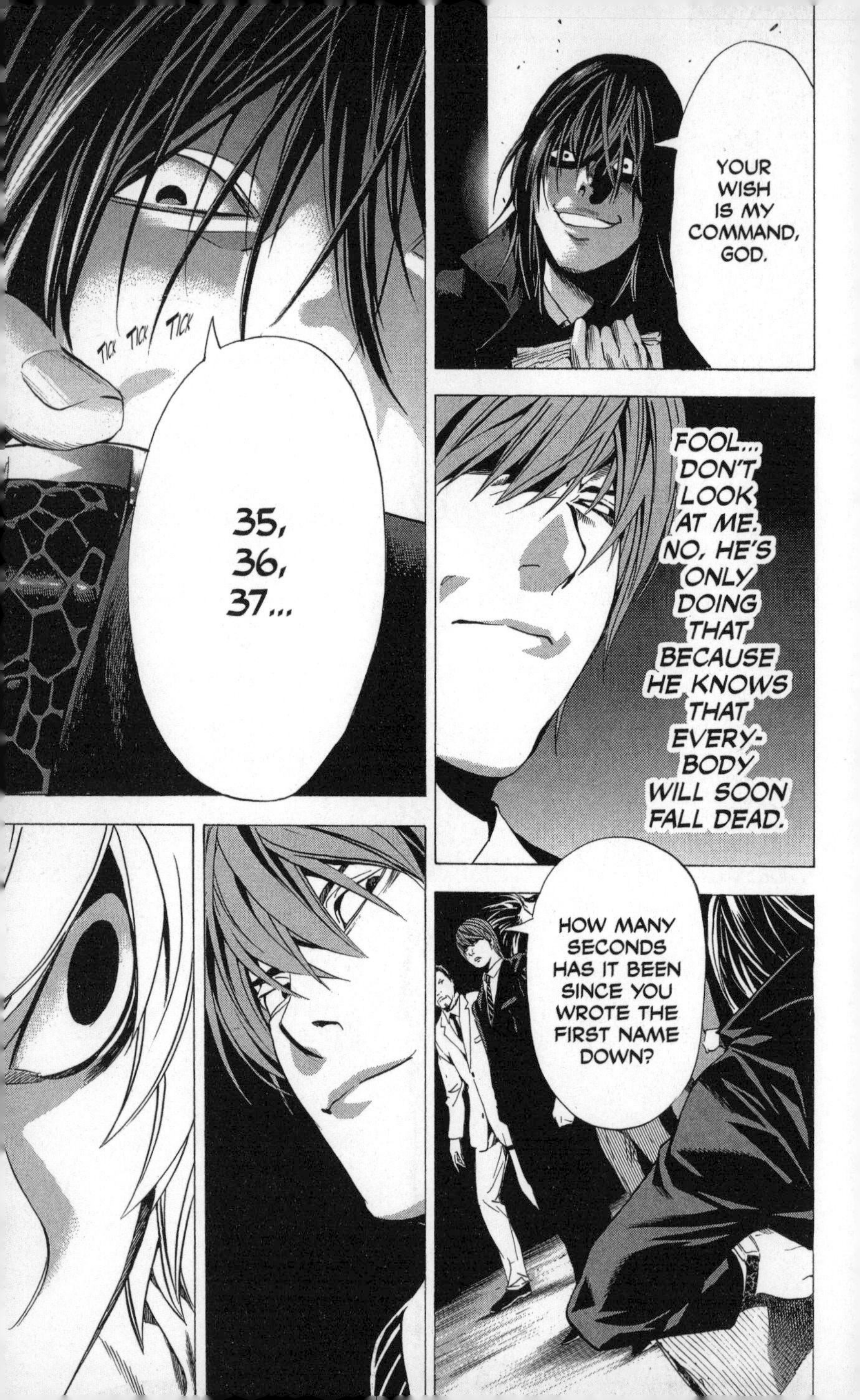
YOUR WISH IS MY COMMAND, GOD.
FOOL... DON'T LOOK AT ME. NO, HE'S ONLY DOING THAT BECAUSE HE KNOWS THAT EVERY-BODY WILL SOON FALL DEAD.
TICK TICK TICK
35, 36, 37...
HOW MANY SECONDS HAS IT BEEN SINCE YOU WROTE THE FIRST NAME DOWN?

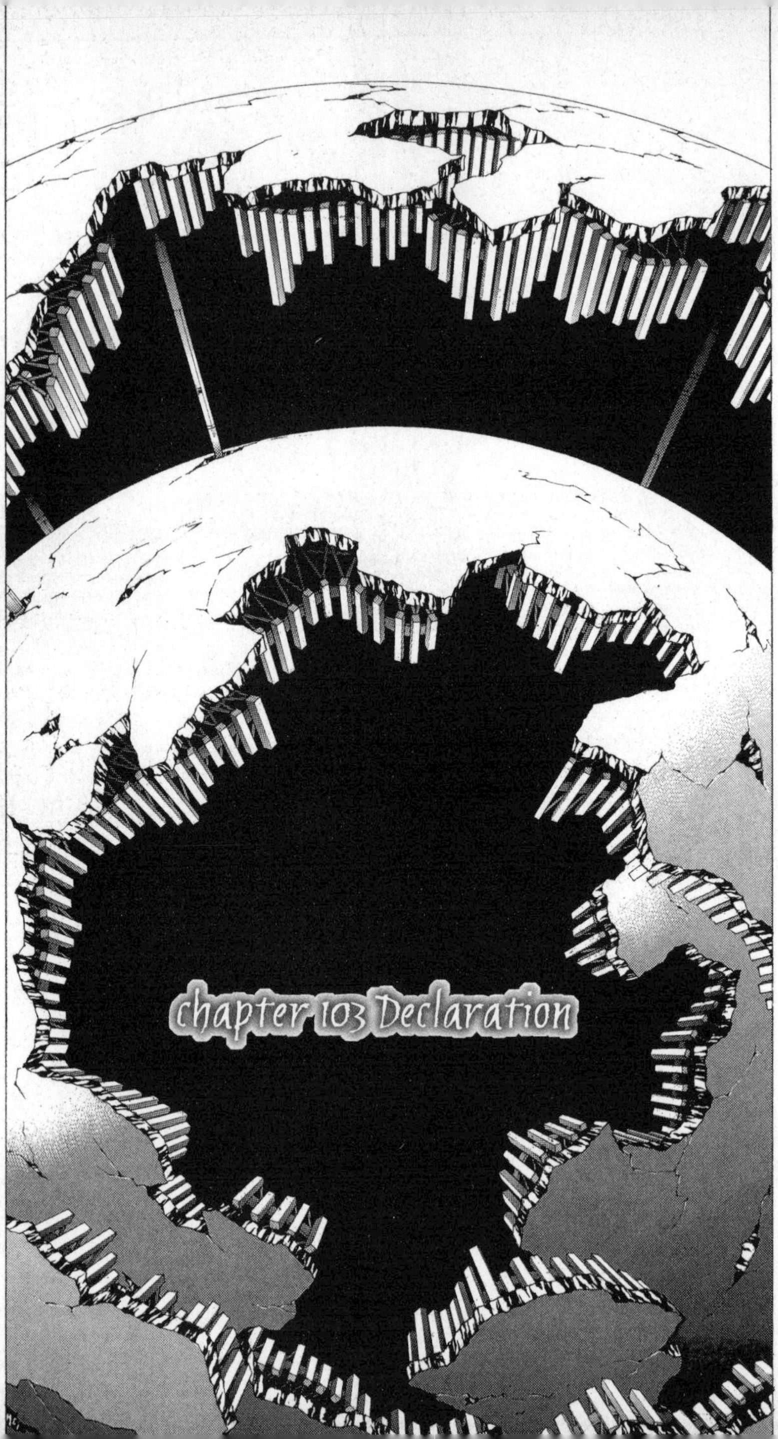
chapter 103 Declaration

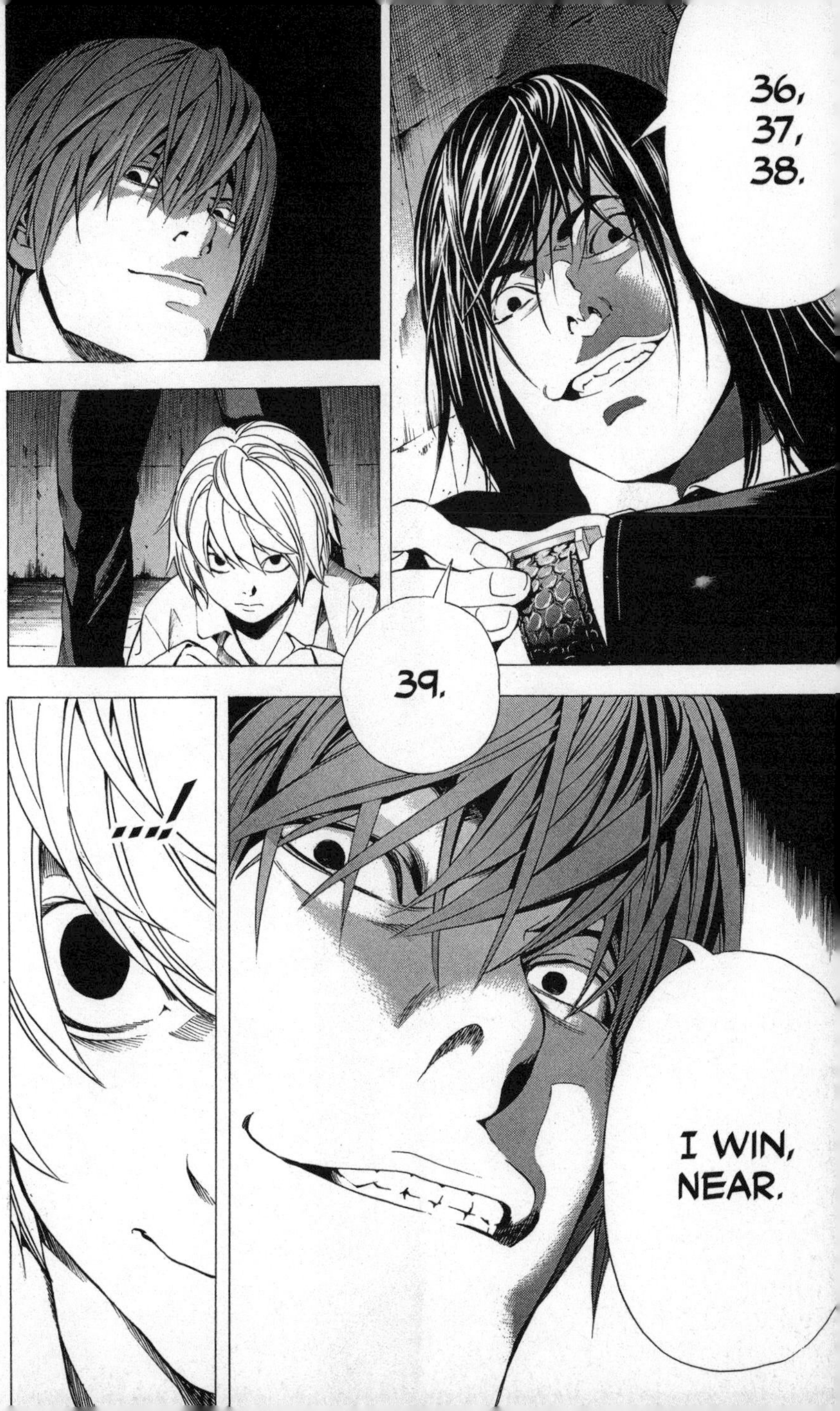
36,
37,
38.
39.
I WIN,
NEAR.
...!

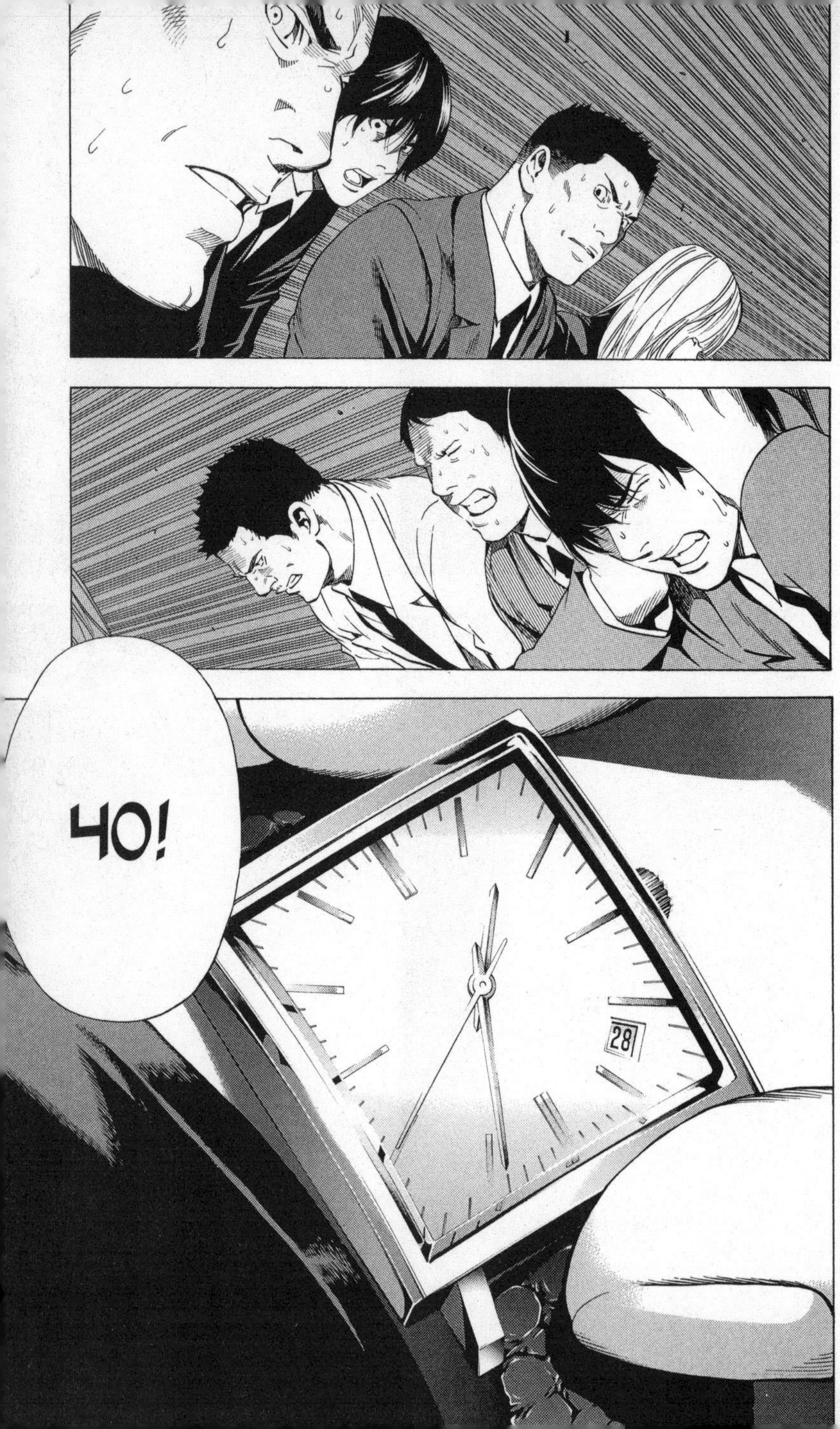
40!

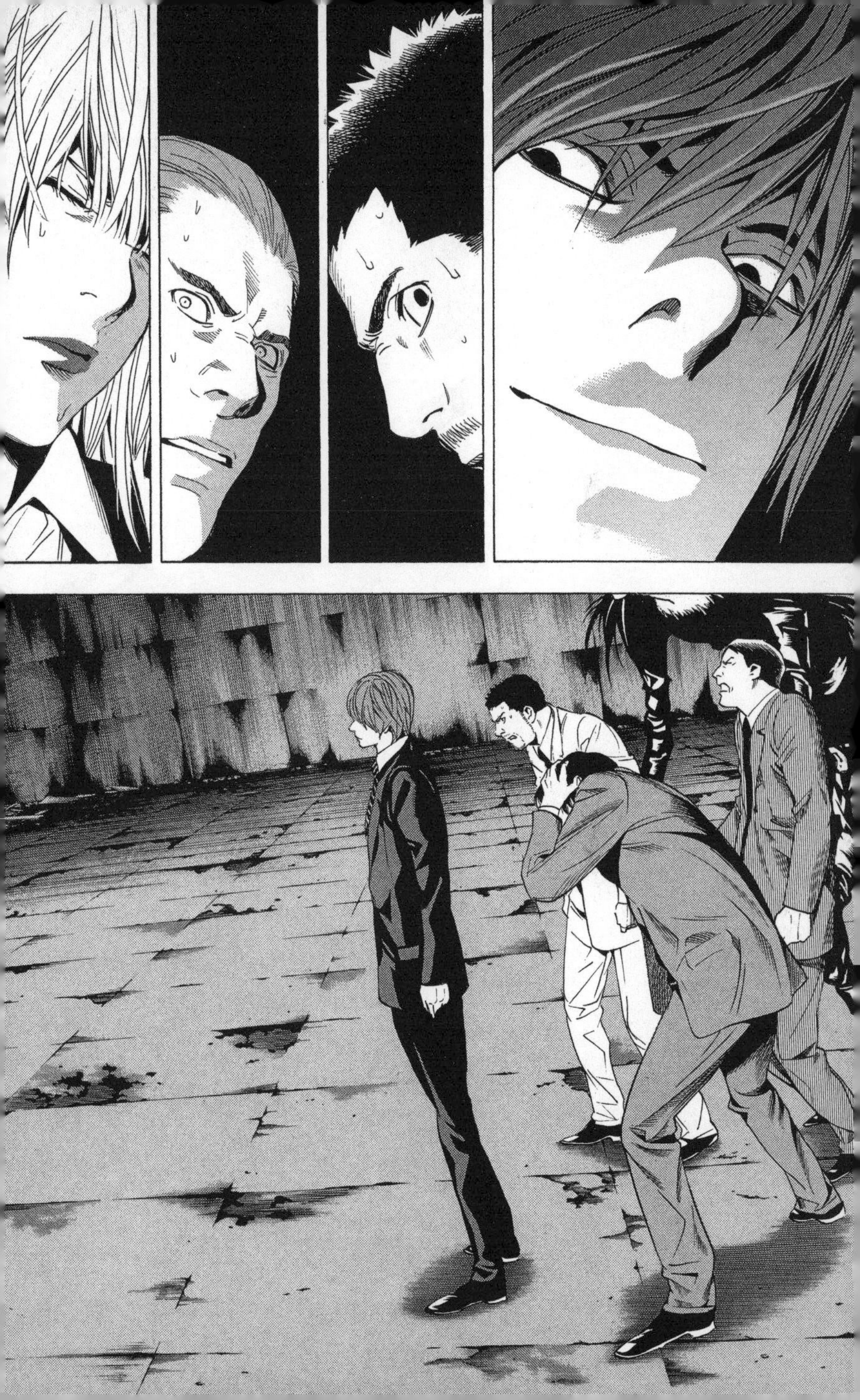

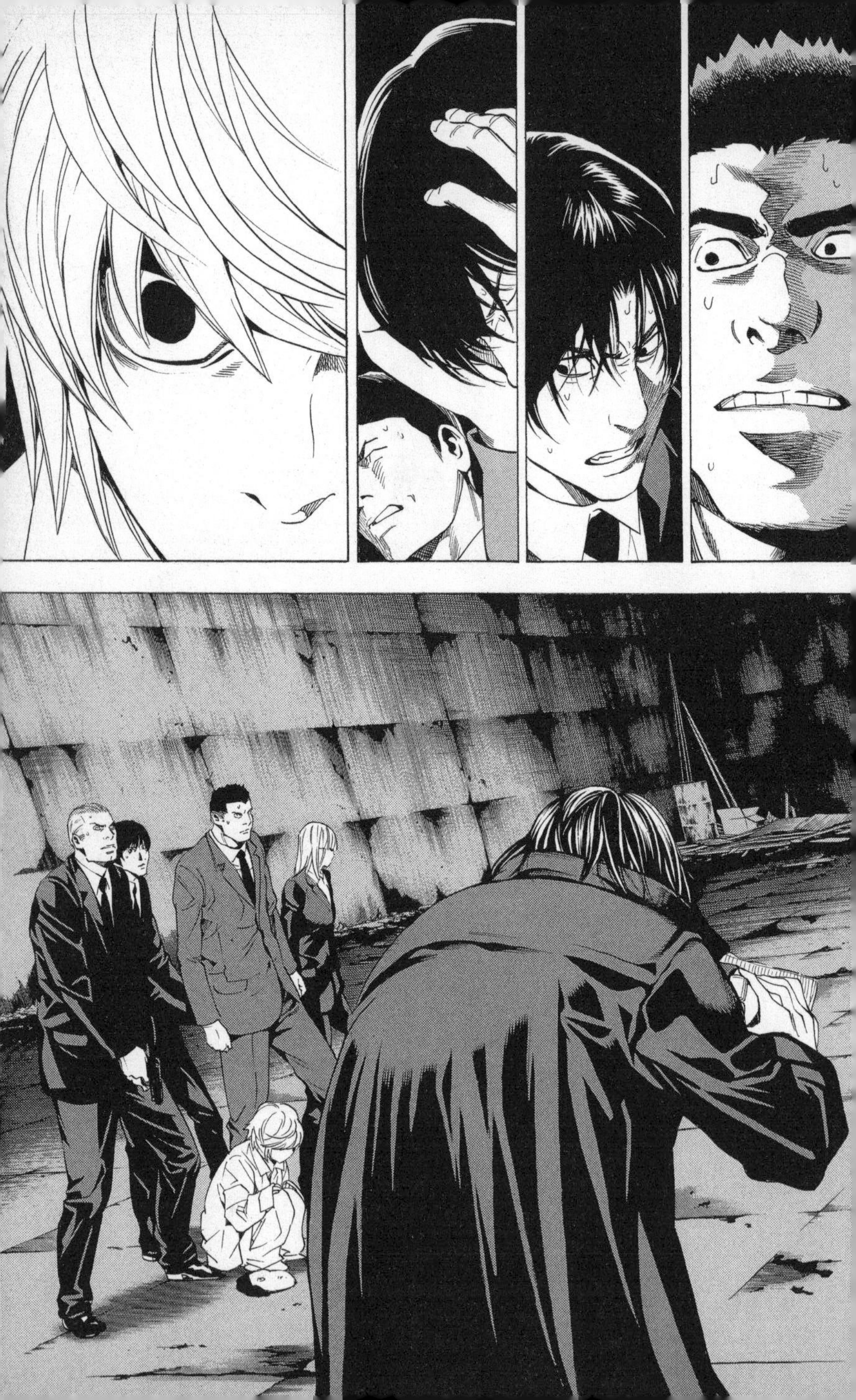

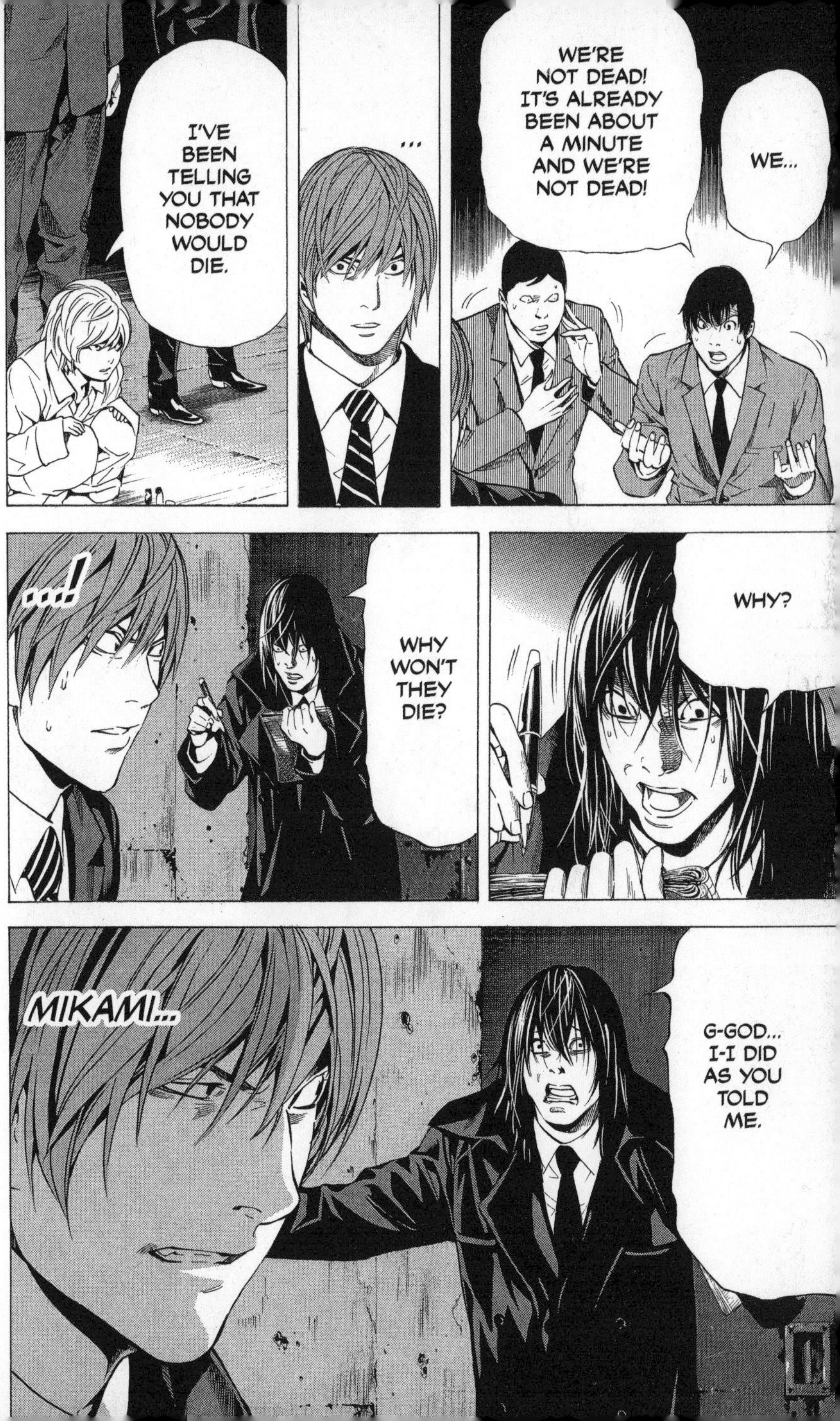
WE...
WE'RE NOT DEAD! IT'S ALREADY BEEN ABOUT A MINUTE AND WE'RE NOT DEAD!
...
I'VE BEEN TELLING YOU THAT NOBODY WOULD DIE.
WHY?
WHY WON'T THEY DIE?
...!
G-GOD... I-I DID AS YOU TOLD ME.
MIKAMI...

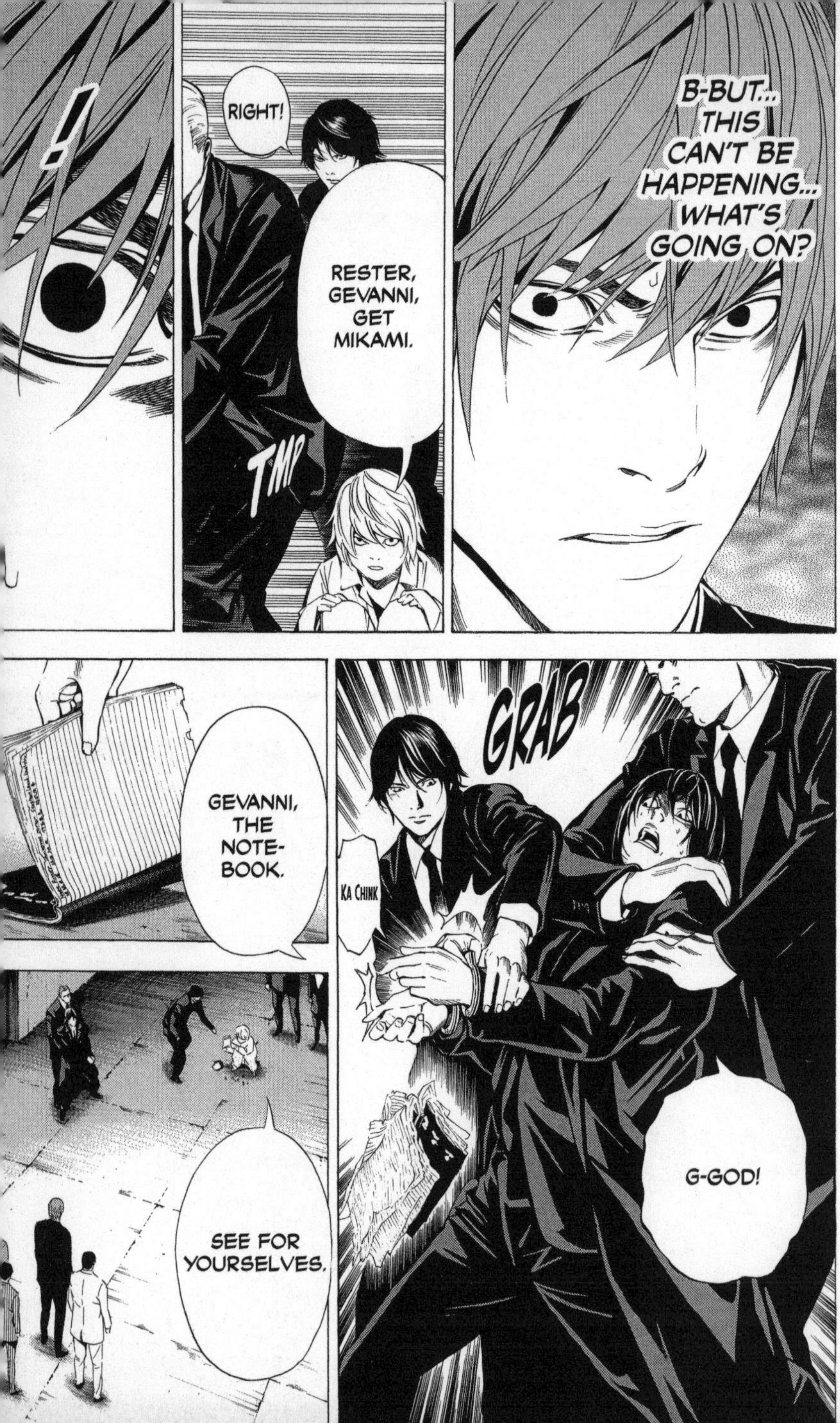

B-BUT... THIS CAN'T BE HAPPENING... WHAT'S GOING ON?
RESTER, GEVANNI, GET MIKAMI.
RIGHT!
TMP
!
GRAB
KA CHINK
G-GOD!
GEVANNI, THE NOTE-BOOK.
SEE FOR YOURSELVES.

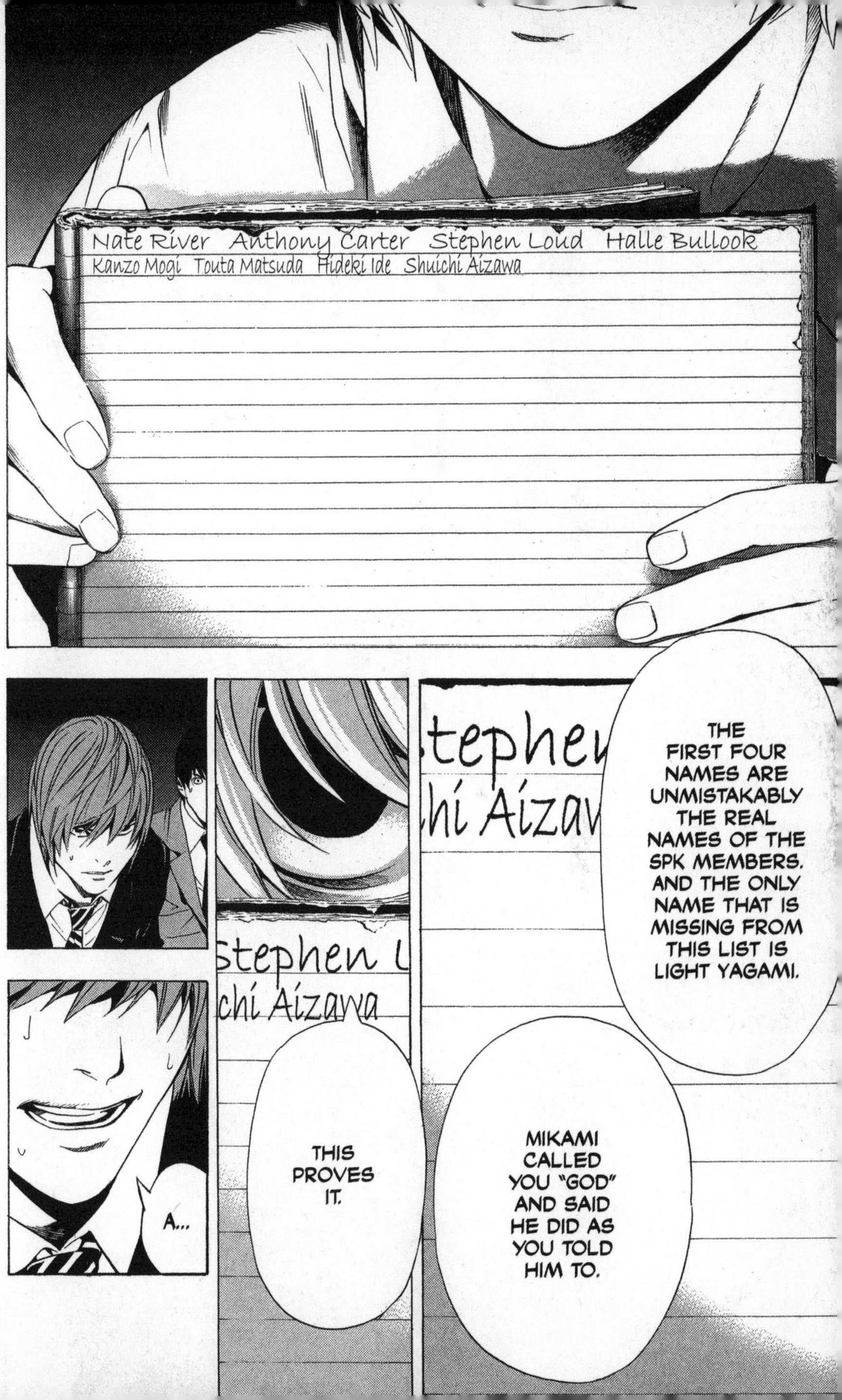
Nate River Anthony Carter Stephen Loud Halle Bullook
Kanzo Mogi Touta Matsuda Hideki Ide Shuichi Aizawa
THE FIRST FOUR NAMES ARE UNMISTAKABLY THE REAL NAMES OF THE SPK MEMBERS. AND THE ONLY NAME THAT IS MISSING FROM THIS LIST IS LIGHT YAGAMI.
MIKAMI CALLED YOU "GOD" AND SAID HE DID AS YOU TOLD HIM TO.
THIS PROVES IT.
A...

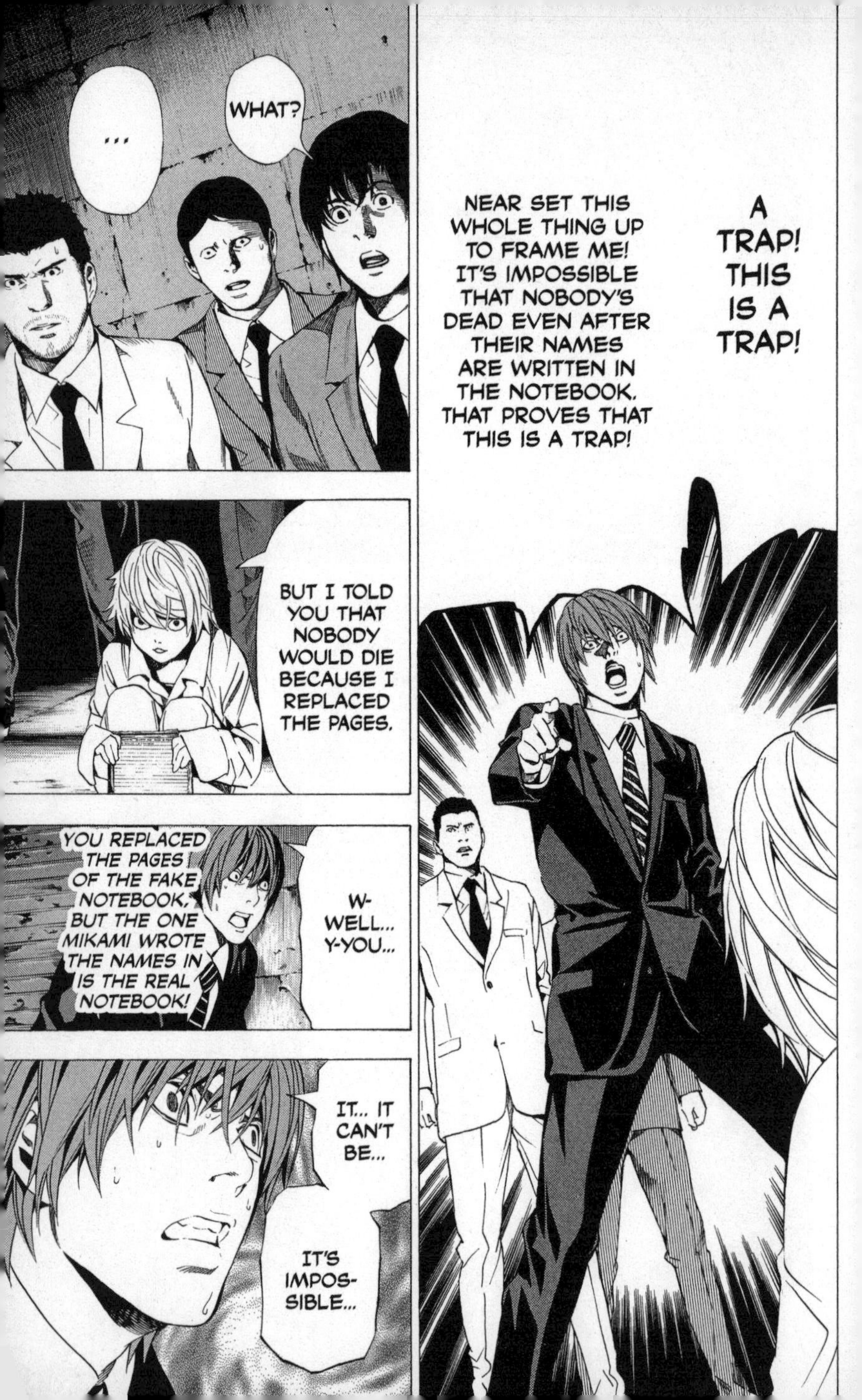
A TRAP! THIS IS A TRAP!
NEAR SET THIS WHOLE THING UP TO FRAME ME! IT'S IMPOSSIBLE THAT NOBODY'S DEAD EVEN AFTER THEIR NAMES ARE WRITTEN IN THE NOTEBOOK. THAT PROVES THAT THIS IS A TRAP!
WHAT?
...
BUT I TOLD YOU THAT NOBODY WOULD DIE BECAUSE I REPLACED THE PAGES.
W-WELL... Y-YOU...
YOU REPLACED THE PAGES OF THE FAKE NOTEBOOK, BUT THE ONE MIKAMI WROTE THE NAMES IN IS THE REAL NOTEBOOK!
IT... IT CAN'T BE...
IT'S IMPOSSIBLE...

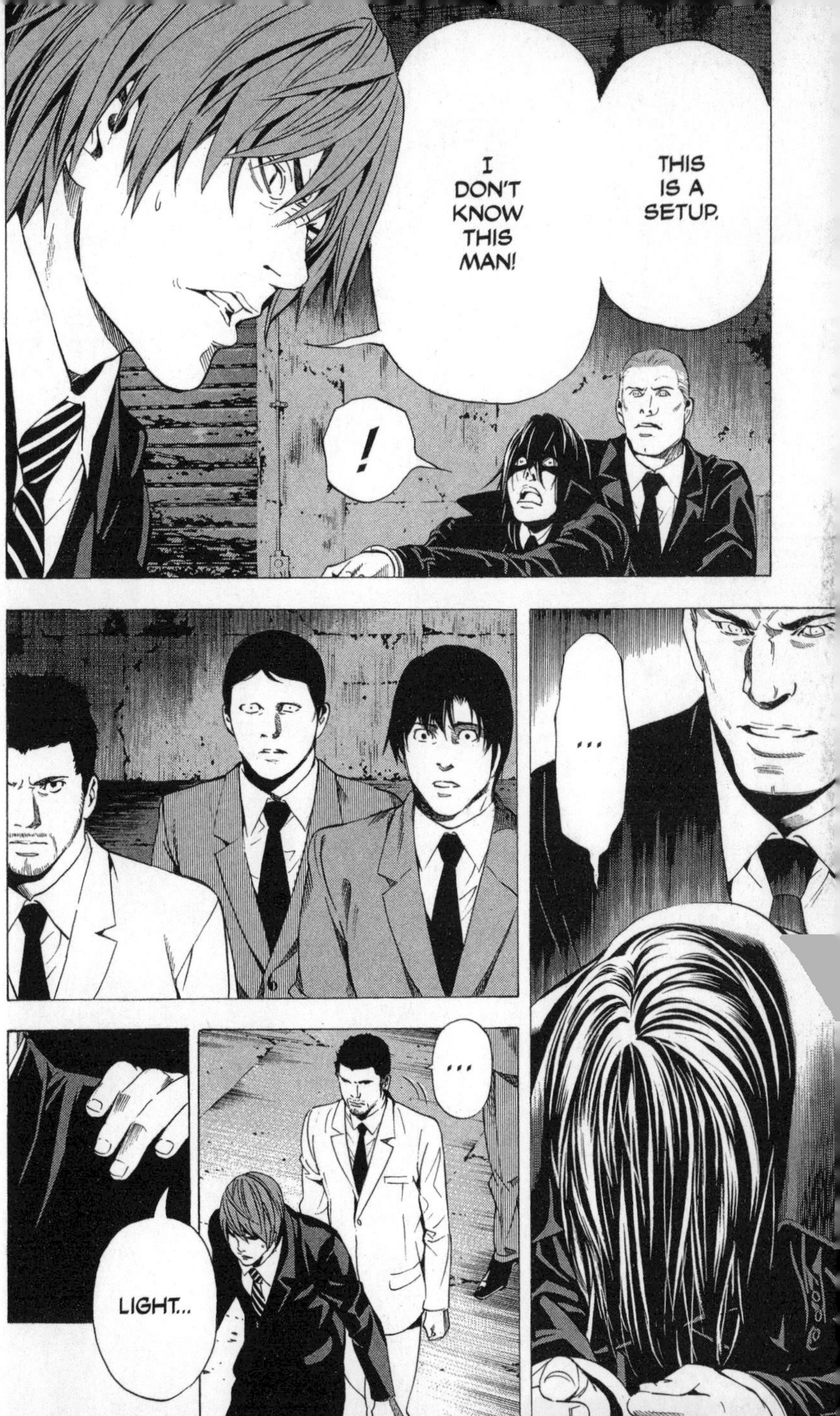
THIS IS A SETUP.
I DON'T KNOW THIS MAN!
!
...
...
LIGHT...

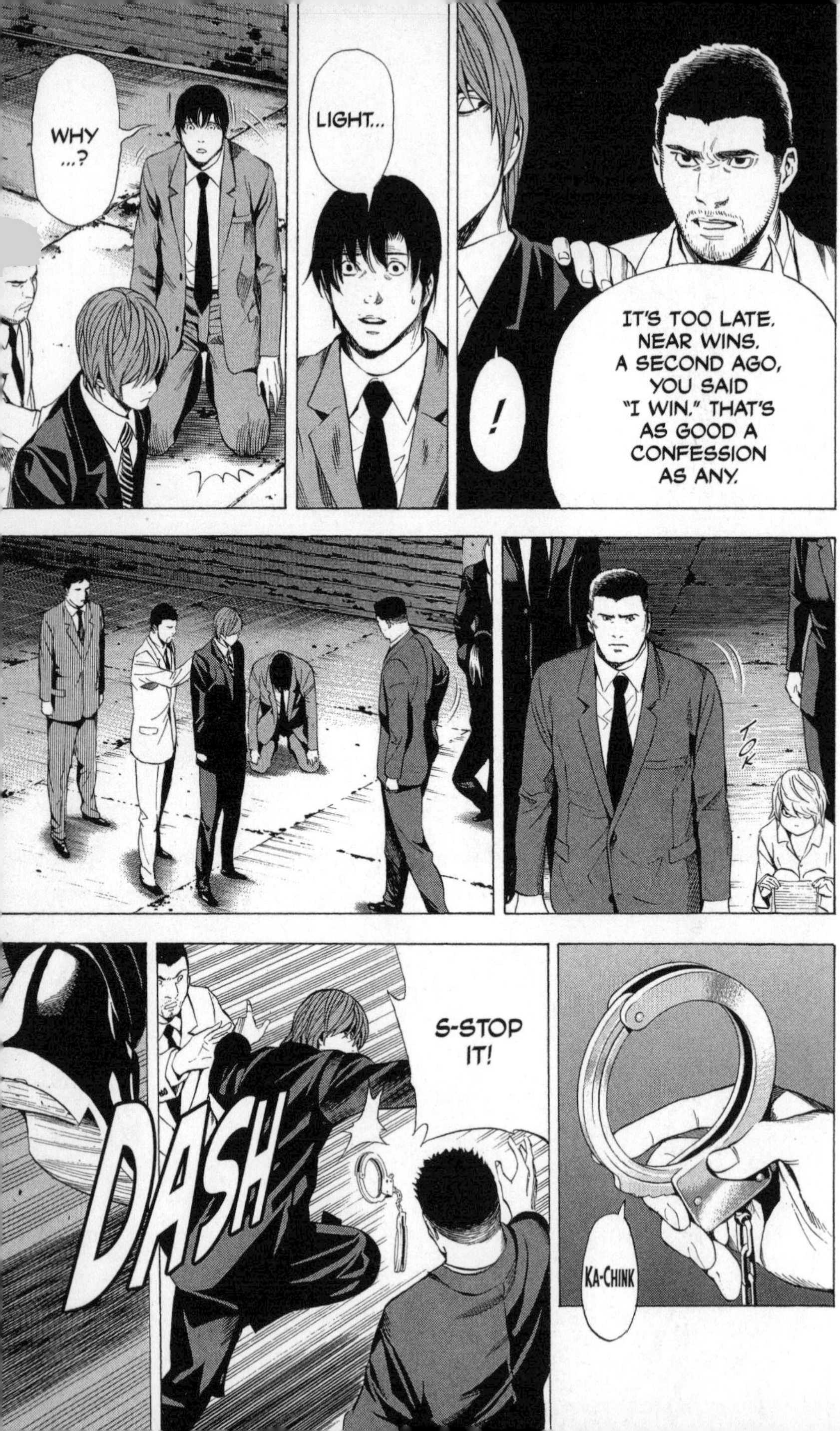
IT'S TOO LATE. NEAR WINS. A SECOND AGO, YOU SAID "I WIN." THAT'S AS GOOD A CONFESSION AS ANY.
!
LIGHT...
WHY ...?
TOK
KA-CHINK
S-STOP IT!
DASH

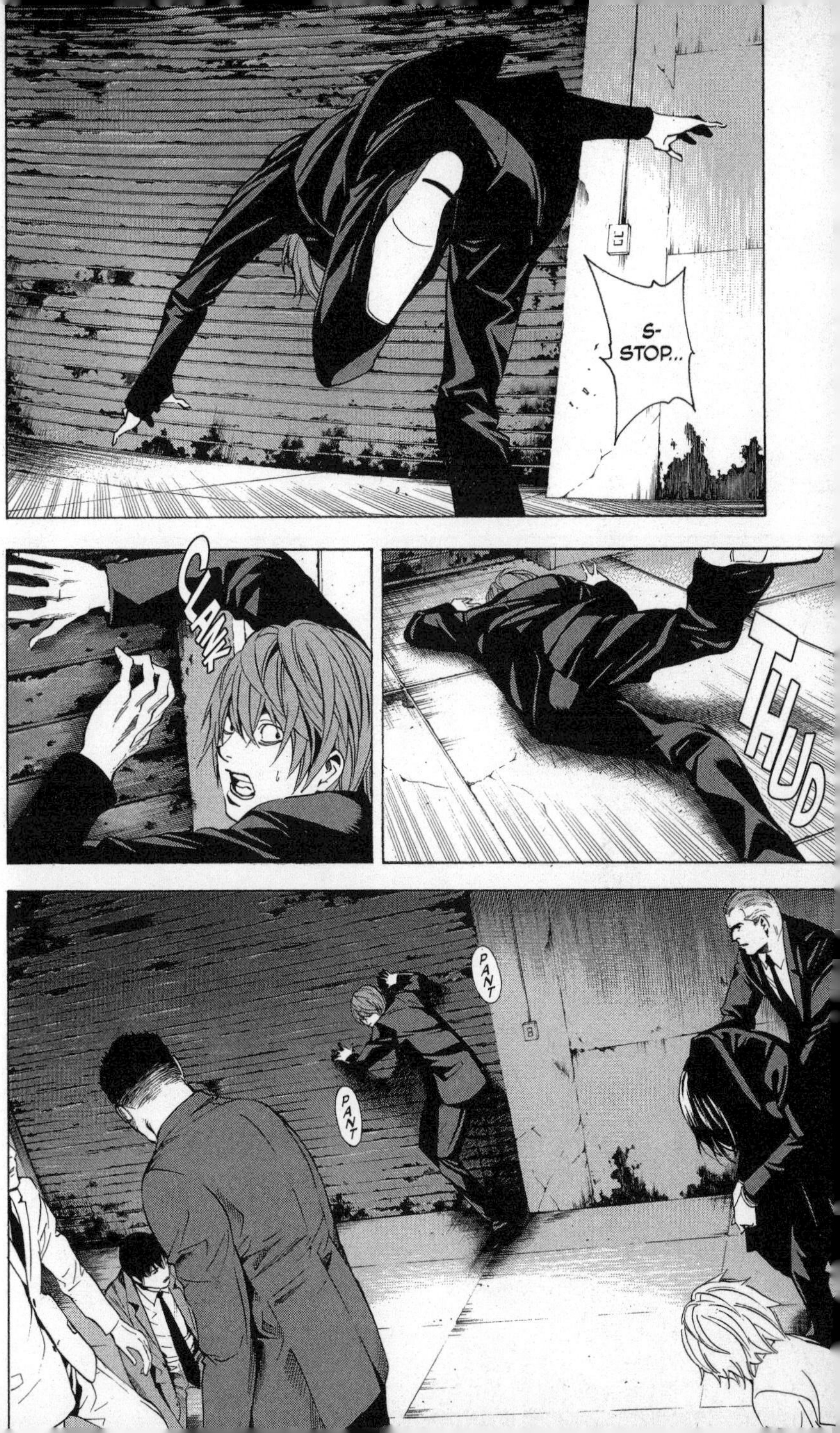
S-
STOP...
THUD
CLANK
PANT
PANT

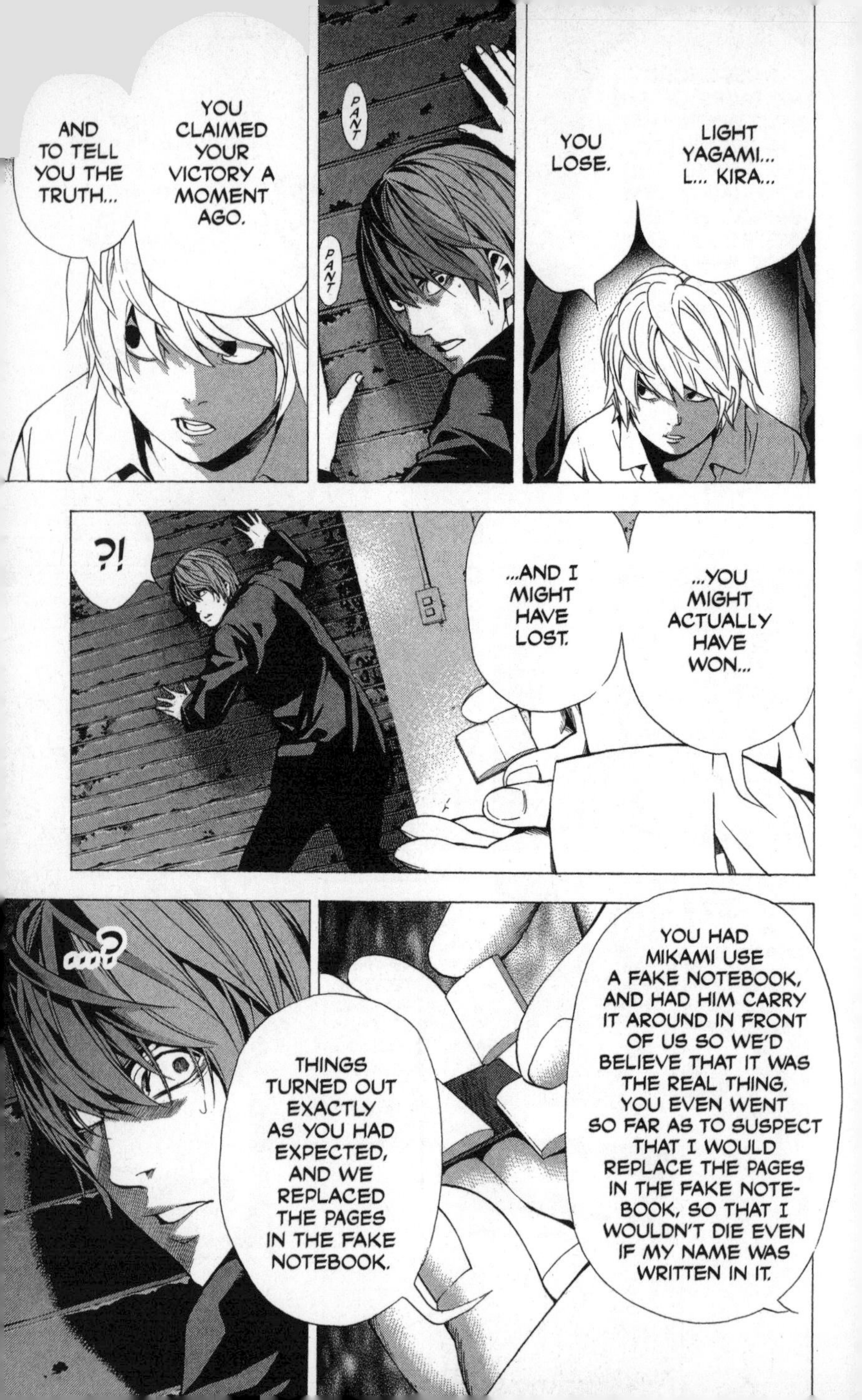
LIGHT YAGAMI... L... KIRA...
YOU LOSE.
PANT
PANT
YOU CLAIMED YOUR VICTORY A MOMENT AGO.
AND TO TELL YOU THE TRUTH...
...YOU MIGHT ACTUALLY HAVE WON...
...AND I MIGHT HAVE LOST.
?!
YOU HAD MIKAMI USE A FAKE NOTEBOOK, AND HAD HIM CARRY IT AROUND IN FRONT OF US SO WE'D BELIEVE THAT IT WAS THE REAL THING. YOU EVEN WENT SO FAR AS TO SUSPECT THAT I WOULD REPLACE THE PAGES IN THE FAKE NOTE-BOOK, SO THAT I WOULDN'T DIE EVEN IF MY NAME WAS WRITTEN IN IT.
THINGS TURNED OUT EXACTLY AS YOU HAD EXPECTED, AND WE REPLACED THE PAGES IN THE FAKE NOTEBOOK.
...?

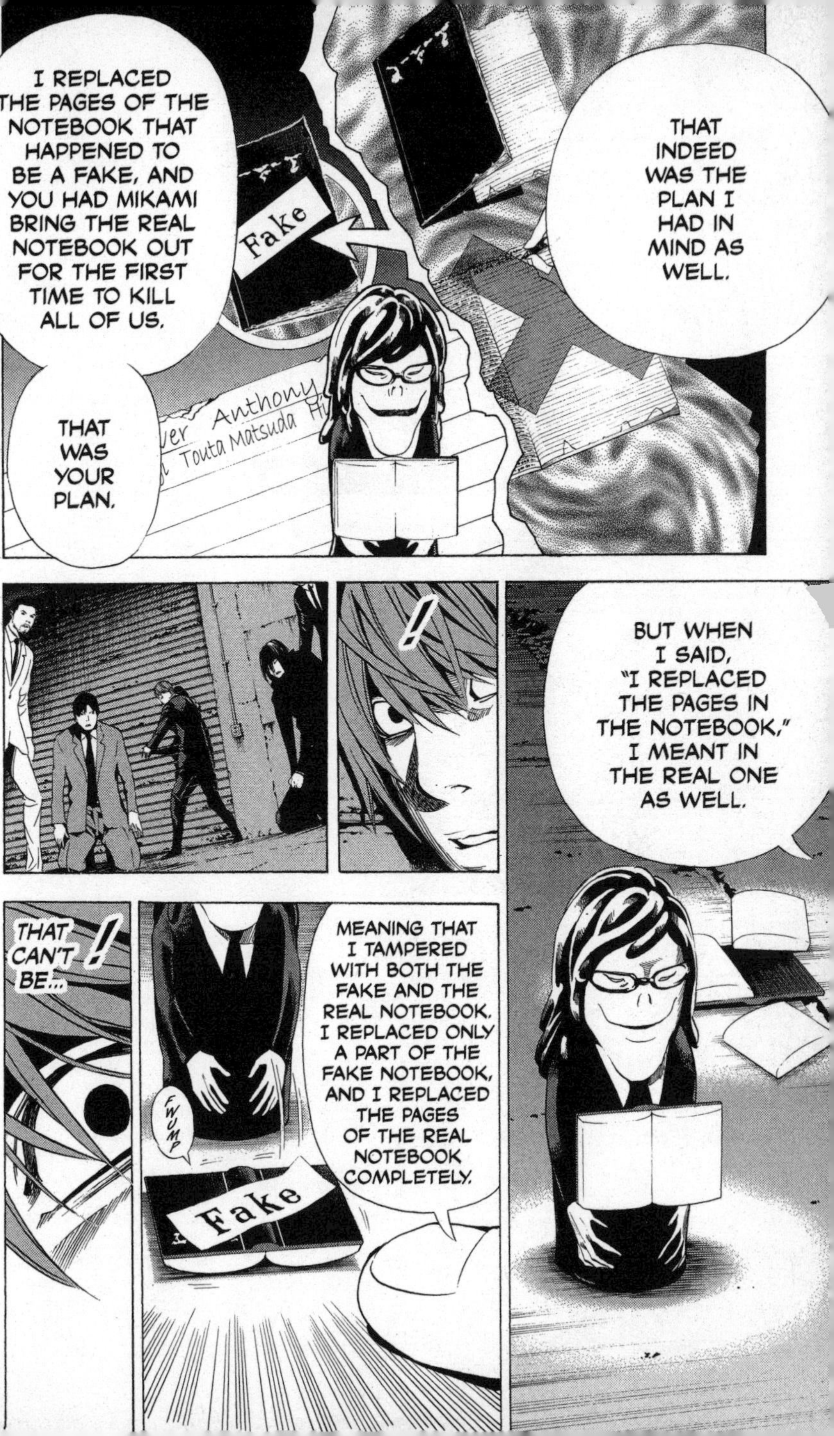
I REPLACED THE PAGES OF THE NOTEBOOK THAT HAPPENED TO BE A FAKE, AND YOU HAD MIKAMI BRING THE REAL NOTEBOOK OUT FOR THE FIRST TIME TO KILL ALL OF US.
Fake
THAT WAS YOUR PLAN.
THAT INDEED WAS THE PLAN I HAD IN MIND AS WELL.
BUT WHEN I SAID, "I REPLACED THE PAGES IN THE NOTEBOOK," I MEANT IN THE REAL ONE AS WELL.
!
MEANING THAT I TAMPERED WITH BOTH THE FAKE AND THE REAL NOTEBOOK. I REPLACED ONLY A PART OF THE FAKE NOTEBOOK, AND I REPLACED THE PAGES OF THE REAL NOTEBOOK COMPLETELY.
FWUMP
Fake
THAT CAN'T BE...
!

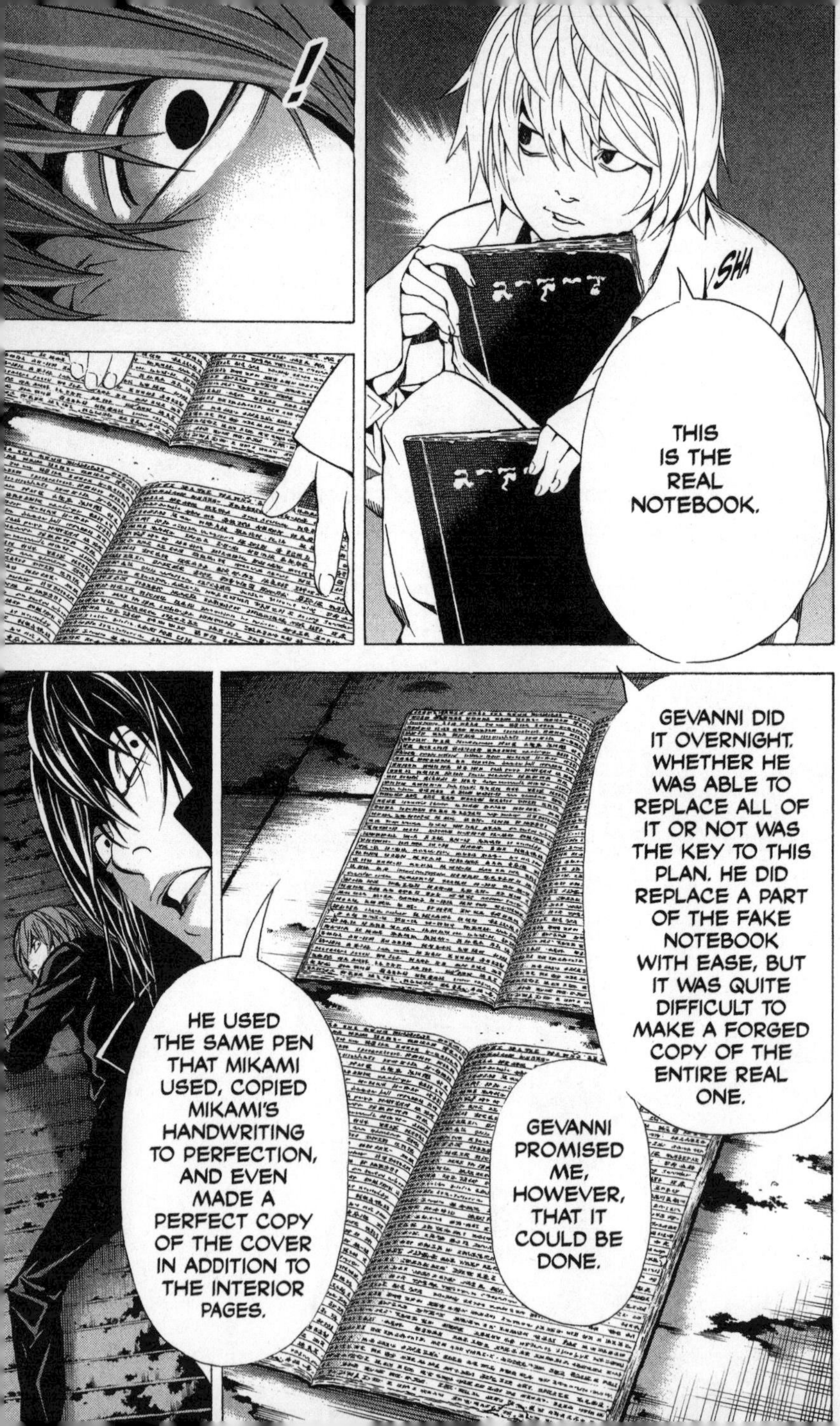SHA
THIS IS THE REAL NOTEBOOK.
!
GEVANNI DID IT OVERNIGHT. WHETHER HE WAS ABLE TO REPLACE ALL OF IT OR NOT WAS THE KEY TO THIS PLAN. HE DID REPLACE A PART OF THE FAKE NOTEBOOK WITH EASE, BUT IT WAS QUITE DIFFICULT TO MAKE A FORGED COPY OF THE ENTIRE REAL ONE.
GEVANNI PROMISED ME, HOWEVER, THAT IT COULD BE DONE.
HE USED THE SAME PEN THAT MIKAMI USED, COPIED MIKAMI'S HANDWRITING TO PERFECTION, AND EVEN MADE A PERFECT COPY OF THE COVER IN ADDITION TO THE INTERIOR PAGES.

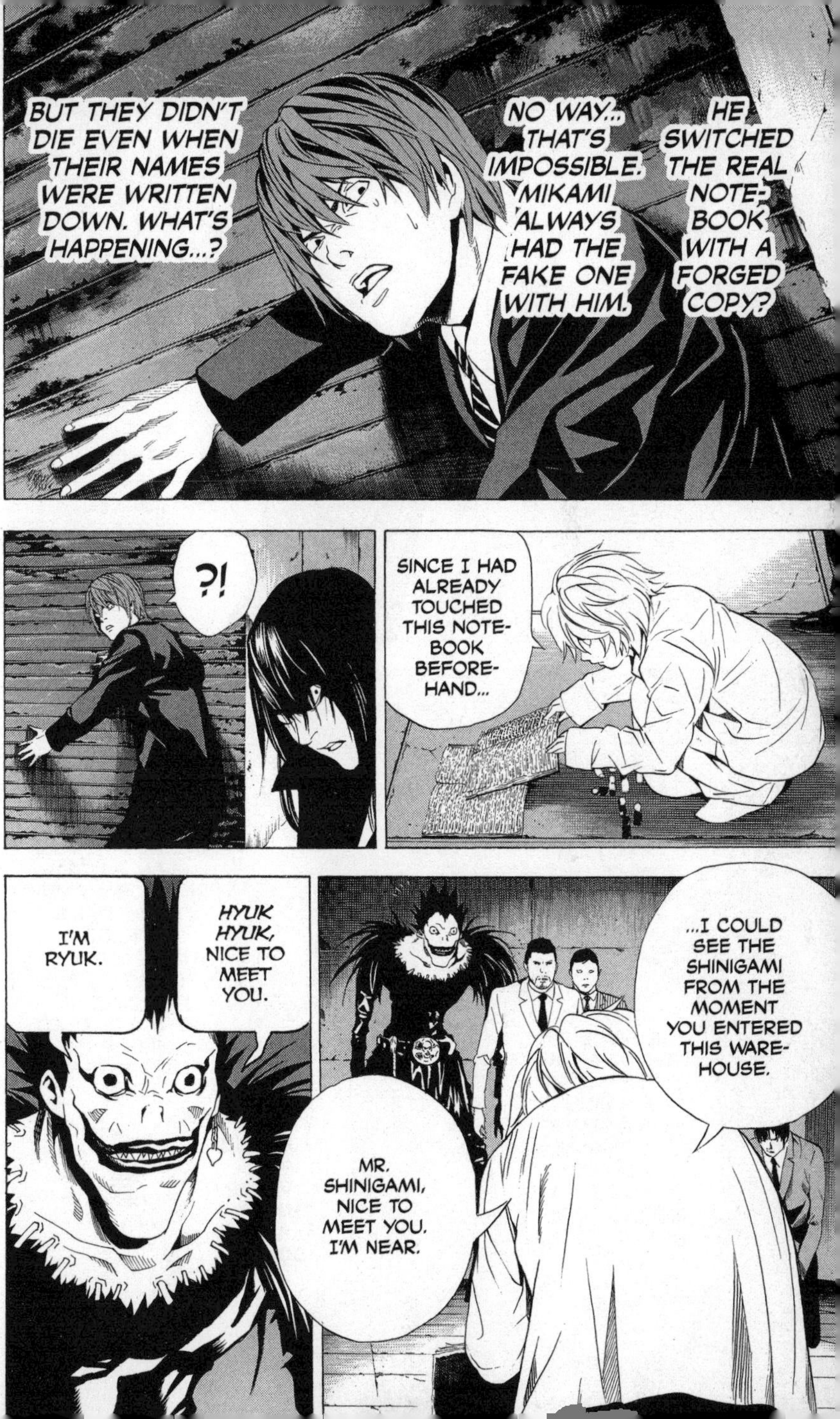
HE SWITCHED THE REAL NOTEBOOK WITH A FORGED COPY?
NO WAY... THAT'S IMPOSSIBLE. MIKAMI ALWAYS HAD THE FAKE ONE WITH HIM.
BUT THEY DIDN'T DIE EVEN WHEN THEIR NAMES WERE WRITTEN DOWN. WHAT'S HAPPENING...?
SINCE I HAD ALREADY TOUCHED THIS NOTEBOOK BEFOREHAND...
?!
...I COULD SEE THE SHINIGAMI FROM THE MOMENT YOU ENTERED THIS WAREHOUSE.
MR. SHINIGAMI, NICE TO MEET YOU. I'M NEAR.
HYUK HYUK, NICE TO MEET YOU.
I'M RYUK.

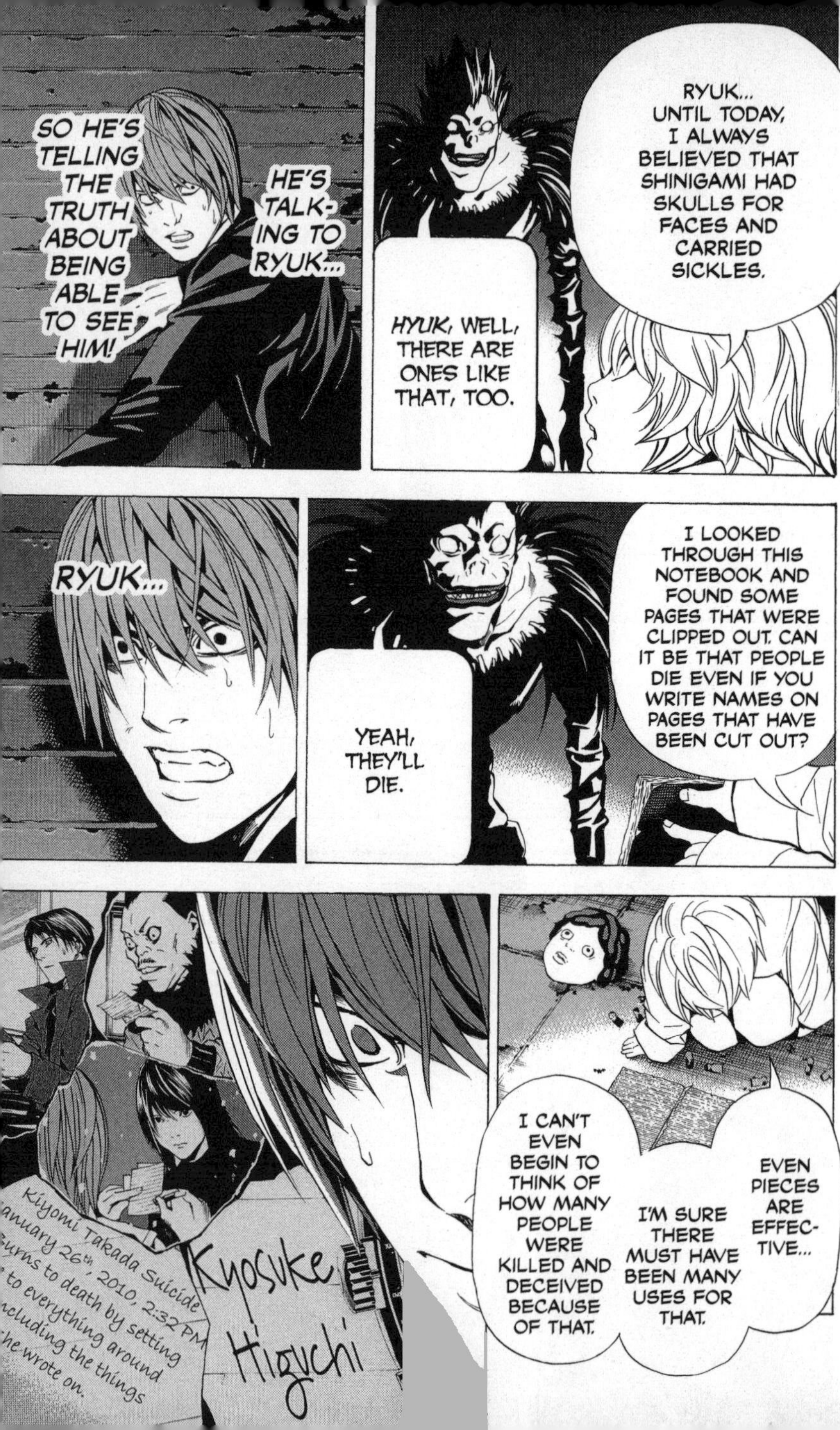
RYUK... UNTIL TODAY, I ALWAYS BELIEVED THAT SHINIGAMI HAD SKULLS FOR FACES AND CARRIED SICKLES.
HYUK, WELL, THERE ARE ONES LIKE THAT, TOO.
HE'S TALKING TO RYUK...
SO HE'S TELLING THE TRUTH ABOUT BEING ABLE TO SEE HIM!
I LOOKED THROUGH THIS NOTEBOOK AND FOUND SOME PAGES THAT WERE CLIPPED OUT. CAN IT BE THAT PEOPLE DIE EVEN IF YOU WRITE NAMES ON PAGES THAT HAVE BEEN CUT OUT?
YEAH, THEY'LL DIE.
RYUK...
EVEN PIECES ARE EFFECTIVE...
I'M SURE THERE MUST HAVE BEEN MANY USES FOR THAT.
I CAN'T EVEN BEGIN TO THINK OF HOW MANY PEOPLE WERE KILLED AND DECEIVED BECAUSE OF THAT.
Kyosuke Higuchi
Kiyomi Takada Suicide
anuary 26th, 2010, 2:32 PM
urns to death by setting
to everything around
ncluding the things
he wrote on.

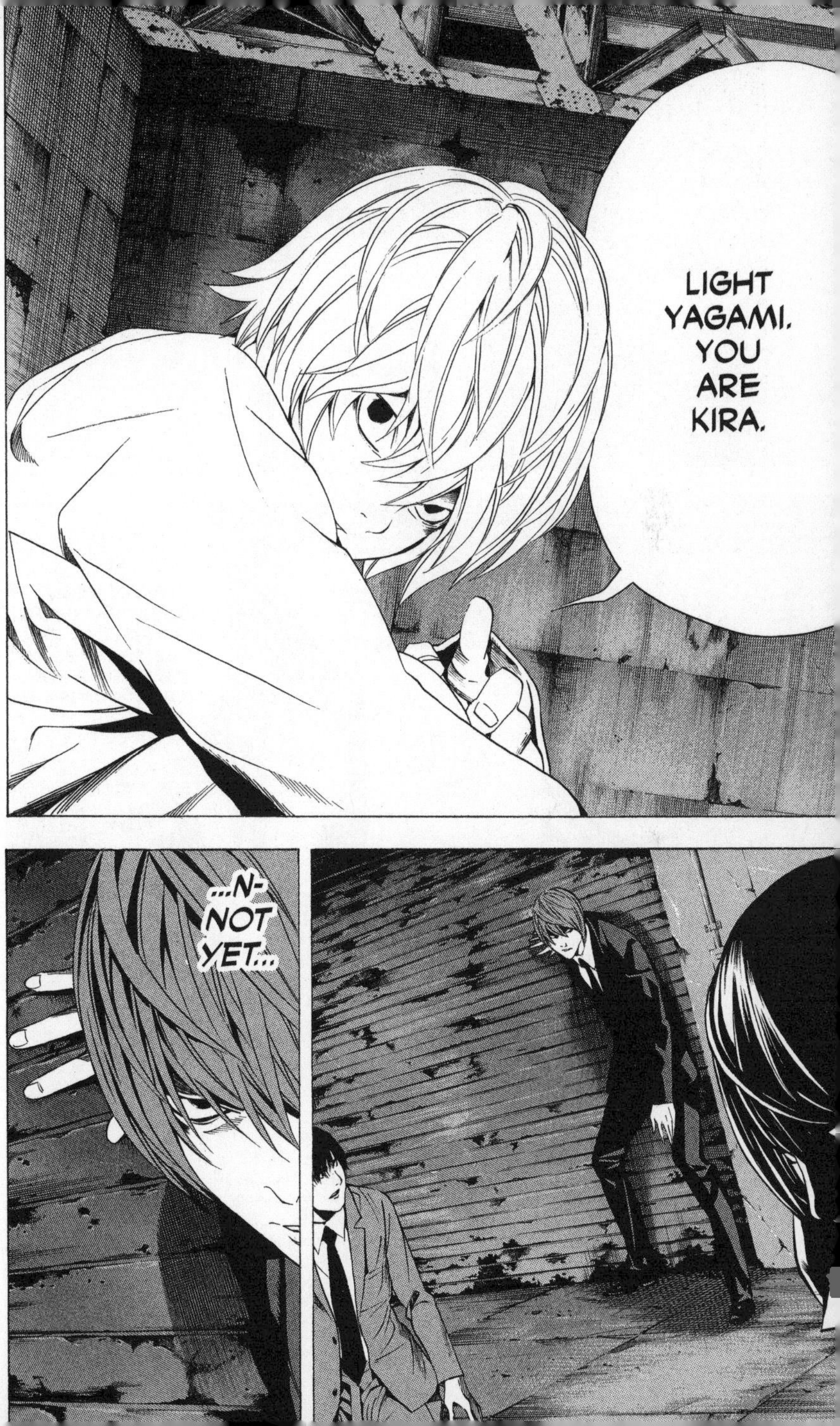
LIGHT YAGAMI. YOU ARE KIRA.
...N-NOT YET...

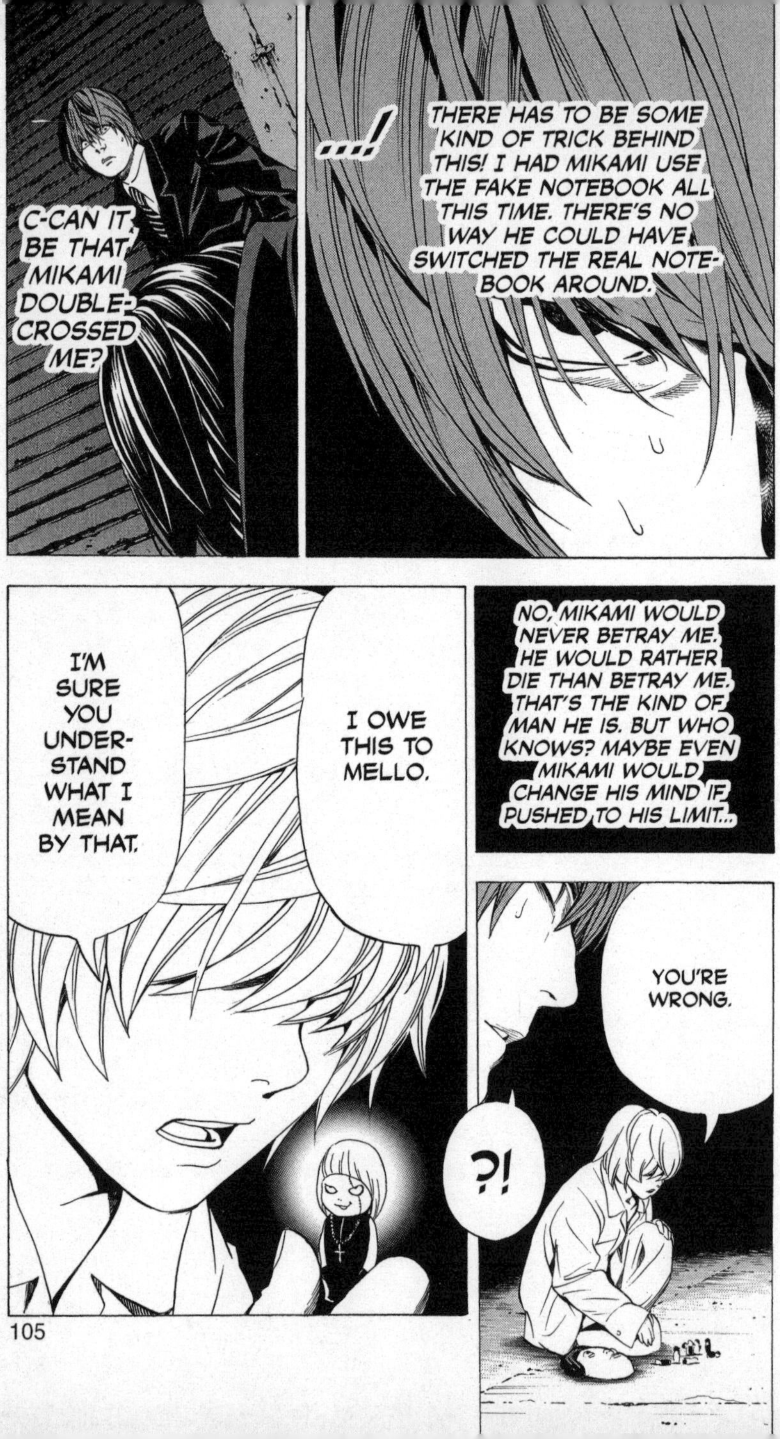
...!
THERE HAS TO BE SOME KIND OF TRICK BEHIND THIS! I HAD MIKAMI USE THE FAKE NOTEBOOK ALL THIS TIME. THERE'S NO WAY HE COULD HAVE SWITCHED THE REAL NOTE-BOOK AROUND.
C-CAN IT BE THAT MIKAMI DOUBLE-CROSSED ME?
NO, MIKAMI WOULD NEVER BETRAY ME. HE WOULD RATHER DIE THAN BETRAY ME. THAT'S THE KIND OF MAN HE IS. BUT WHO KNOWS? MAYBE EVEN MIKAMI WOULD CHANGE HIS MIND IF PUSHED TO HIS LIMIT...
YOU'RE WRONG.
?!
I OWE THIS TO MELLO.
I'M SURE YOU UNDERSTAND WHAT I MEAN BY THAT.

chapter 104 The Answer

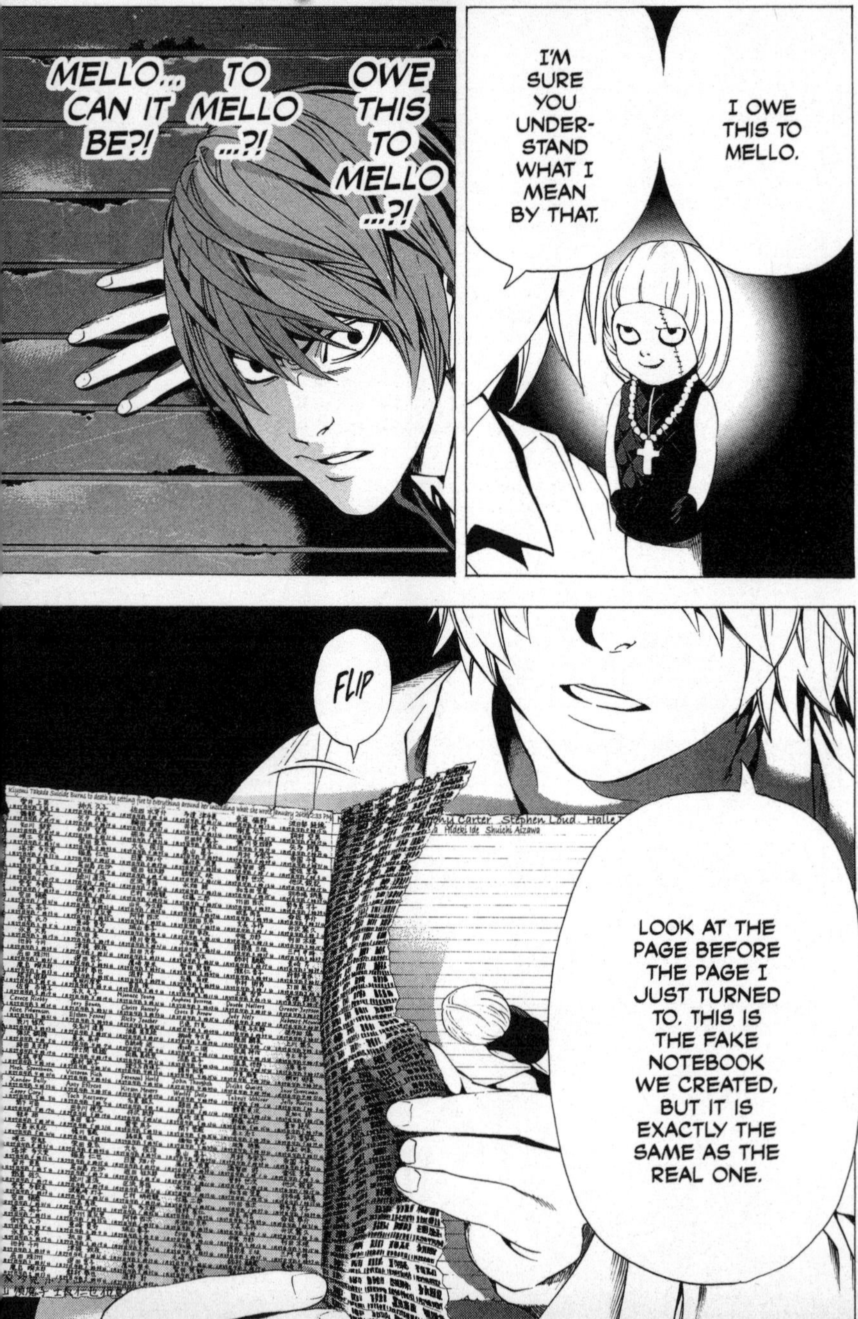
I OWE THIS TO MELLO.
I'M SURE YOU UNDERSTAND WHAT I MEAN BY THAT.
OWE THIS TO MELLO ...?!
TO MELLO ...?!
MELLO... CAN IT BE?!
FLIP
LOOK AT THE PAGE BEFORE THE PAGE I JUST TURNED TO. THIS IS THE FAKE NOTEBOOK WE CREATED, BUT IT IS EXACTLY THE SAME AS THE REAL ONE.

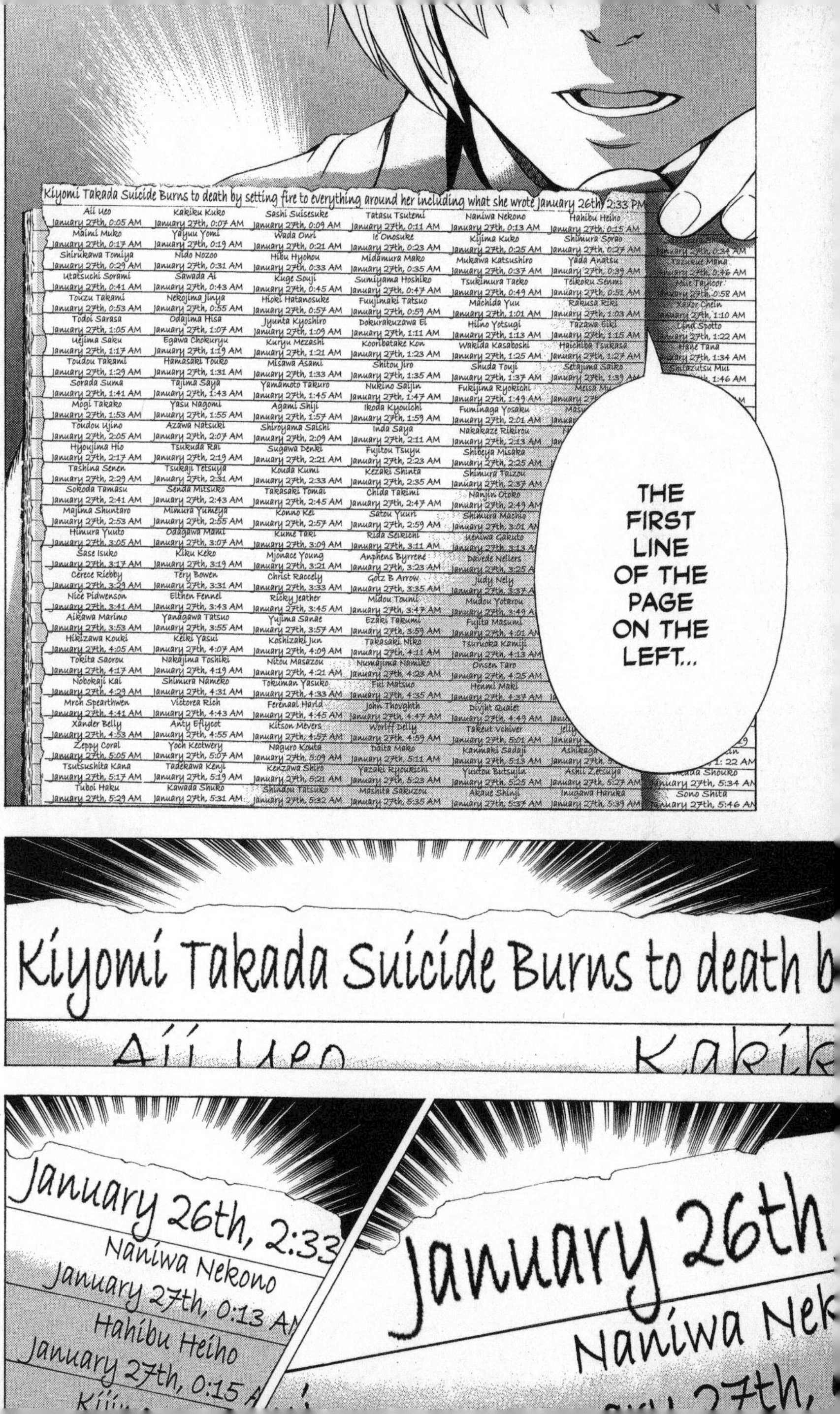

Kiyomi Takada Suicide Burns to death by setting fire to everything around her including what she wrote January 26th 2:33 PM

Aii Ueo January 27th, 0:05 AM	Kakiku Kuko January 27th, 0:07 AM	Sashi Suisesuke January 27th, 0:09 AM	Tatasu Tsutemi January 27th, 0:11 AM	Naniwa Nekono January 27th, 0:13 AM	Hahibu Heiho January 27th, 0:15 AM	
Maimi Muko January 27th, 0:17 AM	Yujuu Yoni January 27th, 0:19 AM	Wada Onri January 27th, 0:21 AM	Ie Onosuke January 27th, 0:23 AM	Kijima Kuko January 27th, 0:25 AM	Shimura Sorao January 27th, 0:27 AM	Tazawa Mina January 27th, 0:34 AM
Shirukawa Tomiya January 27th, 0:29 AM	Nido Nozoo January 27th, 0:31 AM	Hibu Hyohou January 27th, 0:33 AM	Midamura Mako January 27th, 0:35 AM	Mukawa Katsushiro January 27th, 0:37 AM	Yada Anatsu January 27th, 0:39 AM	Takuma Mina January 27th, 0:46 AM
Uratsuchi Sorami January 27th, 0:41 AM	Sawada Ai January 27th, 0:43 AM	Kuge Souji January 27th, 0:45 AM	Sumiyama Hoshiko January 27th, 0:47 AM	Tsukimura Taeko January 27th, 0:49 AM	Takoku Senmi January 27th, 0:51 AM	Mue Tayioor January 27th, 0:58 AM
Touza Takami January 27th, 0:53 AM	Nekojima Jinya January 27th, 0:55 AM	Hioki Hatanosuke January 27th, 0:57 AM	Fuujimaki Tatsuo January 27th, 0:59 AM	Michida Yuu January 27th, 1:01 AM	Rawusa Reki January 27th, 1:03 AM	Xavior Chein January 27th, 1:10 AM
Todoi Sarasa January 27th, 1:05 AM	Odajima Hisa January 27th, 1:07 AM	Jyunta Kyoshiro January 27th, 1:09 AM	Dokurakuzawa Ei January 27th, 1:11 AM	Hiino Yotsugi January 27th, 1:13 AM	Tazawa Eiki January 27th, 1:15 AM	Lind Spotto January 27th, 1:22 AM
Uejima Saku January 27th, 1:17 AM	Egawa Chokuryu January 27th, 1:19 AM	Kuryu Mizashi January 27th, 1:21 AM	Koonbatake Kon January 27th, 1:23 AM	Wakida Kasaboshi January 27th, 1:25 AM	Haishibe Tsukasa January 27th, 1:27 AM	Vigod Tina January 27th, 1:34 AM
Taudou Takami January 27th, 1:29 AM	Hamasaki Touko January 27th, 1:31 AM	Misawa Azami January 27th, 1:33 AM	Shitou Jiro January 27th, 1:35 AM	Shuda Touji January 27th, 1:37 AM	Setajima Sairo January 27th, 1:39 AM	Suuzuduku Mui January 27th, 1:46 AM
Sorada Suuna January 27th, 1:41 AM	Tajima Saya January 27th, 1:43 AM	Yamaheto Takuro January 27th, 1:45 AM	Nakuno Seijin January 27th, 1:47 AM	Fukujima Ryuuichi January 27th, 1:49 AM	Meisa Maa	
Mogi Takako January 27th, 1:53 AM	Yasu Nagomi January 27th, 1:55 AM	Agami Shiji January 27th, 1:57 AM	Ikeda Kiyouichi January 27th, 1:59 AM	Fumikasa Yosaku January 27th, 2:01 AM	MBS	
Tsudou Ujino January 27th, 2:05 AM	Azawa Natsuki January 27th, 2:07 AM	Shiroyama Saisin January 27th, 2:09 AM	Inda Saya January 27th, 2:11 AM	Nakarazz Rikiro January 27th, 2:13 AM		
Hyoujima Hio January 27th, 2:17 AM	Tsukuda Rai January 27th, 2:19 AM	Sugawa Benki January 27th, 2:21 AM	Fujitou Tsuiju January 27th, 2:23 AM	Shiteya Misoro January 27th, 2:25 AM		
Tashina Senon January 27th, 2:29 AM	Tsukiji Tetsuya January 27th, 2:31 AM	Kouda Kumi January 27th, 2:33 AM	Kezaki Shiata January 27th, 2:35 AM	Shimura Tbuzou January 27th, 2:37 AM		
Sokoda Tamasu January 27th, 2:41 AM	Senda Mitsuko January 27th, 2:43 AM	Takasaki Tomai January 27th, 2:45 AM	Chida Takami January 27th, 2:47 AM	Nanjin Ozeko January 27th, 2:49 AM		
Majima Shintaro January 27th, 2:53 AM	Mimura Touboku January 27th, 2:55 AM	Konno Kei January 27th, 2:57 AM	Satou Yuuri January 27th, 2:59 AM	Shimura Machio January 27th, 3:01 AM		
Himura Yuuto January 27th, 3:05 AM	Odagawa Mami January 27th, 3:07 AM	Kama Taks January 27th, 3:09 AM	Ruda Sekisai January 27th, 3:11 AM	Ueuwa Gakuto January 27th, 3:13 AM		
Sase Isuko January 27th, 3:17 AM	Kiku Kebo January 27th, 3:19 AM	Mjonace Young January 27th, 3:21 AM	Anphens Byrrené January 27th, 3:23 AM	Davede Nelleres January 27th, 3:25 AM		
Ceroce Riebby January 27th, 3:29 AM	Terji Bowen January 27th, 3:31 AM	Christ Raecelly January 27th, 3:33 AM	Gotz B Arrow January 27th, 3:35 AM	Judij Nelej January 27th, 3:37 AM		
Nice Pawenson January 27th, 3:42 AM	Elthen Fennel January 27th, 3:43 AM	Ricky Jeather January 27th, 3:45 AM	Midou Taumi January 27th, 3:47 AM	Mudou Yotorru January 27th, 3:49 AM		
Aikawa Marino January 27th, 3:53 AM	Yanadawa Tatsuo January 27th, 3:55 AM	Yujima Sanat January 27th, 3:57 AM	Ezaki Yukio January 27th, 3:59 AM	Fujita Matsuou January 27th, 4:01 AM		
Hikizawa Kasuki January 27th, 4:05 AM	Keiki Yasui January 27th, 4:07 AM	Koshizaki Jun January 27th, 4:09 AM	Takasaki Niko January 27th, 4:11 AM	Tsunoko Kanaji January 27th, 4:13 AM		
Tokita Saorin January 27th, 4:17 AM	Nakajima Tsuiki January 27th, 4:19 AM	Nitsu Masazou January 27th, 4:21 AM	Numajima Namuko January 27th, 4:23 AM	Onsato Taro January 27th, 4:25 AM		
Nobokaji Kai January 27th, 4:29 AM	Shimura Nameko January 27th, 4:31 AM	Tokuman Yasuke January 27th, 4:33 AM	Fui Matsui January 27th, 4:35 AM	Hnami Moki January 27th, 4:37 AM		
Mroh Spearthmen January 27th, 4:41 AM	Victoria Rish January 27th, 4:43 AM	Ferdnand Harld January 27th, 4:45 AM	John Thevjoth January 27th, 4:47 AM	Divjet Qualté January 27th, 4:49 AM	Jeli	
Xander Belly January 27th, 4:53 AM	Anty Erlyzet January 27th, 4:55 AM	Kitson Movers January 27th, 4:57 AM	Wbriff Deluy January 27th, 4:59 AM	Takout Vasivet January 27th, 5:01 AM	Ashkeagra	
Zeppu Coral January 27th, 5:05 AM	Yoah Keetwery January 27th, 5:07 AM	Naguro Kouski January 27th, 5:09 AM	Datta Mako January 27th, 5:11 AM	Kawmami Sadaji January 27th, 5:13 AM		1: 22 AM
Tsutsushita Kana January 27th, 5:17 AM	Tadekawa Kenji January 27th, 5:19 AM	Konzawa Shun January 27th, 5:21 AM	Yazaki Ryuuchi January 27th, 5:23 AM	Yuutba Butsujin January 27th, 5:25 AM	Akuu Zeshin January 27th, 5:27 AM	Amada Shouको January 27th, 5:34 AM
Tuboi Haku January 27th, 5:29 AM	Kawada Shuro January 27th, 5:31 AM	Shindou Tatsuke January 27th, 5:32 AM	Mashita Sakuzou January 27th, 5:35 AM	Akawa Shinji January 27th, 5:37 AM	Inugawa Haruka January 27th, 5:39 AM	Sono Shita January 27th, 5:46 AM

THE FIRST LINE OF THE PAGE ON THE LEFT...

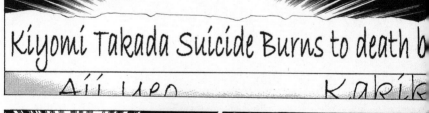

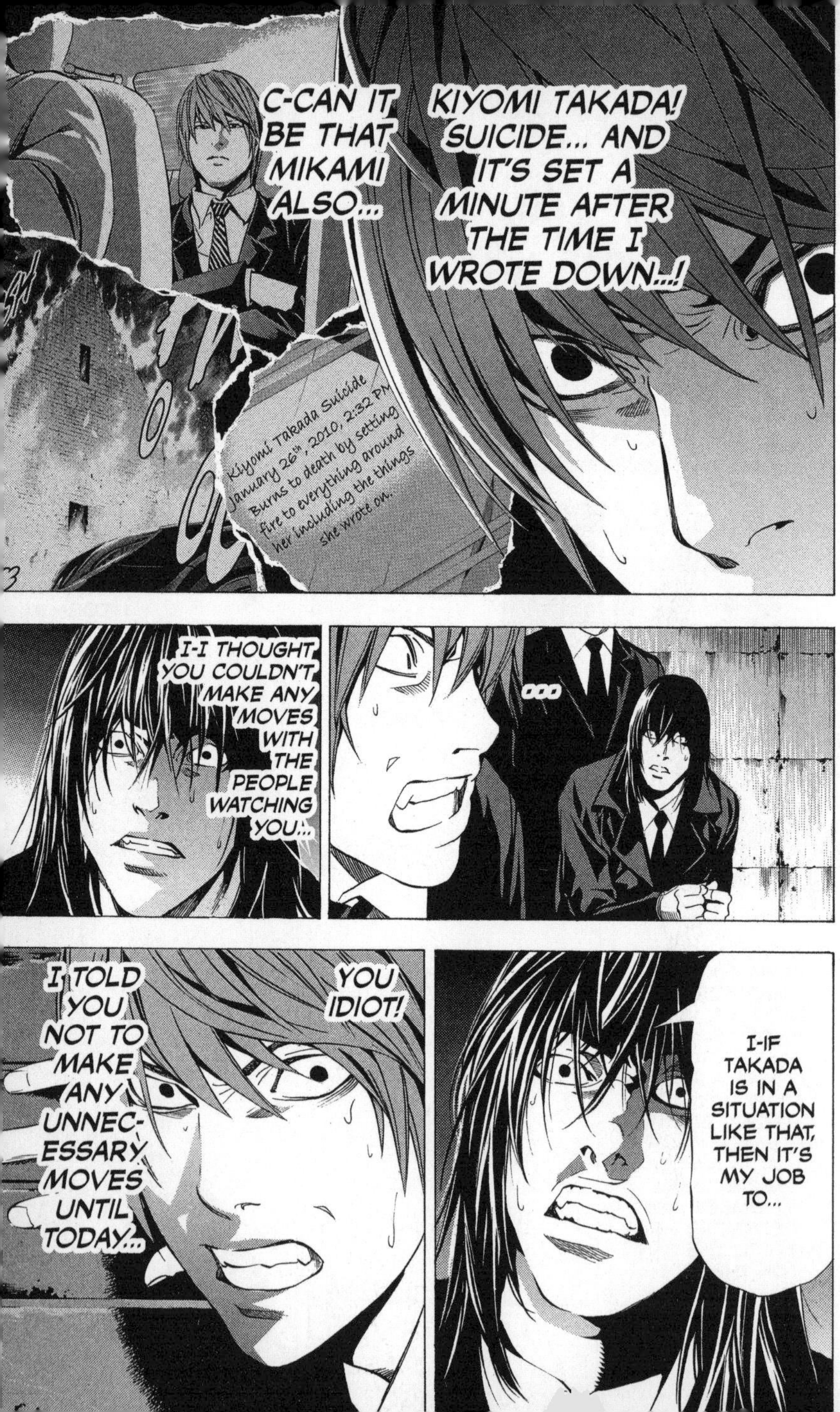
KIYOMI TAKADA! SUICIDE... AND IT'S SET A MINUTE AFTER THE TIME I WROTE DOWN...!
C-CAN IT BE THAT MIKAMI ALSO...
Kiyomi Takada Suicide
January 26th, 2010, 2:32 PM
Burns to death by setting fire to everything around her including the things she wrote on.
...
I-I THOUGHT YOU COULDN'T MAKE ANY MOVES WITH THE PEOPLE WATCHING YOU...
I-IF TAKADA IS IN A SITUATION LIKE THAT, THEN IT'S MY JOB TO...
YOU IDIOT!
I TOLD YOU NOT TO MAKE ANY UNNECESSARY MOVES UNTIL TODAY...

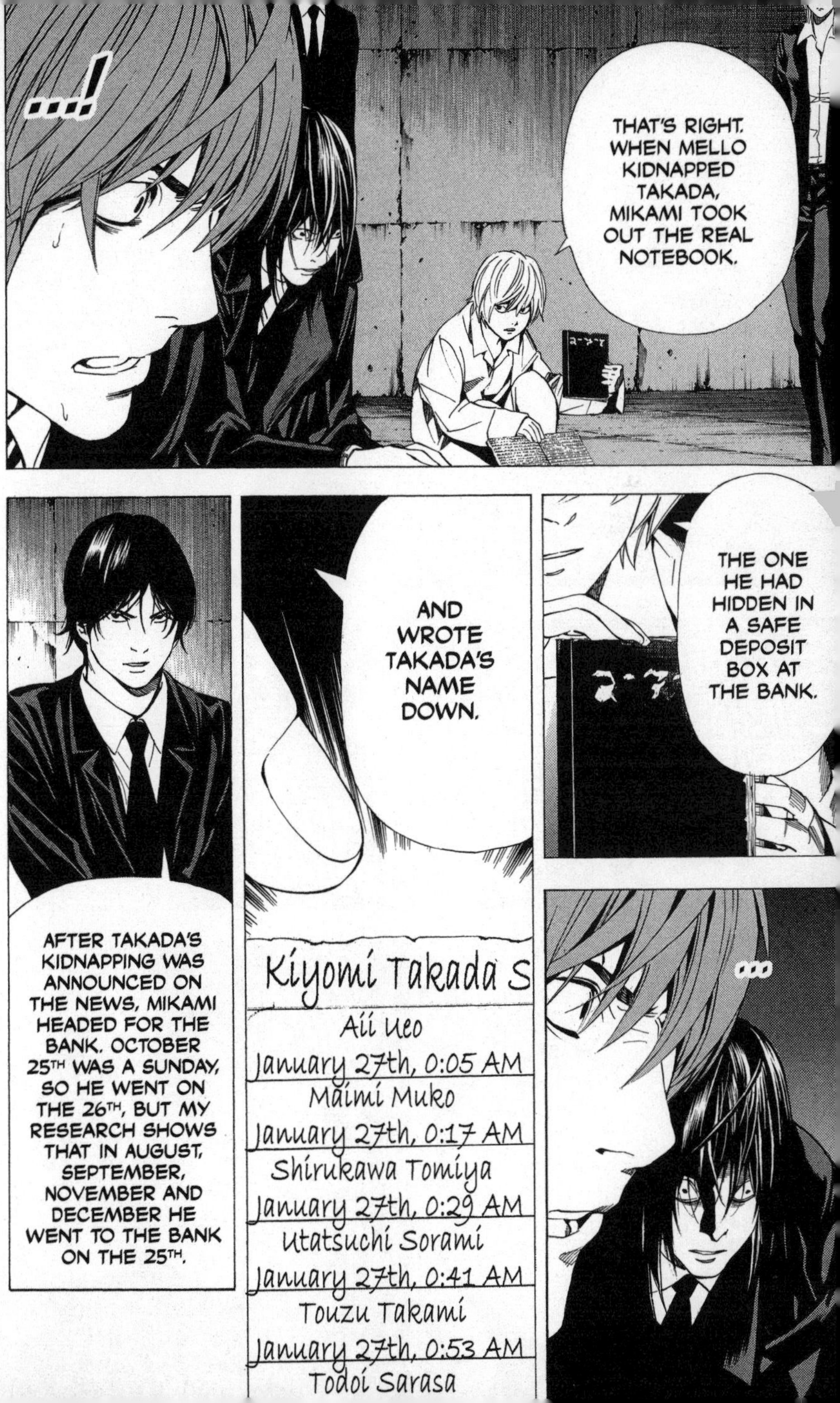
THAT'S RIGHT. WHEN MELLO KIDNAPPED TAKADA, MIKAMI TOOK OUT THE REAL NOTEBOOK.
...!
THE ONE HE HAD HIDDEN IN A SAFE DEPOSIT BOX AT THE BANK.
AND WROTE TAKADA'S NAME DOWN.
...
Kiyomi Takada S
Aii Ueo
January 27th, 0:05 AM
Maimi Muko
January 27th, 0:17 AM
Shirukawa Tomiya
January 27th, 0:29 AM
Utatsuchi Sorami
January 27th, 0:41 AM
Touzu Takami
January 27th, 0:53 AM
Todoi Sarasa
AFTER TAKADA'S KIDNAPPING WAS ANNOUNCED ON THE NEWS, MIKAMI HEADED FOR THE BANK. OCTOBER 25TH WAS A SUNDAY, SO HE WENT ON THE 26TH, BUT MY RESEARCH SHOWS THAT IN AUGUST, SEPTEMBER, NOVEMBER AND DECEMBER HE WENT TO THE BANK ON THE 25TH.

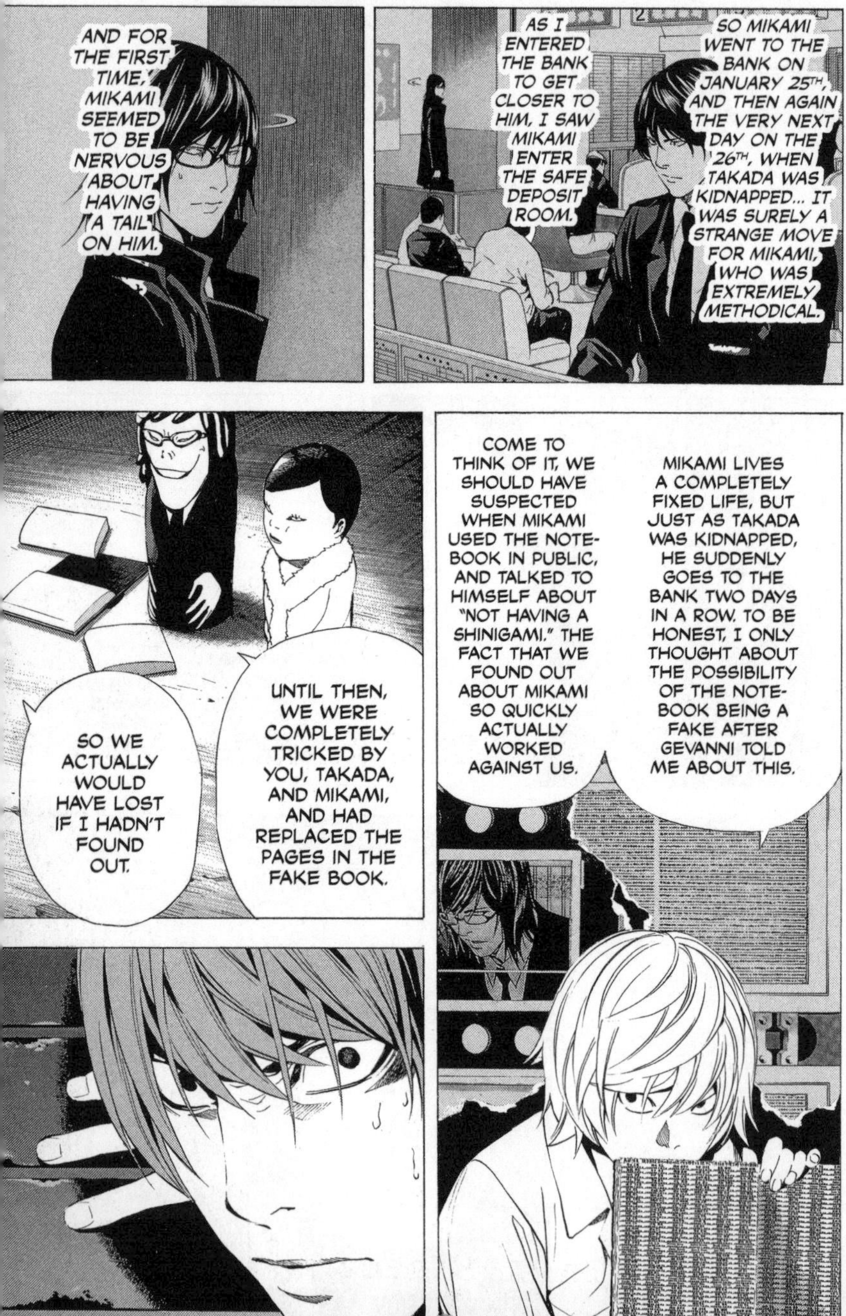
SO MIKAMI WENT TO THE BANK ON JANUARY 25TH, AND THEN AGAIN THE VERY NEXT DAY ON THE 26TH, WHEN TAKADA WAS KIDNAPPED... IT WAS SURELY A STRANGE MOVE FOR MIKAMI, WHO WAS EXTREMELY METHODICAL.
AS I ENTERED THE BANK TO GET CLOSER TO HIM, I SAW MIKAMI ENTER THE SAFE DEPOSIT ROOM.
AND FOR THE FIRST TIME, MIKAMI SEEMED TO BE NERVOUS ABOUT HAVING A TAIL ON HIM.
MIKAMI LIVES A COMPLETELY FIXED LIFE, BUT JUST AS TAKADA WAS KIDNAPPED, HE SUDDENLY GOES TO THE BANK TWO DAYS IN A ROW. TO BE HONEST, I ONLY THOUGHT ABOUT THE POSSIBILITY OF THE NOTE-BOOK BEING A FAKE AFTER GEVANNI TOLD ME ABOUT THIS.
COME TO THINK OF IT, WE SHOULD HAVE SUSPECTED WHEN MIKAMI USED THE NOTE-BOOK IN PUBLIC, AND TALKED TO HIMSELF ABOUT "NOT HAVING A SHINIGAMI." THE FACT THAT WE FOUND OUT ABOUT MIKAMI SO QUICKLY ACTUALLY WORKED AGAINST US.
UNTIL THEN, WE WERE COMPLETELY TRICKED BY YOU, TAKADA, AND MIKAMI, AND HAD REPLACED THE PAGES IN THE FAKE BOOK.
SO WE ACTUALLY WOULD HAVE LOST IF I HADN'T FOUND OUT.

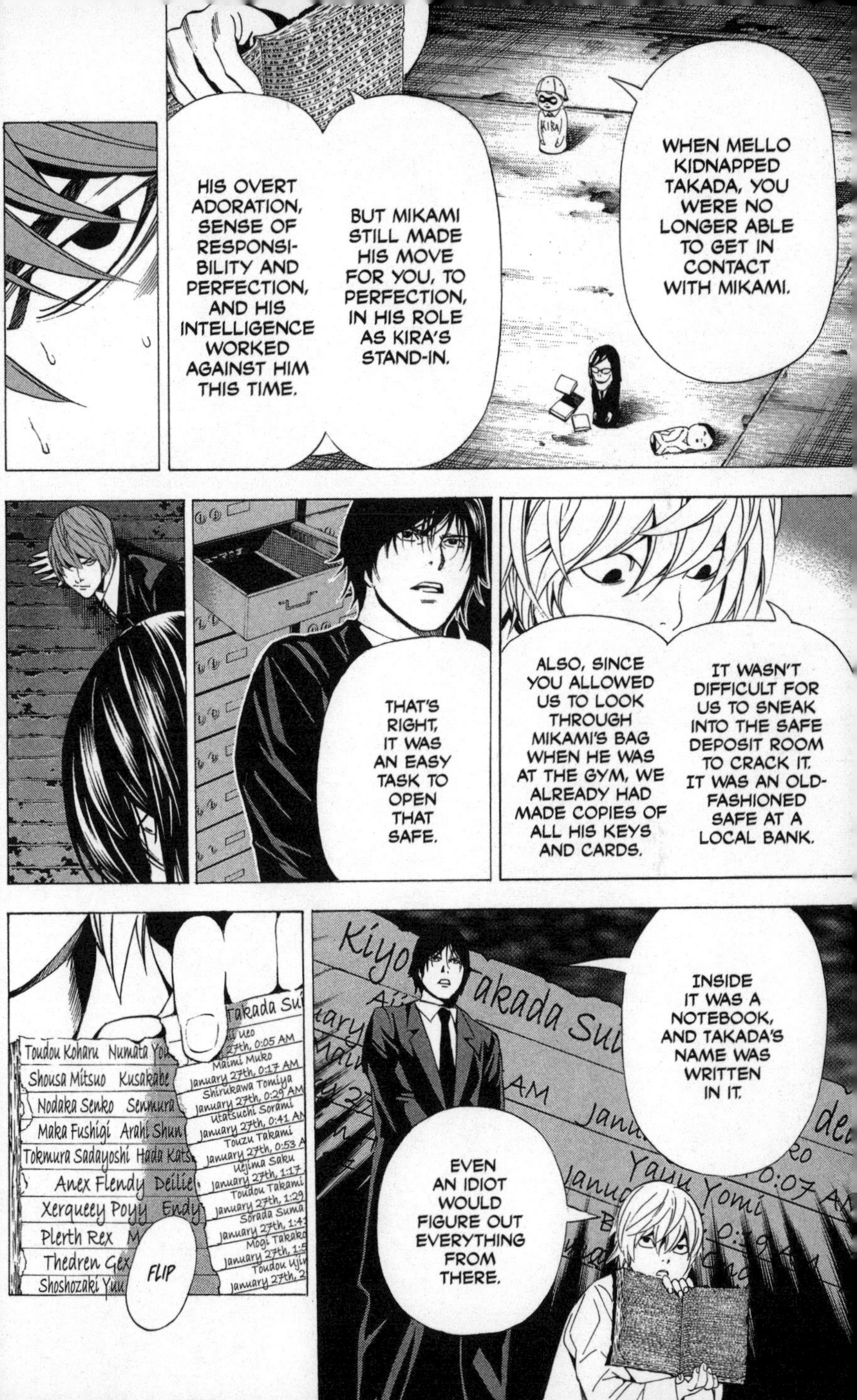
WHEN MELLO KIDNAPPED TAKADA, YOU WERE NO LONGER ABLE TO GET IN CONTACT WITH MIKAMI.
BUT MIKAMI STILL MADE HIS MOVE FOR YOU, TO PERFECTION, IN HIS ROLE AS KIRA'S STAND-IN.
HIS OVERT ADORATION, SENSE OF RESPONSIBILITY AND PERFECTION, AND HIS INTELLIGENCE WORKED AGAINST HIM THIS TIME.
IT WASN'T DIFFICULT FOR US TO SNEAK INTO THE SAFE DEPOSIT ROOM TO CRACK IT. IT WAS AN OLD-FASHIONED SAFE AT A LOCAL BANK.
ALSO, SINCE YOU ALLOWED US TO LOOK THROUGH MIKAMI'S BAG WHEN HE WAS AT THE GYM, WE ALREADY HAD MADE COPIES OF ALL HIS KEYS AND CARDS.
THAT'S RIGHT, IT WAS AN EASY TASK TO OPEN THAT SAFE.
INSIDE IT WAS A NOTEBOOK, AND TAKADA'S NAME WAS WRITTEN IN IT.
EVEN AN IDIOT WOULD FIGURE OUT EVERYTHING FROM THERE.
FLIP

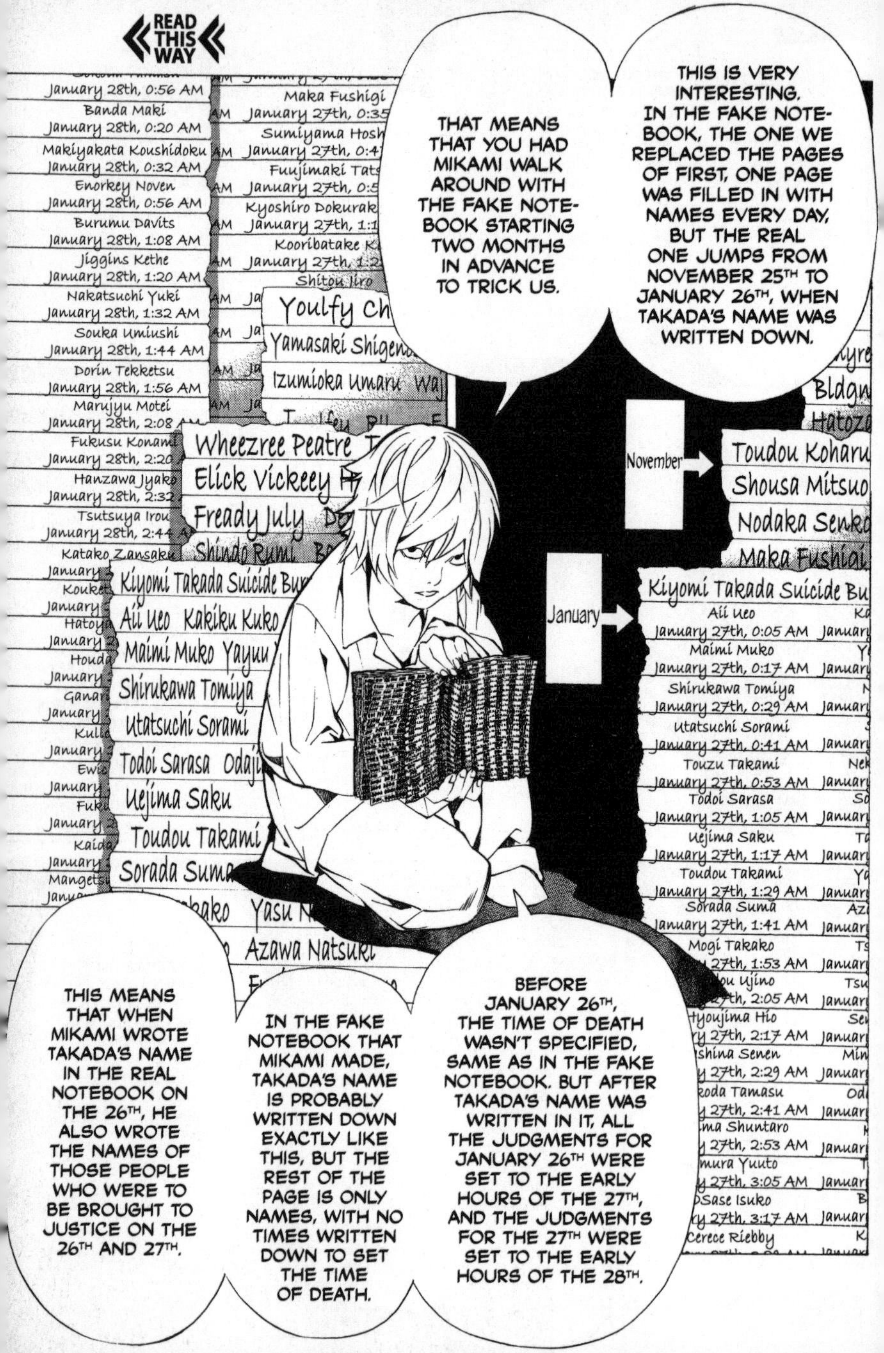
READ THIS WAY
THIS IS VERY INTERESTING. IN THE FAKE NOTEBOOK, THE ONE WE REPLACED THE PAGES OF FIRST, ONE PAGE WAS FILLED IN WITH NAMES EVERY DAY, BUT THE REAL ONE JUMPS FROM NOVEMBER 25TH TO JANUARY 26TH, WHEN TAKADA'S NAME WAS WRITTEN DOWN.
THAT MEANS THAT YOU HAD MIKAMI WALK AROUND WITH THE FAKE NOTEBOOK STARTING TWO MONTHS IN ADVANCE TO TRICK US.
November
January
BEFORE JANUARY 26TH, THE TIME OF DEATH WASN'T SPECIFIED, SAME AS IN THE FAKE NOTEBOOK. BUT AFTER TAKADA'S NAME WAS WRITTEN IN IT, ALL THE JUDGMENTS FOR JANUARY 26TH WERE SET TO THE EARLY HOURS OF THE 27TH, AND THE JUDGMENTS FOR THE 27TH WERE SET TO THE EARLY HOURS OF THE 28TH.
IN THE FAKE NOTEBOOK THAT MIKAMI MADE, TAKADA'S NAME IS PROBABLY WRITTEN DOWN EXACTLY LIKE THIS, BUT THE REST OF THE PAGE IS ONLY NAMES, WITH NO TIMES WRITTEN DOWN TO SET THE TIME OF DEATH.
THIS MEANS THAT WHEN MIKAMI WROTE TAKADA'S NAME IN THE REAL NOTEBOOK ON THE 26TH, HE ALSO WROTE THE NAMES OF THOSE PEOPLE WHO WERE TO BE BROUGHT TO JUSTICE ON THE 26TH AND 27TH.

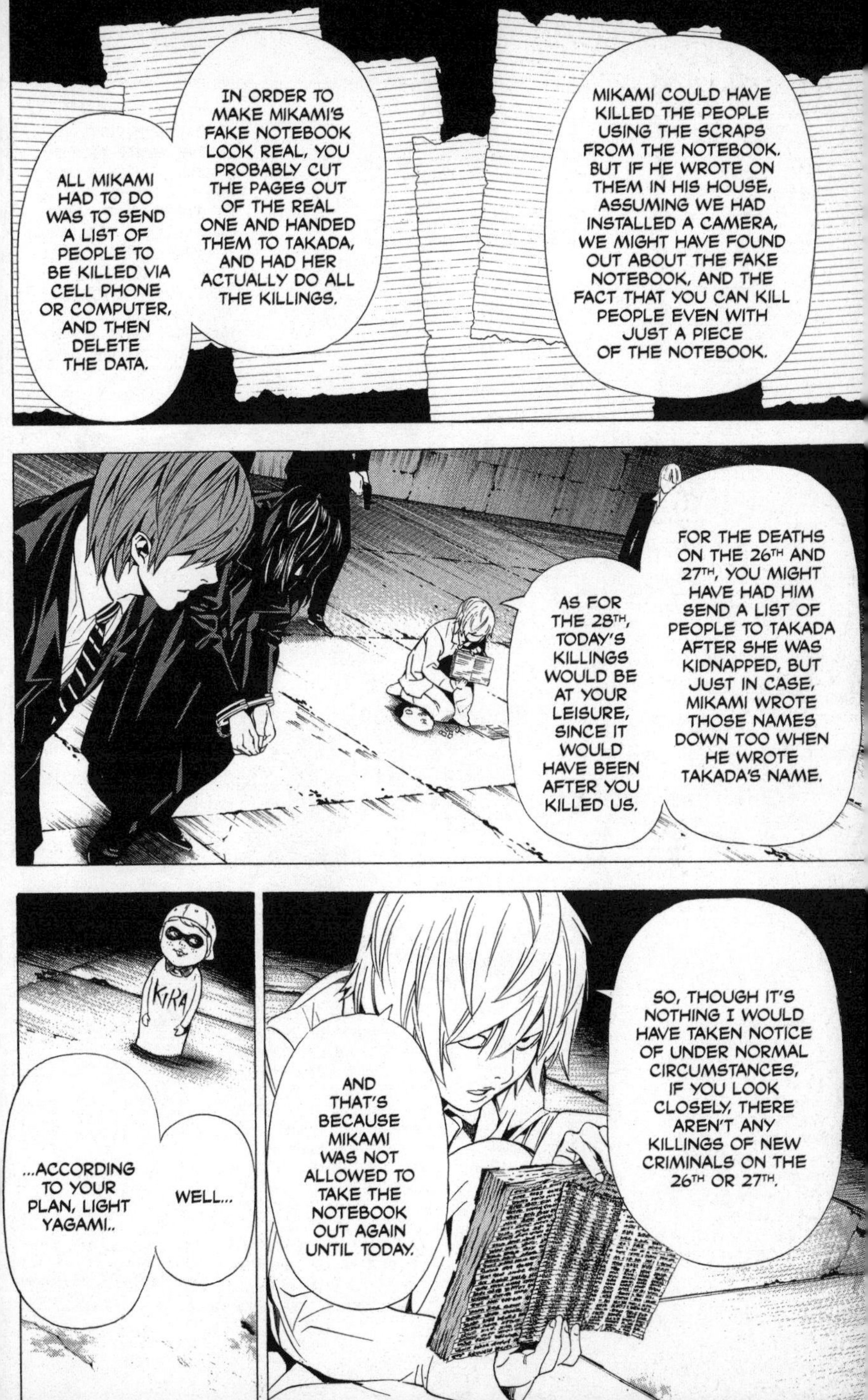
MIKAMI COULD HAVE KILLED THE PEOPLE USING THE SCRAPS FROM THE NOTEBOOK. BUT IF HE WROTE ON THEM IN HIS HOUSE, ASSUMING WE HAD INSTALLED A CAMERA, WE MIGHT HAVE FOUND OUT ABOUT THE FAKE NOTEBOOK, AND THE FACT THAT YOU CAN KILL PEOPLE EVEN WITH JUST A PIECE OF THE NOTEBOOK.
IN ORDER TO MAKE MIKAMI'S FAKE NOTEBOOK LOOK REAL, YOU PROBABLY CUT THE PAGES OUT OF THE REAL ONE AND HANDED THEM TO TAKADA, AND HAD HER ACTUALLY DO ALL THE KILLINGS.
ALL MIKAMI HAD TO DO WAS TO SEND A LIST OF PEOPLE TO BE KILLED VIA CELL PHONE OR COMPUTER, AND THEN DELETE THE DATA.
FOR THE DEATHS ON THE 26TH AND 27TH, YOU MIGHT HAVE HAD HIM SEND A LIST OF PEOPLE TO TAKADA AFTER SHE WAS KIDNAPPED, BUT JUST IN CASE, MIKAMI WROTE THOSE NAMES DOWN TOO WHEN HE WROTE TAKADA'S NAME.
AS FOR THE 28TH, TODAY'S KILLINGS WOULD BE AT YOUR LEISURE, SINCE IT WOULD HAVE BEEN AFTER YOU KILLED US.
SO, THOUGH IT'S NOTHING I WOULD HAVE TAKEN NOTICE OF UNDER NORMAL CIRCUMSTANCES, IF YOU LOOK CLOSELY, THERE AREN'T ANY KILLINGS OF NEW CRIMINALS ON THE 26TH OR 27TH.
AND THAT'S BECAUSE MIKAMI WAS NOT ALLOWED TO TAKE THE NOTEBOOK OUT AGAIN UNTIL TODAY.
KIRA
WELL...
...ACCORDING TO YOUR PLAN, LIGHT YAGAMI..

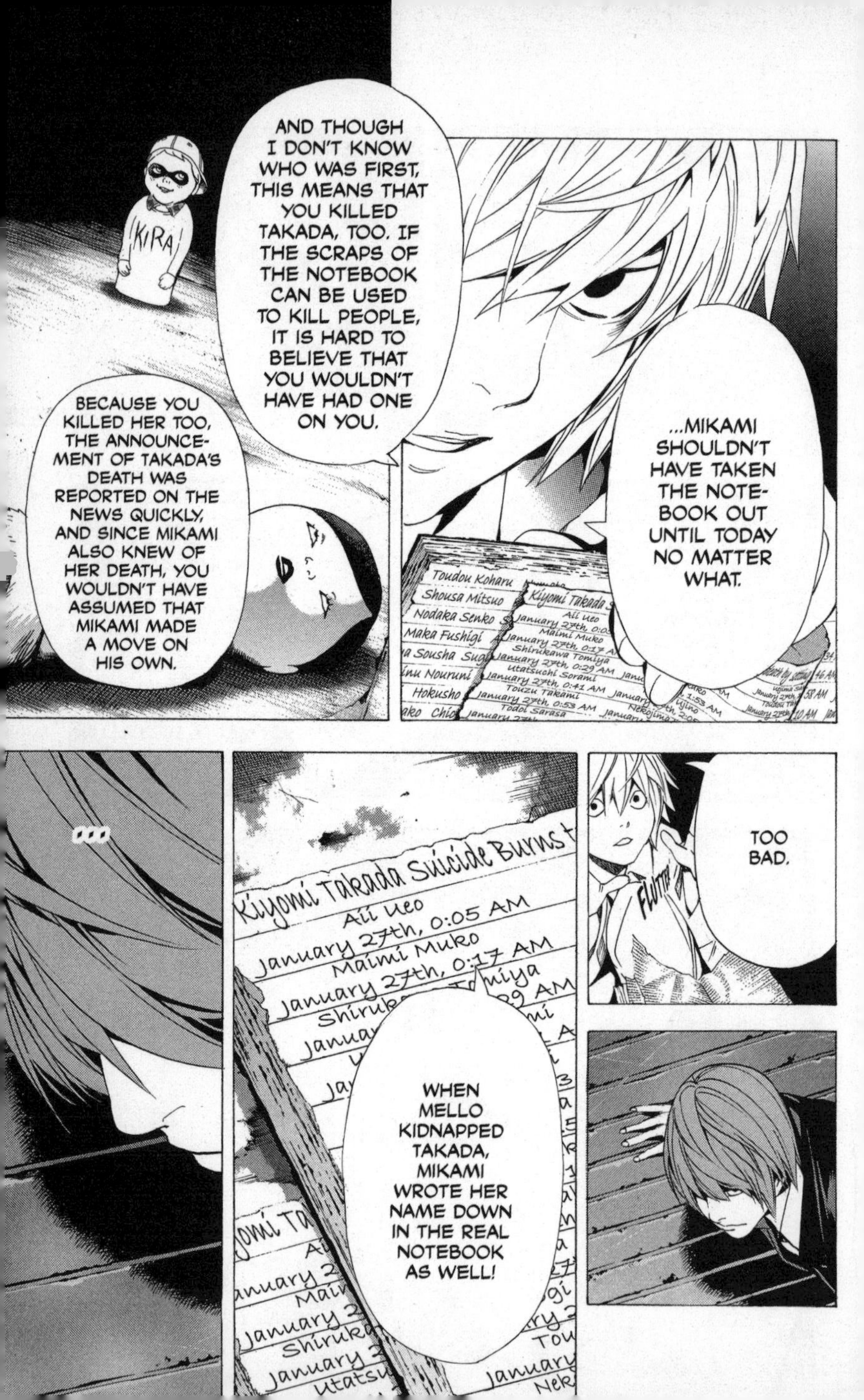

...MIKAMI SHOULDN'T HAVE TAKEN THE NOTE-BOOK OUT UNTIL TODAY NO MATTER WHAT.
AND THOUGH I DON'T KNOW WHO WAS FIRST, THIS MEANS THAT YOU KILLED TAKADA, TOO. IF THE SCRAPS OF THE NOTEBOOK CAN BE USED TO KILL PEOPLE, IT IS HARD TO BELIEVE THAT YOU WOULDN'T HAVE HAD ONE ON YOU.
BECAUSE YOU KILLED HER TOO, THE ANNOUNCE-MENT OF TAKADA'S DEATH WAS REPORTED ON THE NEWS QUICKLY, AND SINCE MIKAMI ALSO KNEW OF HER DEATH, YOU WOULDN'T HAVE ASSUMED THAT MIKAMI MADE A MOVE ON HIS OWN.
KIRA
TOO BAD.
FLUTTER
Kiyomi Takada Suicide Burns
Aii Ueo
January 27th, 0:05 AM
Maimi Muko
January 27th, 0:17 AM
WHEN MELLO KIDNAPPED TAKADA, MIKAMI WROTE HER NAME DOWN IN THE REAL NOTEBOOK AS WELL!
...

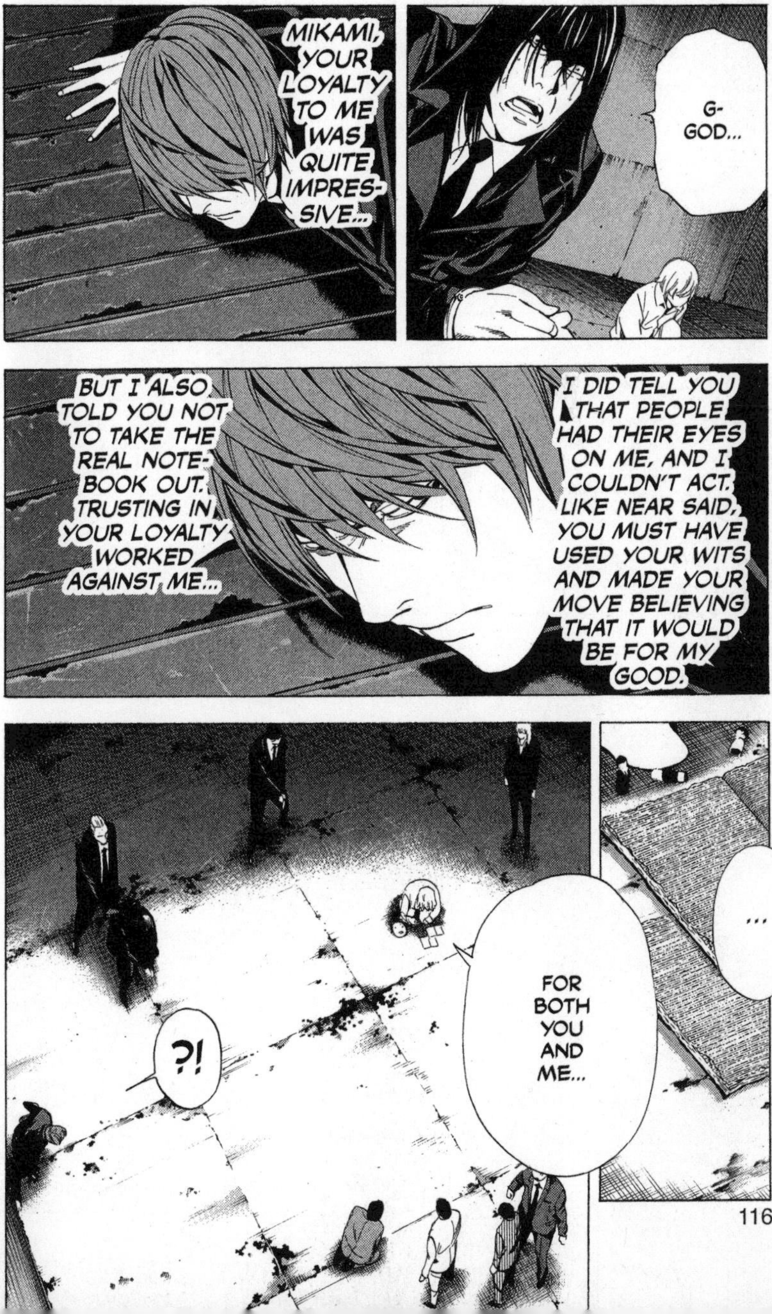
G-GOD...
MIKAMI, YOUR LOYALTY TO ME WAS QUITE IMPRESSIVE...
I DID TELL YOU THAT PEOPLE HAD THEIR EYES ON ME, AND I COULDN'T ACT. LIKE NEAR SAID, YOU MUST HAVE USED YOUR WITS AND MADE YOUR MOVE BELIEVING THAT IT WOULD BE FOR MY GOOD.
BUT I ALSO TOLD YOU NOT TO TAKE THE REAL NOTEBOOK OUT. TRUSTING IN YOUR LOYALTY WORKED AGAINST ME...
...
FOR BOTH YOU AND ME...
?!

READ THIS WAY

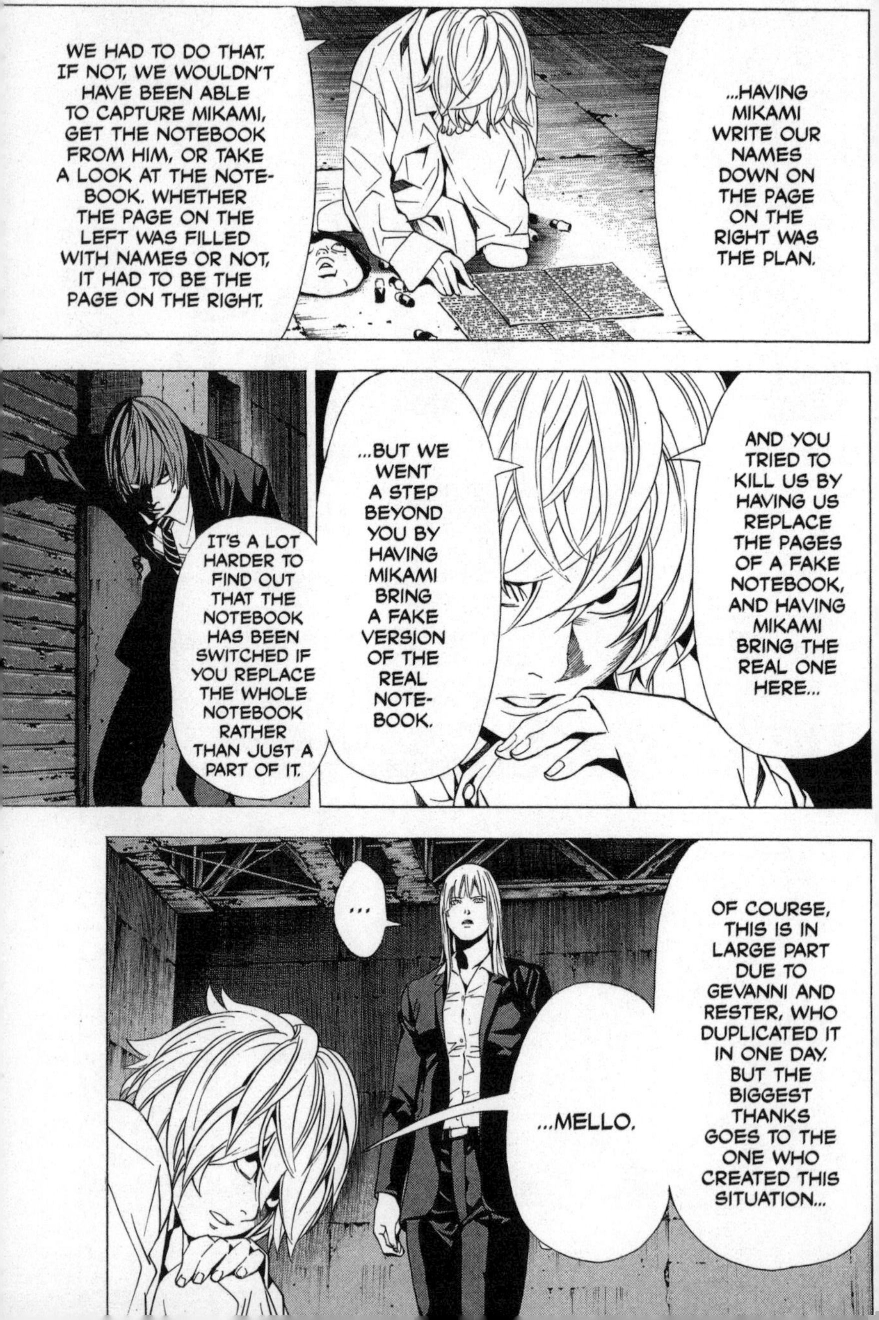

...HAVING MIKAMI WRITE OUR NAMES DOWN ON THE PAGE ON THE RIGHT WAS THE PLAN.
WE HAD TO DO THAT. IF NOT, WE WOULDN'T HAVE BEEN ABLE TO CAPTURE MIKAMI, GET THE NOTEBOOK FROM HIM, OR TAKE A LOOK AT THE NOTE-BOOK. WHETHER THE PAGE ON THE LEFT WAS FILLED WITH NAMES OR NOT, IT HAD TO BE THE PAGE ON THE RIGHT.
AND YOU TRIED TO KILL US BY HAVING US REPLACE THE PAGES OF A FAKE NOTEBOOK, AND HAVING MIKAMI BRING THE REAL ONE HERE...
...BUT WE WENT A STEP BEYOND YOU BY HAVING MIKAMI BRING A FAKE VERSION OF THE REAL NOTE-BOOK.
IT'S A LOT HARDER TO FIND OUT THAT THE NOTEBOOK HAS BEEN SWITCHED IF YOU REPLACE THE WHOLE NOTEBOOK RATHER THAN JUST A PART OF IT.
OF COURSE, THIS IS IN LARGE PART DUE TO GEVANNI AND RESTER, WHO DUPLICATED IT IN ONE DAY. BUT THE BIGGEST THANKS GOES TO THE ONE WHO CREATED THIS SITUATION...
...MELLO.
...

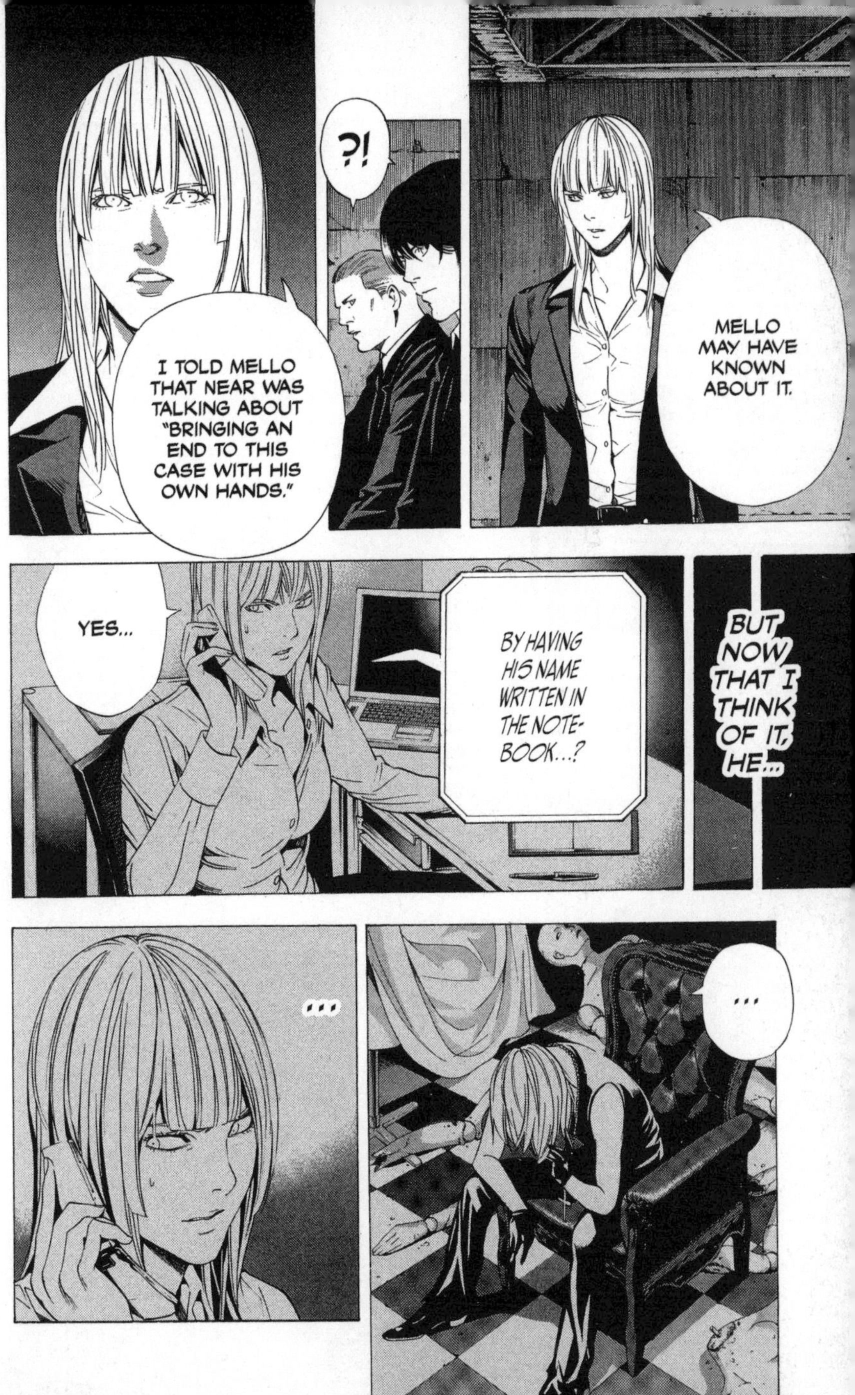
MELLO MAY HAVE KNOWN ABOUT IT.
?!
I TOLD MELLO THAT NEAR WAS TALKING ABOUT "BRINGING AN END TO THIS CASE WITH HIS OWN HANDS."
BUT NOW THAT I THINK OF IT, HE...
BY HAVING HIS NAME WRITTEN IN THE NOTE-BOOK...?
YES...
...
...

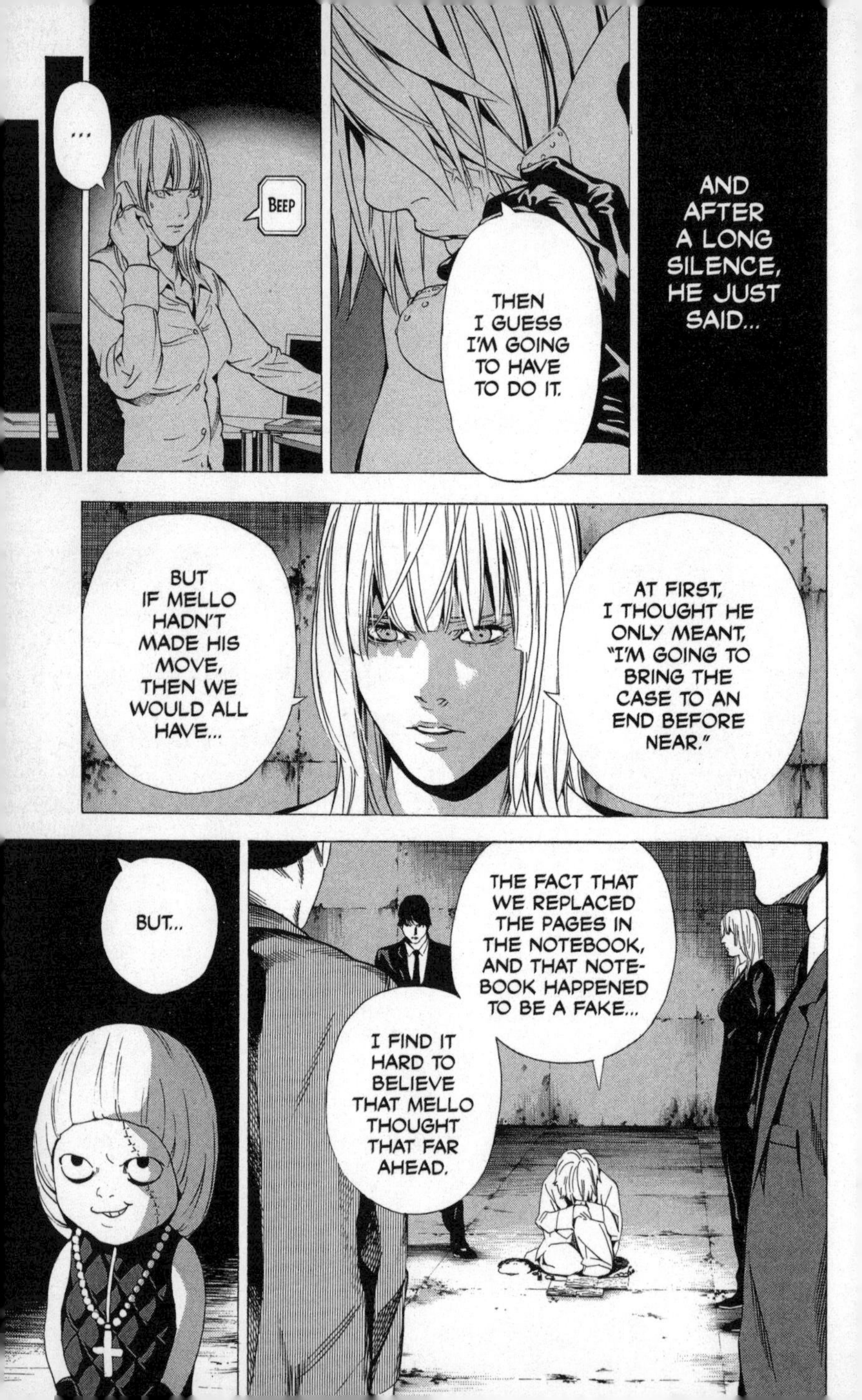
AND AFTER A LONG SILENCE, HE JUST SAID...
THEN I GUESS I'M GOING TO HAVE TO DO IT.
BEEP
...
AT FIRST, I THOUGHT HE ONLY MEANT, "I'M GOING TO BRING THE CASE TO AN END BEFORE NEAR."
BUT IF MELLO HADN'T MADE HIS MOVE, THEN WE WOULD ALL HAVE...
THE FACT THAT WE REPLACED THE PAGES IN THE NOTEBOOK, AND THAT NOTE-BOOK HAPPENED TO BE A FAKE...
I FIND IT HARD TO BELIEVE THAT MELLO THOUGHT THAT FAR AHEAD.
BUT...

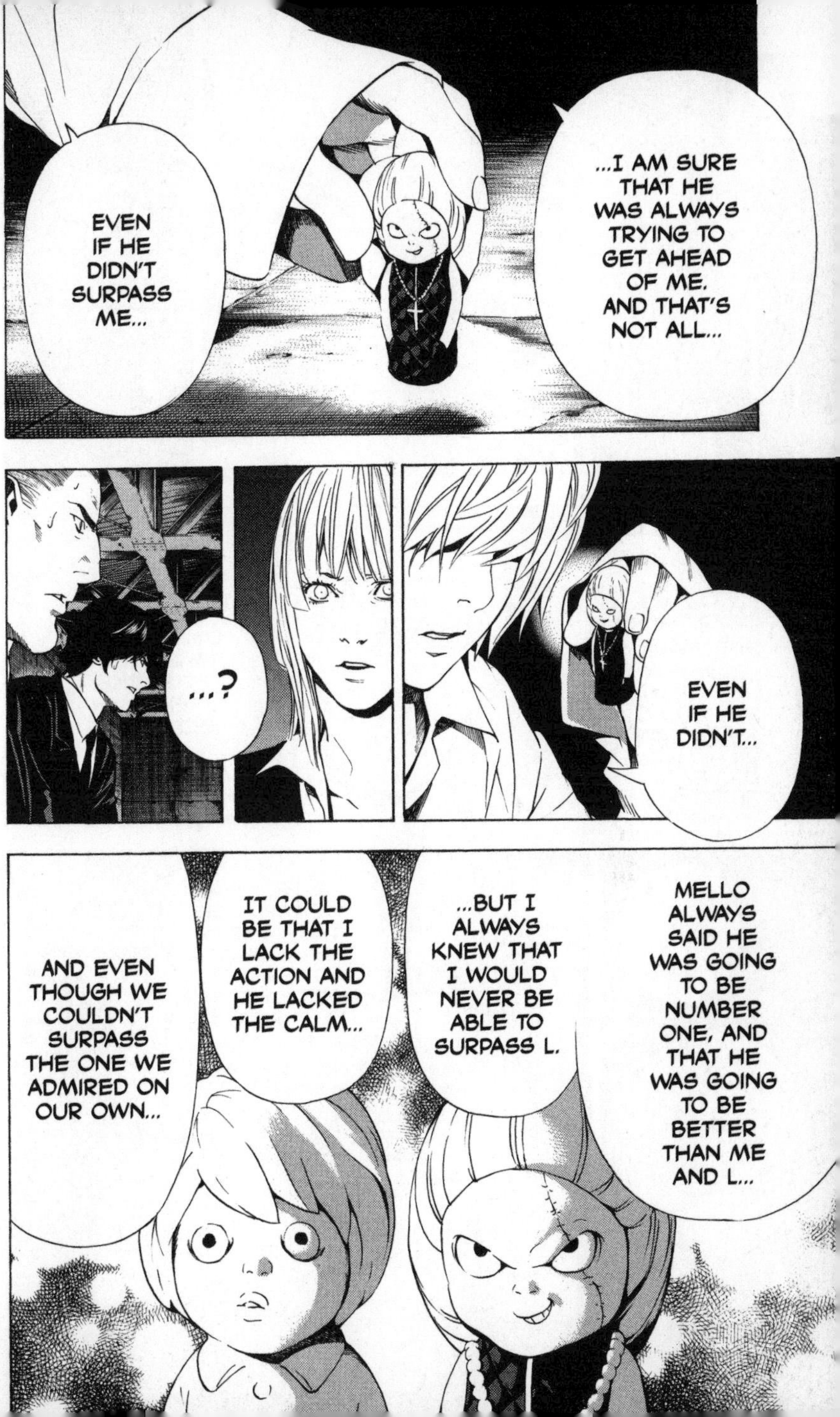
...I AM SURE THAT HE WAS ALWAYS TRYING TO GET AHEAD OF ME. AND THAT'S NOT ALL...
EVEN IF HE DIDN'T SURPASS ME...
EVEN IF HE DIDN'T...
...?
MELLO ALWAYS SAID HE WAS GOING TO BE NUMBER ONE, AND THAT HE WAS GOING TO BE BETTER THAN ME AND L...
...BUT I ALWAYS KNEW THAT I WOULD NEVER BE ABLE TO SURPASS L.
IT COULD BE THAT I LACK THE ACTION AND HE LACKED THE CALM...
AND EVEN THOUGH WE COULDN'T SURPASS THE ONE WE ADMIRED ON OUR OWN...

« READ THIS WAY «

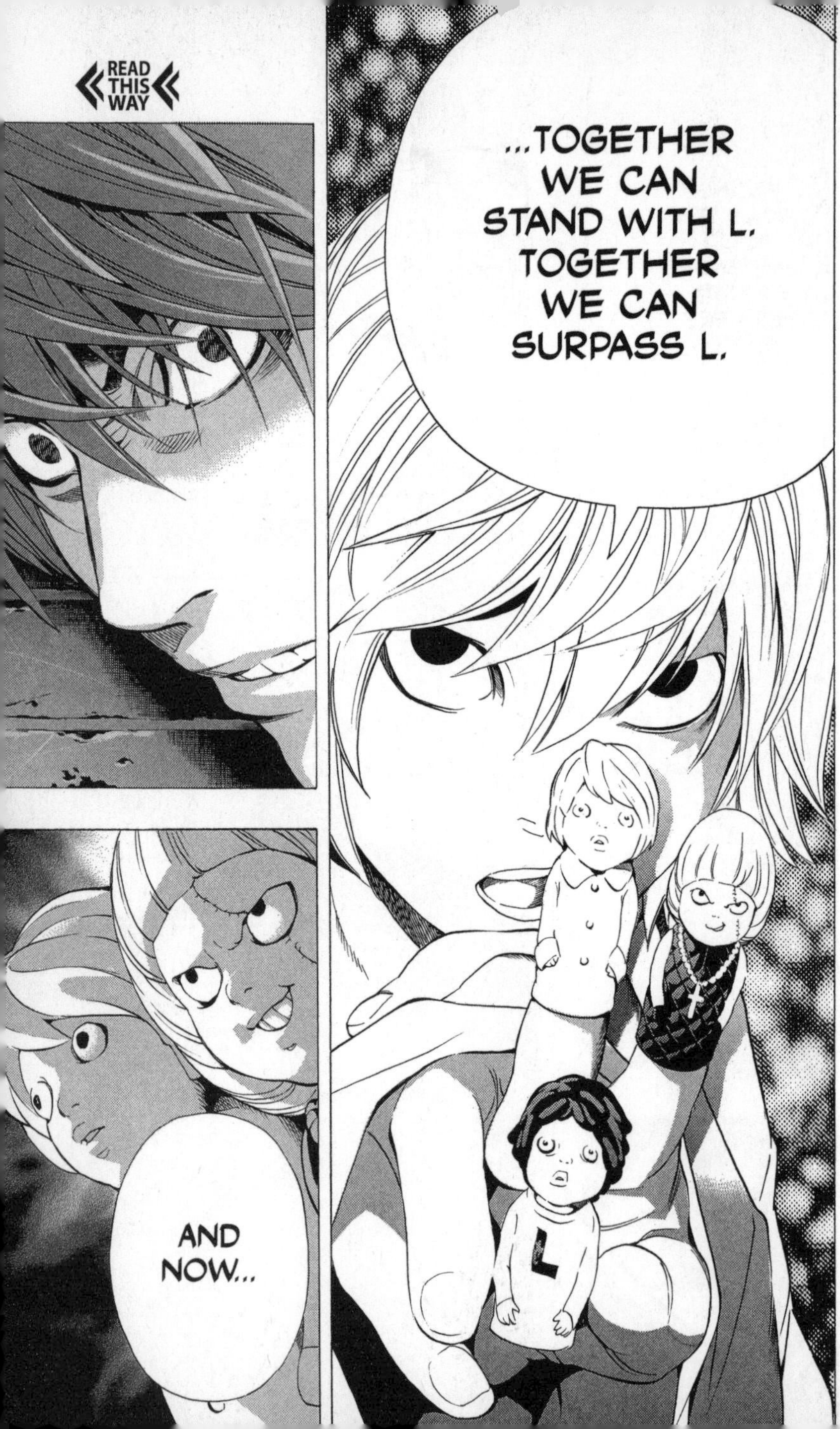
...TOGETHER WE CAN STAND WITH L. TOGETHER WE CAN SURPASS L.
AND NOW...

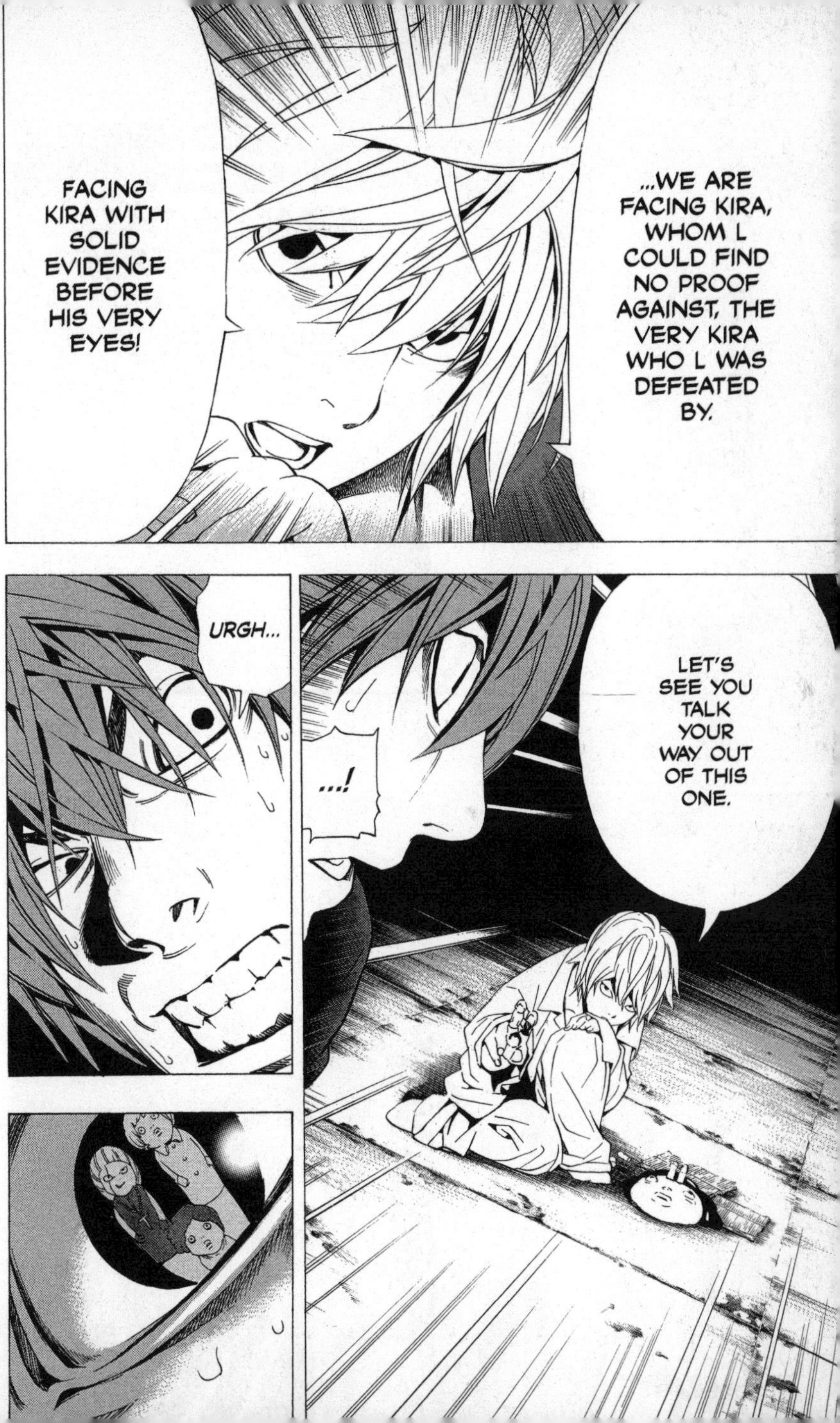
...WE ARE FACING KIRA, WHOM L COULD FIND NO PROOF AGAINST, THE VERY KIRA WHO L WAS DEFEATED BY.
FACING KIRA WITH SOLID EVIDENCE BEFORE HIS VERY EYES!
LET'S SEE YOU TALK YOUR WAY OUT OF THIS ONE.
...!
URGH...

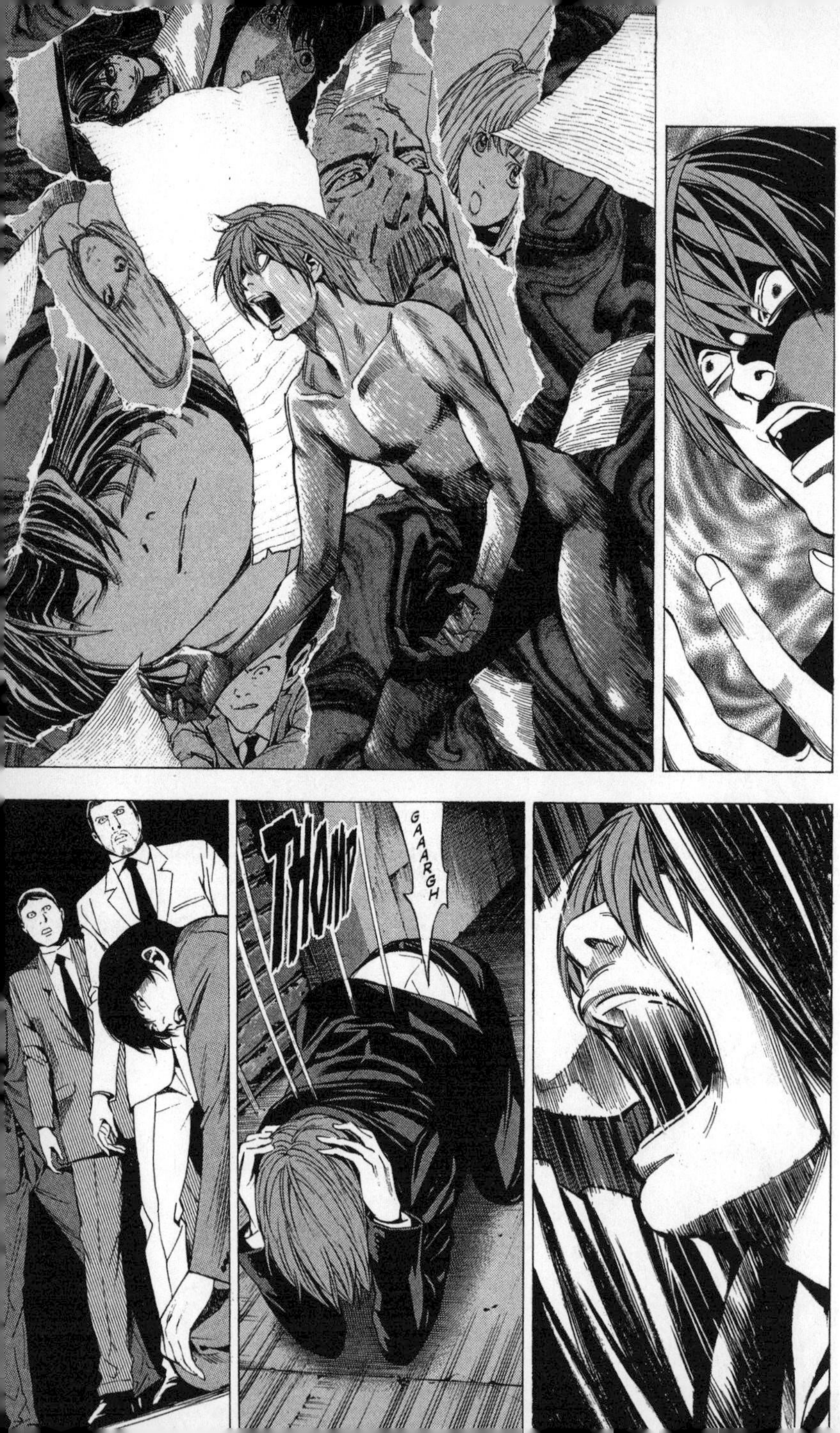
GAAAARGH
THOMP

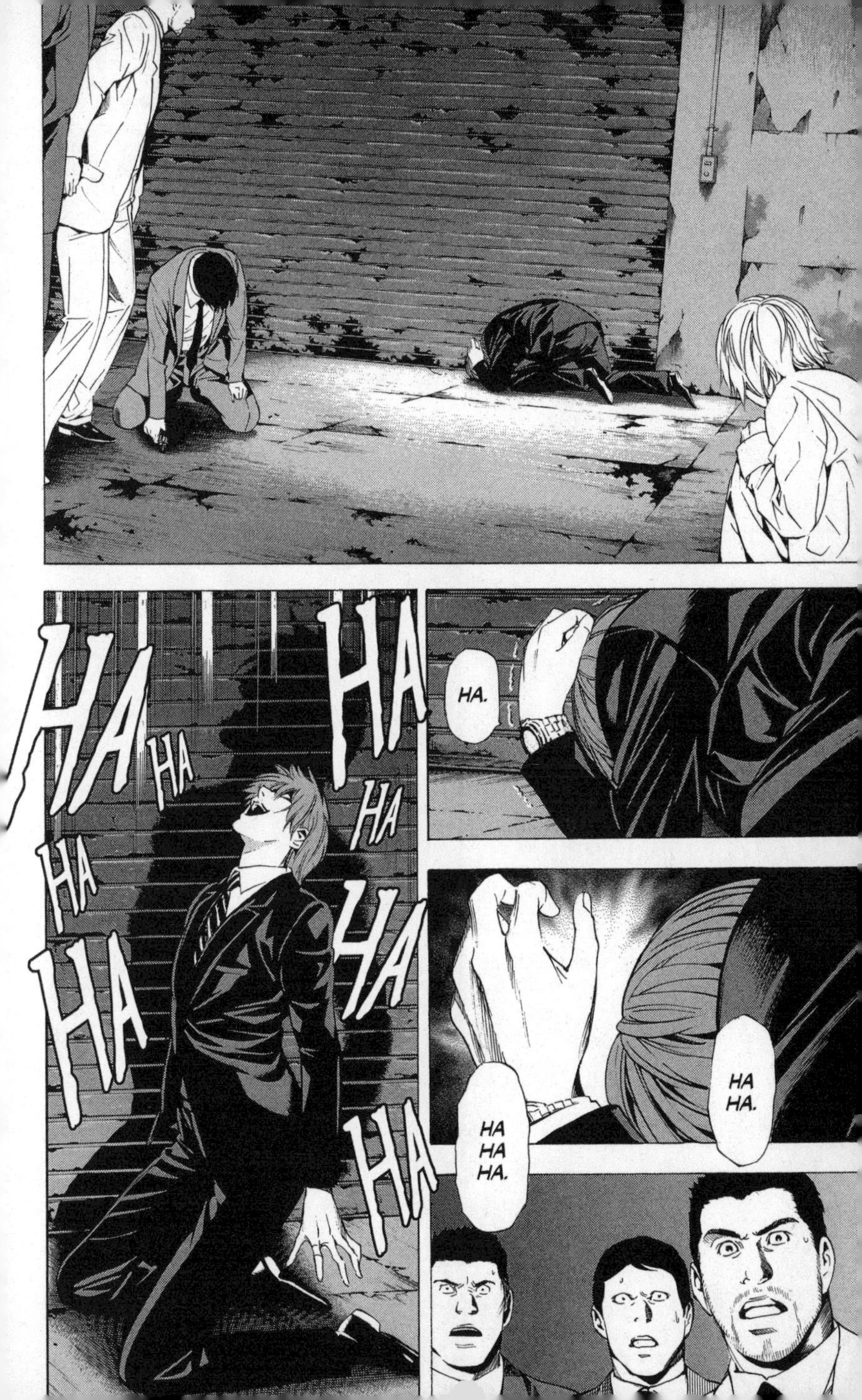
HA.
HA HA.
HA HA HA.
HA
HA
HA
HA
HA
HA
HA
HA
HA

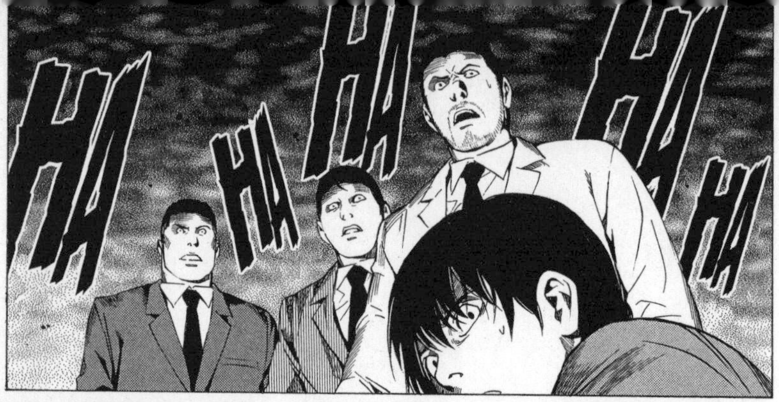
HA HA HA HA HA HA
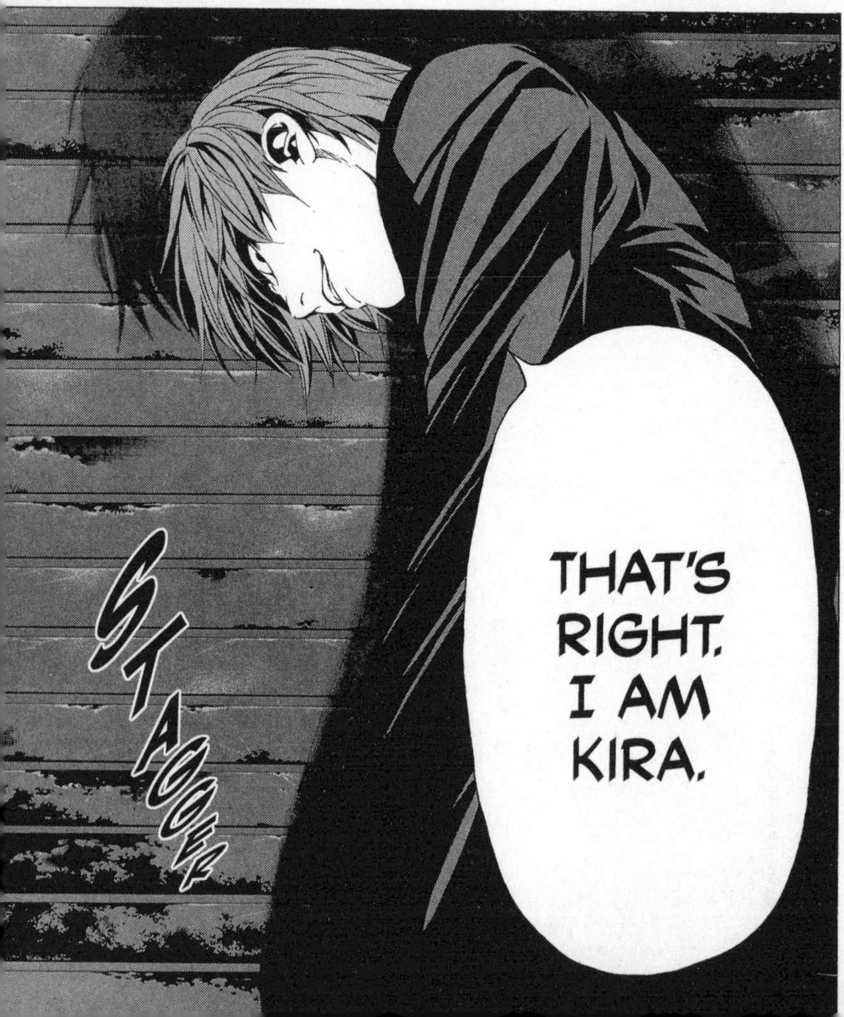
THAT'S RIGHT. I AM KIRA.

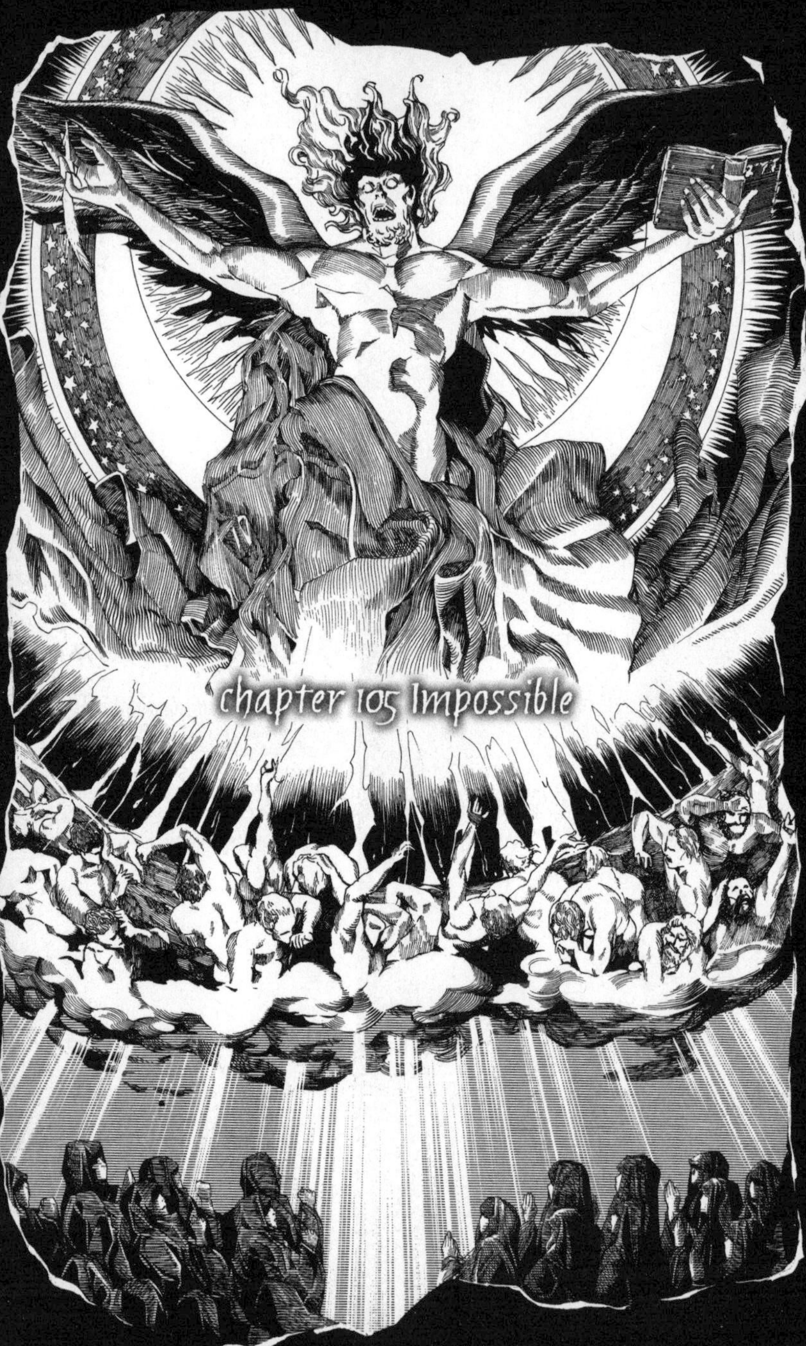
chapter 105 Impossible

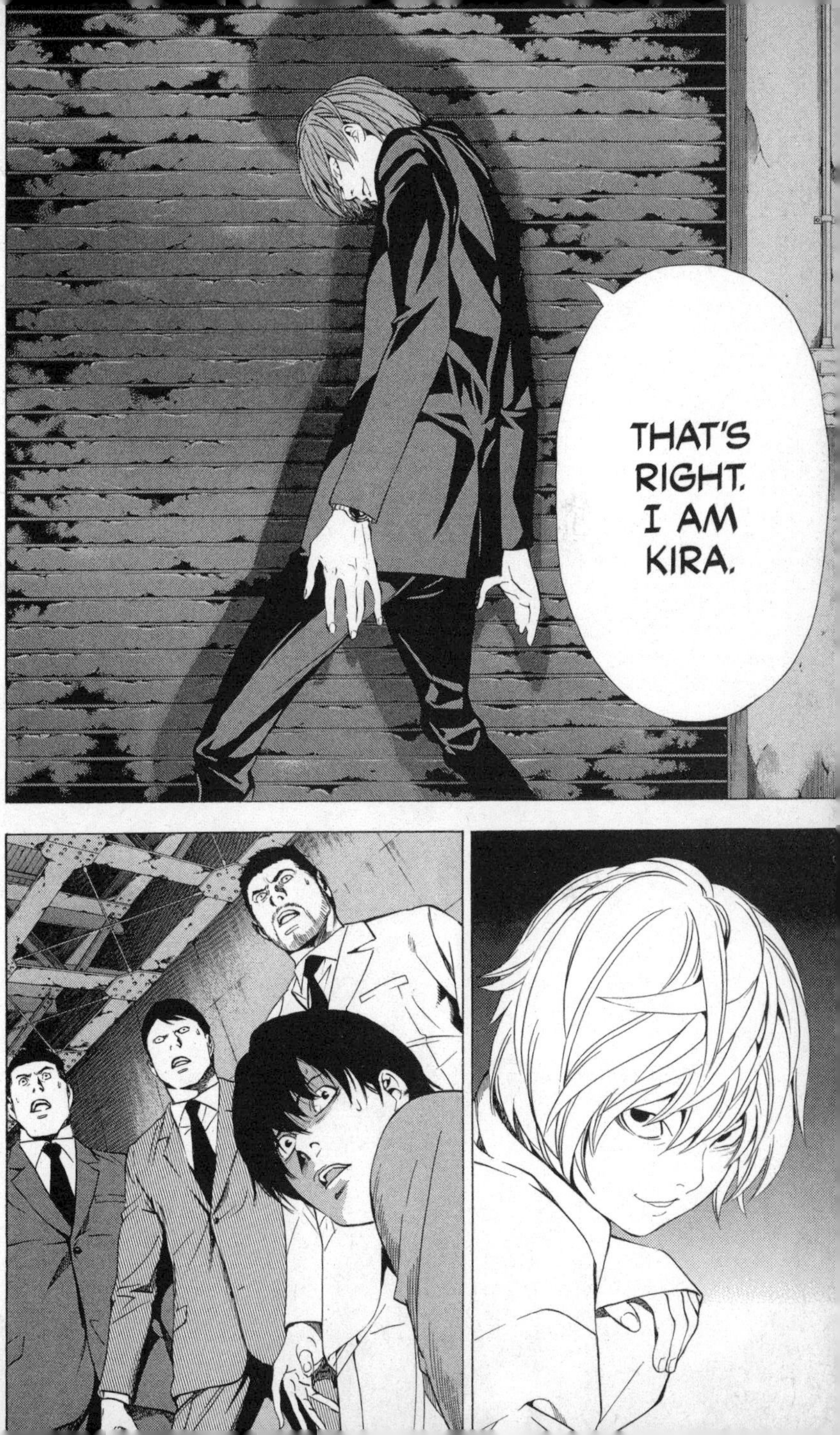
THAT'S RIGHT. I AM KIRA.

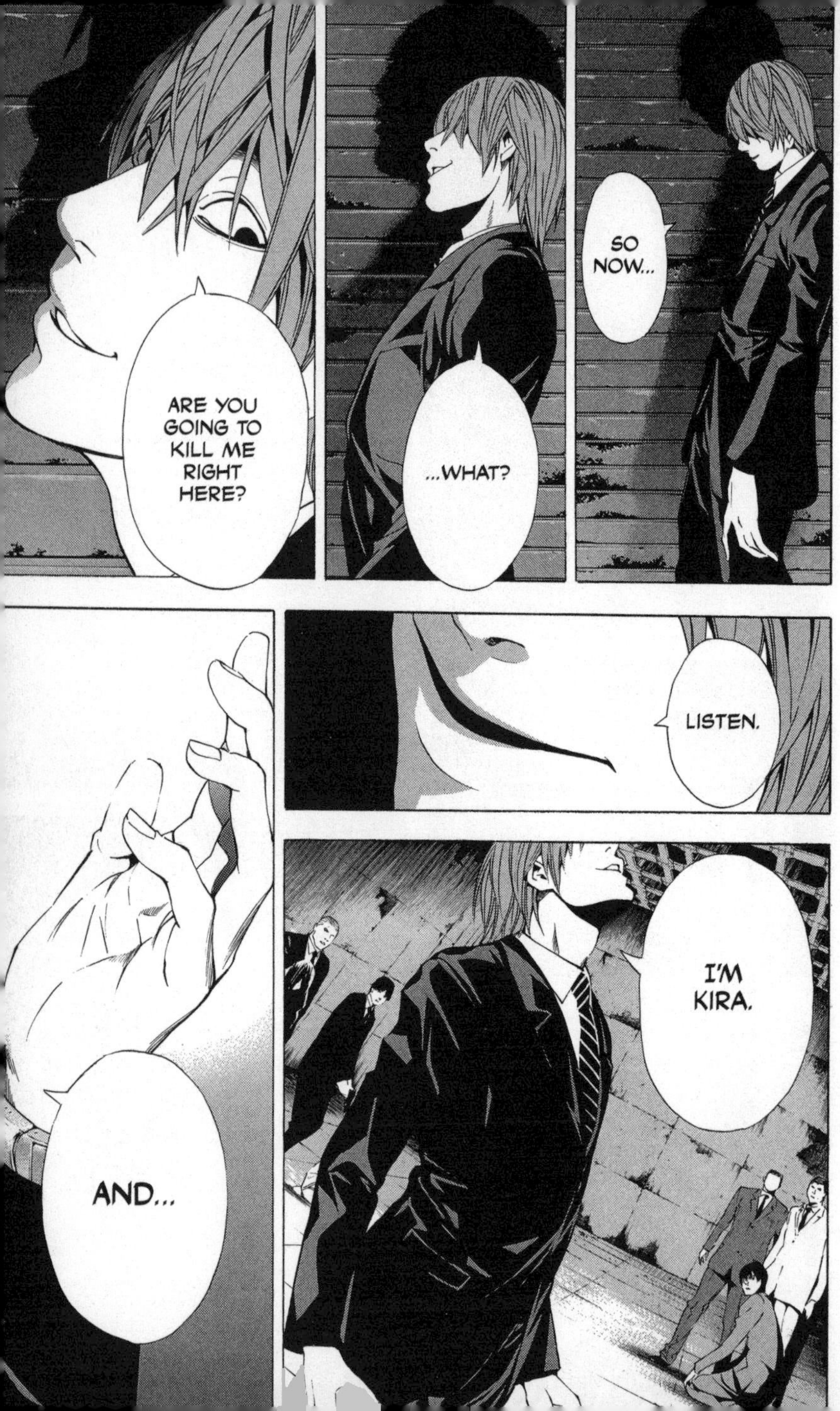
SO NOW...
...WHAT?
ARE YOU GOING TO KILL ME RIGHT HERE?
LISTEN.
I'M KIRA.
AND...

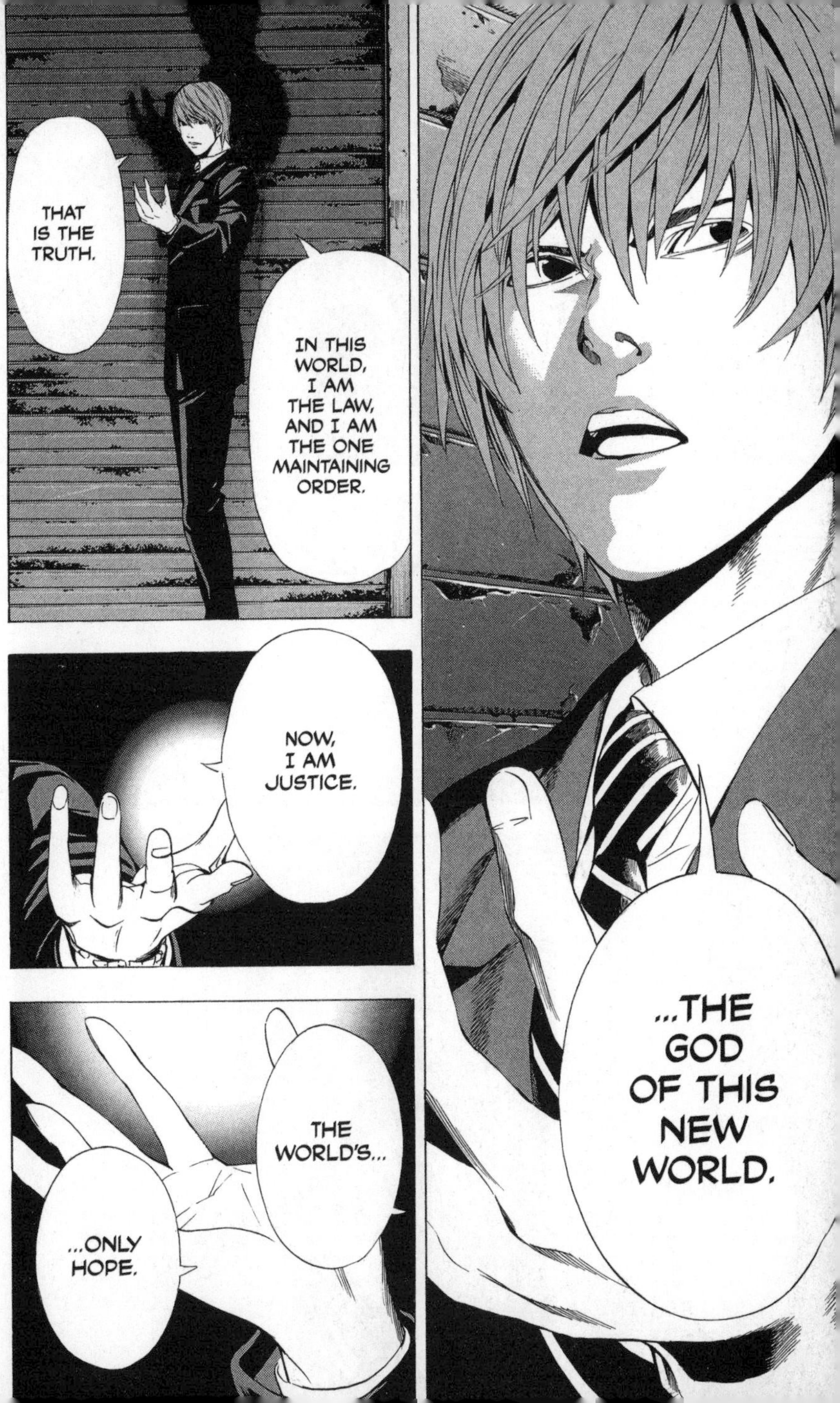
THAT IS THE TRUTH.
IN THIS WORLD, I AM THE LAW, AND I AM THE ONE MAINTAINING ORDER.
NOW, I AM JUSTICE.
THE WORLD'S...
...ONLY HOPE.
...THE GOD OF THIS NEW WORLD.

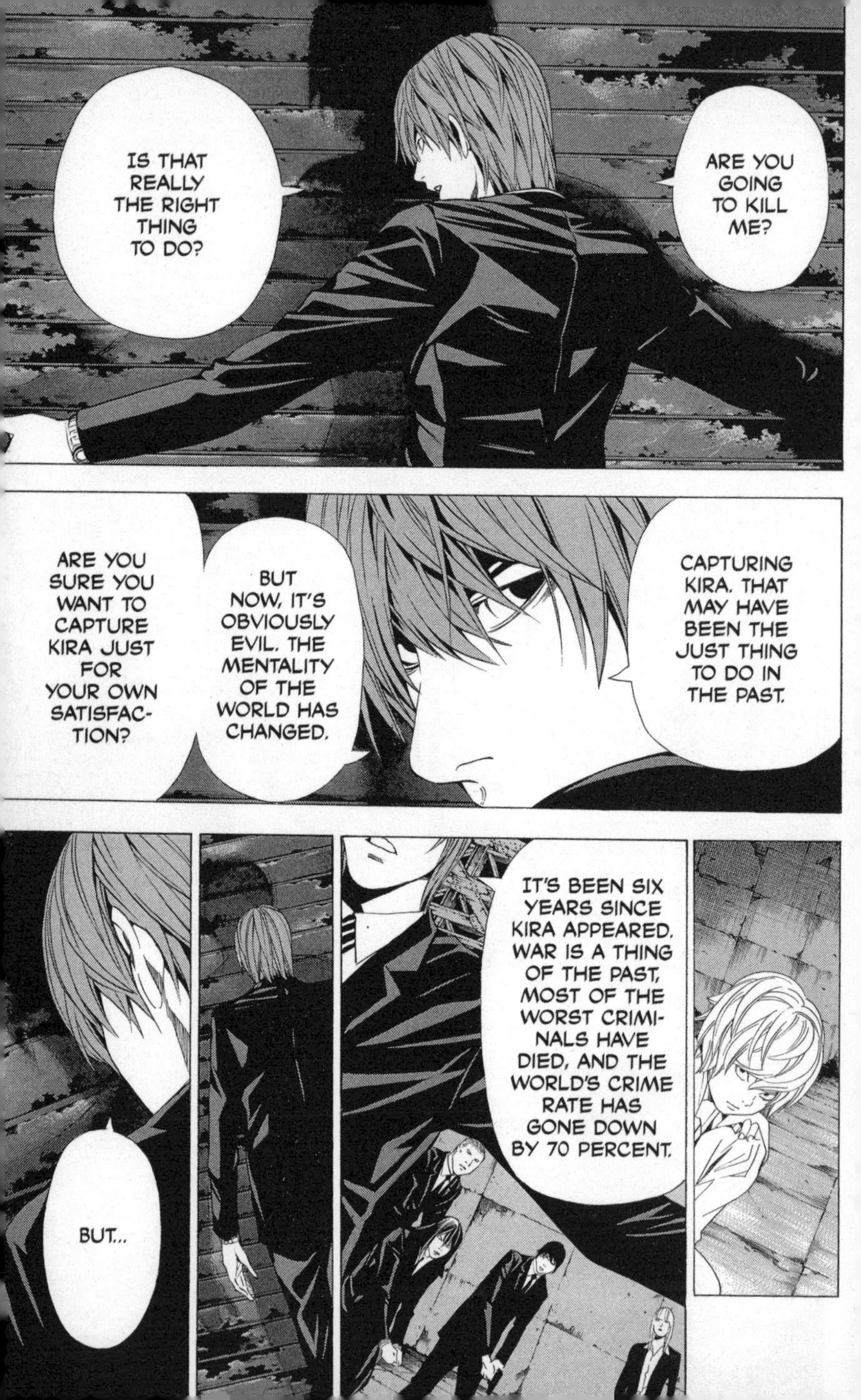
ARE YOU GOING TO KILL ME?
IS THAT REALLY THE RIGHT THING TO DO?
CAPTURING KIRA. THAT MAY HAVE BEEN THE JUST THING TO DO IN THE PAST.
BUT NOW, IT'S OBVIOUSLY EVIL. THE MENTALITY OF THE WORLD HAS CHANGED.
ARE YOU SURE YOU WANT TO CAPTURE KIRA JUST FOR YOUR OWN SATISFACTION?
IT'S BEEN SIX YEARS SINCE KIRA APPEARED. WAR IS A THING OF THE PAST, MOST OF THE WORST CRIMINALS HAVE DIED, AND THE WORLD'S CRIME RATE HAS GONE DOWN BY 70 PERCENT.
BUT...

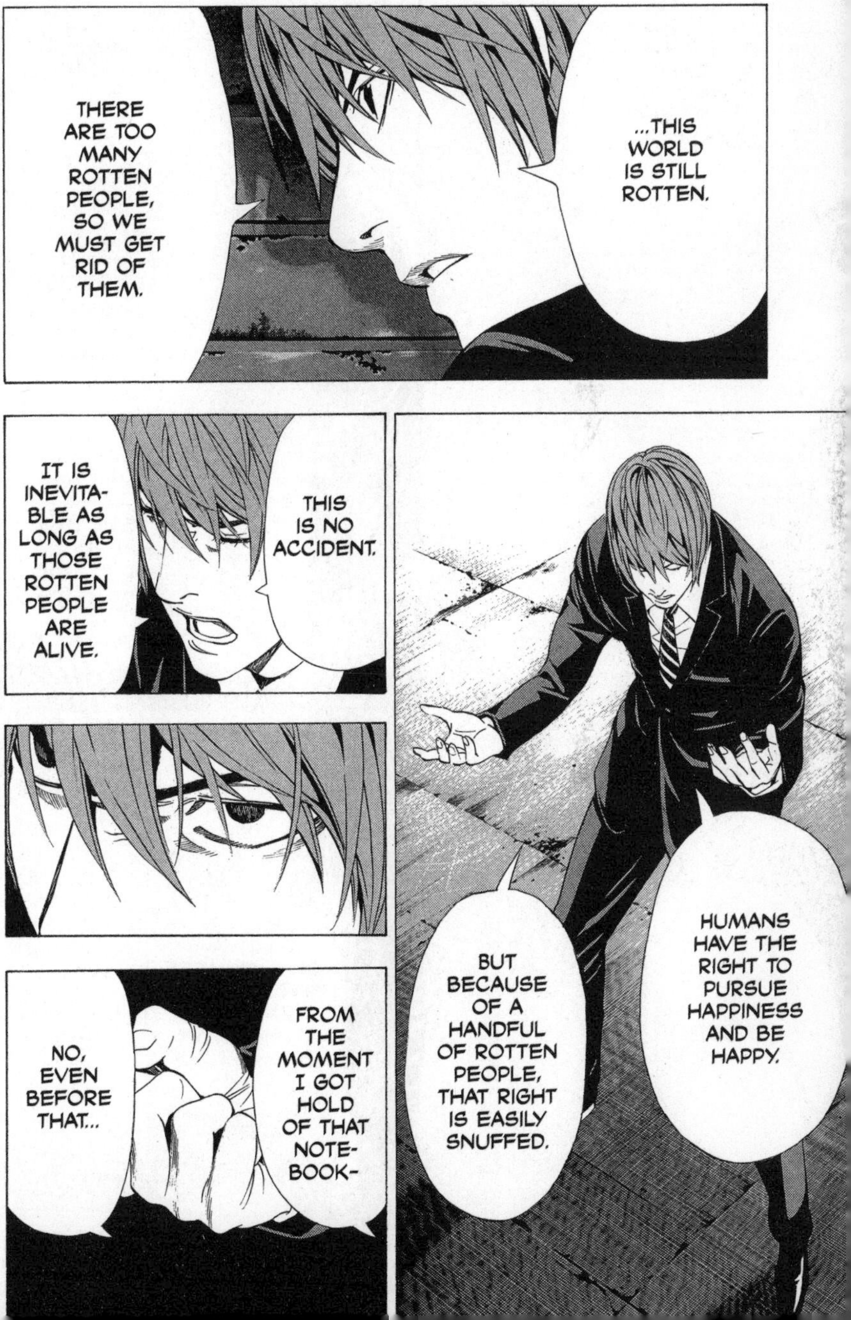
...THIS WORLD IS STILL ROTTEN.
THERE ARE TOO MANY ROTTEN PEOPLE, SO WE MUST GET RID OF THEM.
HUMANS HAVE THE RIGHT TO PURSUE HAPPINESS AND BE HAPPY.
BUT BECAUSE OF A HANDFUL OF ROTTEN PEOPLE, THAT RIGHT IS EASILY SNUFFED.
THIS IS NO ACCIDENT.
IT IS INEVITABLE AS LONG AS THOSE ROTTEN PEOPLE ARE ALIVE.
FROM THE MOMENT I GOT HOLD OF THAT NOTEBOOK-
NO, EVEN BEFORE THAT...

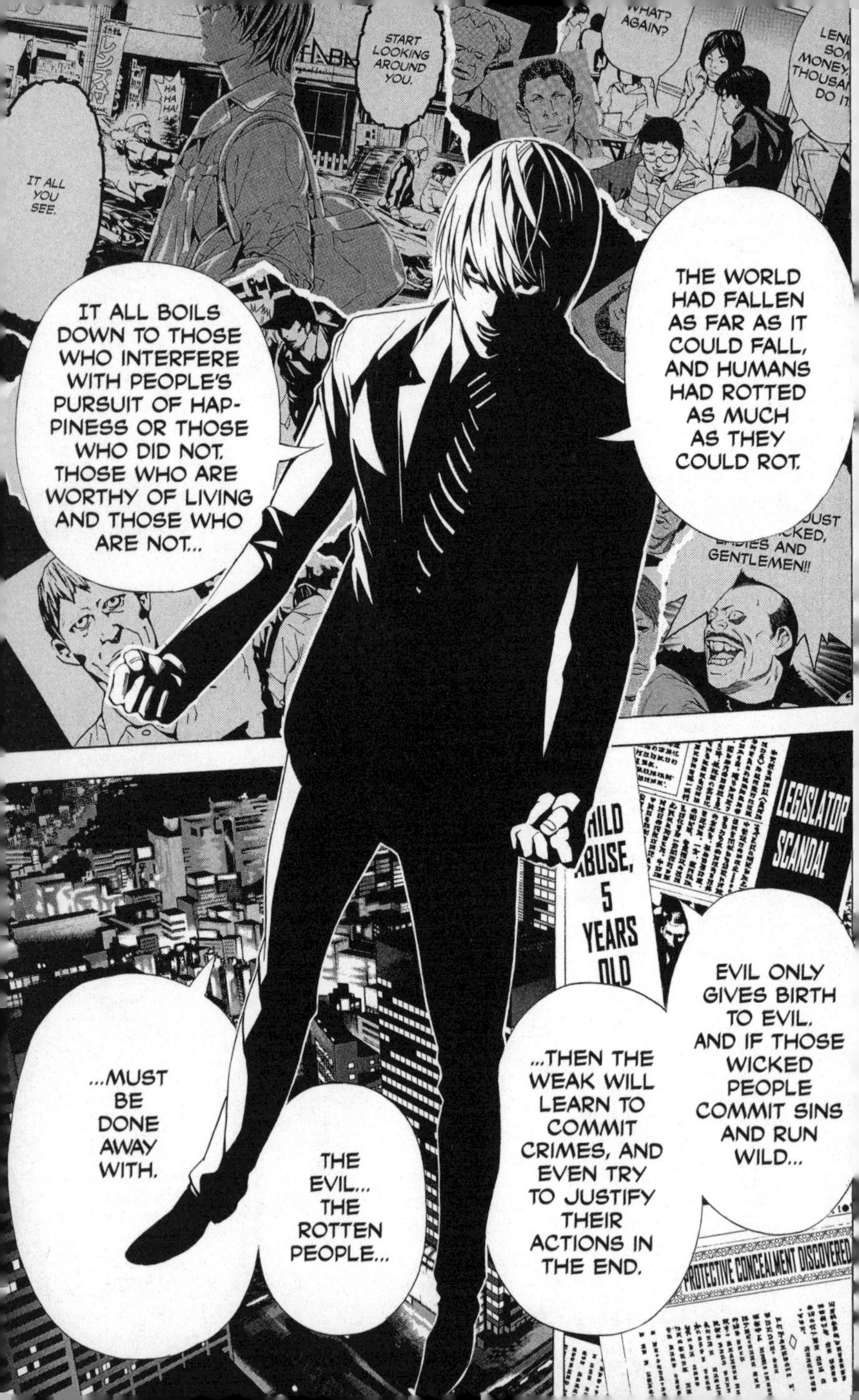
WHAT? AGAIN?
START LOOKING AROUND YOU.
HA HA HA!
IT ALL YOU SEE.
THE WORLD HAD FALLEN AS FAR AS IT COULD FALL, AND HUMANS HAD ROTTED AS MUCH AS THEY COULD ROT.
IT ALL BOILS DOWN TO THOSE WHO INTERFERE WITH PEOPLE'S PURSUIT OF HAP-PINESS OR THOSE WHO DID NOT. THOSE WHO ARE WORTHY OF LIVING AND THOSE WHO ARE NOT...
GENTLEMEN!!
LEGISLATOR SCANDAL
EVIL ONLY GIVES BIRTH TO EVIL. AND IF THOSE WICKED PEOPLE COMMIT SINS AND RUN WILD...
...THEN THE WEAK WILL LEARN TO COMMIT CRIMES, AND EVEN TRY TO JUSTIFY THEIR ACTIONS IN THE END.
THE EVIL... THE ROTTEN PEOPLE...
...MUST BE DONE AWAY WITH.
PROTECTIVE CONCEALMENT DISCOVERED

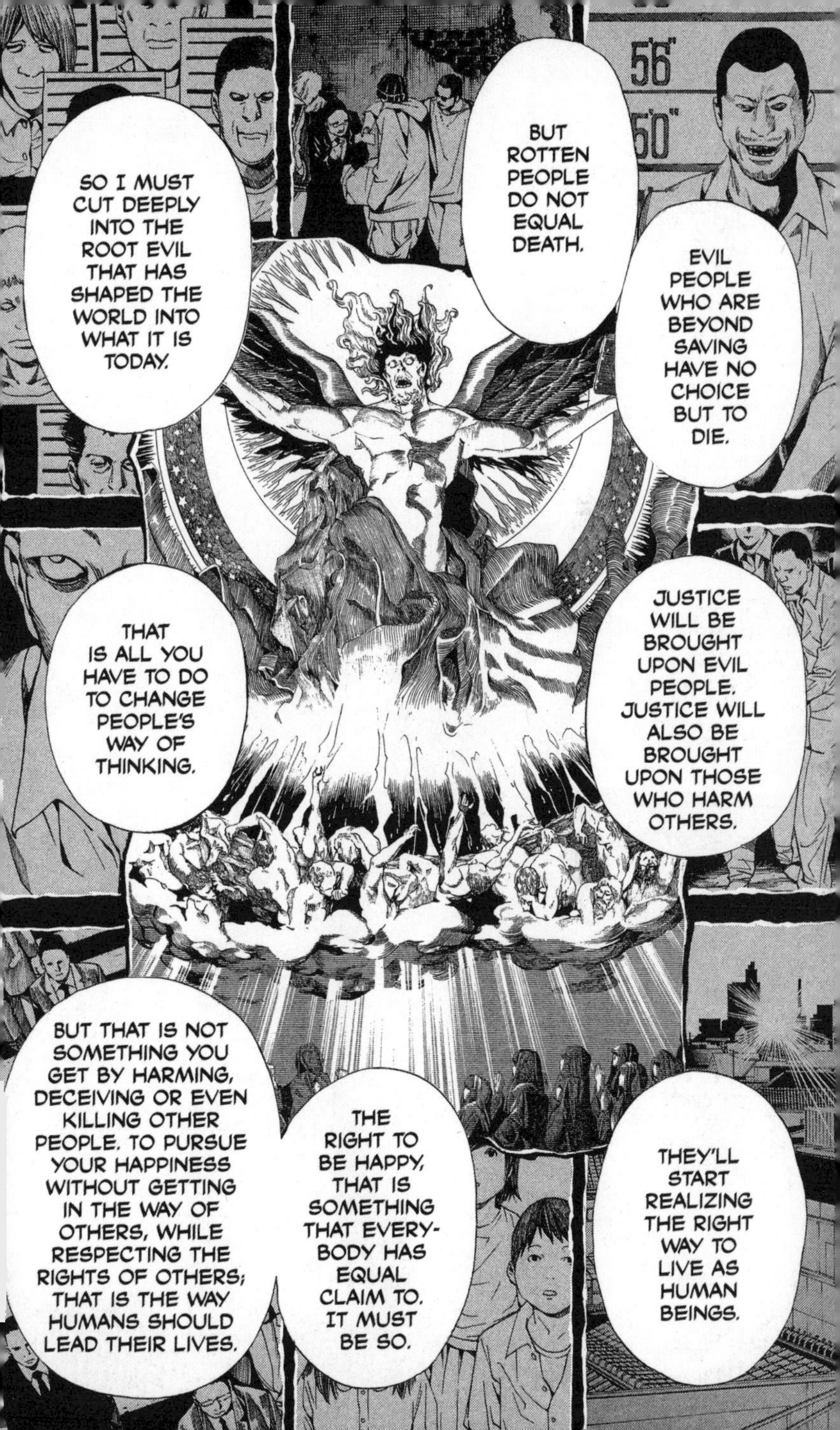
EVIL PEOPLE WHO ARE BEYOND SAVING HAVE NO CHOICE BUT TO DIE.
BUT ROTTEN PEOPLE DO NOT EQUAL DEATH.
SO I MUST CUT DEEPLY INTO THE ROOT EVIL THAT HAS SHAPED THE WORLD INTO WHAT IT IS TODAY.
JUSTICE WILL BE BROUGHT UPON EVIL PEOPLE. JUSTICE WILL ALSO BE BROUGHT UPON THOSE WHO HARM OTHERS.
THAT IS ALL YOU HAVE TO DO TO CHANGE PEOPLE'S WAY OF THINKING.
THEY'LL START REALIZING THE RIGHT WAY TO LIVE AS HUMAN BEINGS.
THE RIGHT TO BE HAPPY, THAT IS SOMETHING THAT EVERY-BODY HAS EQUAL CLAIM TO. IT MUST BE SO.
BUT THAT IS NOT SOMETHING YOU GET BY HARMING, DECEIVING OR EVEN KILLING OTHER PEOPLE. TO PURSUE YOUR HAPPINESS WITHOUT GETTING IN THE WAY OF OTHERS, WHILE RESPECTING THE RIGHTS OF OTHERS; THAT IS THE WAY HUMANS SHOULD LEAD THEIR LIVES.

READ THIS WAY

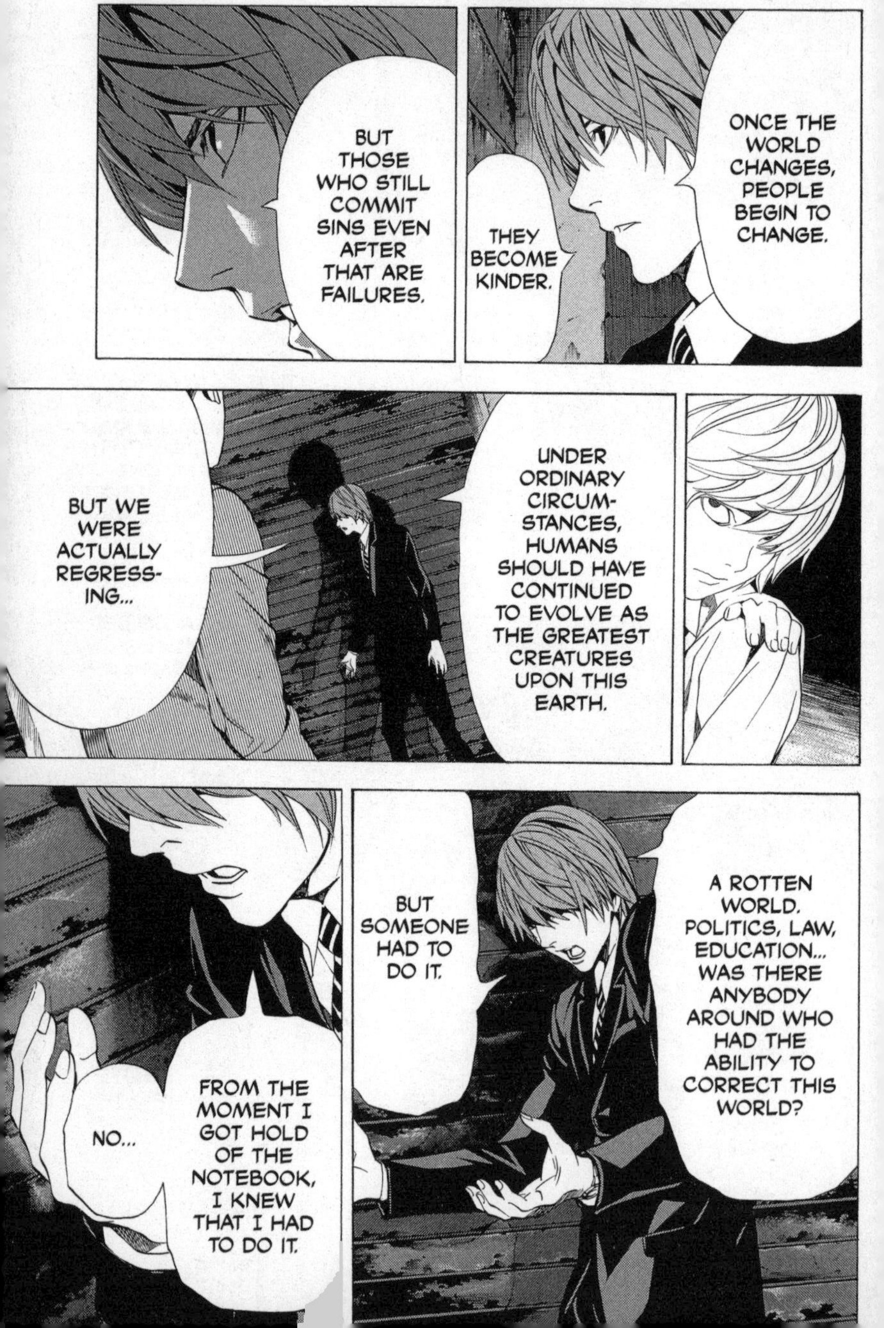
ONCE THE WORLD CHANGES, PEOPLE BEGIN TO CHANGE.
THEY BECOME KINDER.
BUT THOSE WHO STILL COMMIT SINS EVEN AFTER THAT ARE FAILURES.
UNDER ORDINARY CIRCUM-STANCES, HUMANS SHOULD HAVE CONTINUED TO EVOLVE AS THE GREATEST CREATURES UPON THIS EARTH.
BUT WE WERE ACTUALLY REGRESS-ING...
A ROTTEN WORLD. POLITICS, LAW, EDUCATION... WAS THERE ANYBODY AROUND WHO HAD THE ABILITY TO CORRECT THIS WORLD?
BUT SOMEONE HAD TO DO IT.
NO...
FROM THE MOMENT I GOT HOLD OF THE NOTEBOOK, I KNEW THAT I HAD TO DO IT.

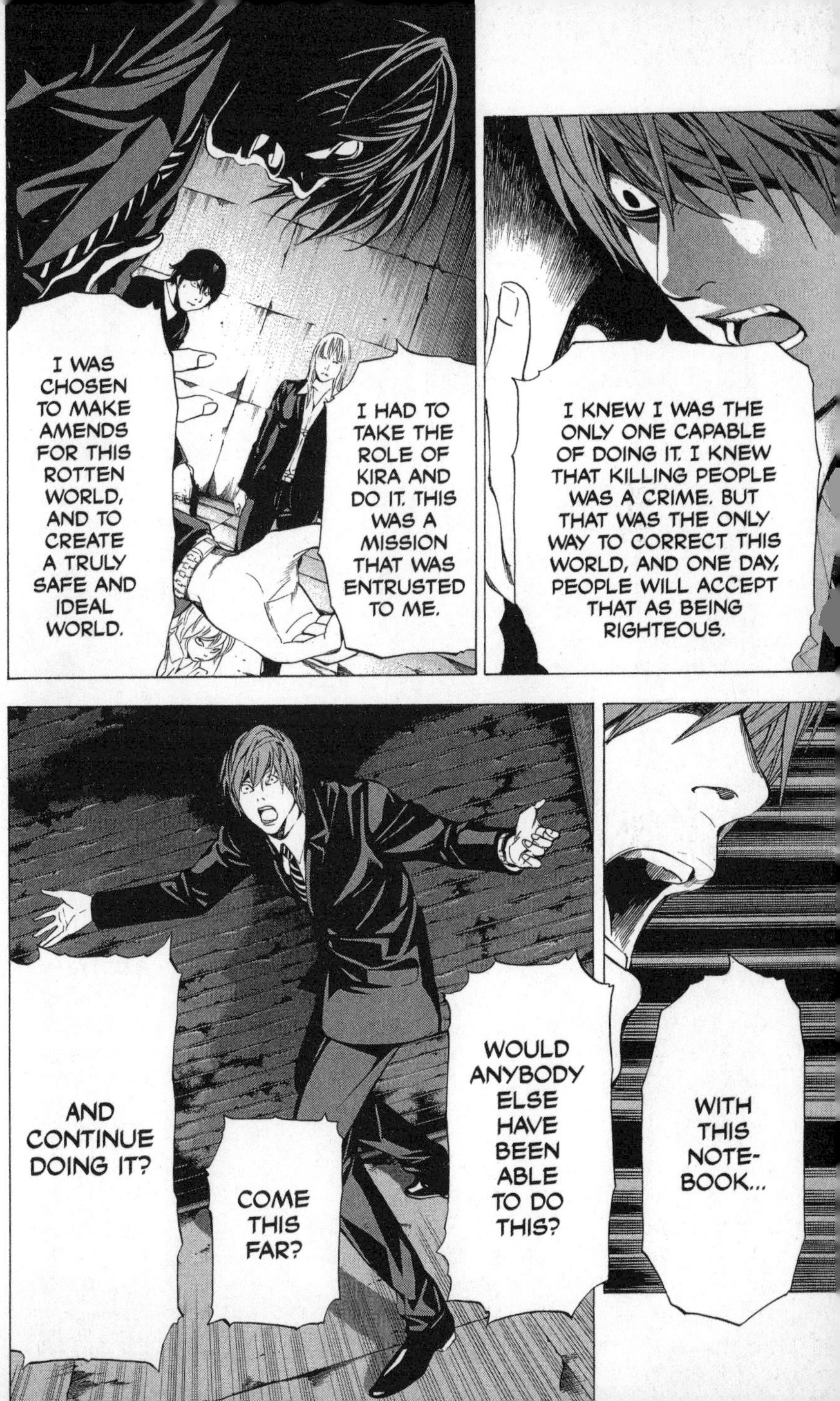
I KNEW I WAS THE ONLY ONE CAPABLE OF DOING IT. I KNEW THAT KILLING PEOPLE WAS A CRIME. BUT THAT WAS THE ONLY WAY TO CORRECT THIS WORLD, AND ONE DAY, PEOPLE WILL ACCEPT THAT AS BEING RIGHTEOUS.
I HAD TO TAKE THE ROLE OF KIRA AND DO IT. THIS WAS A MISSION THAT WAS ENTRUSTED TO ME.
I WAS CHOSEN TO MAKE AMENDS FOR THIS ROTTEN WORLD, AND TO CREATE A TRULY SAFE AND IDEAL WORLD.
WITH THIS NOTE-BOOK...
WOULD ANYBODY ELSE HAVE BEEN ABLE TO DO THIS?
COME THIS FAR?
AND CONTINUE DOING IT?

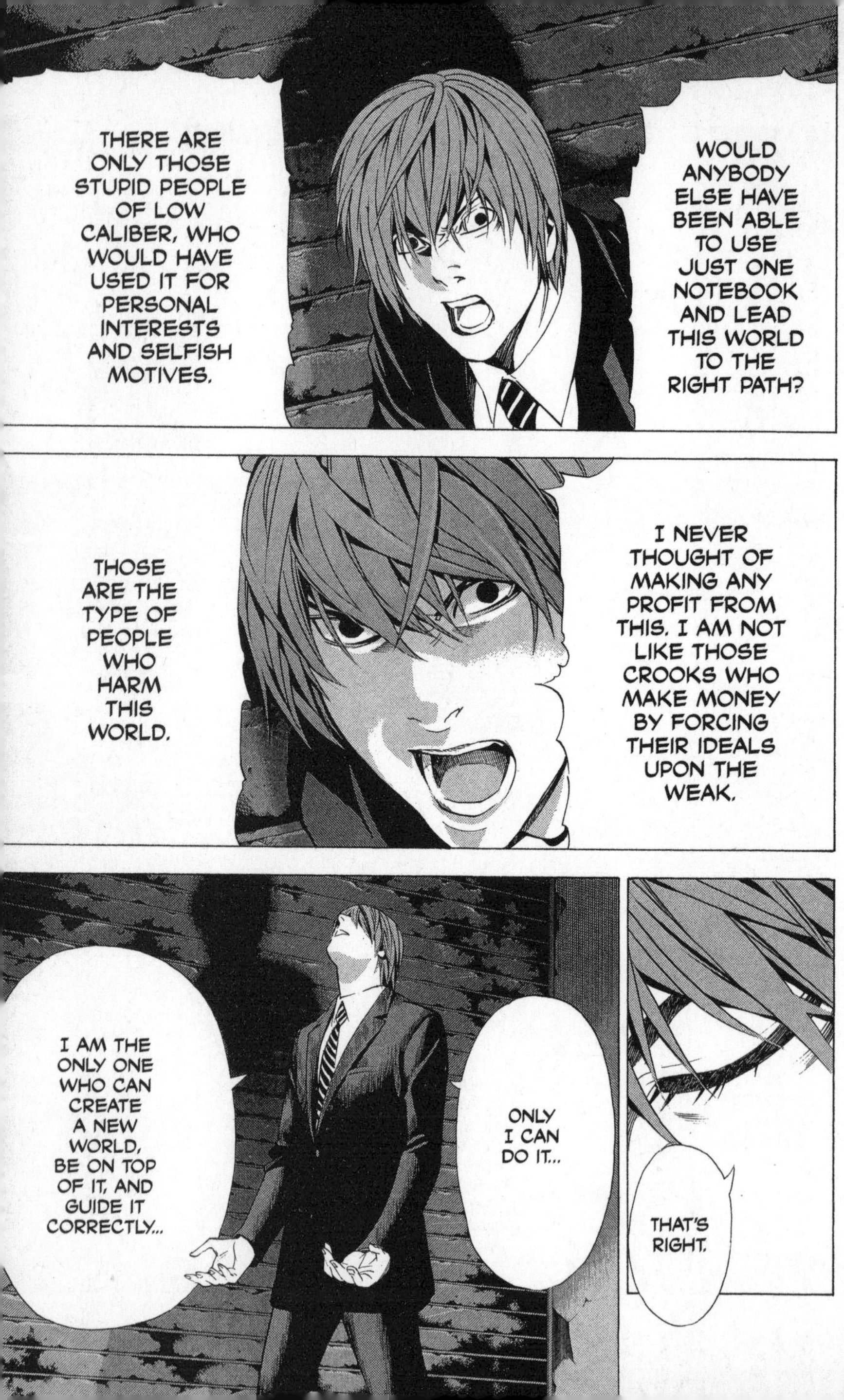
WOULD ANYBODY ELSE HAVE BEEN ABLE TO USE JUST ONE NOTEBOOK AND LEAD THIS WORLD TO THE RIGHT PATH?
THERE ARE ONLY THOSE STUPID PEOPLE OF LOW CALIBER, WHO WOULD HAVE USED IT FOR PERSONAL INTERESTS AND SELFISH MOTIVES.
I NEVER THOUGHT OF MAKING ANY PROFIT FROM THIS. I AM NOT LIKE THOSE CROOKS WHO MAKE MONEY BY FORCING THEIR IDEALS UPON THE WEAK.
THOSE ARE THE TYPE OF PEOPLE WHO HARM THIS WORLD.
THAT'S RIGHT.
ONLY I CAN DO IT...
I AM THE ONLY ONE WHO CAN CREATE A NEW WORLD, BE ON TOP OF IT, AND GUIDE IT CORRECTLY...

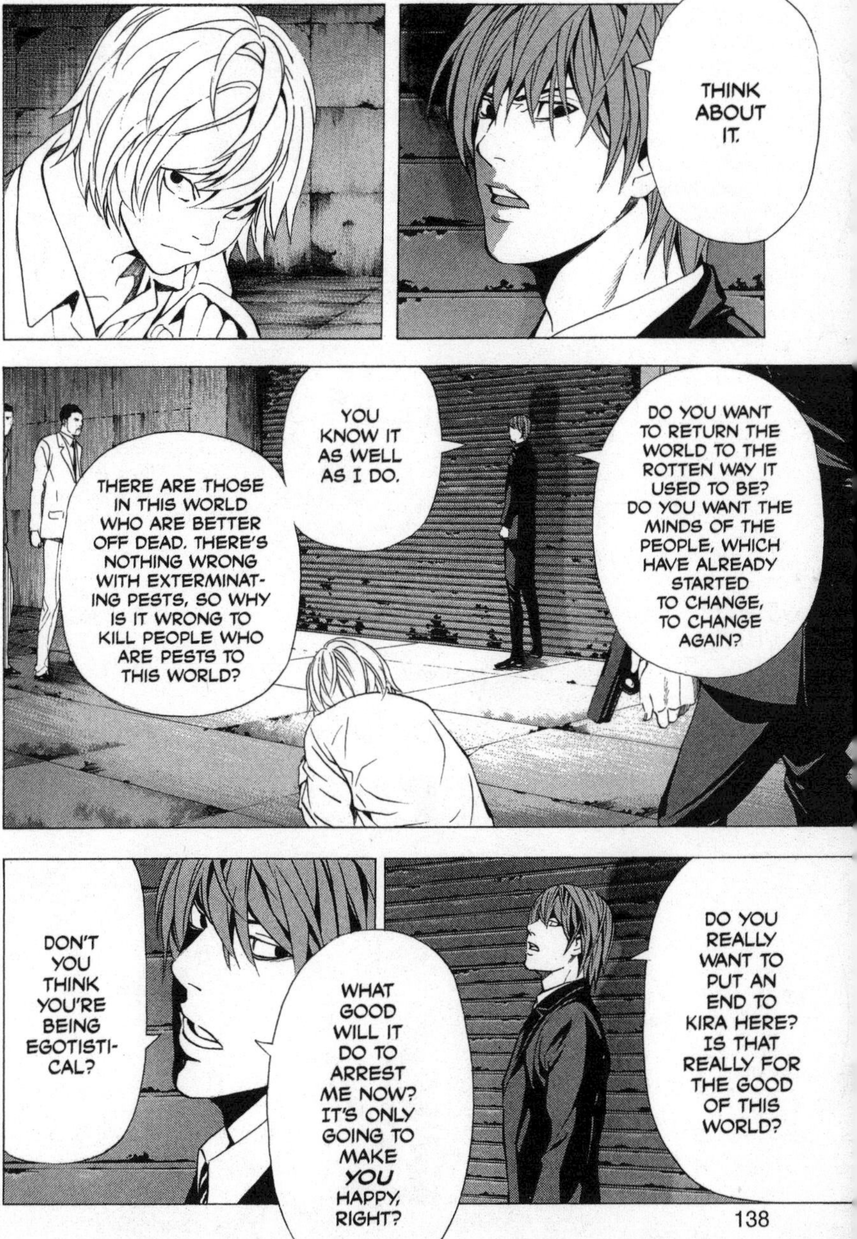
THINK ABOUT IT.
DO YOU WANT TO RETURN THE WORLD TO THE ROTTEN WAY IT USED TO BE? DO YOU WANT THE MINDS OF THE PEOPLE, WHICH HAVE ALREADY STARTED TO CHANGE, TO CHANGE AGAIN?
YOU KNOW IT AS WELL AS I DO.
THERE ARE THOSE IN THIS WORLD WHO ARE BETTER OFF DEAD. THERE'S NOTHING WRONG WITH EXTERMINAT-ING PESTS, SO WHY IS IT WRONG TO KILL PEOPLE WHO ARE PESTS TO THIS WORLD?
DO YOU REALLY WANT TO PUT AN END TO KIRA HERE? IS THAT REALLY FOR THE GOOD OF THIS WORLD?
WHAT GOOD WILL IT DO TO ARREST ME NOW? IT'S ONLY GOING TO MAKE *YOU* HAPPY, RIGHT?
DON'T YOU THINK YOU'RE BEING EGOTISTI-CAL?

READ THIS WAY

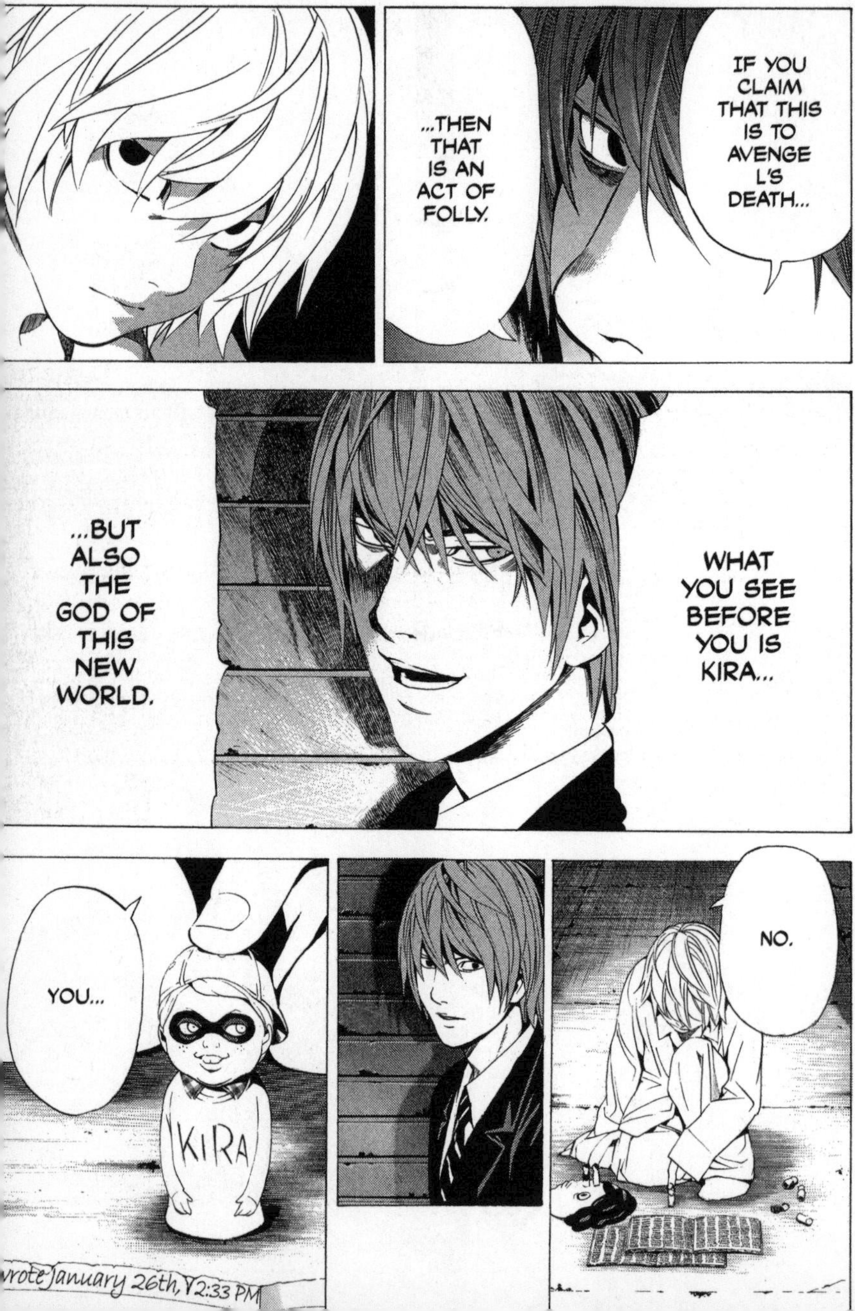
IF YOU CLAIM THAT THIS IS TO AVENGE L'S DEATH...
...THEN THAT IS AN ACT OF FOLLY.
WHAT YOU SEE BEFORE YOU IS KIRA...
...BUT ALSO THE GOD OF THIS NEW WORLD.
NO.
YOU...
KIRA
wrote January 26th, 12:33 PM

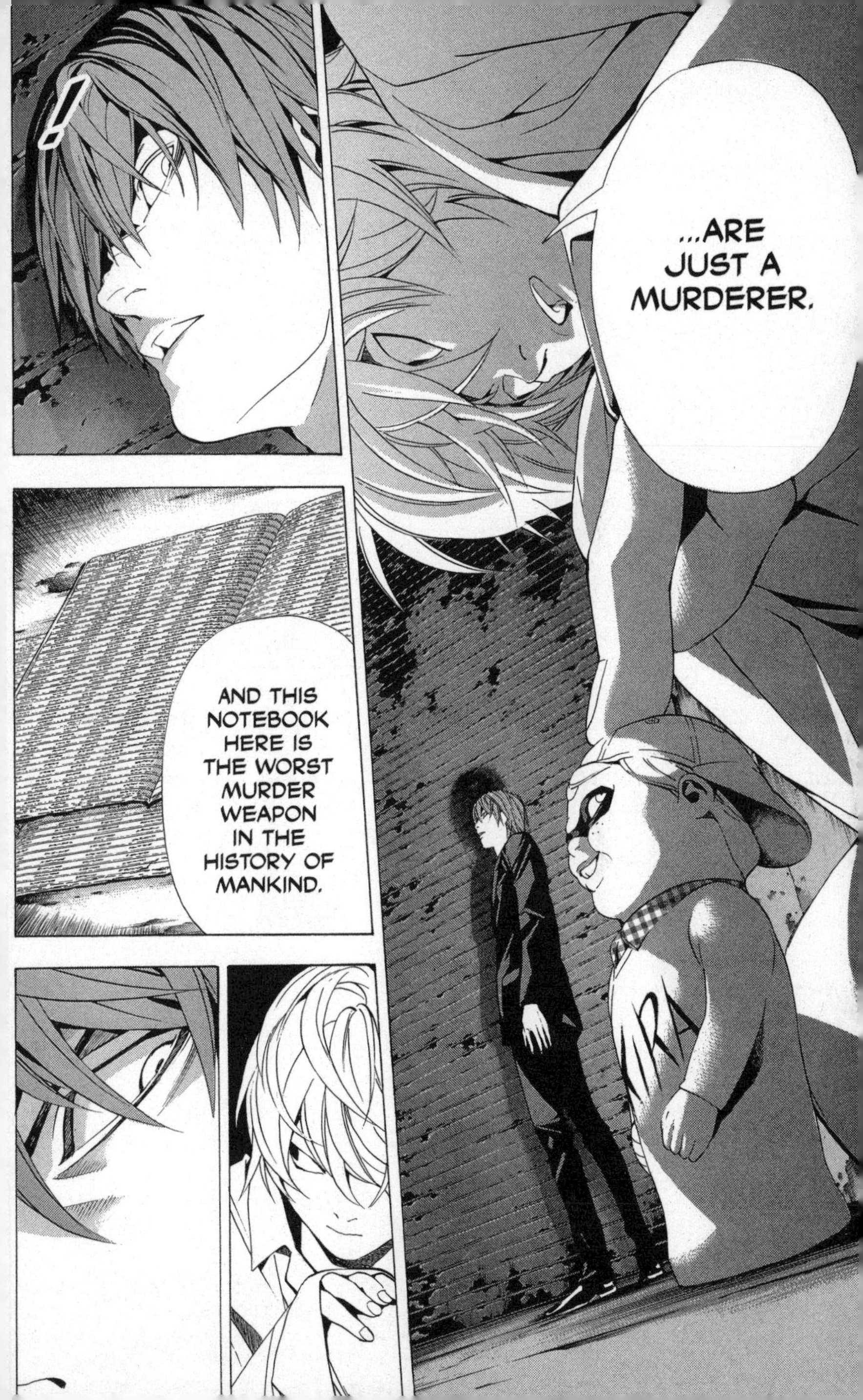
...ARE JUST A MURDERER.
!
AND THIS NOTEBOOK HERE IS THE WORST MURDER WEAPON IN THE HISTORY OF MANKIND.

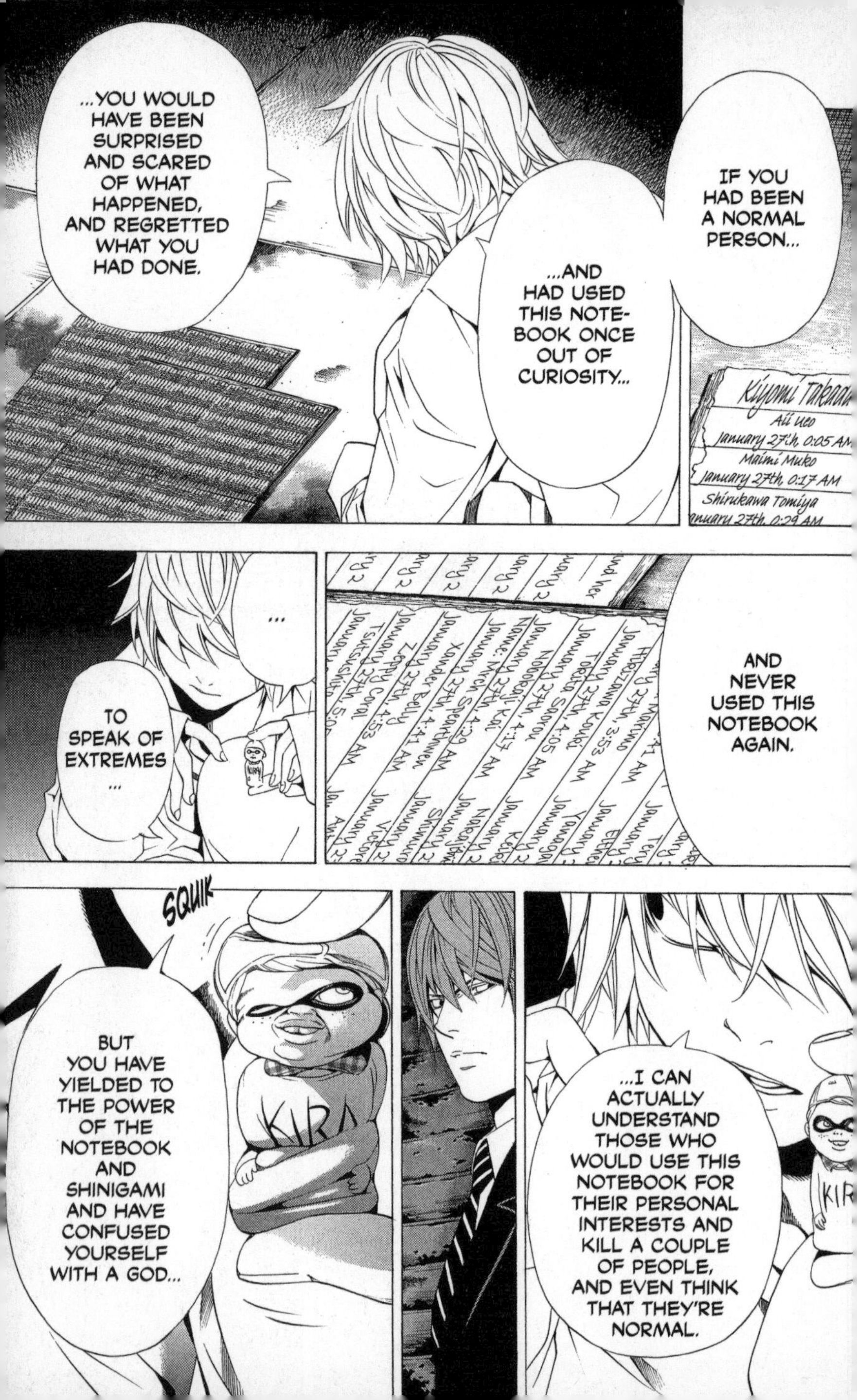
IF YOU HAD BEEN A NORMAL PERSON...
...AND HAD USED THIS NOTE-BOOK ONCE OUT OF CURIOSITY...
...YOU WOULD HAVE BEEN SURPRISED AND SCARED OF WHAT HAPPENED, AND REGRETTED WHAT YOU HAD DONE.
Aii uco
January 27th 0:05 AM
Maimi Muko
January 27th 0:17 AM
Shirukawa Tomiya
AND NEVER USED THIS NOTEBOOK AGAIN.
...
TO SPEAK OF EXTREMES ...
...I CAN ACTUALLY UNDERSTAND THOSE WHO WOULD USE THIS NOTEBOOK FOR THEIR PERSONAL INTERESTS AND KILL A COUPLE OF PEOPLE, AND EVEN THINK THAT THEY'RE NORMAL.
SQUIK
BUT YOU HAVE YIELDED TO THE POWER OF THE NOTEBOOK AND SHINIGAMI AND HAVE CONFUSED YOURSELF WITH A GOD...

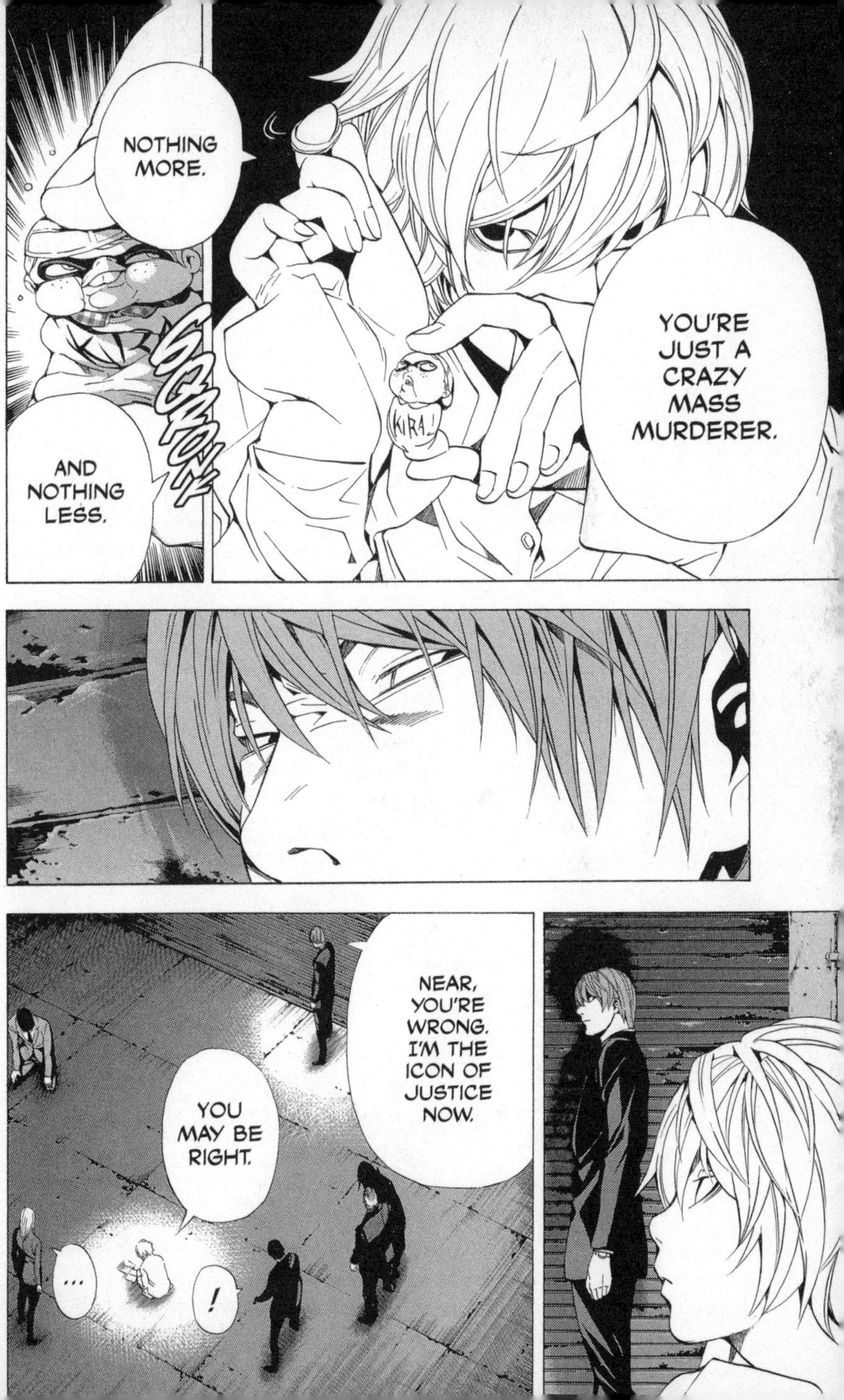
YOU'RE JUST A CRAZY MASS MURDERER.
KIRA!
NOTHING MORE.
AND NOTHING LESS.
NEAR, YOU'RE WRONG. I'M THE ICON OF JUSTICE NOW.
YOU MAY BE RIGHT.
!
...

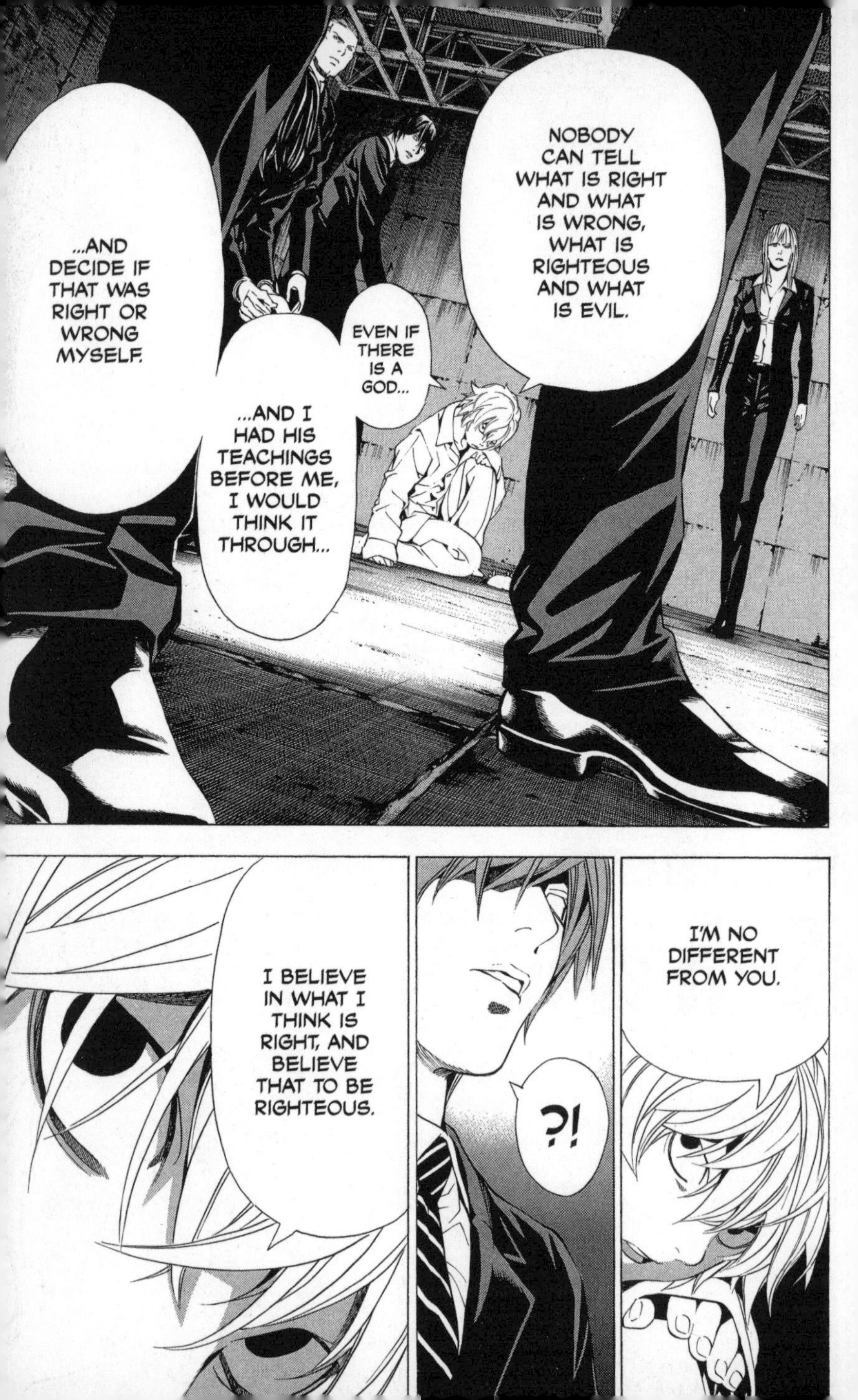
NOBODY CAN TELL WHAT IS RIGHT AND WHAT IS WRONG, WHAT IS RIGHTEOUS AND WHAT IS EVIL.
EVEN IF THERE IS A GOD...
...AND I HAD HIS TEACHINGS BEFORE ME, I WOULD THINK IT THROUGH...
...AND DECIDE IF THAT WAS RIGHT OR WRONG MYSELF.
I'M NO DIFFERENT FROM YOU.
?!
I BELIEVE IN WHAT I THINK IS RIGHT, AND BELIEVE THAT TO BE RIGHTEOUS.

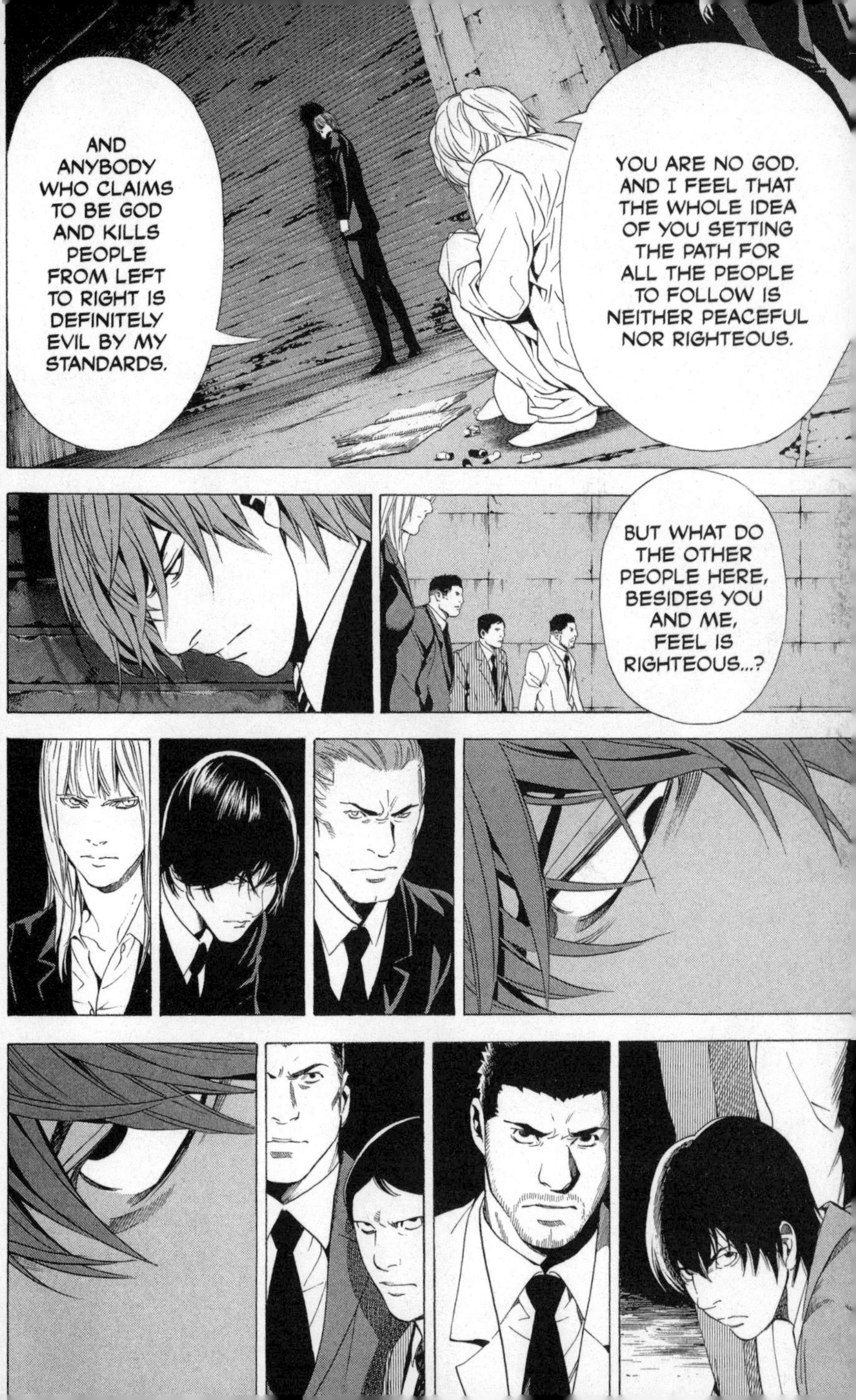
YOU ARE NO GOD. AND I FEEL THAT THE WHOLE IDEA OF YOU SETTING THE PATH FOR ALL THE PEOPLE TO FOLLOW IS NEITHER PEACEFUL NOR RIGHTEOUS.
AND ANYBODY WHO CLAIMS TO BE GOD AND KILLS PEOPLE FROM LEFT TO RIGHT IS DEFINITELY EVIL BY MY STANDARDS.
BUT WHAT DO THE OTHER PEOPLE HERE, BESIDES YOU AND ME, FEEL IS RIGHTEOUS...?

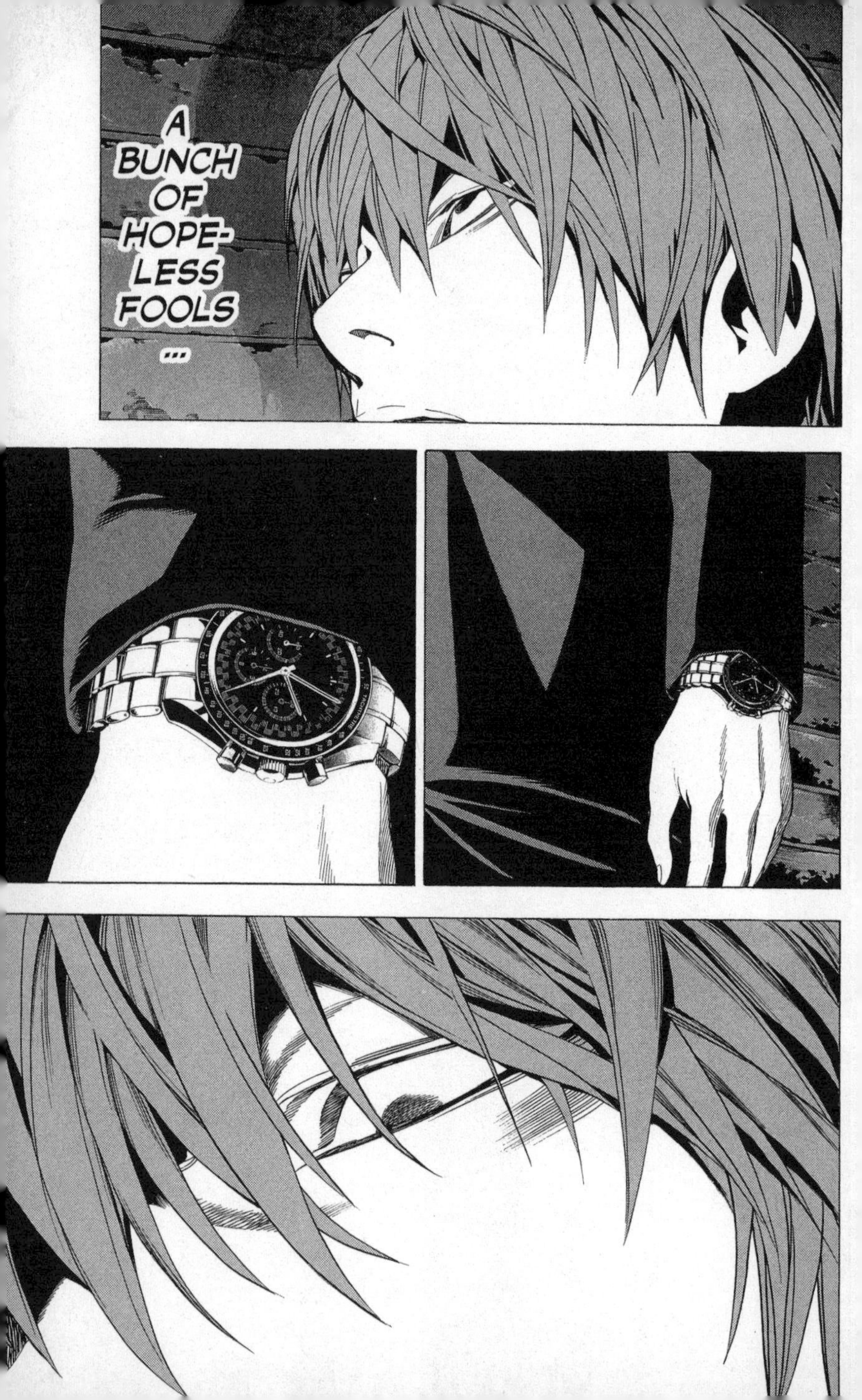
A BUNCH OF HOPE-LESS FOOLS ...

chapter 106 Intent to Kill

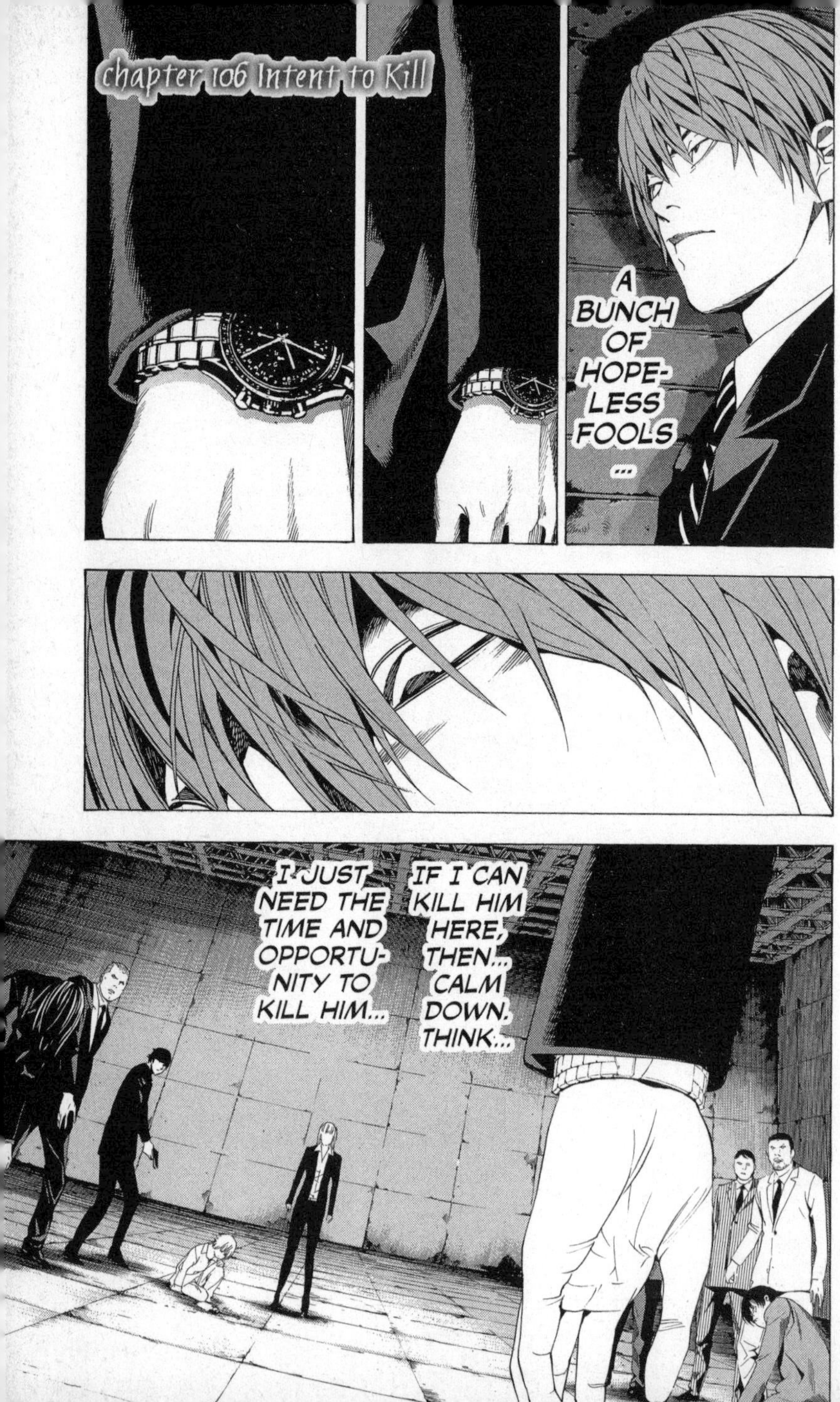
A BUNCH OF HOPELESS FOOLS ...
IF I CAN KILL HIM HERE, THEN... CALM DOWN. THINK...
I JUST NEED THE TIME AND OPPORTUNITY TO KILL HIM...

chapter 106 Intent to Kill

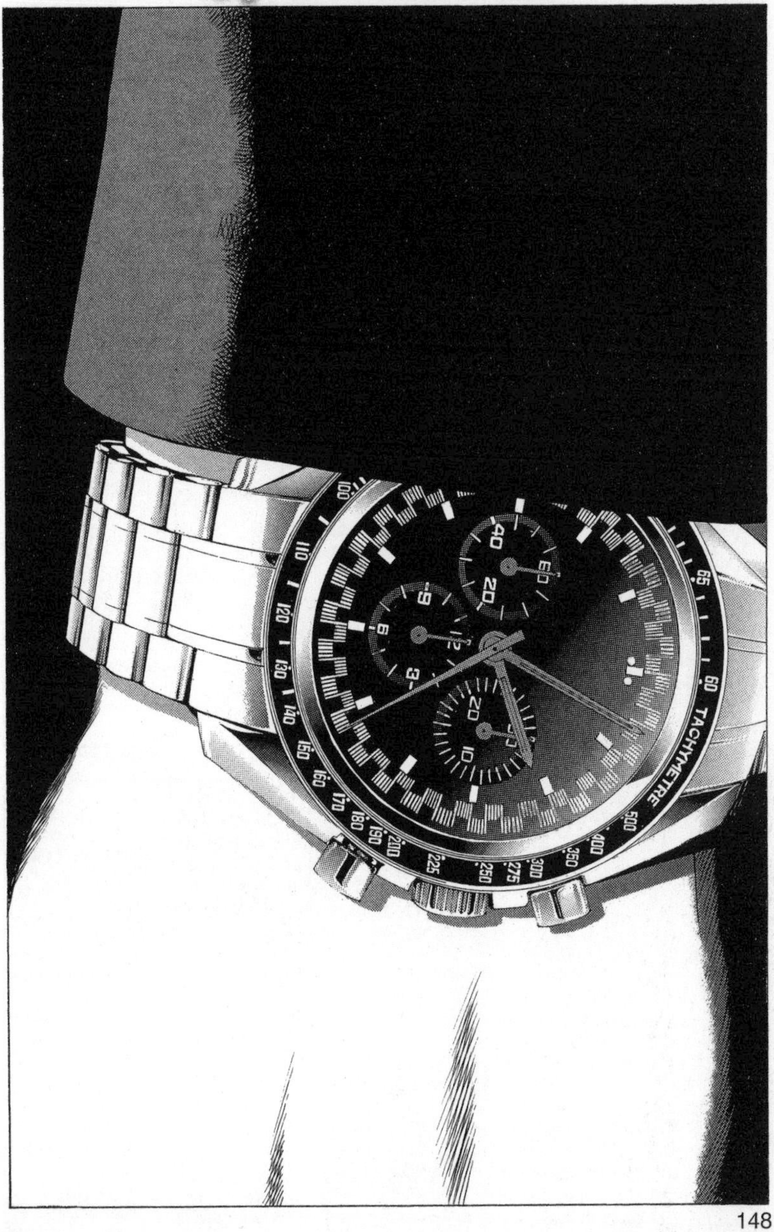
TACHYMETRE

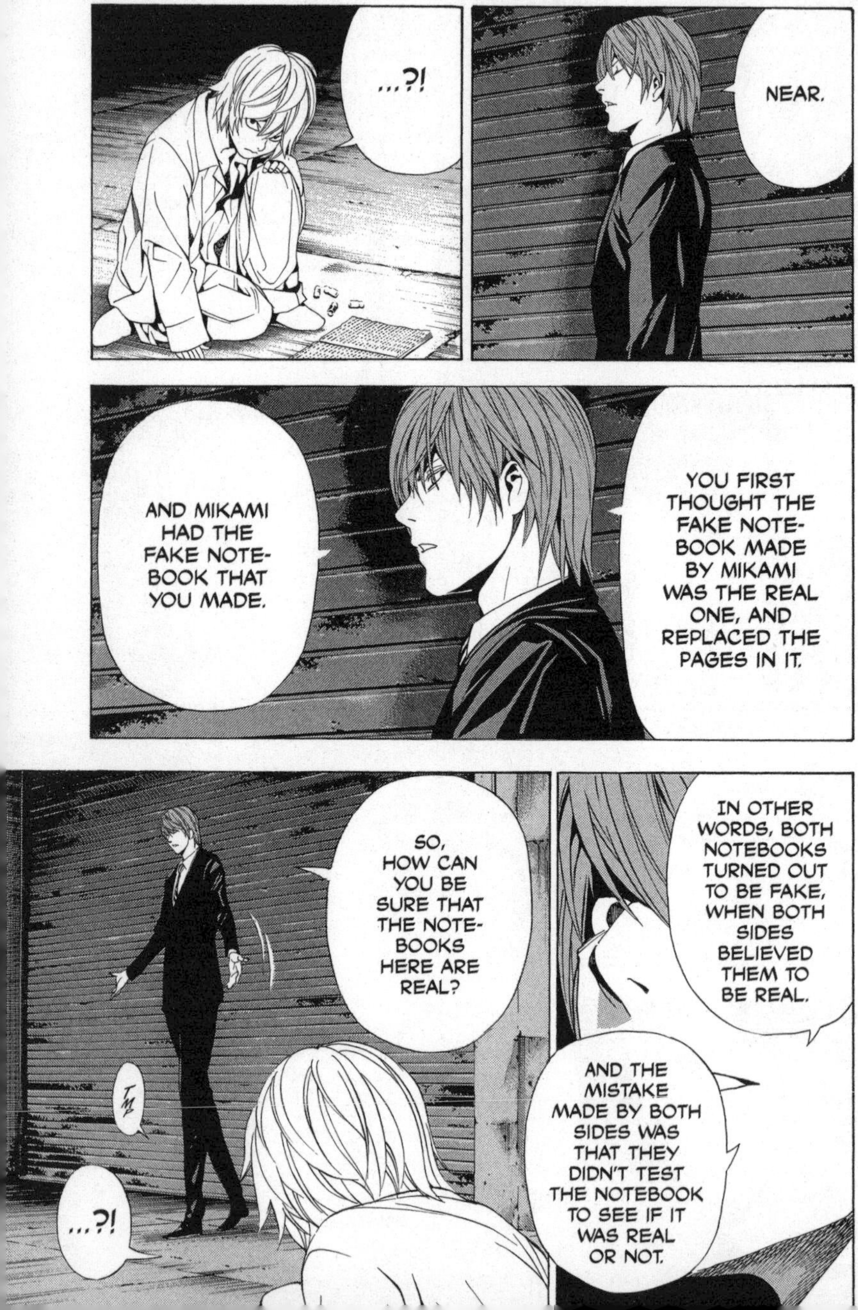
NEAR.
...?!
YOU FIRST THOUGHT THE FAKE NOTE-BOOK MADE BY MIKAMI WAS THE REAL ONE, AND REPLACED THE PAGES IN IT.
AND MIKAMI HAD THE FAKE NOTE-BOOK THAT YOU MADE.
IN OTHER WORDS, BOTH NOTEBOOKS TURNED OUT TO BE FAKE, WHEN BOTH SIDES BELIEVED THEM TO BE REAL.
AND THE MISTAKE MADE BY BOTH SIDES WAS THAT THEY DIDN'T TEST THE NOTEBOOK TO SEE IF IT WAS REAL OR NOT.
SO, HOW CAN YOU BE SURE THAT THE NOTE-BOOKS HERE ARE REAL?
TMP
...?!

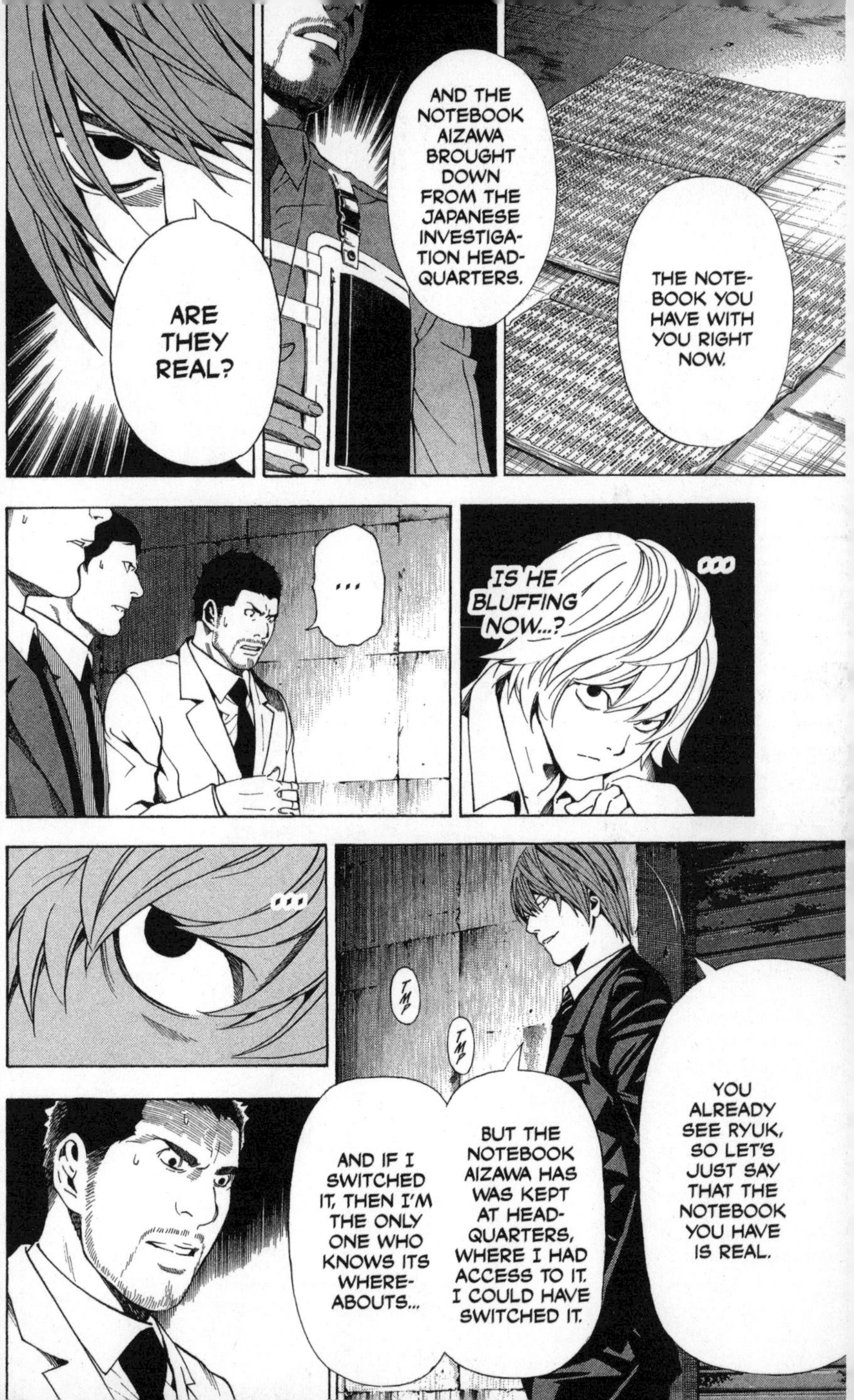
THE NOTEBOOK YOU HAVE WITH YOU RIGHT NOW.
AND THE NOTEBOOK AIZAWA BROUGHT DOWN FROM THE JAPANESE INVESTIGATION HEADQUARTERS.
ARE THEY REAL?
IS HE BLUFFING NOW...?
...
...
TMP
TMP
YOU ALREADY SEE RYUK, SO LET'S JUST SAY THAT THE NOTEBOOK YOU HAVE IS REAL.
BUT THE NOTEBOOK AIZAWA HAS WAS KEPT AT HEADQUARTERS, WHERE I HAD ACCESS TO IT. I COULD HAVE SWITCHED IT.
AND IF I SWITCHED IT, THEN I'M THE ONLY ONE WHO KNOWS ITS WHEREABOUTS...
...

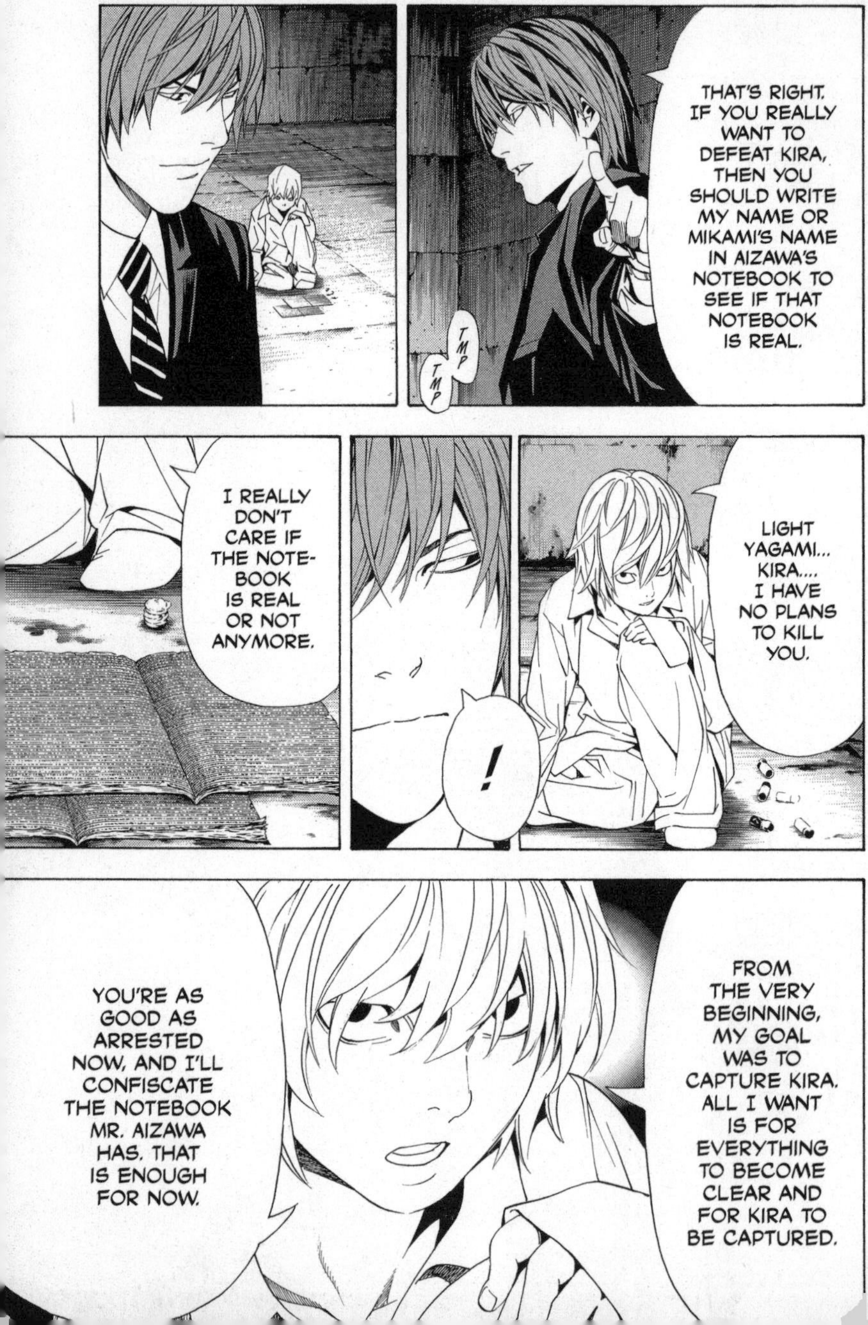
THAT'S RIGHT. IF YOU REALLY WANT TO DEFEAT KIRA, THEN YOU SHOULD WRITE MY NAME OR MIKAMI'S NAME IN AIZAWA'S NOTEBOOK TO SEE IF THAT NOTEBOOK IS REAL.
TMP TMP
LIGHT YAGAMI... KIRA.... I HAVE NO PLANS TO KILL YOU.
!
I REALLY DON'T CARE IF THE NOTE-BOOK IS REAL OR NOT ANYMORE.
FROM THE VERY BEGINNING, MY GOAL WAS TO CAPTURE KIRA. ALL I WANT IS FOR EVERYTHING TO BECOME CLEAR AND FOR KIRA TO BE CAPTURED.
YOU'RE AS GOOD AS ARRESTED NOW, AND I'LL CONFISCATE THE NOTEBOOK MR. AIZAWA HAS. THAT IS ENOUGH FOR NOW.

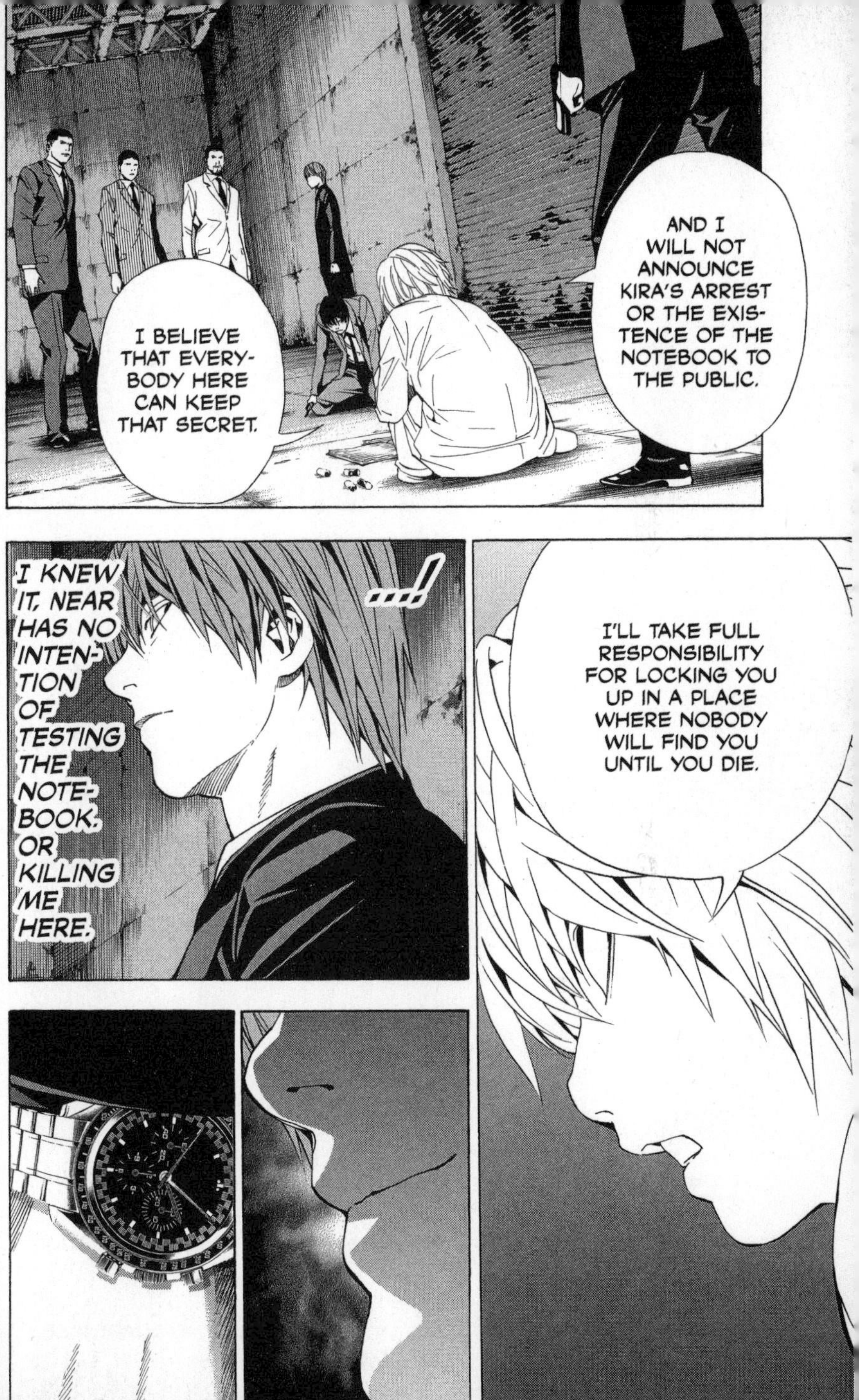
AND I WILL NOT ANNOUNCE KIRA'S ARREST OR THE EXISTENCE OF THE NOTEBOOK TO THE PUBLIC.
I BELIEVE THAT EVERYBODY HERE CAN KEEP THAT SECRET.
I'LL TAKE FULL RESPONSIBILITY FOR LOCKING YOU UP IN A PLACE WHERE NOBODY WILL FIND YOU UNTIL YOU DIE.
...!
I KNEW IT, NEAR HAS NO INTENTION OF TESTING THE NOTEBOOK. OR KILLING ME HERE.

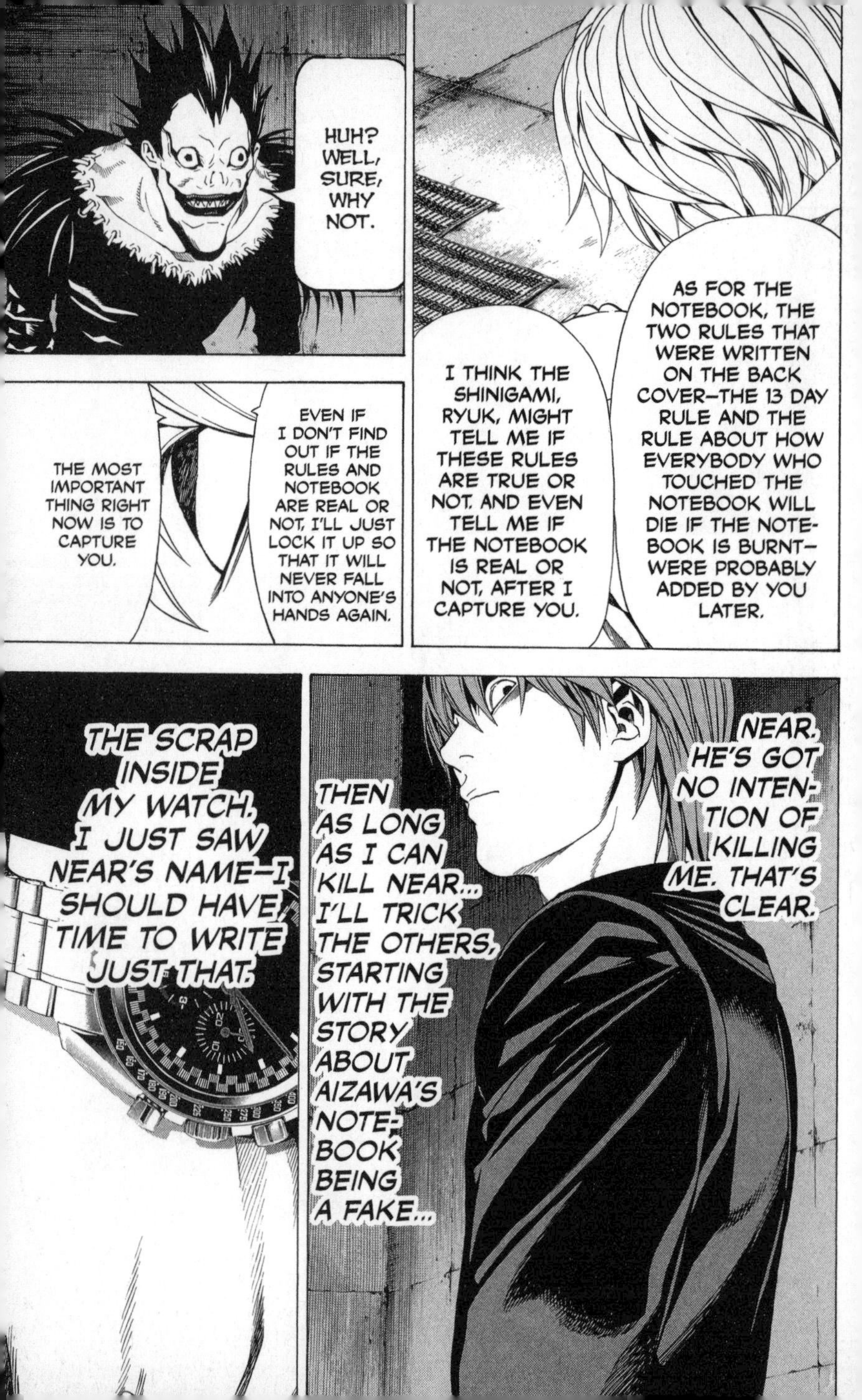
AS FOR THE NOTEBOOK, THE TWO RULES THAT WERE WRITTEN ON THE BACK COVER—THE 13 DAY RULE AND THE RULE ABOUT HOW EVERYBODY WHO TOUCHED THE NOTEBOOK WILL DIE IF THE NOTE-BOOK IS BURNT—WERE PROBABLY ADDED BY YOU LATER.
I THINK THE SHINIGAMI, RYUK, MIGHT TELL ME IF THESE RULES ARE TRUE OR NOT. AND EVEN TELL ME IF THE NOTEBOOK IS REAL OR NOT, AFTER I CAPTURE YOU.
HUH? WELL, SURE, WHY NOT.
EVEN IF I DON'T FIND OUT IF THE RULES AND NOTEBOOK ARE REAL OR NOT, I'LL JUST LOCK IT UP SO THAT IT WILL NEVER FALL INTO ANYONE'S HANDS AGAIN.
THE MOST IMPORTANT THING RIGHT NOW IS TO CAPTURE YOU.
NEAR. HE'S GOT NO INTEN-TION OF KILLING ME. THAT'S CLEAR.
THEN AS LONG AS I CAN KILL NEAR... I'LL TRICK THE OTHERS, STARTING WITH THE STORY ABOUT AIZAWA'S NOTE-BOOK BEING A FAKE...
THE SCRAP INSIDE MY WATCH. I JUST SAW NEAR'S NAME—I SHOULD HAVE TIME TO WRITE JUST THAT.

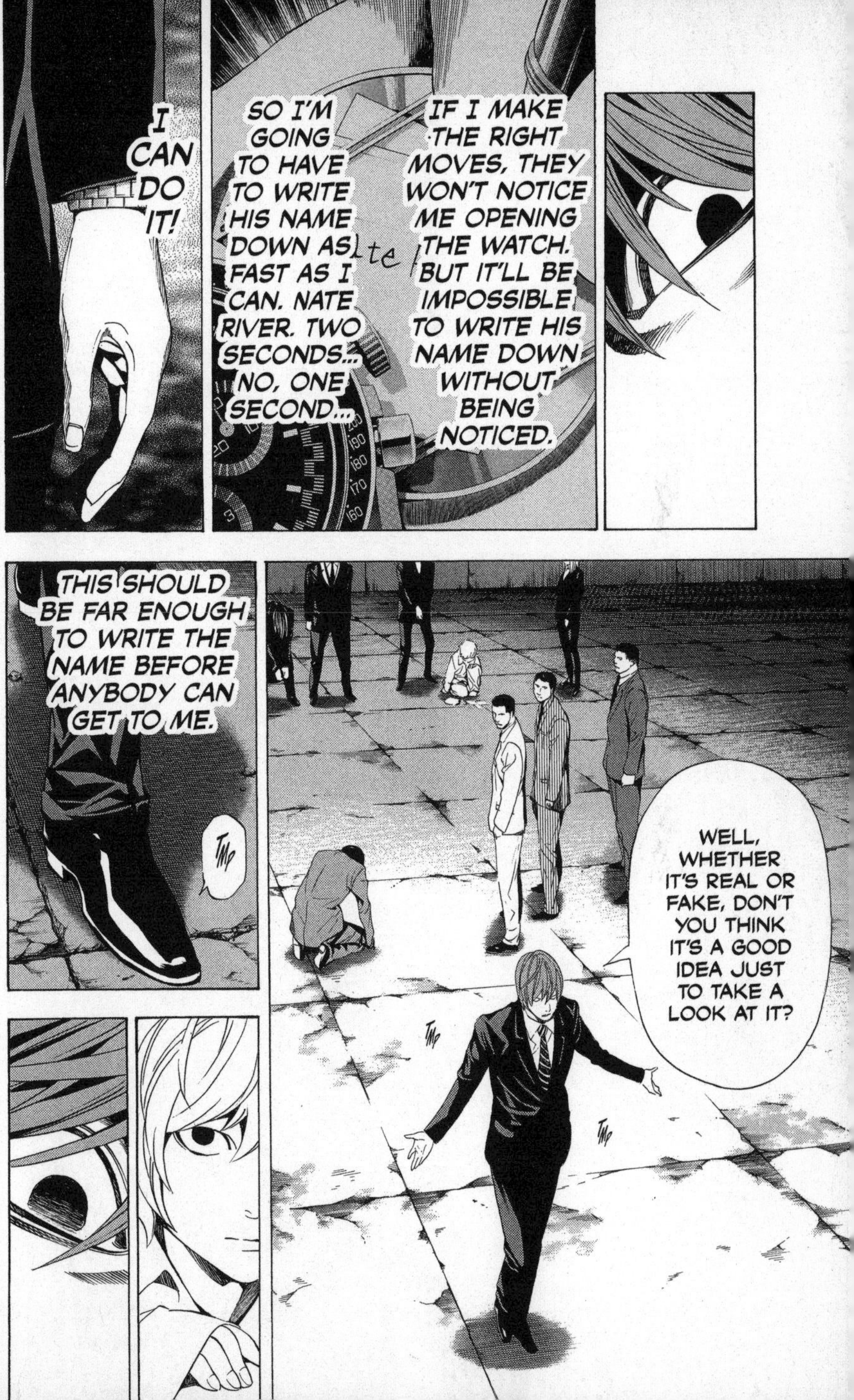
IF I MAKE THE RIGHT MOVES, THEY WON'T NOTICE ME OPENING THE WATCH. BUT IT'LL BE IMPOSSIBLE TO WRITE HIS NAME DOWN WITHOUT BEING NOTICED.
SO I'M GOING TO HAVE TO WRITE HIS NAME DOWN AS FAST AS I CAN. NATE RIVER. TWO SECONDS... NO, ONE SECOND...
I CAN DO IT!
WELL, WHETHER IT'S REAL OR FAKE, DON'T YOU THINK IT'S A GOOD IDEA JUST TO TAKE A LOOK AT IT?
TMP
TMP
THIS SHOULD BE FAR ENOUGH TO WRITE THE NAME BEFORE ANYBODY CAN GET TO ME.
TMP

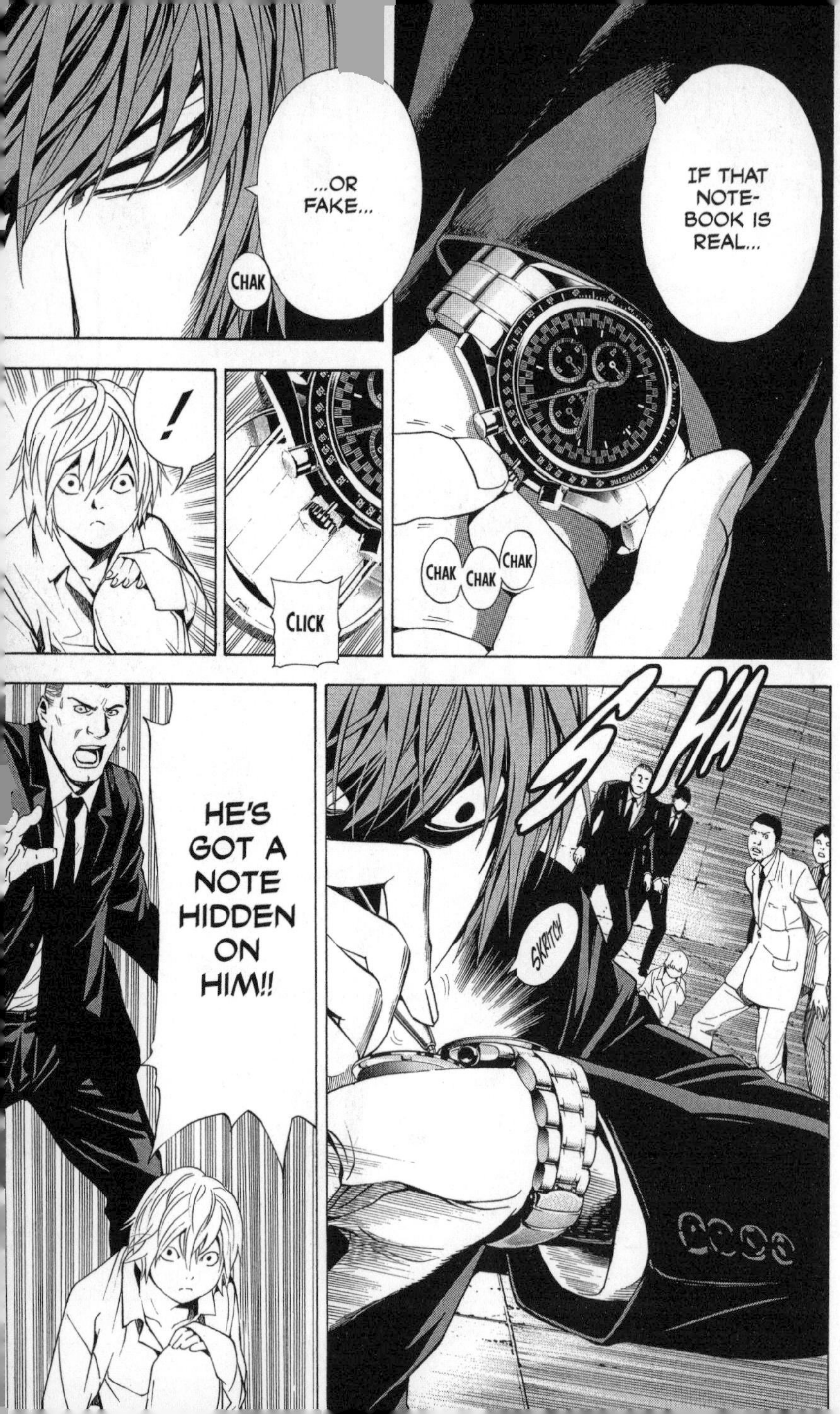
IF THAT NOTE-
BOOK IS REAL...
...OR FAKE...
CHAK
CHAK
CHAK
CHAK
CLICK
!
SHA
SKRITCH
HE'S GOT A NOTE HIDDEN ON HIM!!

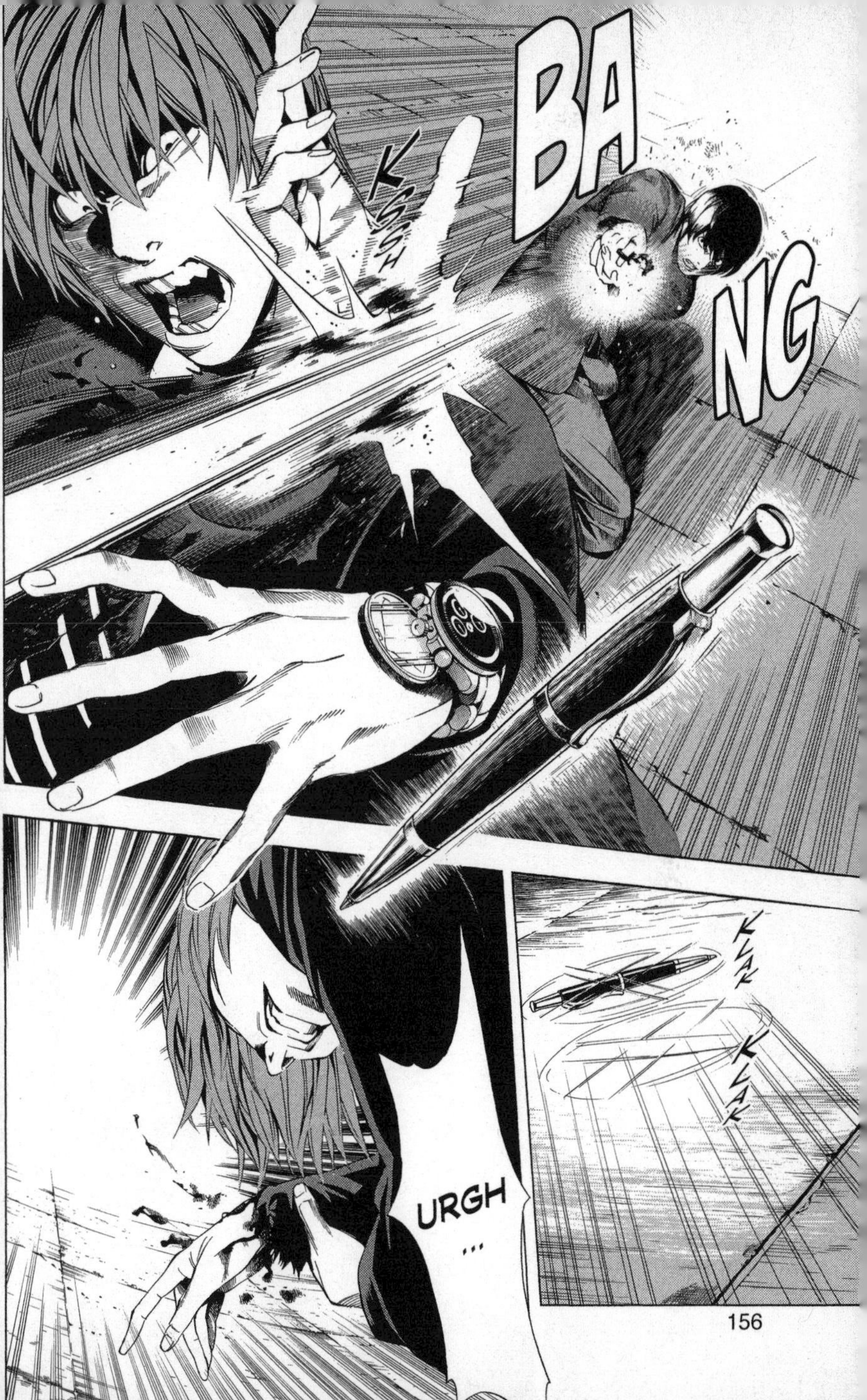
BANG
KSSH
KLAK
KLAK
URGH...

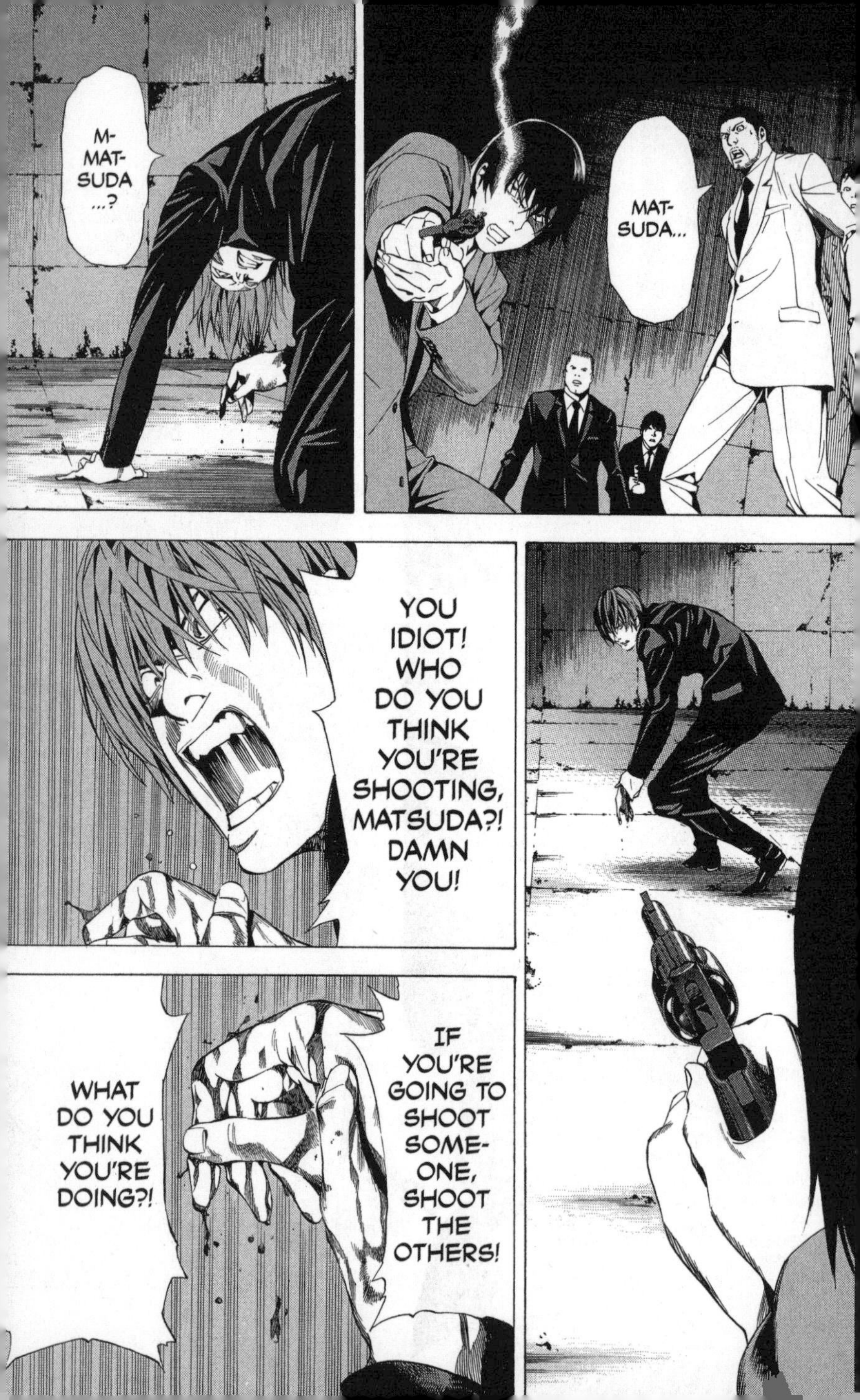
MAT-SUDA...
M-MAT-SUDA ...?
YOU IDIOT! WHO DO YOU THINK YOU'RE SHOOTING, MATSUDA?! DAMN YOU!
IF YOU'RE GOING TO SHOOT SOME-ONE, SHOOT THE OTHERS!
WHAT DO YOU THINK YOU'RE DOING?!

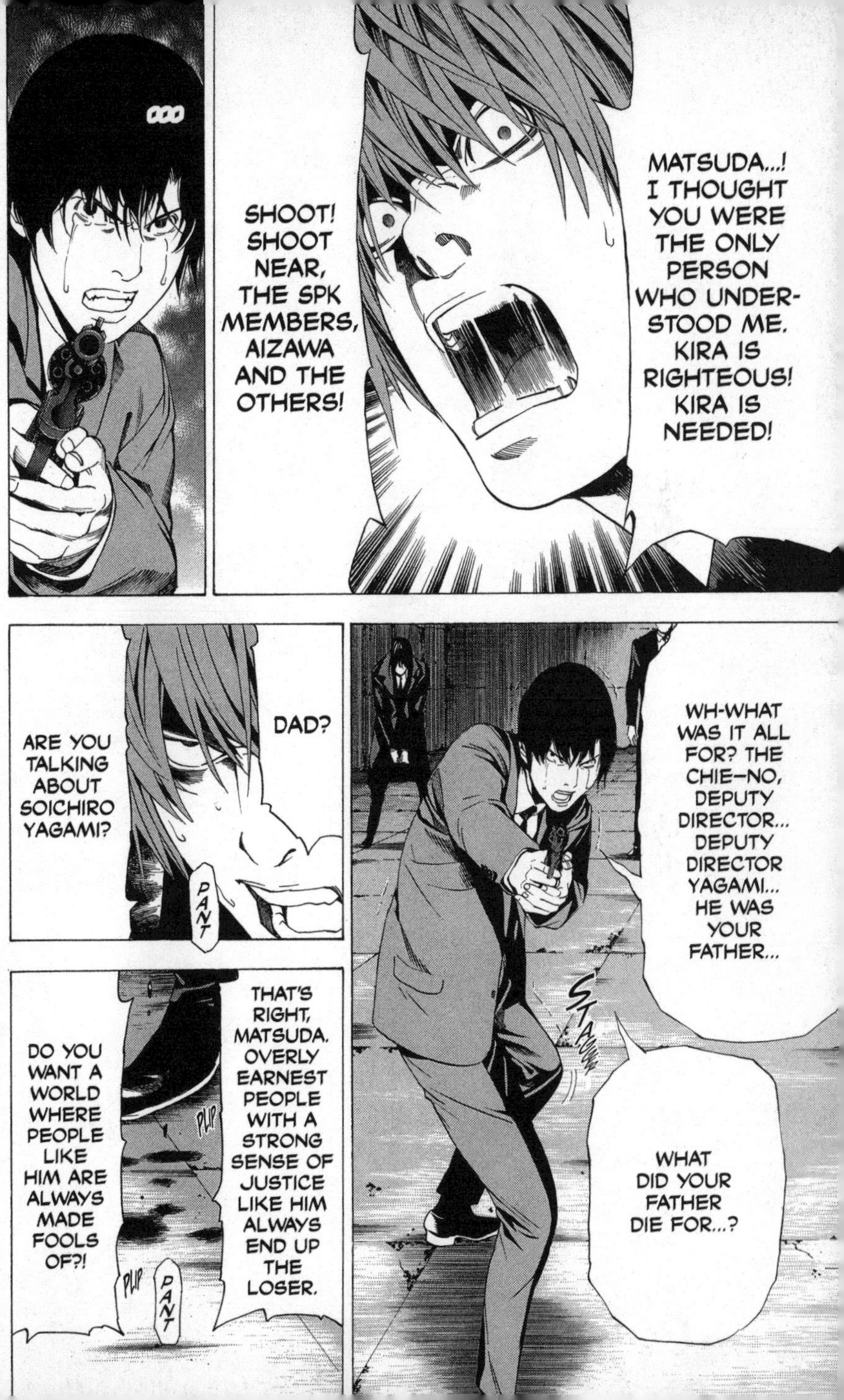
MATSUDA...! I THOUGHT YOU WERE THE ONLY PERSON WHO UNDER-STOOD ME. KIRA IS RIGHTEOUS! KIRA IS NEEDED!
SHOOT! SHOOT NEAR, THE SPK MEMBERS, AIZAWA AND THE OTHERS!
...
WH-WHAT WAS IT ALL FOR? THE CHIE–NO, DEPUTY DIRECTOR... DEPUTY DIRECTOR YAGAMI... HE WAS YOUR FATHER...
STACOOM
WHAT DID YOUR FATHER DIE FOR...?
DAD?
ARE YOU TALKING ABOUT SOICHIRO YAGAMI?
PANT PANT
THAT'S RIGHT, MATSUDA. OVERLY EARNEST PEOPLE WITH A STRONG SENSE OF JUSTICE LIKE HIM ALWAYS END UP THE LOSER.
DO YOU WANT A WORLD WHERE PEOPLE LIKE HIM ARE ALWAYS MADE FOOLS OF?!
PLIP
PLIP
PANT

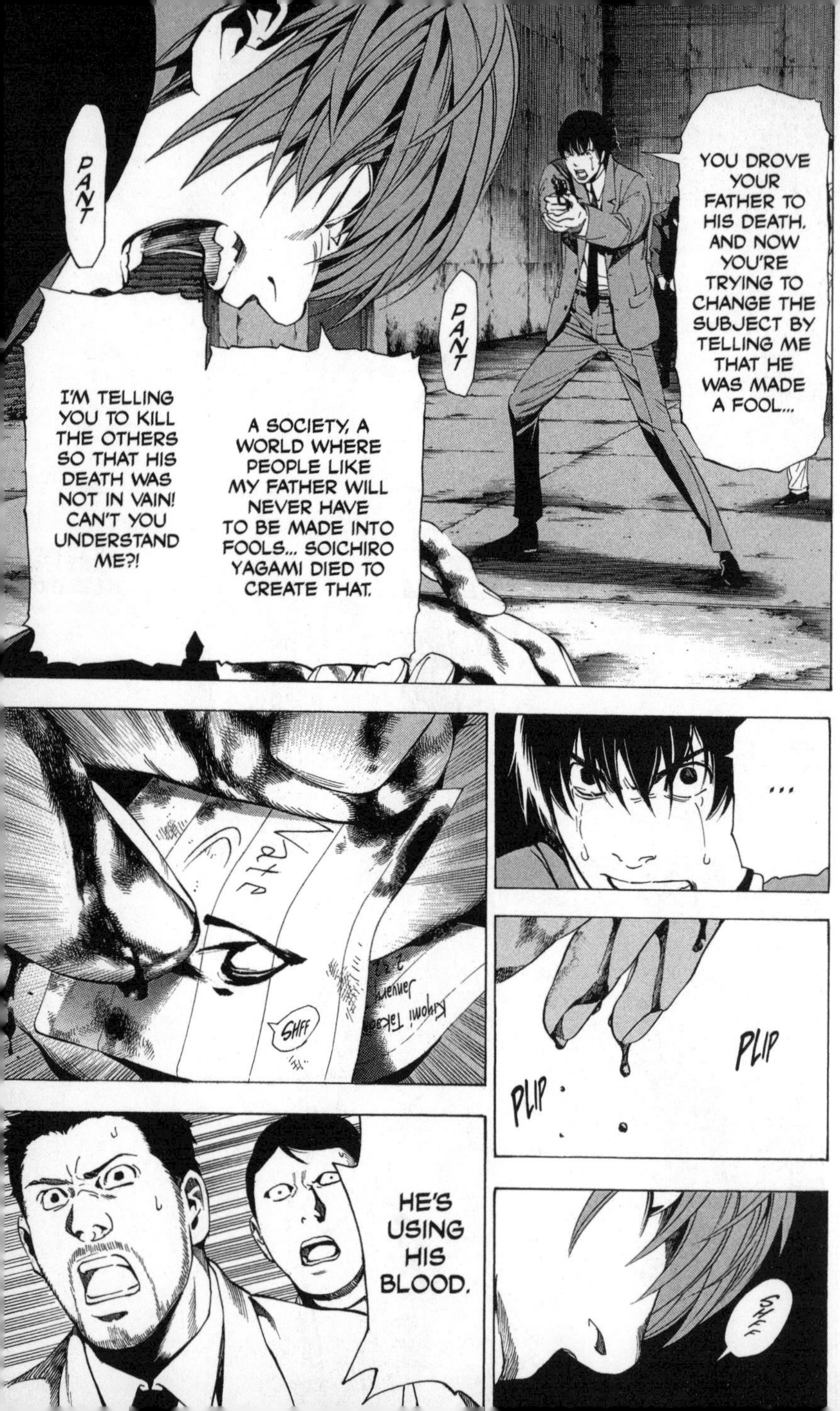

YOU DROVE YOUR FATHER TO HIS DEATH. AND NOW YOU'RE TRYING TO CHANGE THE SUBJECT BY TELLING ME THAT HE WAS MADE A FOOL...
PANT
A SOCIETY, A WORLD WHERE PEOPLE LIKE MY FATHER WILL NEVER HAVE TO BE MADE INTO FOOLS... SOICHIRO YAGAMI DIED TO CREATE THAT.
PANT
I'M TELLING YOU TO KILL THE OTHERS SO THAT HIS DEATH WAS NOT IN VAIN! CAN'T YOU UNDERSTAND ME?!
...
PLIP
PLIP
SHFF
SHFF
HE'S USING HIS BLOOD.

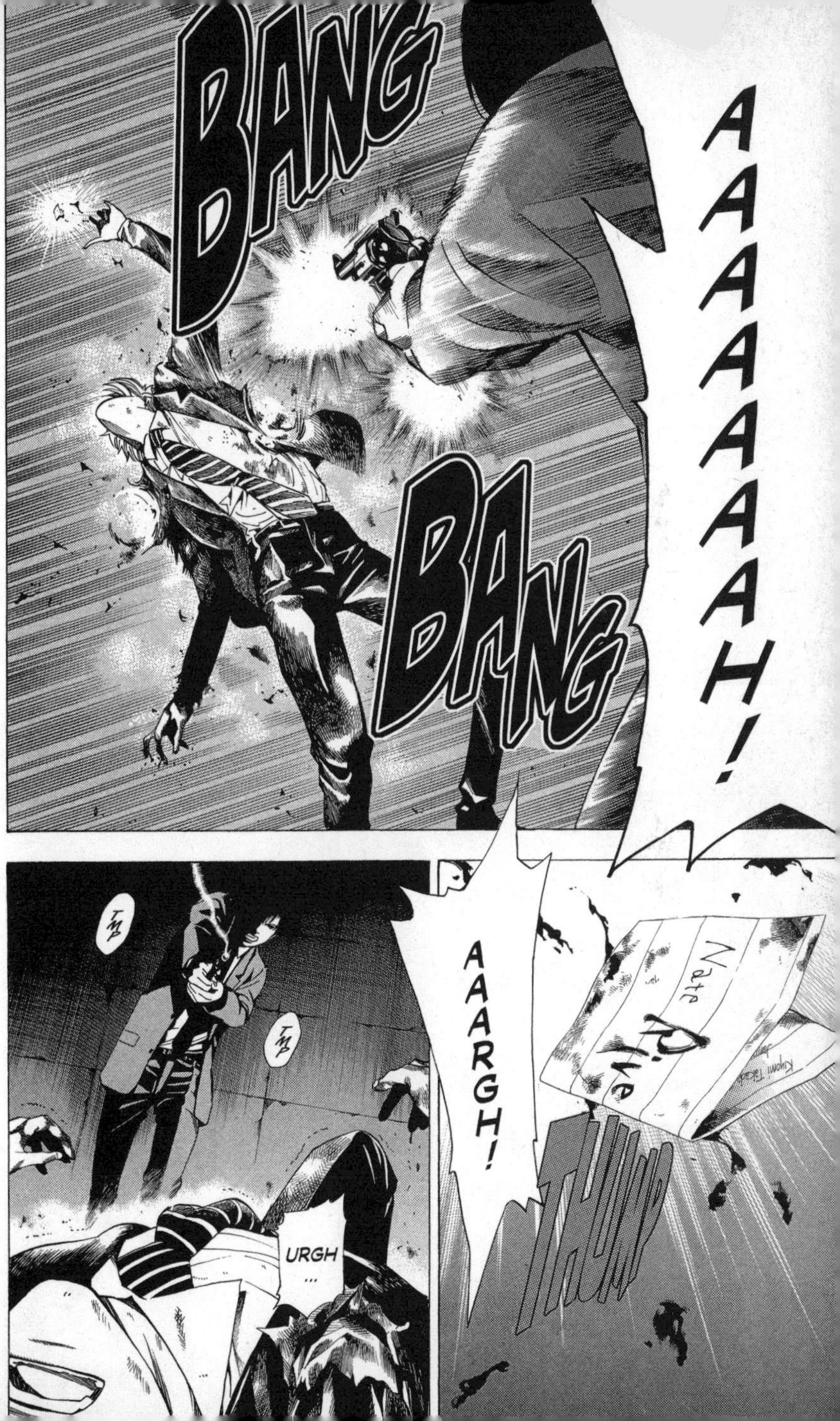
BANG
BANG
AAAAAAAAH!
AAAARGH!
THUD
TMP
TMP
URGH
...

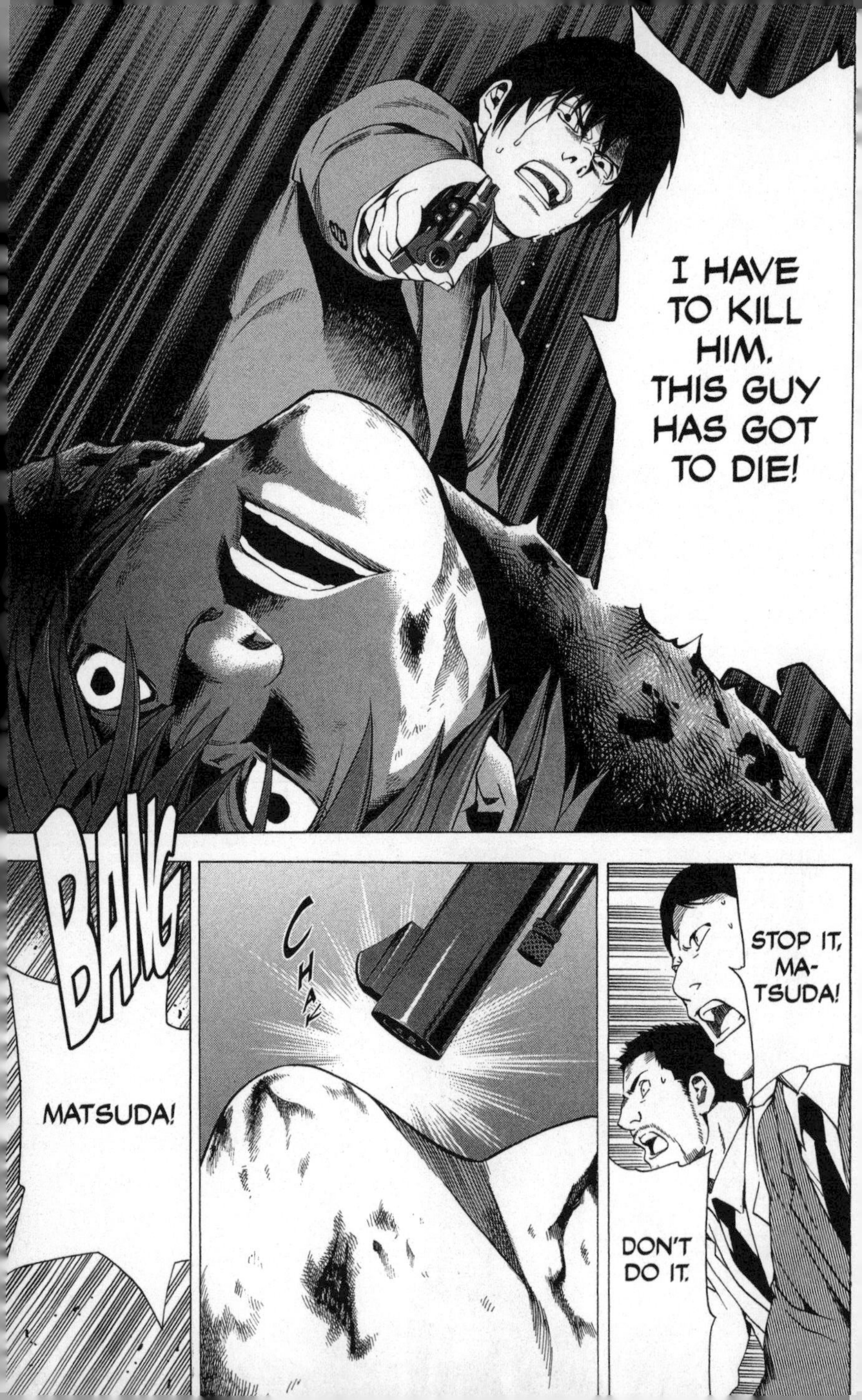
I HAVE TO KILL HIM. THIS GUY HAS GOT TO DIE!
STOP IT, MA-TSUDA!
DON'T DO IT.
CHAK
BANG
MATSUDA!

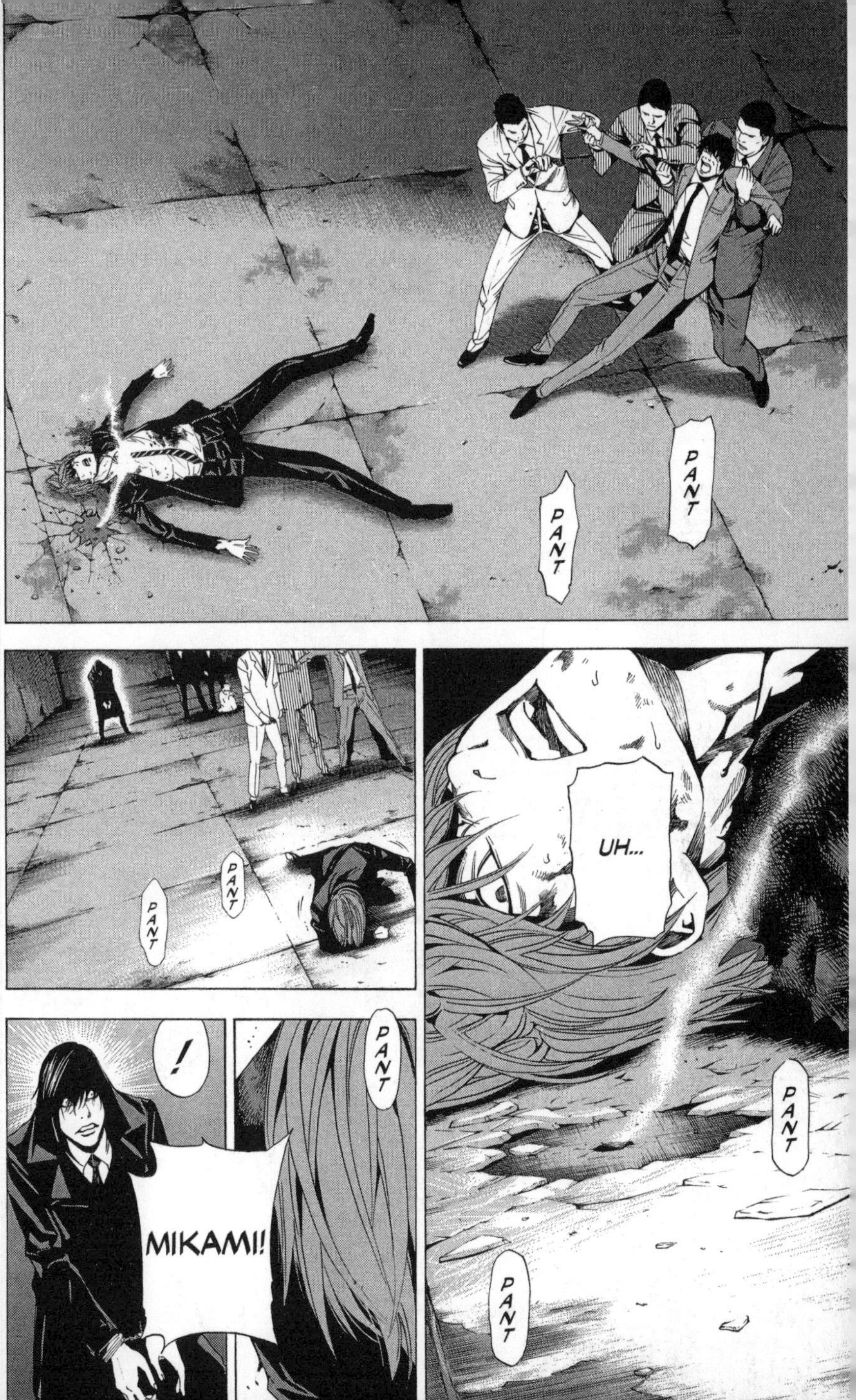
PANT
PANT
UH...
PANT
PANT
PANT
PANT
PANT
!
MIKAMI!

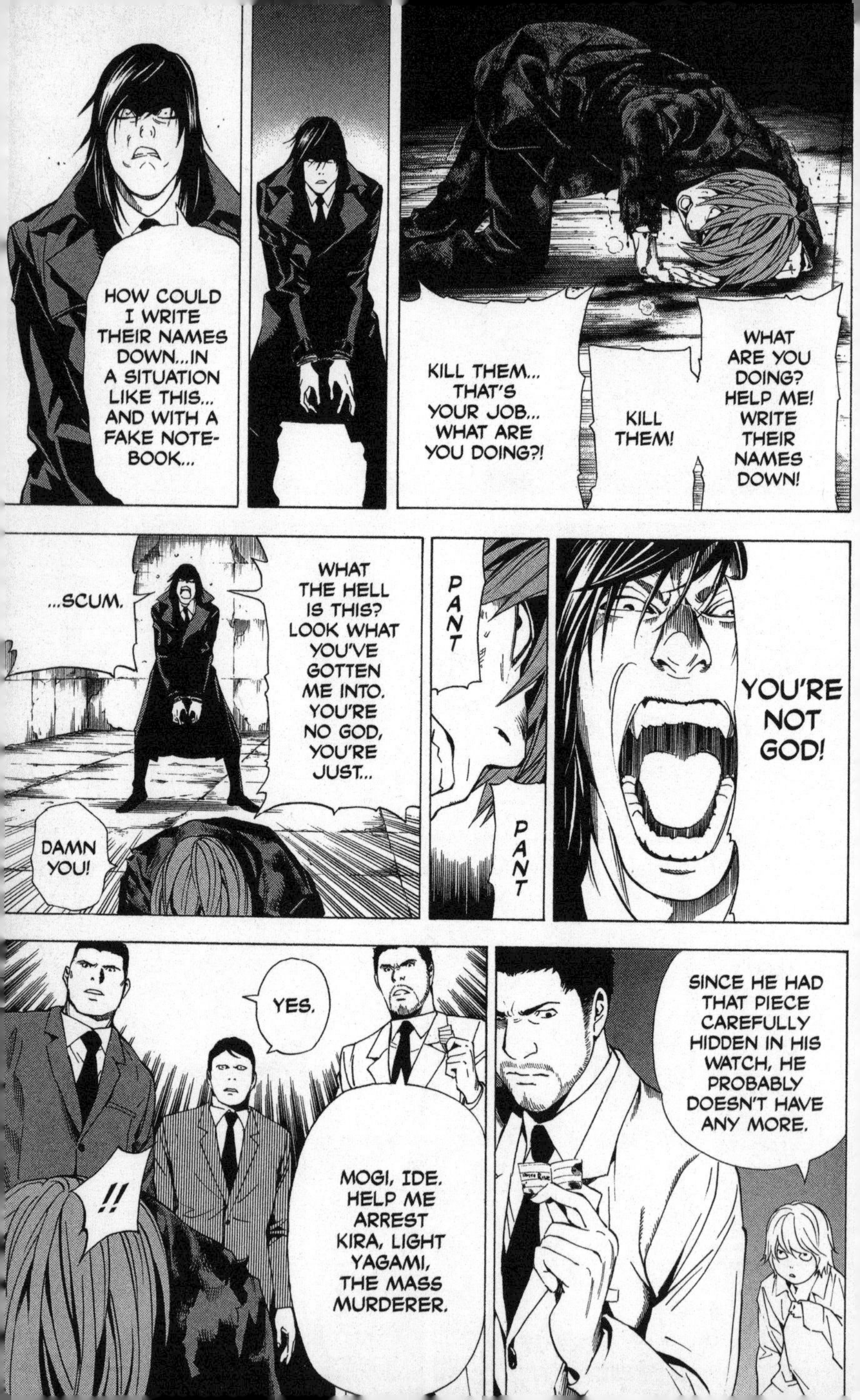
WHAT ARE YOU DOING? HELP ME! WRITE THEIR NAMES DOWN!
KILL THEM!
KILL THEM... THAT'S YOUR JOB... WHAT ARE YOU DOING?!
HOW COULD I WRITE THEIR NAMES DOWN...IN A SITUATION LIKE THIS... AND WITH A FAKE NOTE-BOOK...
YOU'RE NOT GOD!
PANT
PANT
WHAT THE HELL IS THIS? LOOK WHAT YOU'VE GOTTEN ME INTO. YOU'RE NO GOD, YOU'RE JUST...
...SCUM.
DAMN YOU!
SINCE HE HAD THAT PIECE CAREFULLY HIDDEN IN HIS WATCH, HE PROBABLY DOESN'T HAVE ANY MORE.
YES.
MOGI, IDE. HELP ME ARREST KIRA, LIGHT YAGAMI, THE MASS MURDERER.
!!

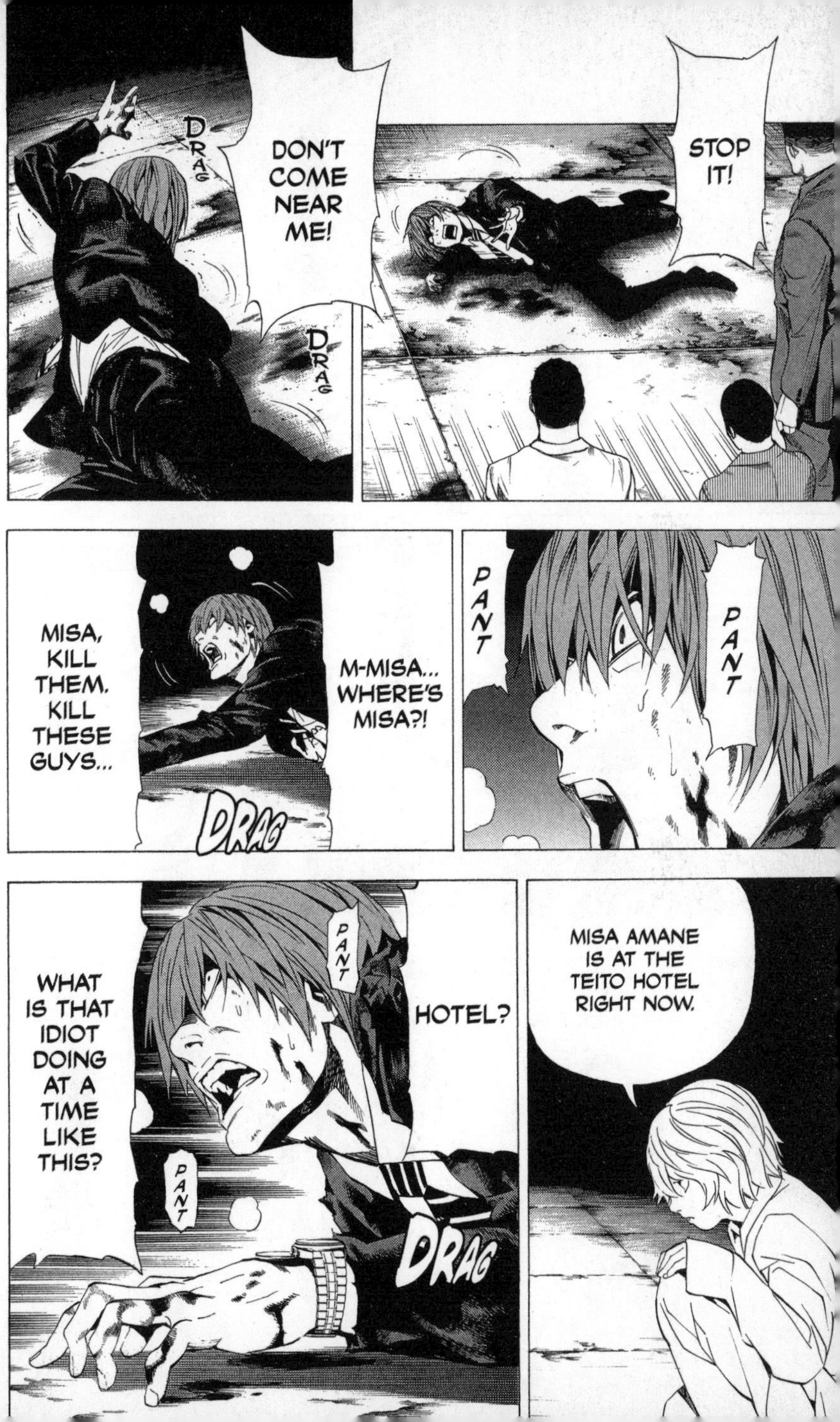
STOP IT!
DRAG
DON'T COME NEAR ME!
DRAG
PANT
PANT
M-MISA... WHERE'S MISA?!
MISA, KILL THEM. KILL THESE GUYS...
DRAG
MISA AMANE IS AT THE TEITO HOTEL RIGHT NOW.
HOTEL?
PANT
WHAT IS THAT IDIOT DOING AT A TIME LIKE THIS?
PANT
DRAG

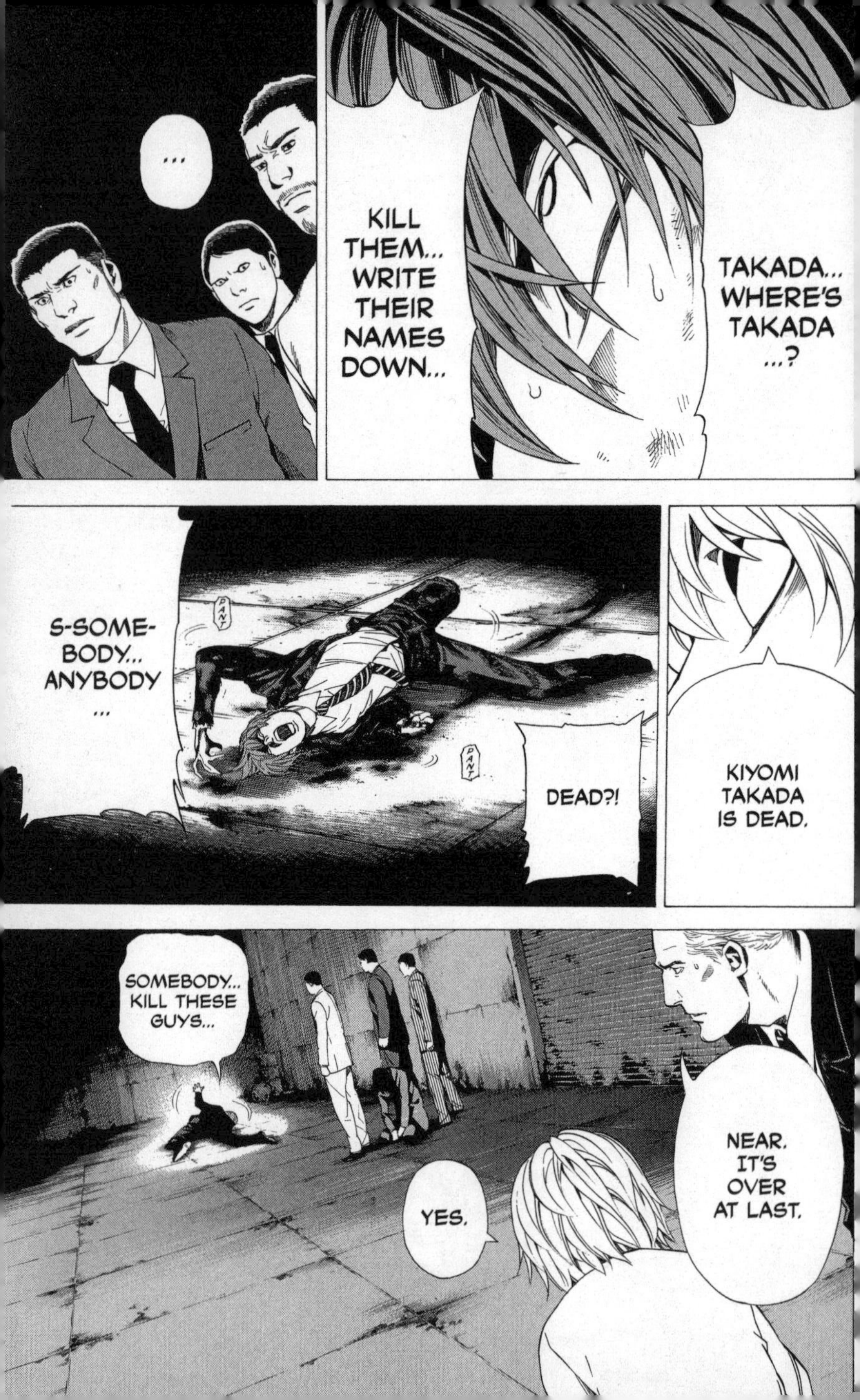
TAKADA... WHERE'S TAKADA ...?
KILL THEM... WRITE THEIR NAMES DOWN...
...
KIYOMI TAKADA IS DEAD.
DEAD?!
PANT
PANT
S-SOME-BODY... ANYBODY ...
NEAR. IT'S OVER AT LAST.
YES.
SOMEBODY... KILL THESE GUYS...

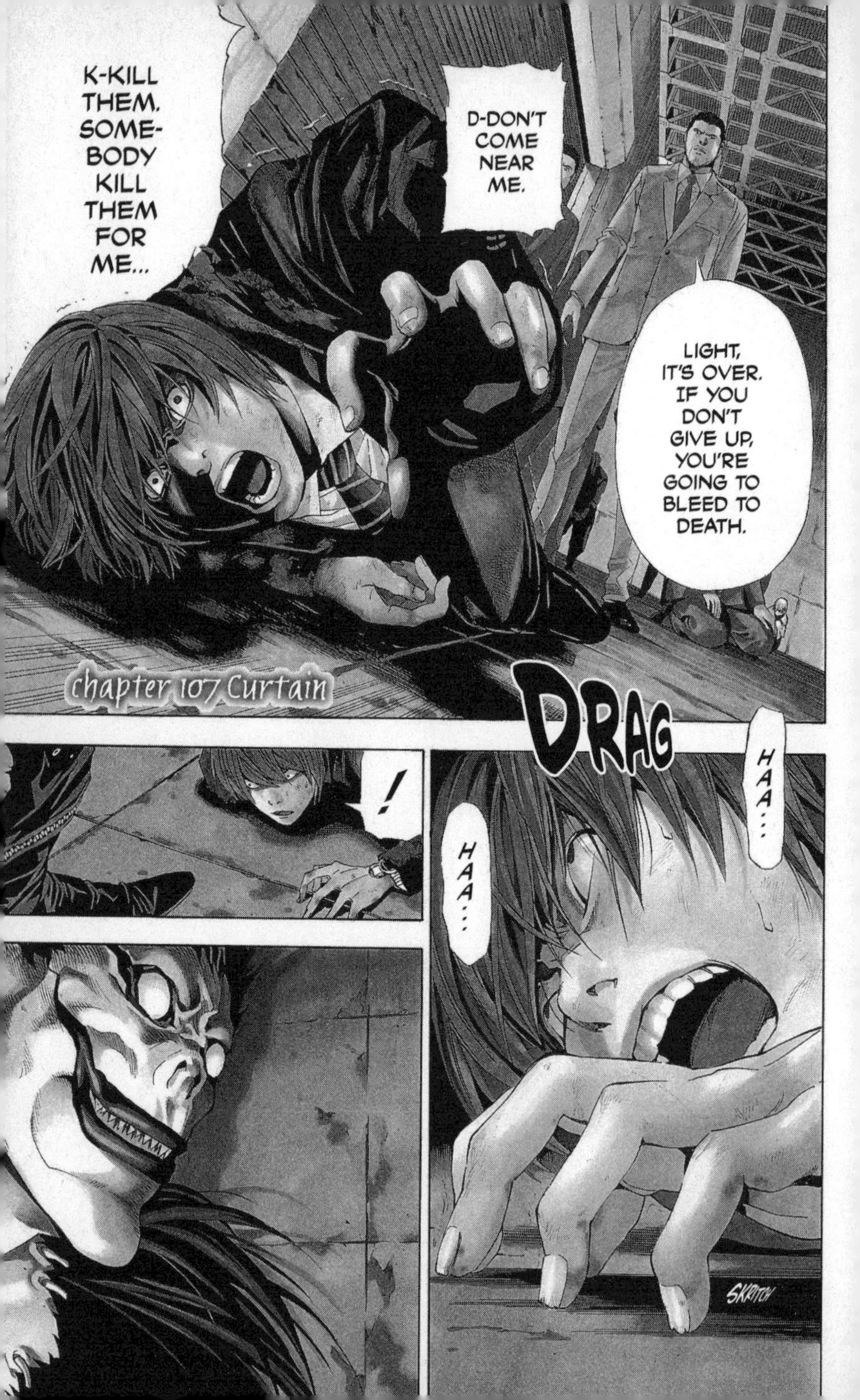
LIGHT, IT'S OVER. IF YOU DON'T GIVE UP, YOU'RE GOING TO BLEED TO DEATH.
D-DON'T COME NEAR ME.
K-KILL THEM. SOME-BODY KILL THEM FOR ME...
chapter 107 Curtain
DRAG
HAA...
HAA...
SKRITCH
!

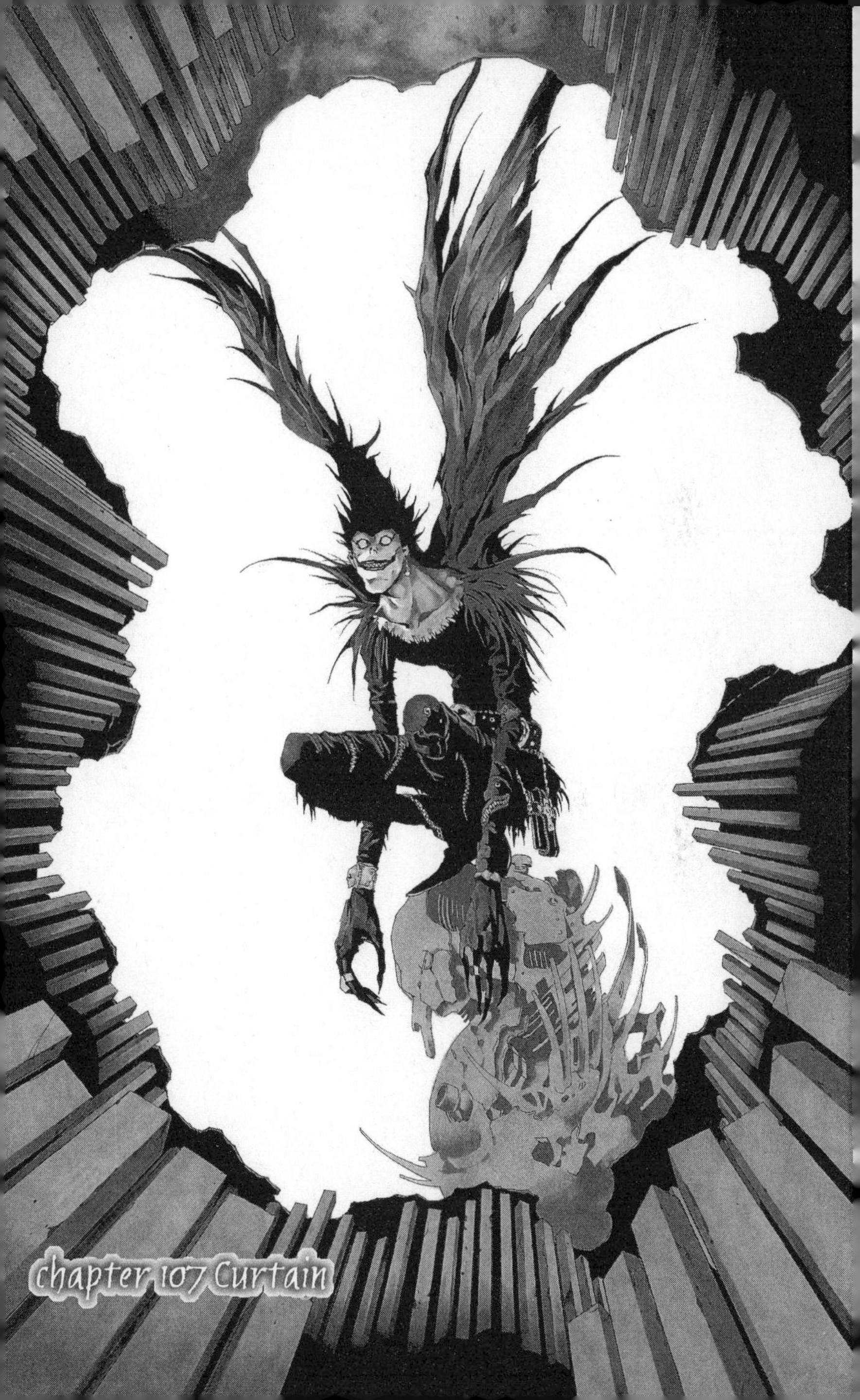
chapter 107 Curtain

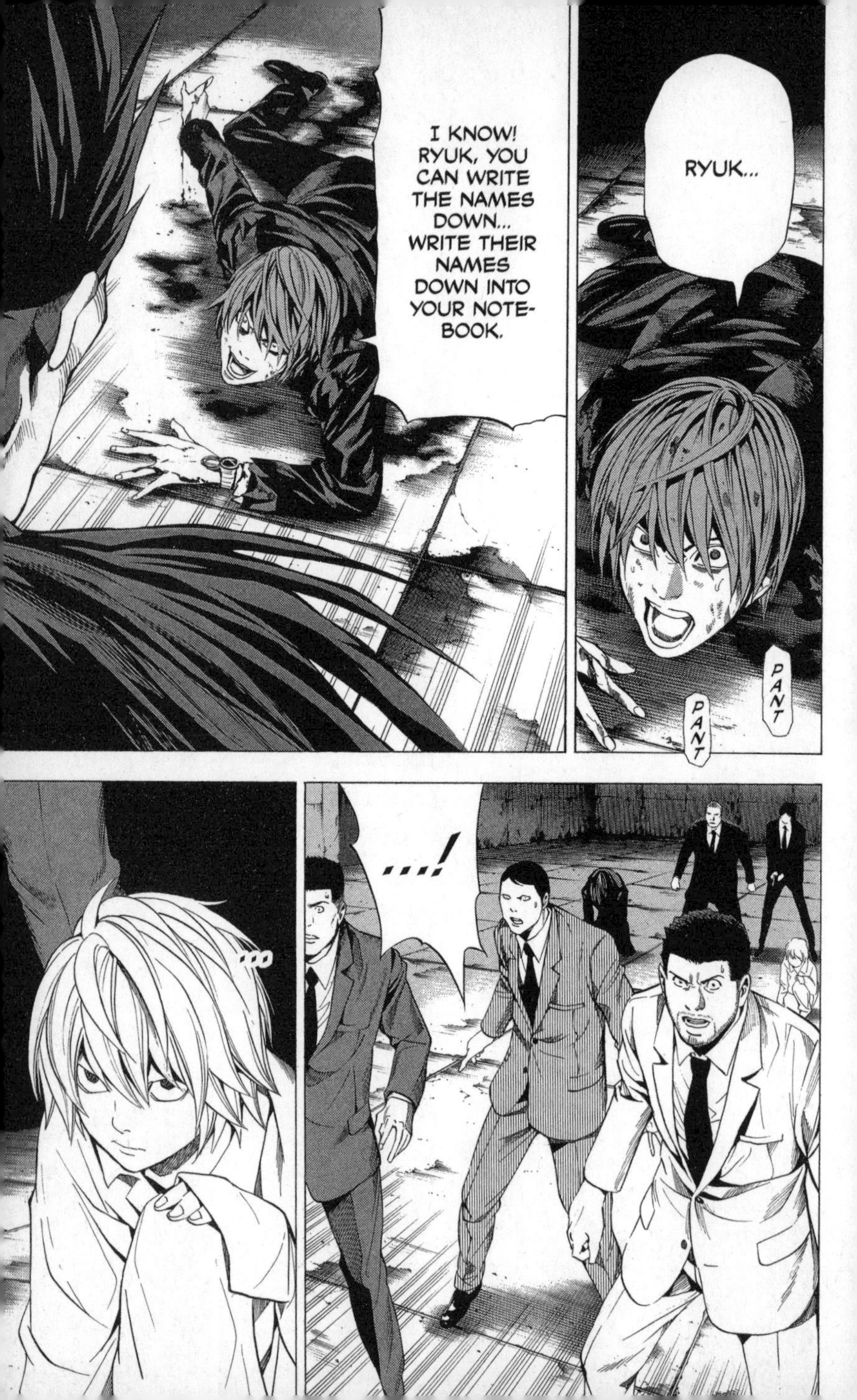
RYUK...
PANT
PANT
I KNOW! RYUK, YOU CAN WRITE THE NAMES DOWN... WRITE THEIR NAMES DOWN INTO YOUR NOTE-BOOK.
...!
...

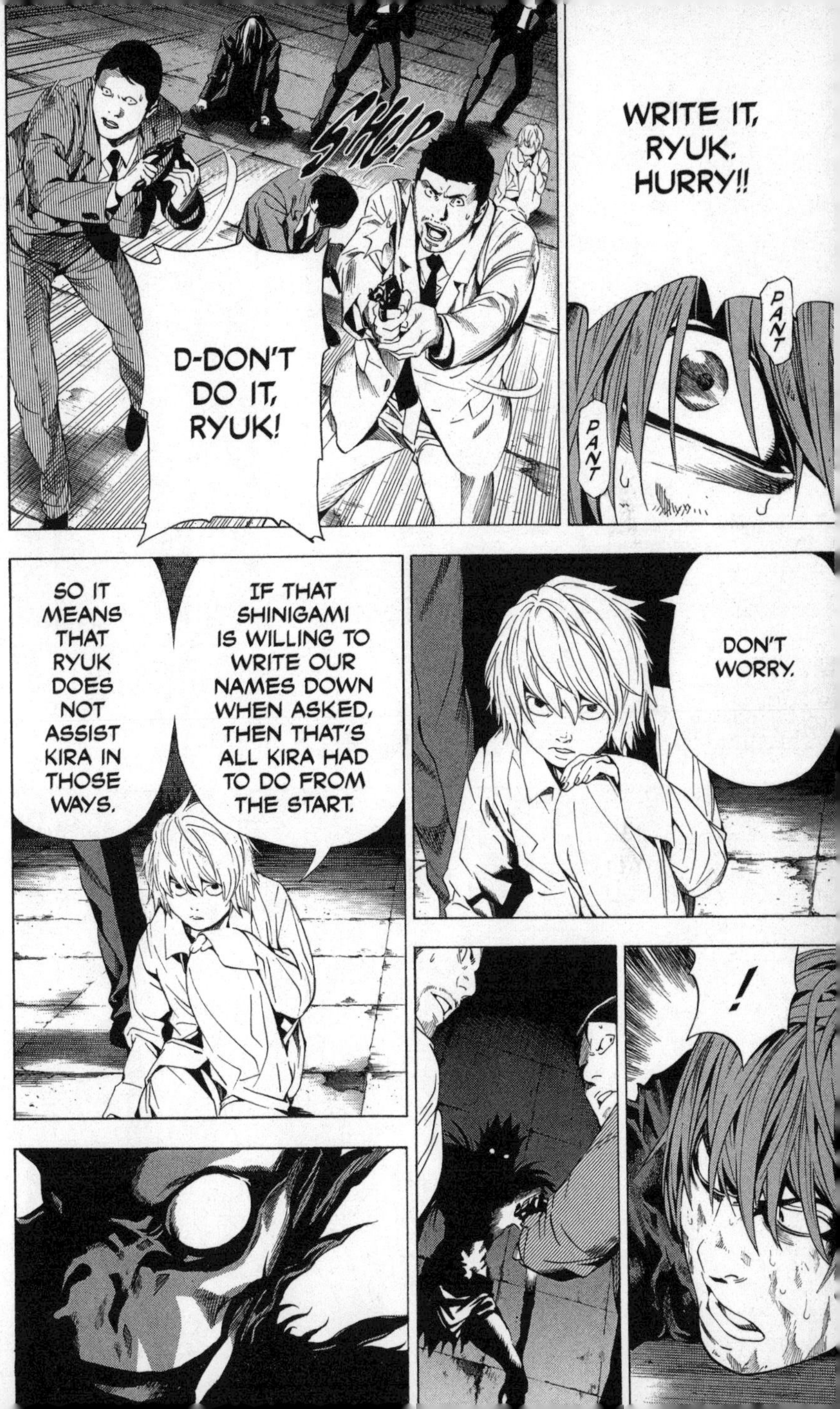
WRITE IT, RYUK. HURRY!!
PANT
PANT
D-DON'T DO IT, RYUK!
DON'T WORRY.
IF THAT SHINIGAMI IS WILLING TO WRITE OUR NAMES DOWN WHEN ASKED, THEN THAT'S ALL KIRA HAD TO DO FROM THE START.
SO IT MEANS THAT RYUK DOES NOT ASSIST KIRA IN THOSE WAYS.
!

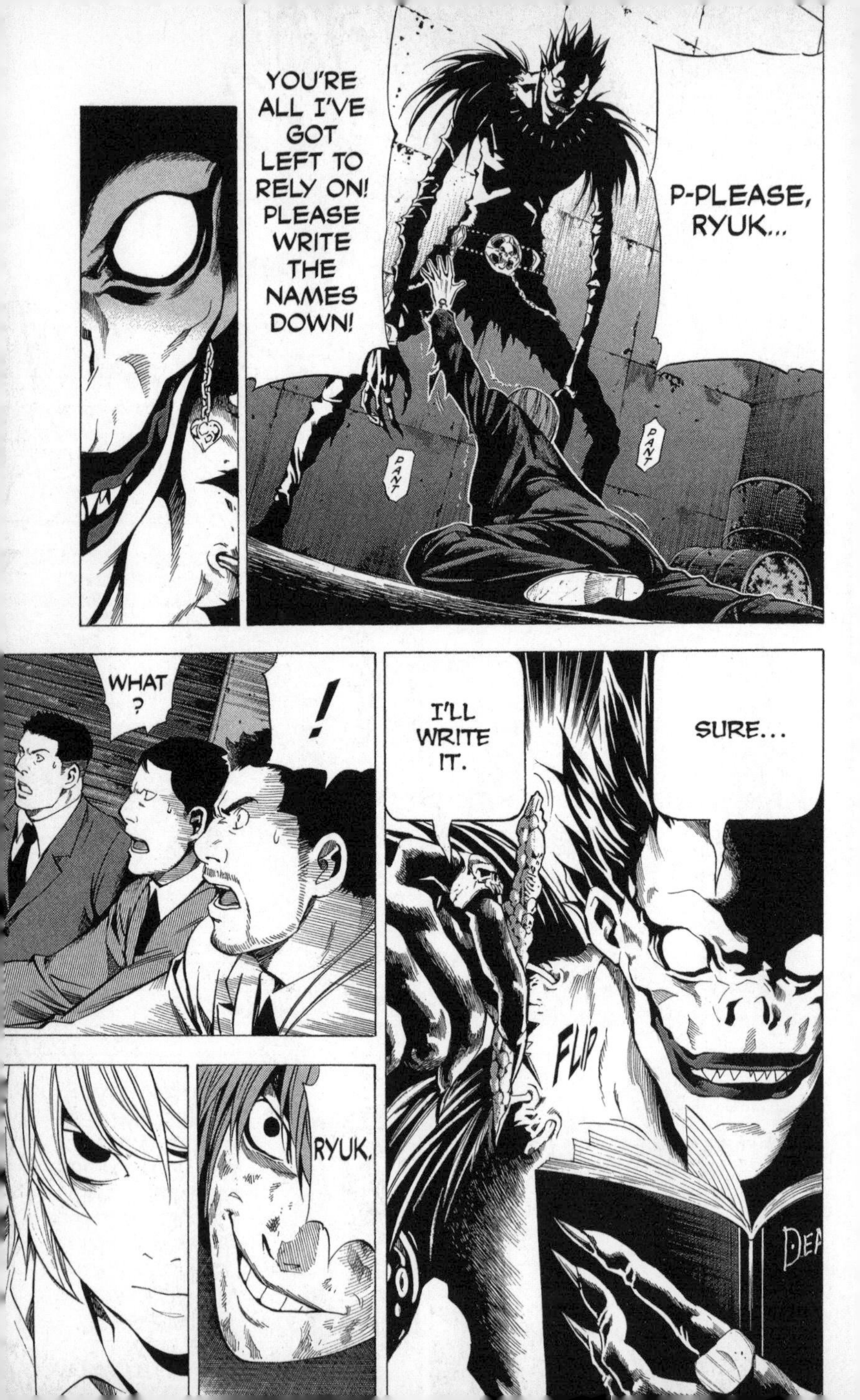
P-PLEASE, RYUK...
YOU'RE ALL I'VE GOT LEFT TO RELY ON! PLEASE WRITE THE NAMES DOWN!
PANT
PANT
SURE...
I'LL WRITE IT.
FLIP
!
WHAT ?
RYUK,

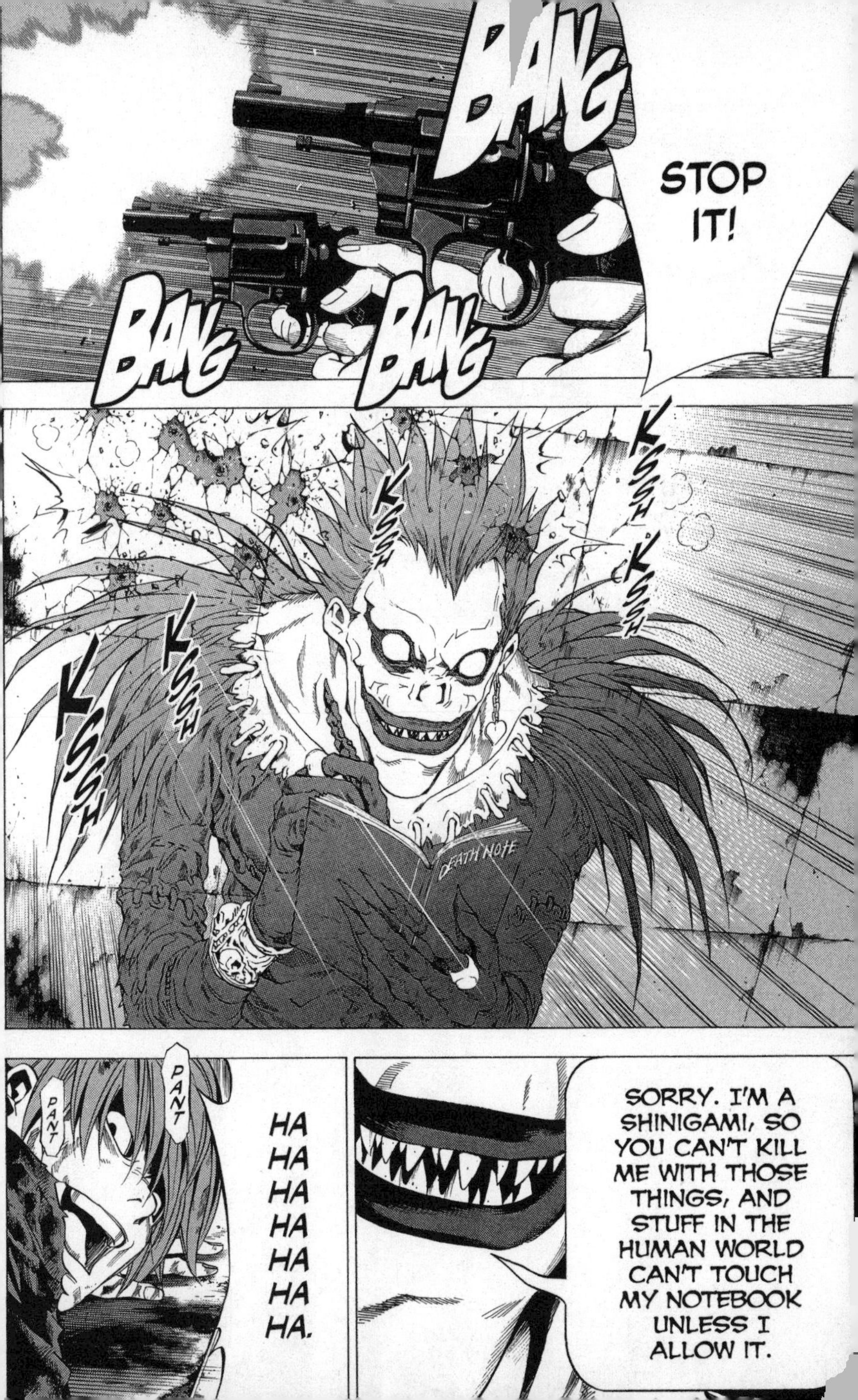
BANG
STOP IT!
BANG
BANG
KSSH
KSSH
KSSH
KSSH
KSSH
SORRY. I'M A SHINIGAMI, SO YOU CAN'T KILL ME WITH THOSE THINGS, AND STUFF IN THE HUMAN WORLD CAN'T TOUCH MY NOTEBOOK UNLESS I ALLOW IT.
HA HA HA HA HA HA HA.
PANT
PANT
DEATH NOTE

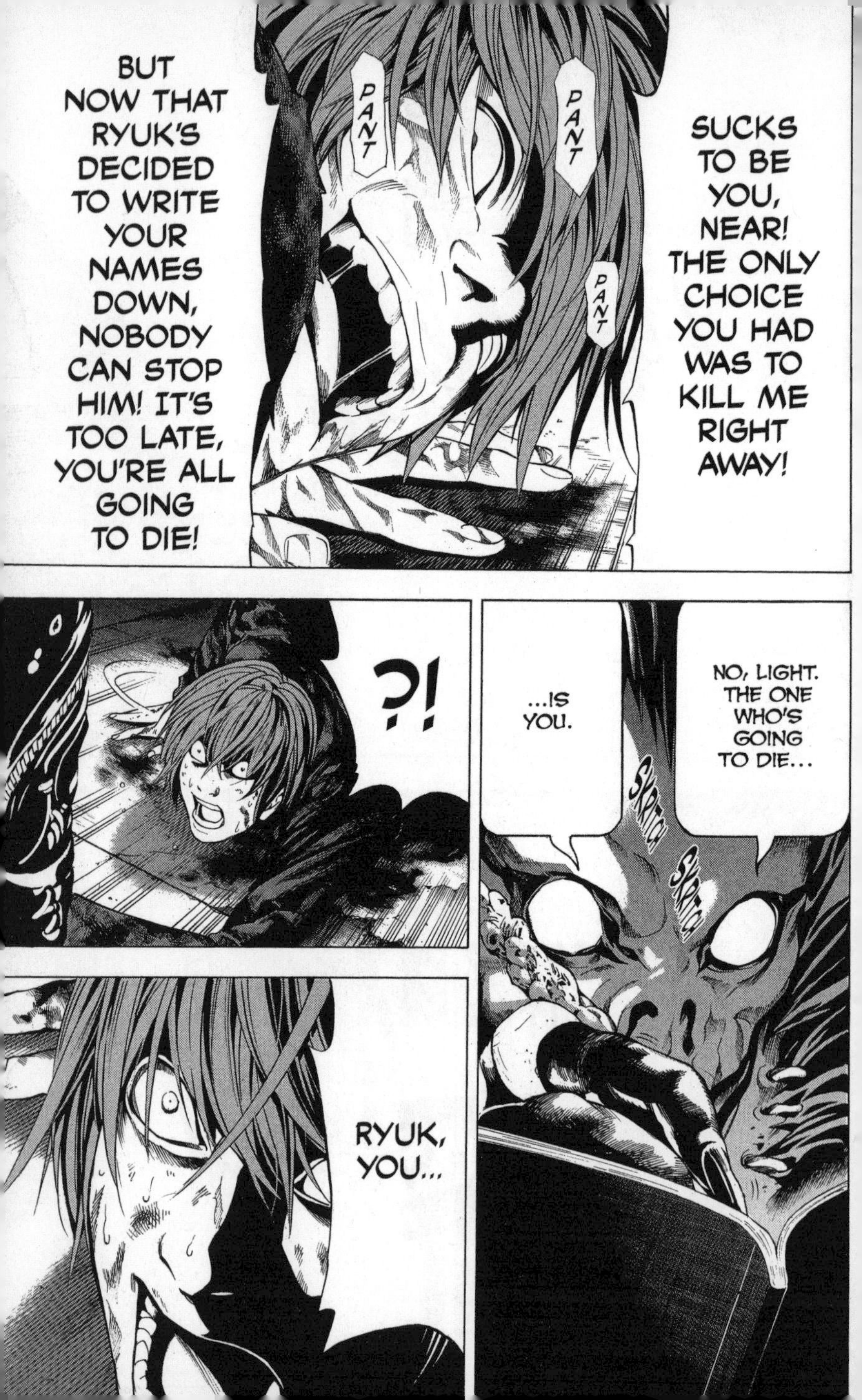

PANT
PANT
PANT
SUCKS TO BE YOU, NEAR! THE ONLY CHOICE YOU HAD WAS TO KILL ME RIGHT AWAY!
BUT NOW THAT RYUK'S DECIDED TO WRITE YOUR NAMES DOWN, NOBODY CAN STOP HIM! IT'S TOO LATE, YOU'RE ALL GOING TO DIE!
NO, LIGHT. THE ONE WHO'S GOING TO DIE...
...IS YOU.
SKRITCH
SKRITCH
?!
RYUK, YOU...

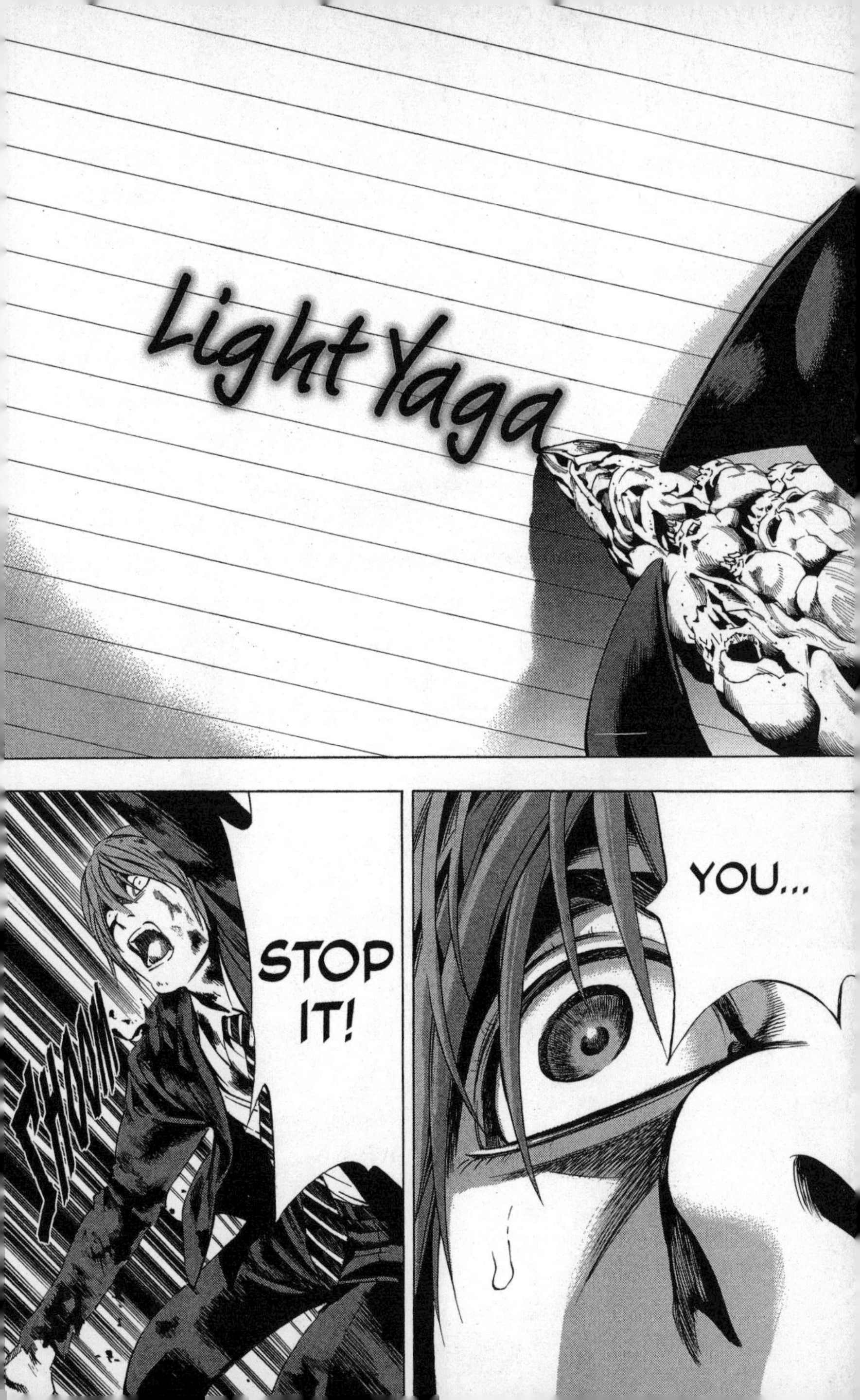
Light Yaga
YOU...
STOP IT!

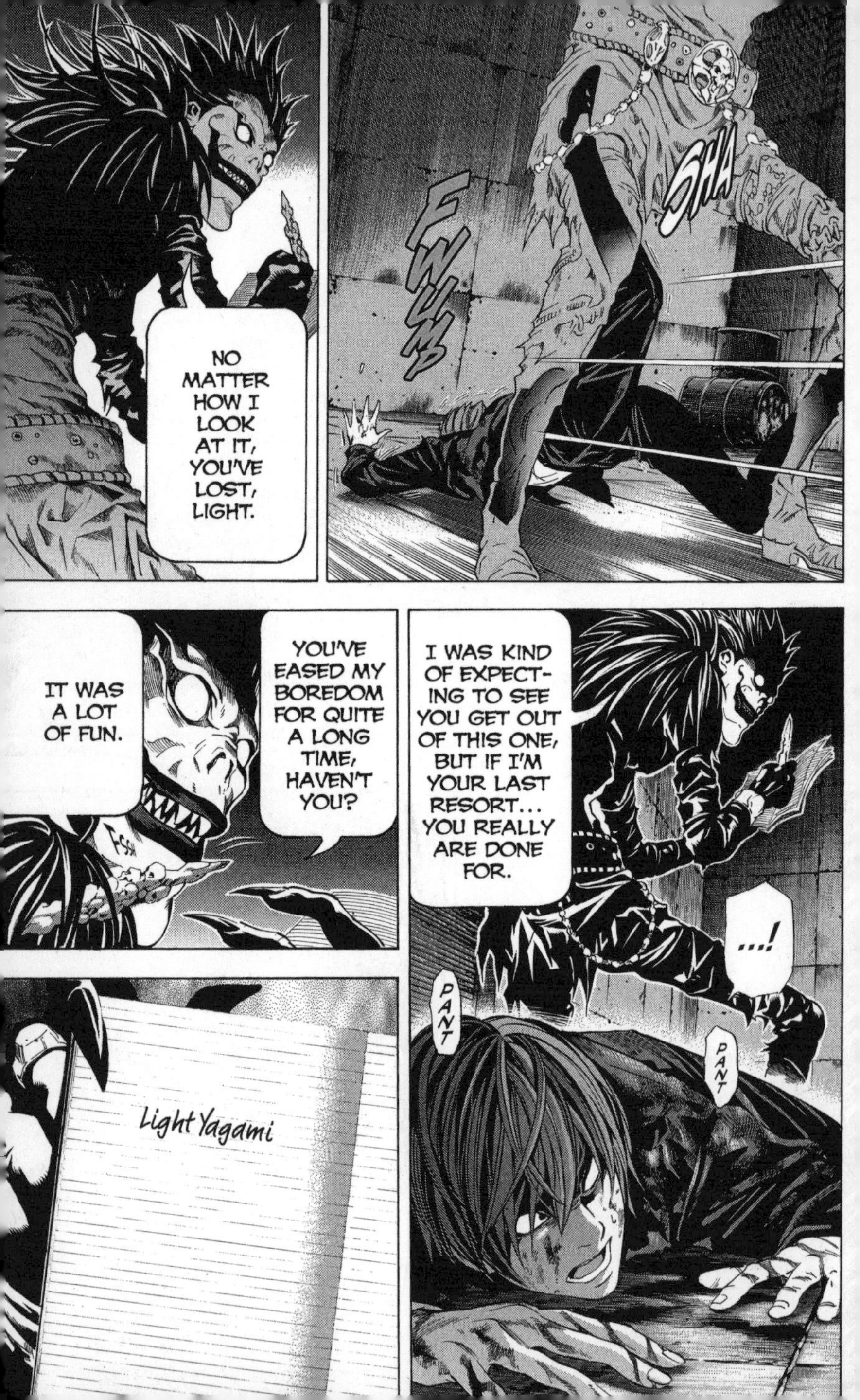
SHA
FWUMP
NO MATTER HOW I LOOK AT IT, YOU'VE LOST, LIGHT.
I WAS KIND OF EXPECT-ING TO SEE YOU GET OUT OF THIS ONE, BUT IF I'M YOUR LAST RESORT... YOU REALLY ARE DONE FOR.
...!
PANT
PANT
YOU'VE EASED MY BOREDOM FOR QUITE A LONG TIME, HAVEN'T YOU?
IT WAS A LOT OF FUN.
FSSH
Light Yagami

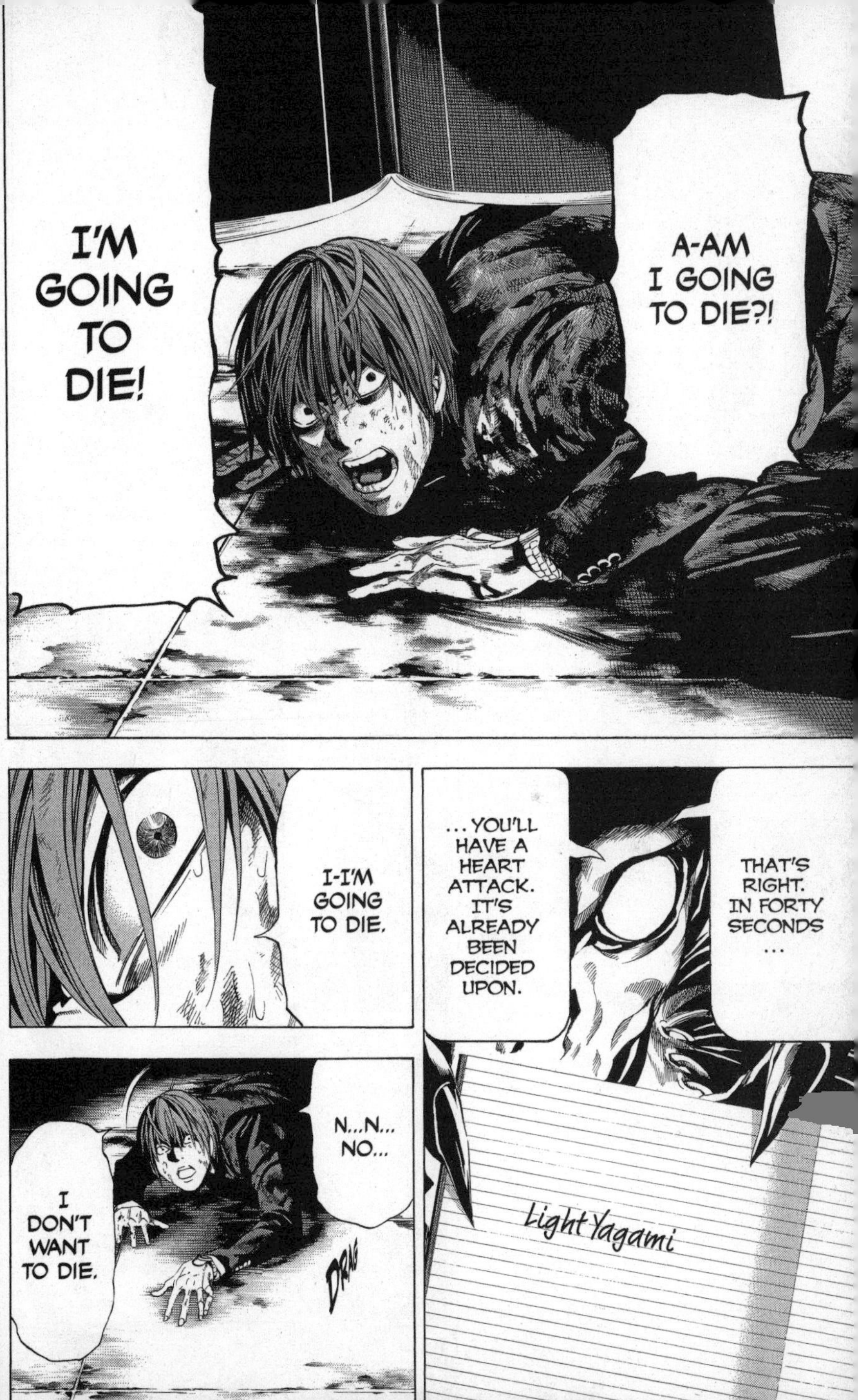
A-AM I GOING TO DIE?!
I'M GOING TO DIE!
THAT'S RIGHT. IN FORTY SECONDS ...
...YOU'LL HAVE A HEART ATTACK. IT'S ALREADY BEEN DECIDED UPON.
Light Yagami
I-I'M GOING TO DIE.
N...N... NO...
I DON'T WANT TO DIE.
DRAG

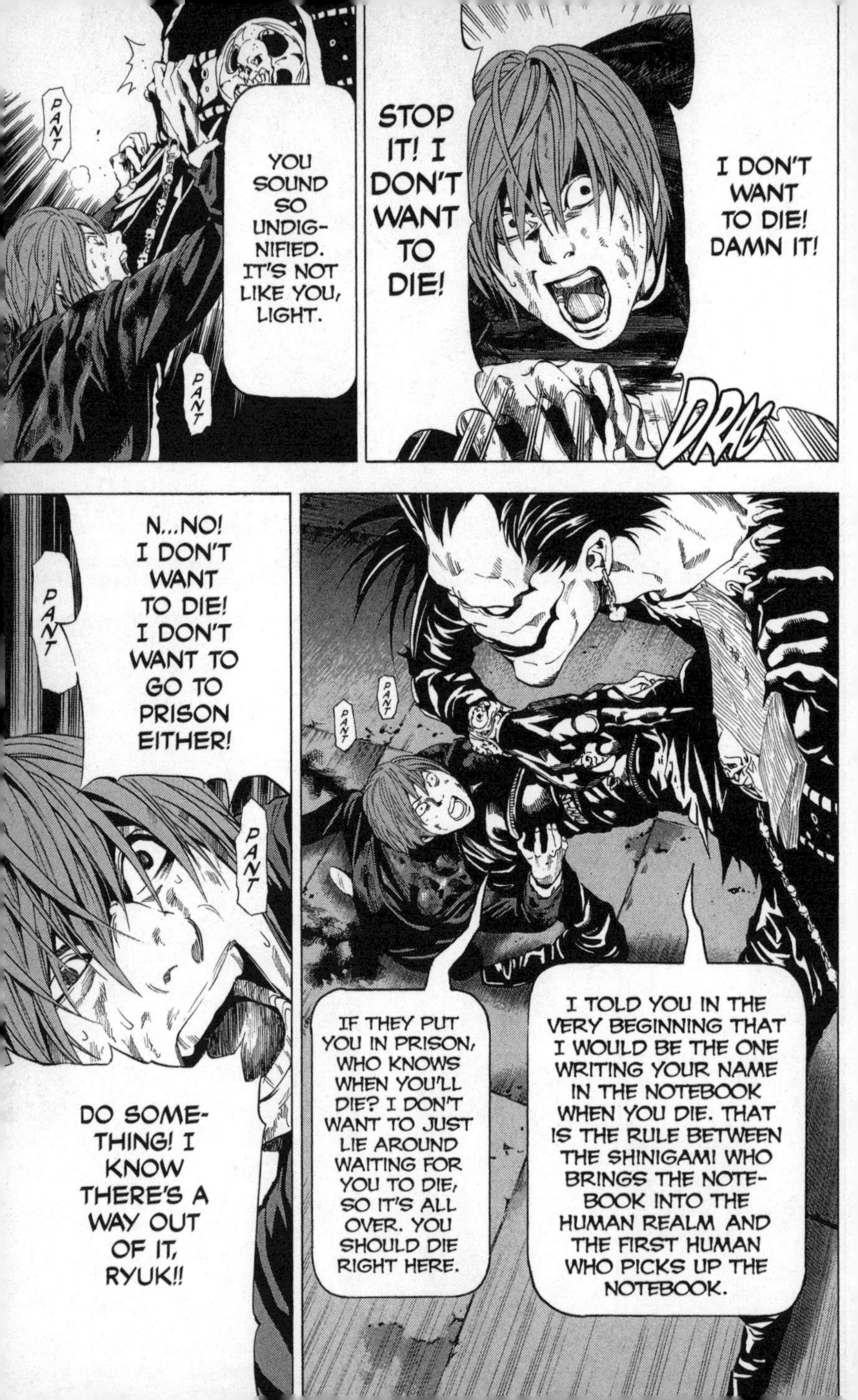

I DON'T WANT TO DIE! DAMN IT!
STOP IT! I DON'T WANT TO DIE!
DRAG
YOU SOUND SO UNDIG-NIFIED. IT'S NOT LIKE YOU, LIGHT.
PANT
PANT
I TOLD YOU IN THE VERY BEGINNING THAT I WOULD BE THE ONE WRITING YOUR NAME IN THE NOTEBOOK WHEN YOU DIE. THAT IS THE RULE BETWEEN THE SHINIGAMI WHO BRINGS THE NOTE-BOOK INTO THE HUMAN REALM AND THE FIRST HUMAN WHO PICKS UP THE NOTEBOOK.
PANT
PANT
IF THEY PUT YOU IN PRISON, WHO KNOWS WHEN YOU'LL DIE? I DON'T WANT TO JUST LIE AROUND WAITING FOR YOU TO DIE, SO IT'S ALL OVER. YOU SHOULD DIE RIGHT HERE.
N...NO! I DON'T WANT TO DIE! I DON'T WANT TO GO TO PRISON EITHER!
PANT
PANT
DO SOME-THING! I KNOW THERE'S A WAY OUT OF IT, RYUK!!

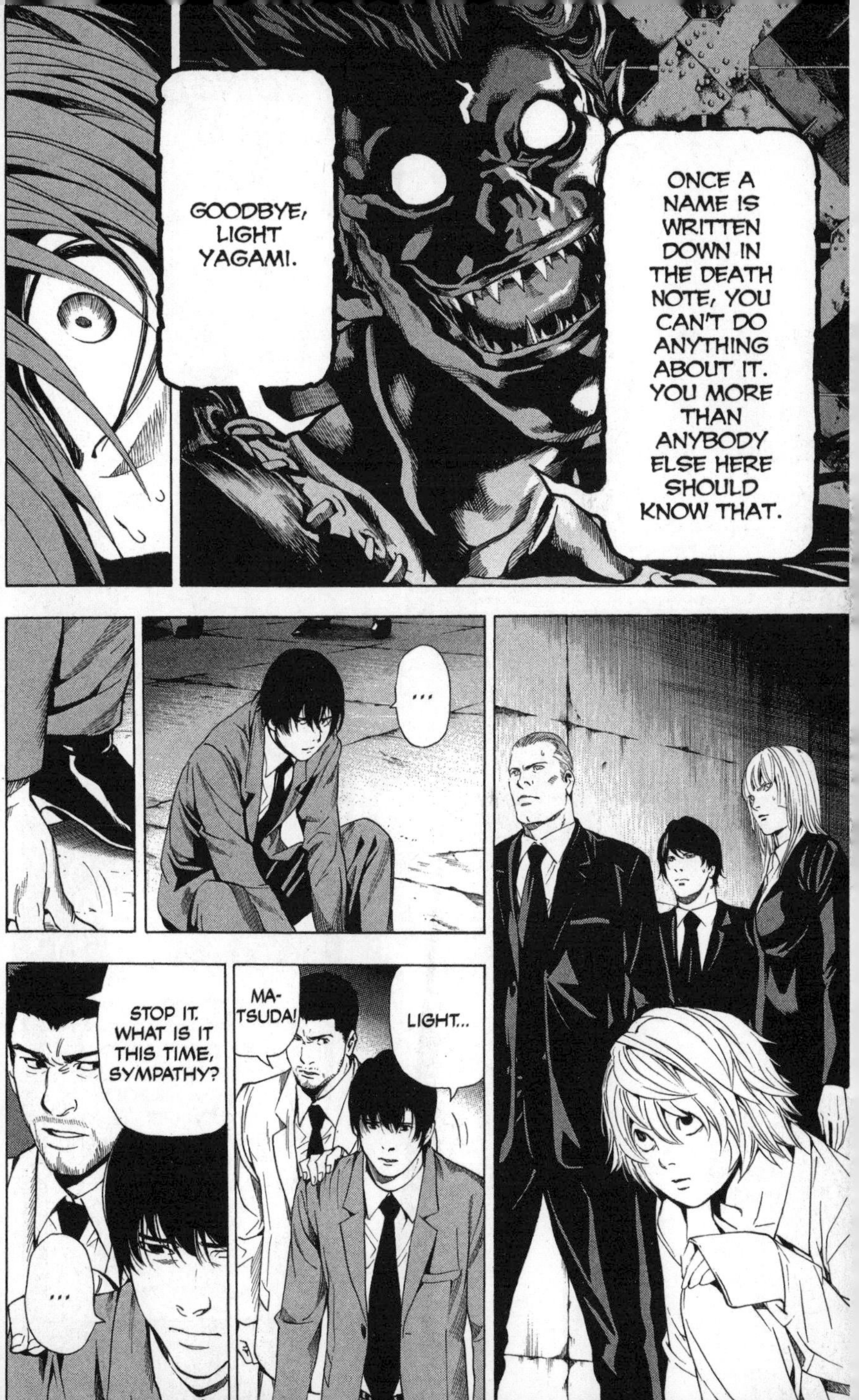
ONCE A NAME IS WRITTEN DOWN IN THE DEATH NOTE, YOU CAN'T DO ANYTHING ABOUT IT. YOU MORE THAN ANYBODY ELSE HERE SHOULD KNOW THAT.
GOODBYE, LIGHT YAGAMI.
...
LIGHT...
MA-TSUDA!
STOP IT. WHAT IS IT THIS TIME, SYMPATHY?
...

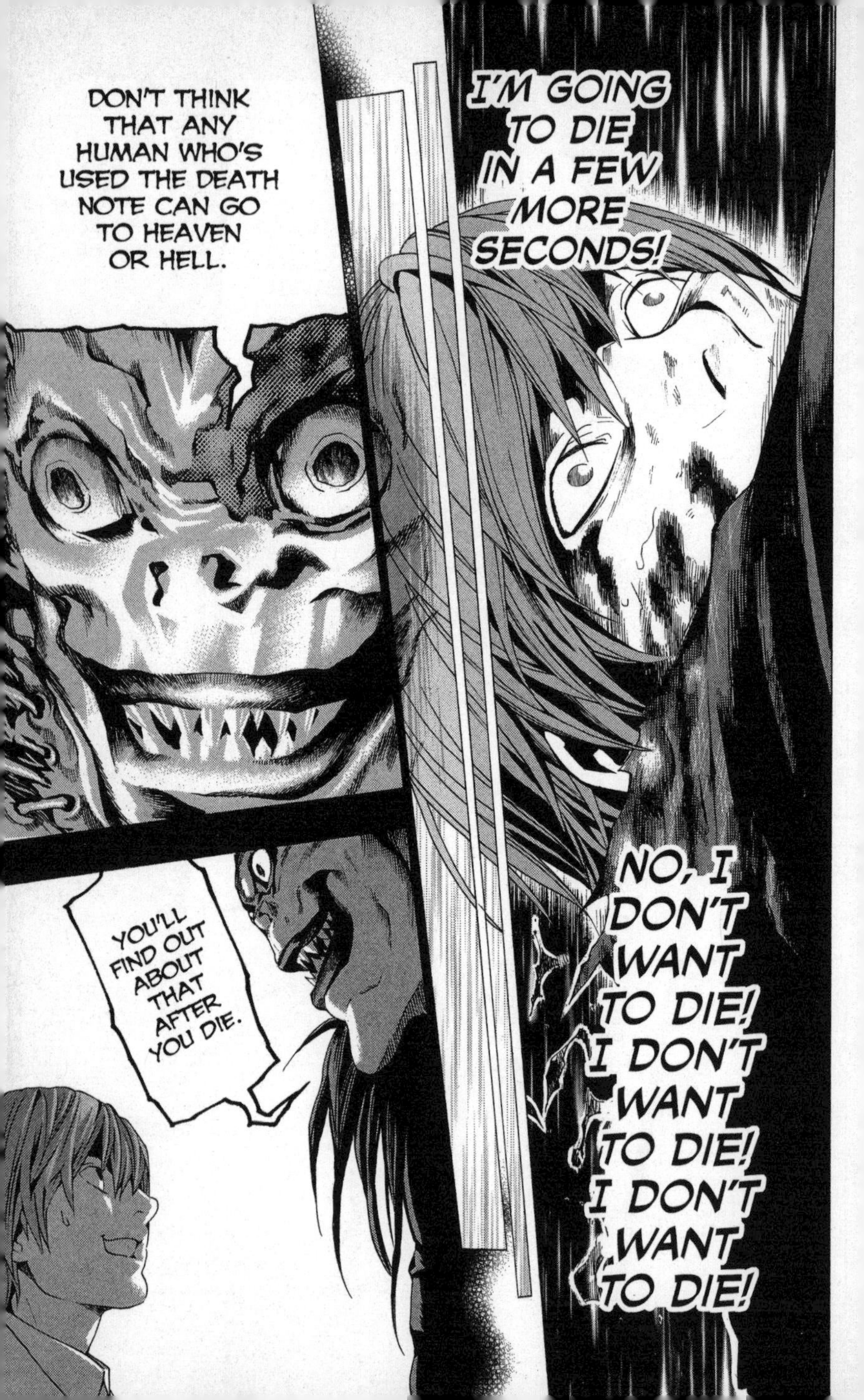
I'M GOING TO DIE IN A FEW MORE SECONDS!
DON'T THINK THAT ANY HUMAN WHO'S USED THE DEATH NOTE CAN GO TO HEAVEN OR HELL.
NO, I DON'T WANT TO DIE! I DON'T WANT TO DIE! I DON'T WANT TO DIE!
YOU'LL FIND OUT ABOUT THAT AFTER YOU DIE.

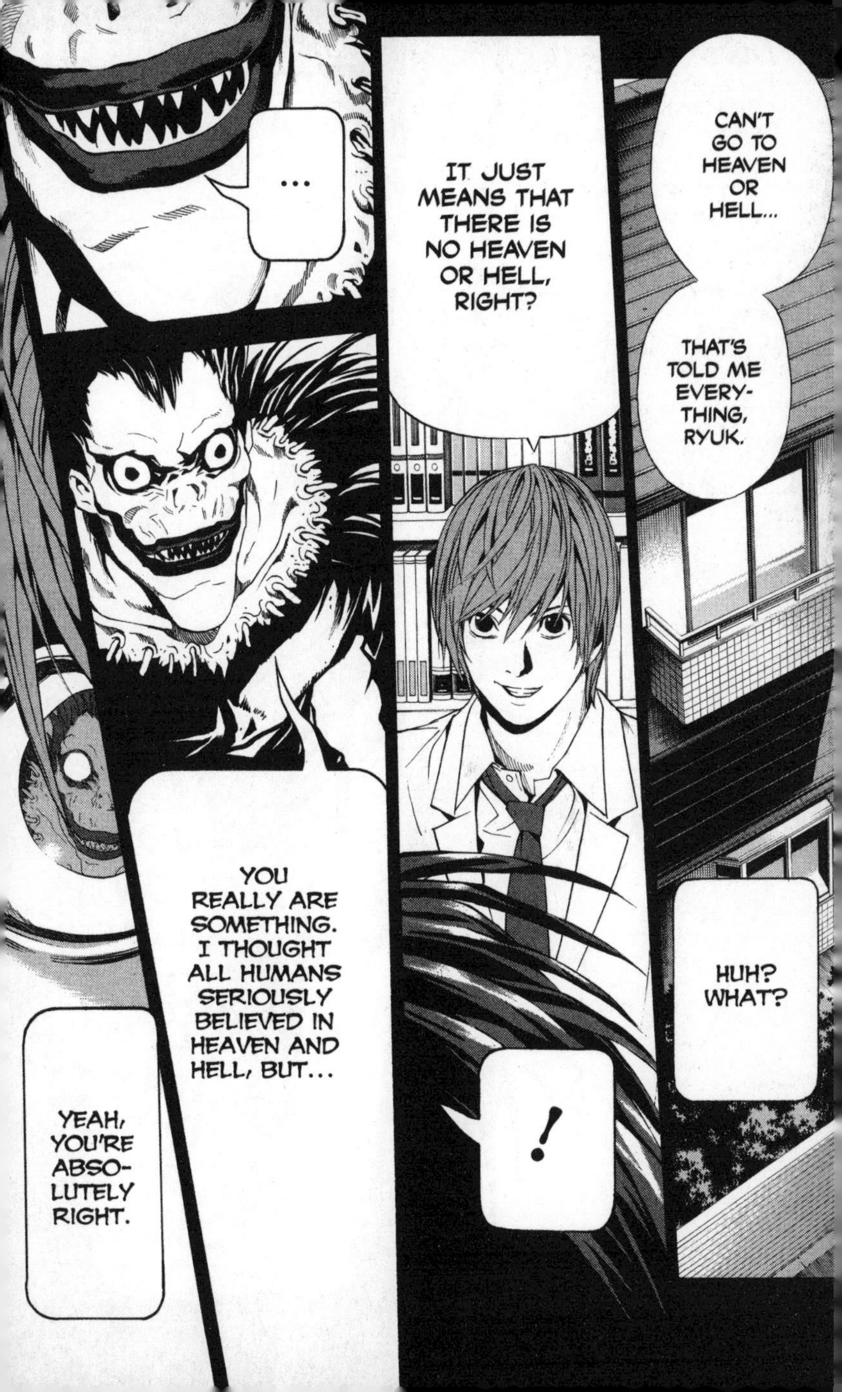
CAN'T GO TO HEAVEN OR HELL...
THAT'S TOLD ME EVERY-THING, RYUK.
HUH? WHAT?
IT JUST MEANS THAT THERE IS NO HEAVEN OR HELL, RIGHT?
!
...
YOU REALLY ARE SOMETHING. I THOUGHT ALL HUMANS SERIOUSLY BELIEVED IN HEAVEN AND HELL, BUT...
YEAH, YOU'RE ABSO-LUTELY RIGHT.

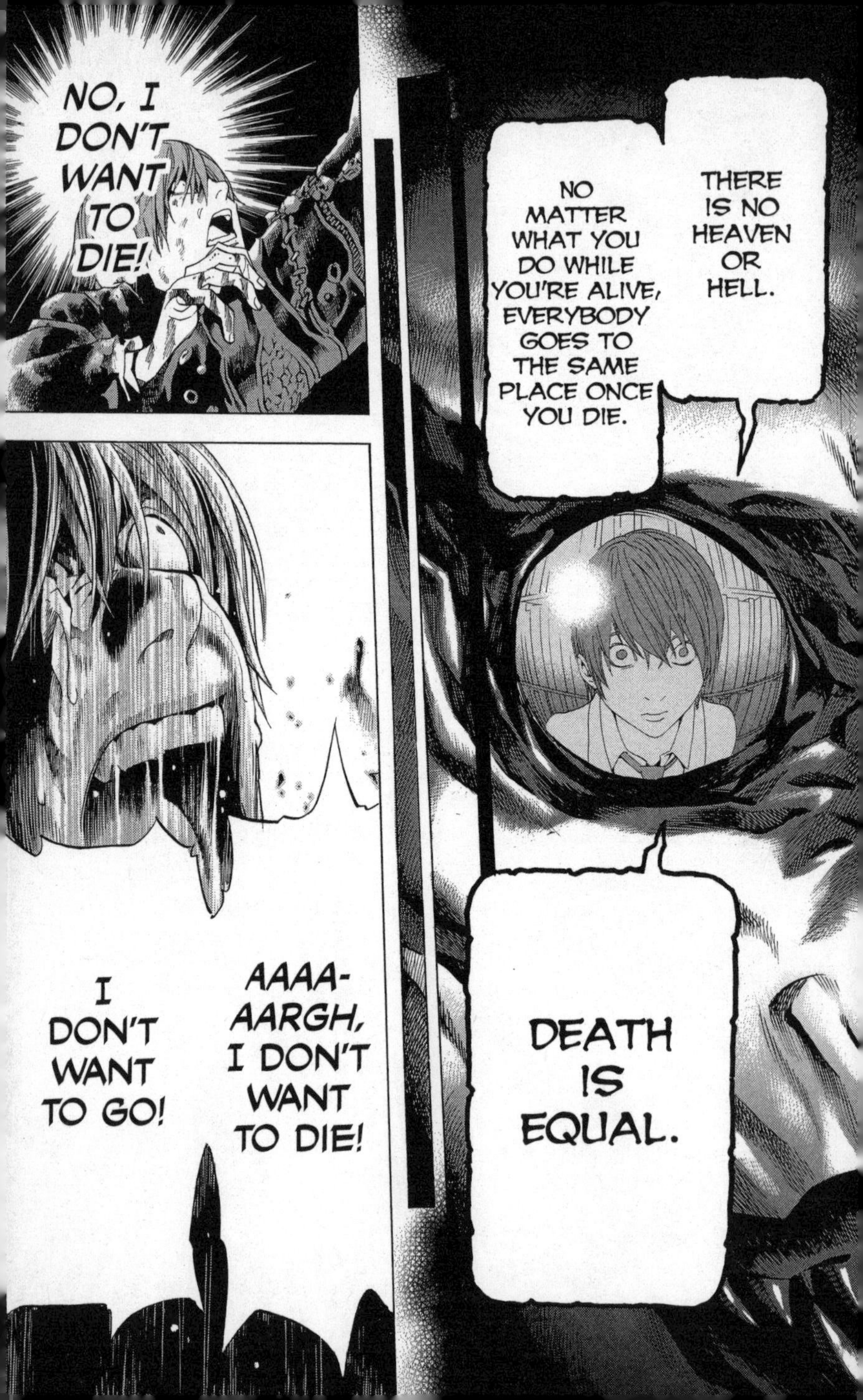
THERE IS NO HEAVEN OR HELL.
NO MATTER WHAT YOU DO WHILE YOU'RE ALIVE, EVERYBODY GOES TO THE SAME PLACE ONCE YOU DIE.
DEATH IS EQUAL.
NO, I DON'T WANT TO DIE!
AAAA-AARGH, I DON'T WANT TO DIE!
I DON'T WANT TO GO!

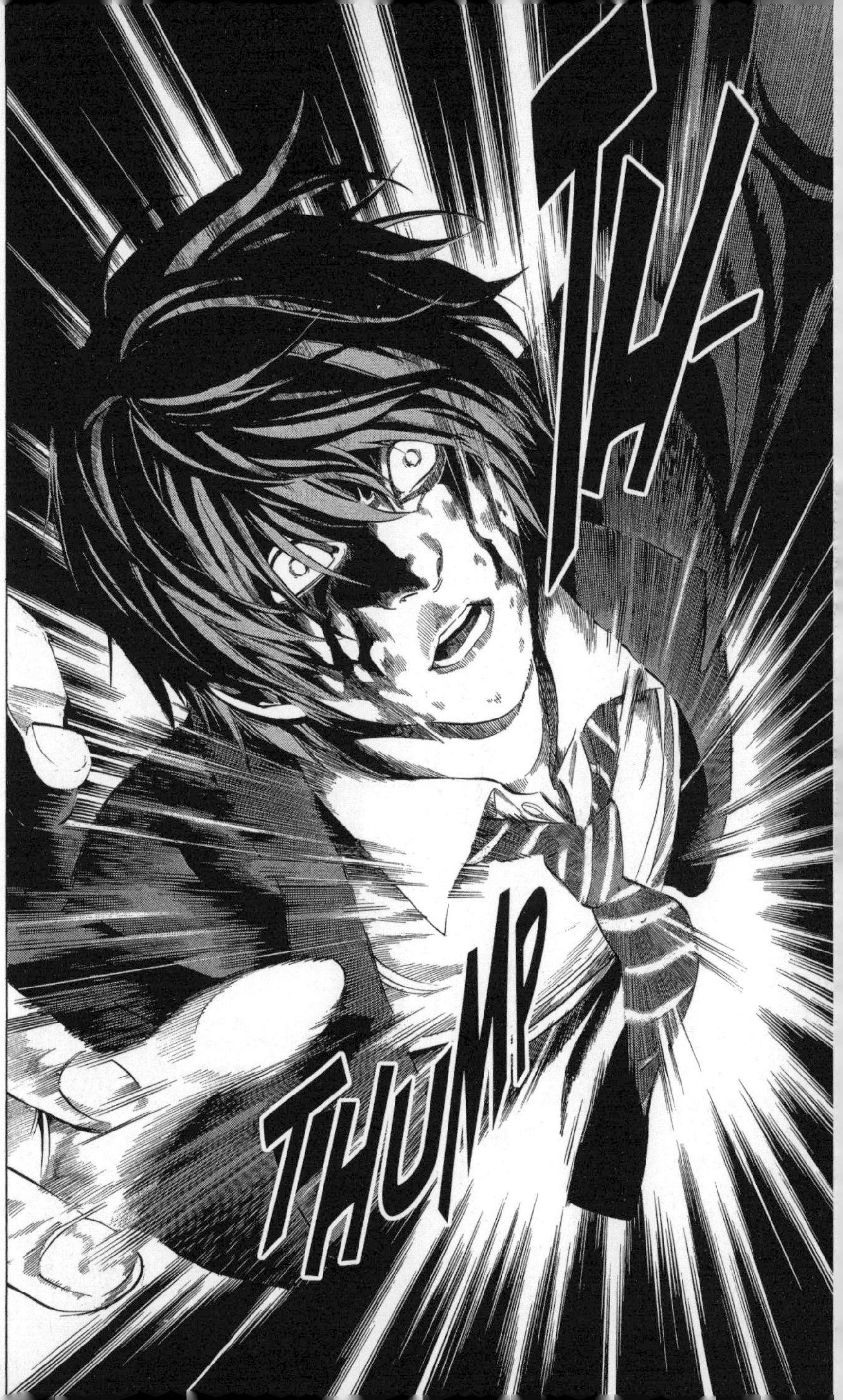
THA
THUMP

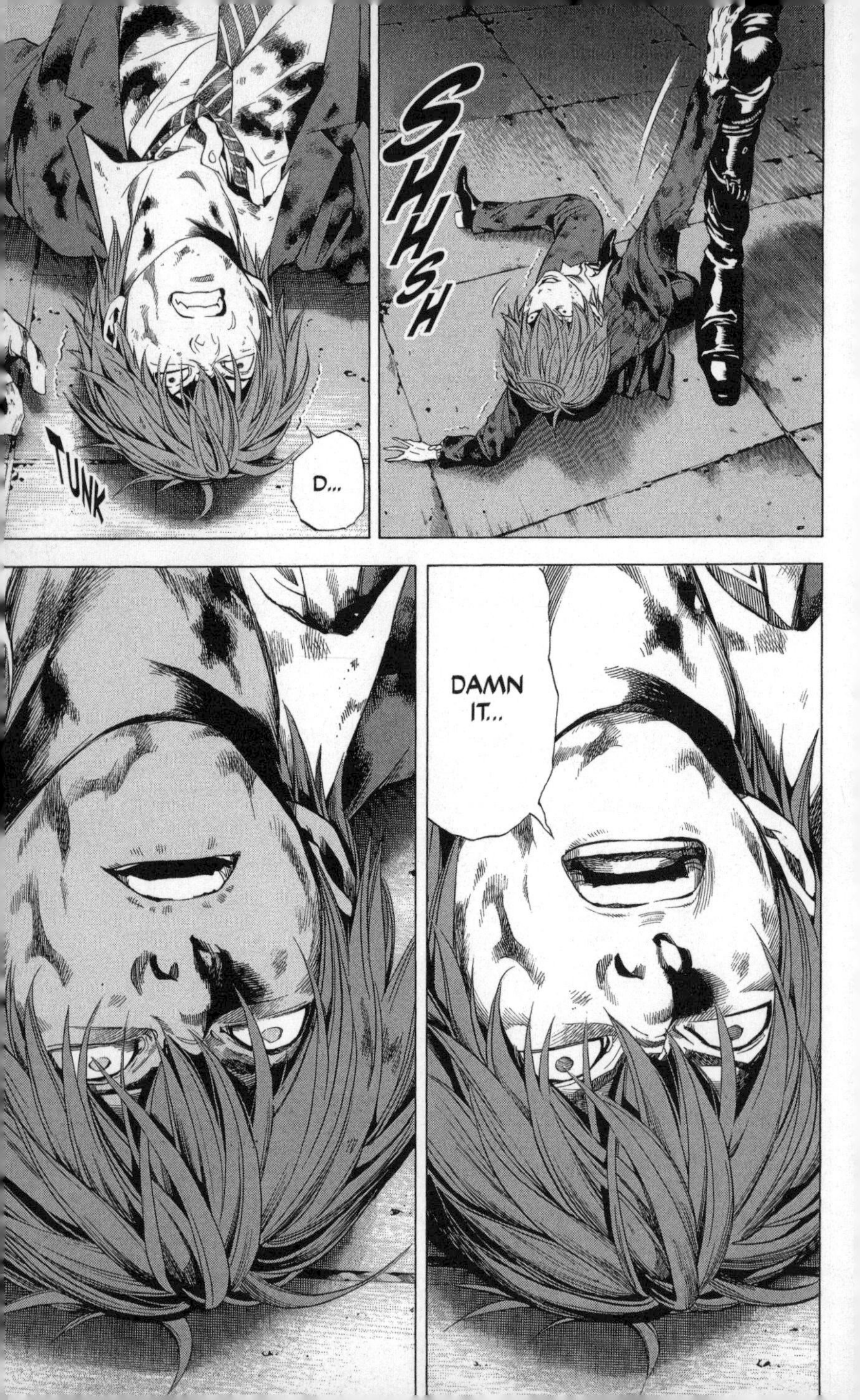
SHHHSH
TUNK
D...
DAMN IT...

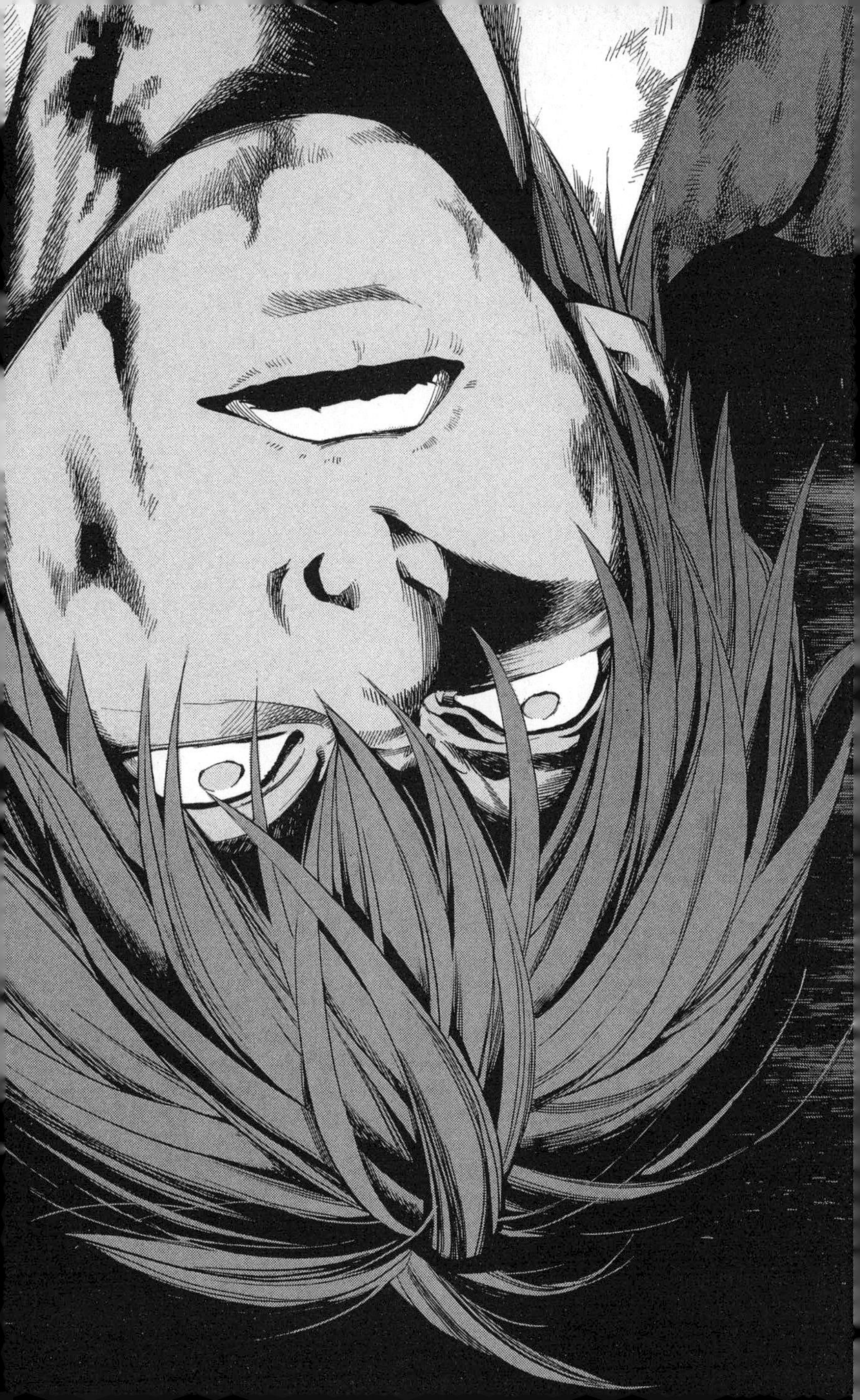

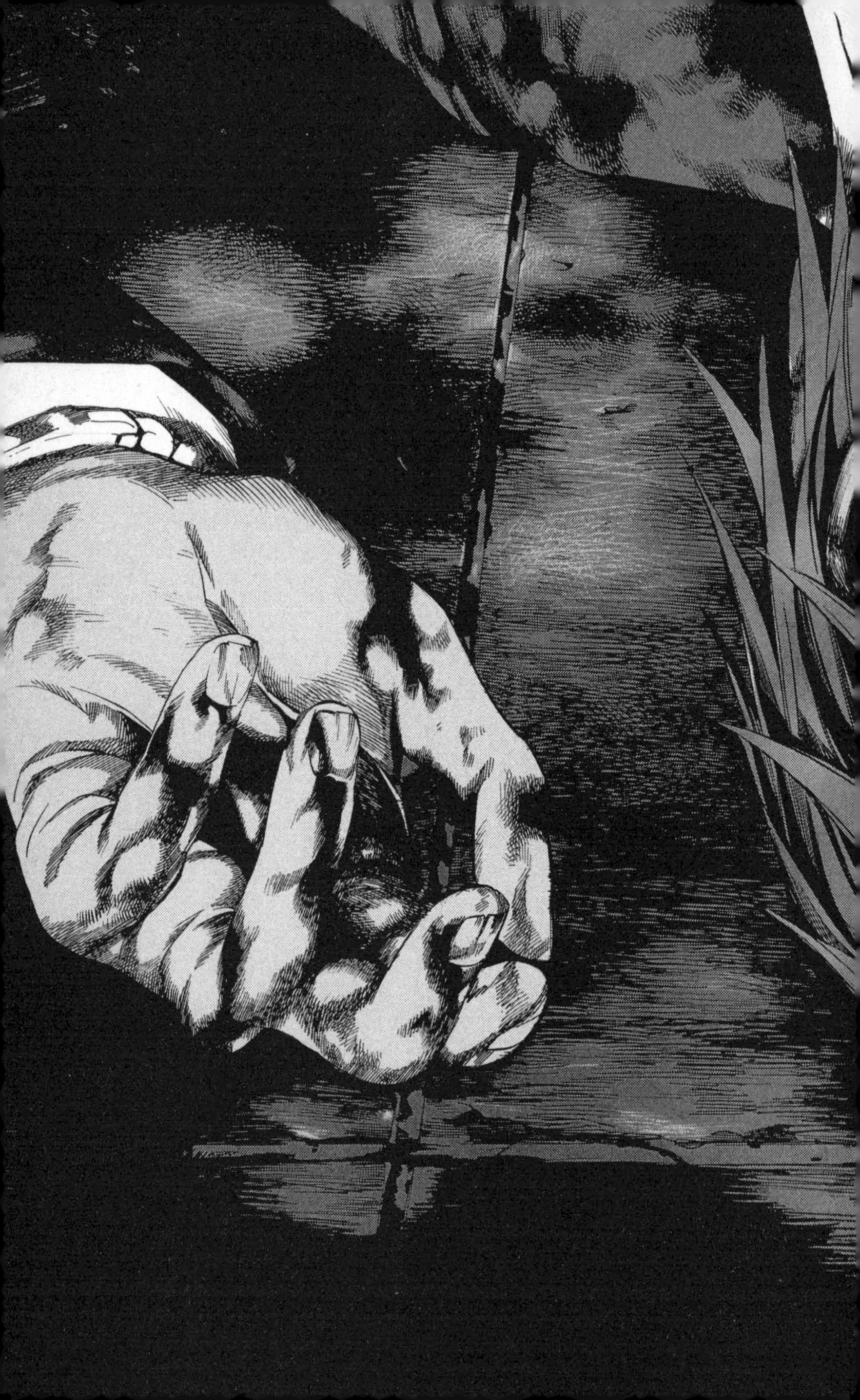

⊙ All humans will, without exception, eventually die.

人間は、いつか必ず死ぬ。

◻ After they die, the place they go is MU.
(Nothingness)

死んだ後にいくところは、無である。

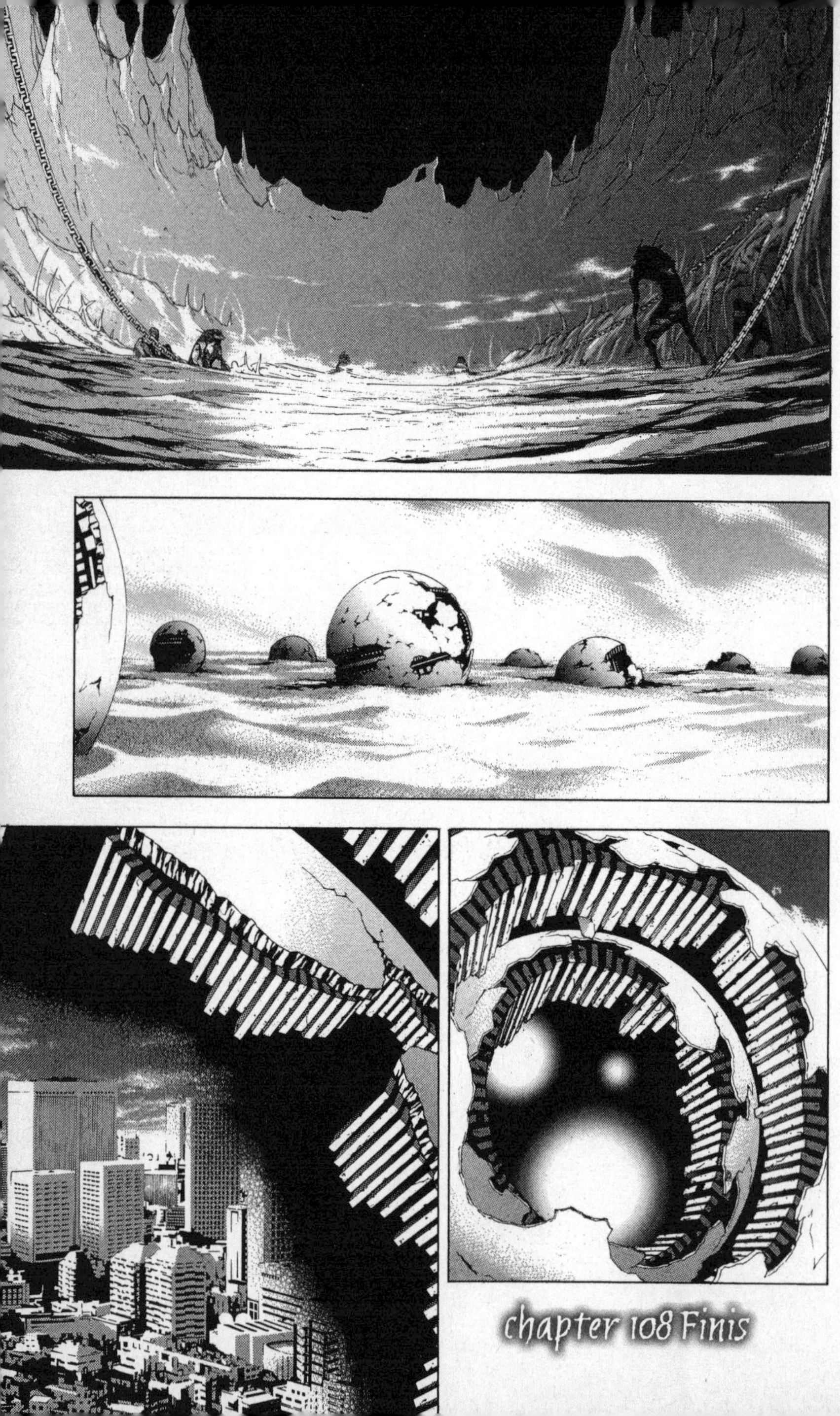

chapter 108 Finis

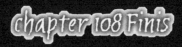

chapter 108 Finis

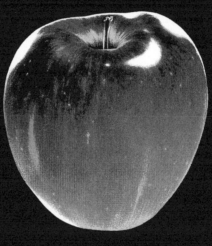

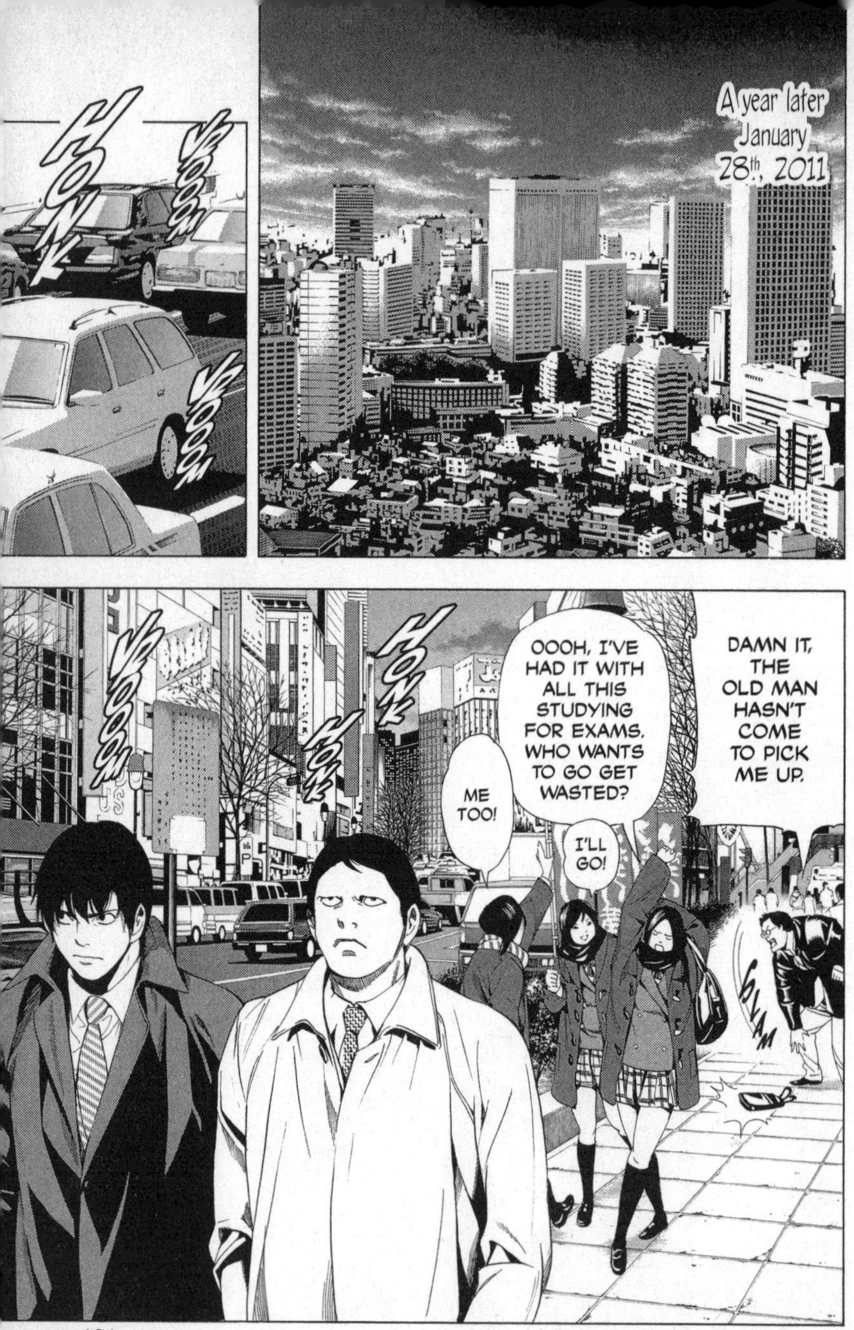
A year later
January
28th, 2011
HONK
VROOOM
VROOOM
DAMN IT, THE OLD MAN HASN'T COME TO PICK ME UP.
OOOH, I'VE HAD IT WITH ALL THIS STUDYING FOR EXAMS. WHO WANTS TO GO GET WASTED?
I'LL GO!
ME TOO!
BLAM
HONK
HONK
VROOOM

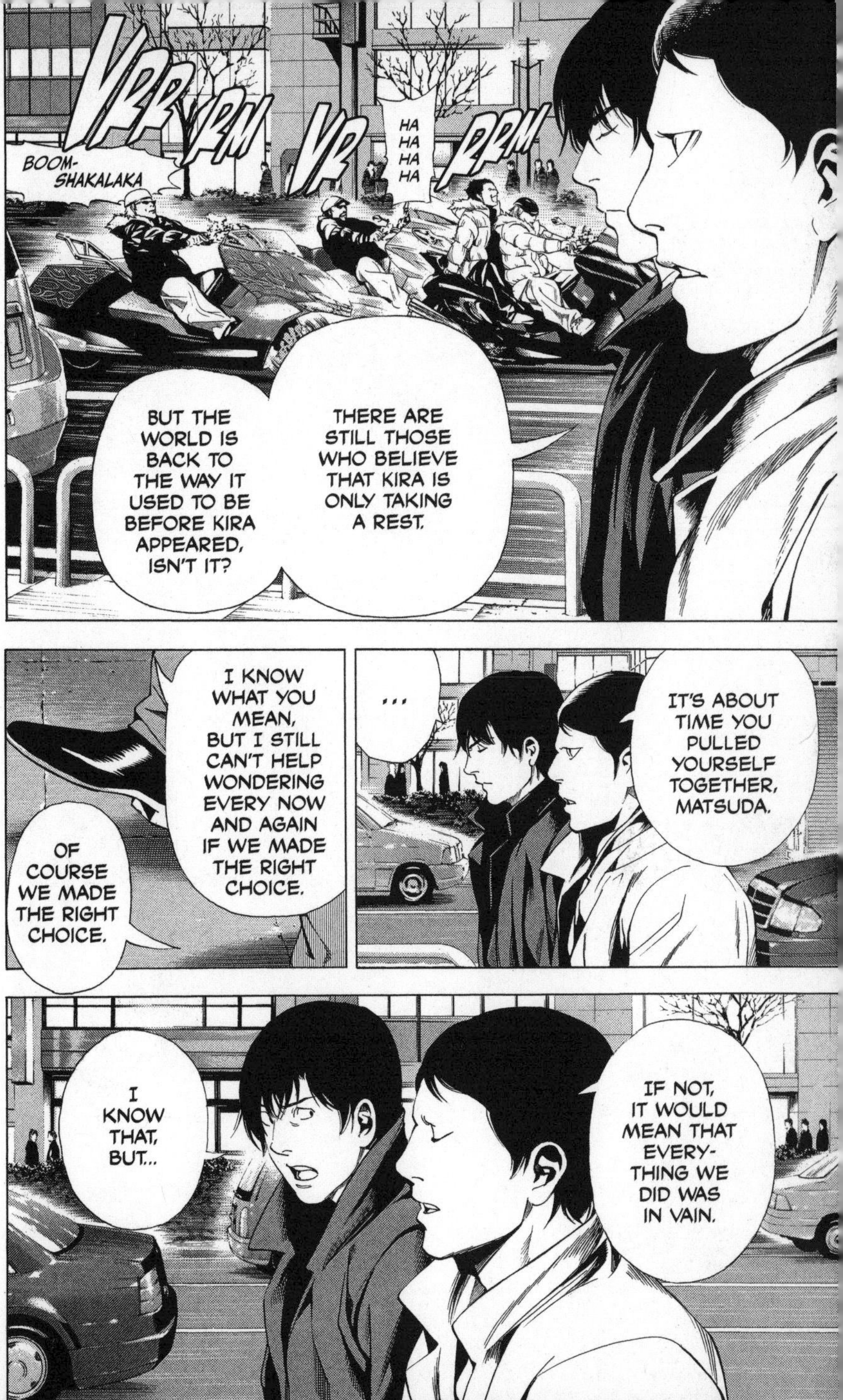
RRM
HA HA HA HA
VR
VRM
VRR
BOOM-SHAKALAKA
THERE ARE STILL THOSE WHO BELIEVE THAT KIRA IS ONLY TAKING A REST.
BUT THE WORLD IS BACK TO THE WAY IT USED TO BE BEFORE KIRA APPEARED, ISN'T IT?
IT'S ABOUT TIME YOU PULLED YOURSELF TOGETHER, MATSUDA.
...
I KNOW WHAT YOU MEAN, BUT I STILL CAN'T HELP WONDERING EVERY NOW AND AGAIN IF WE MADE THE RIGHT CHOICE.
OF COURSE WE MADE THE RIGHT CHOICE.
IF NOT, IT WOULD MEAN THAT EVERYTHING WE DID WAS IN VAIN.
I KNOW THAT, BUT...

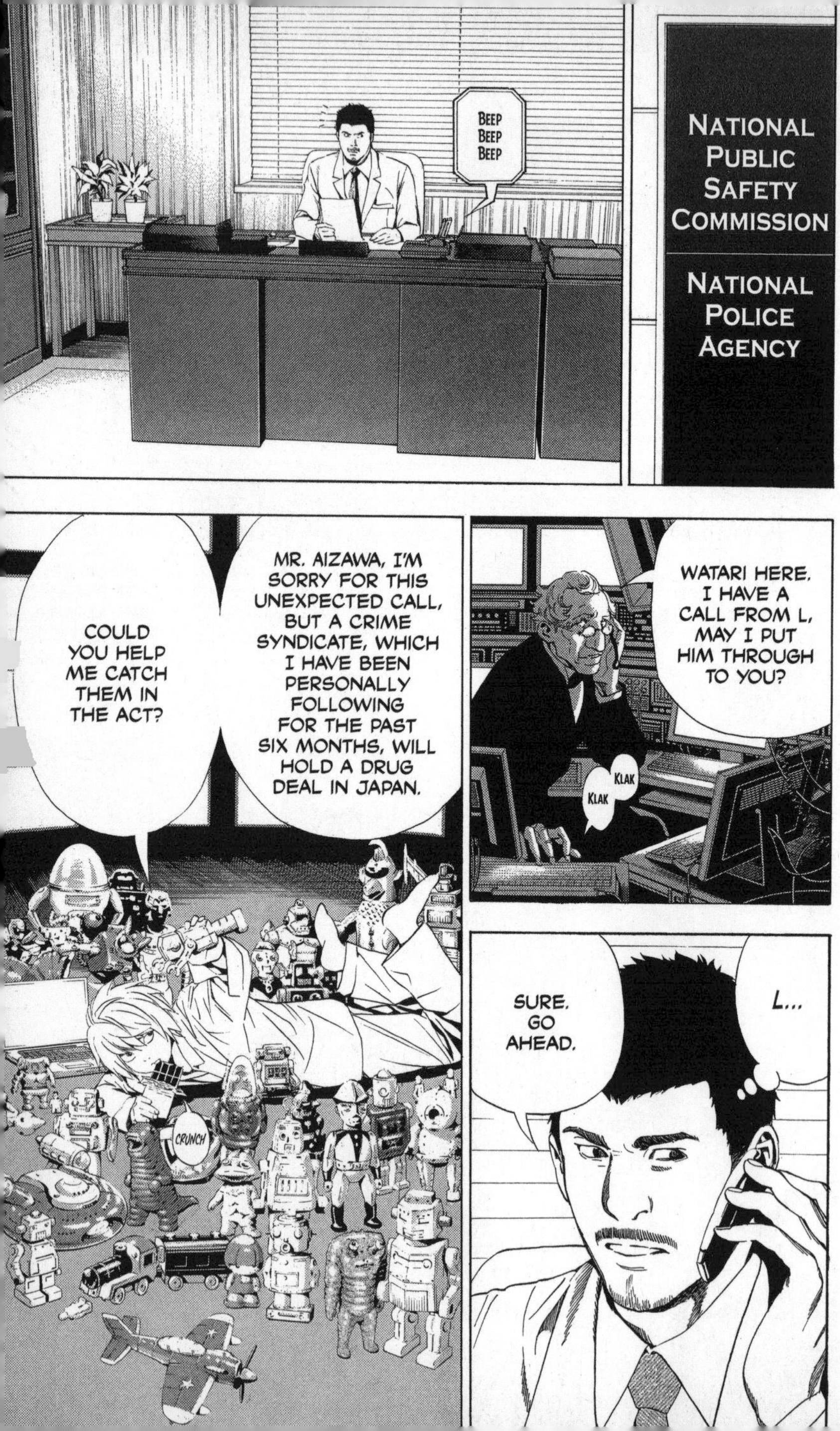
NATIONAL PUBLIC SAFETY COMMISSION
NATIONAL POLICE AGENCY
BEEP BEEP BEEP
WATARI HERE. I HAVE A CALL FROM L, MAY I PUT HIM THROUGH TO YOU?
KLAK KLAK
L...
SURE. GO AHEAD.
MR. AIZAWA, I'M SORRY FOR THIS UNEXPECTED CALL, BUT A CRIME SYNDICATE, WHICH I HAVE BEEN PERSONALLY FOLLOWING FOR THE PAST SIX MONTHS, WILL HOLD A DRUG DEAL IN JAPAN.
COULD YOU HELP ME CATCH THEM IN THE ACT?
CRUNCH

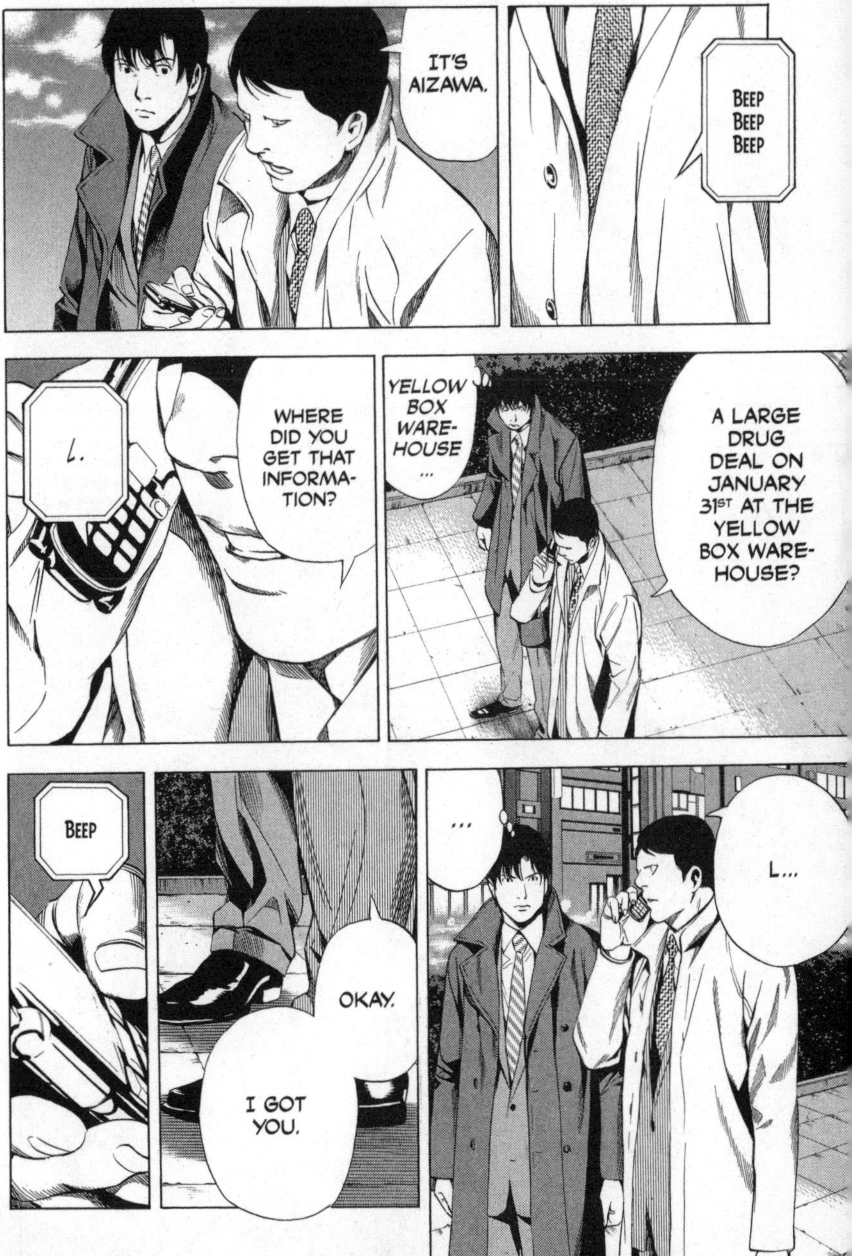
BEEP BEEP BEEP
IT'S AIZAWA.
A LARGE DRUG DEAL ON JANUARY 31ST AT THE YELLOW BOX WAREHOUSE?
YELLOW BOX WAREHOUSE...
WHERE DID YOU GET THAT INFORMATION?
L.
L...
...
OKAY.
I GOT YOU.
BEEP

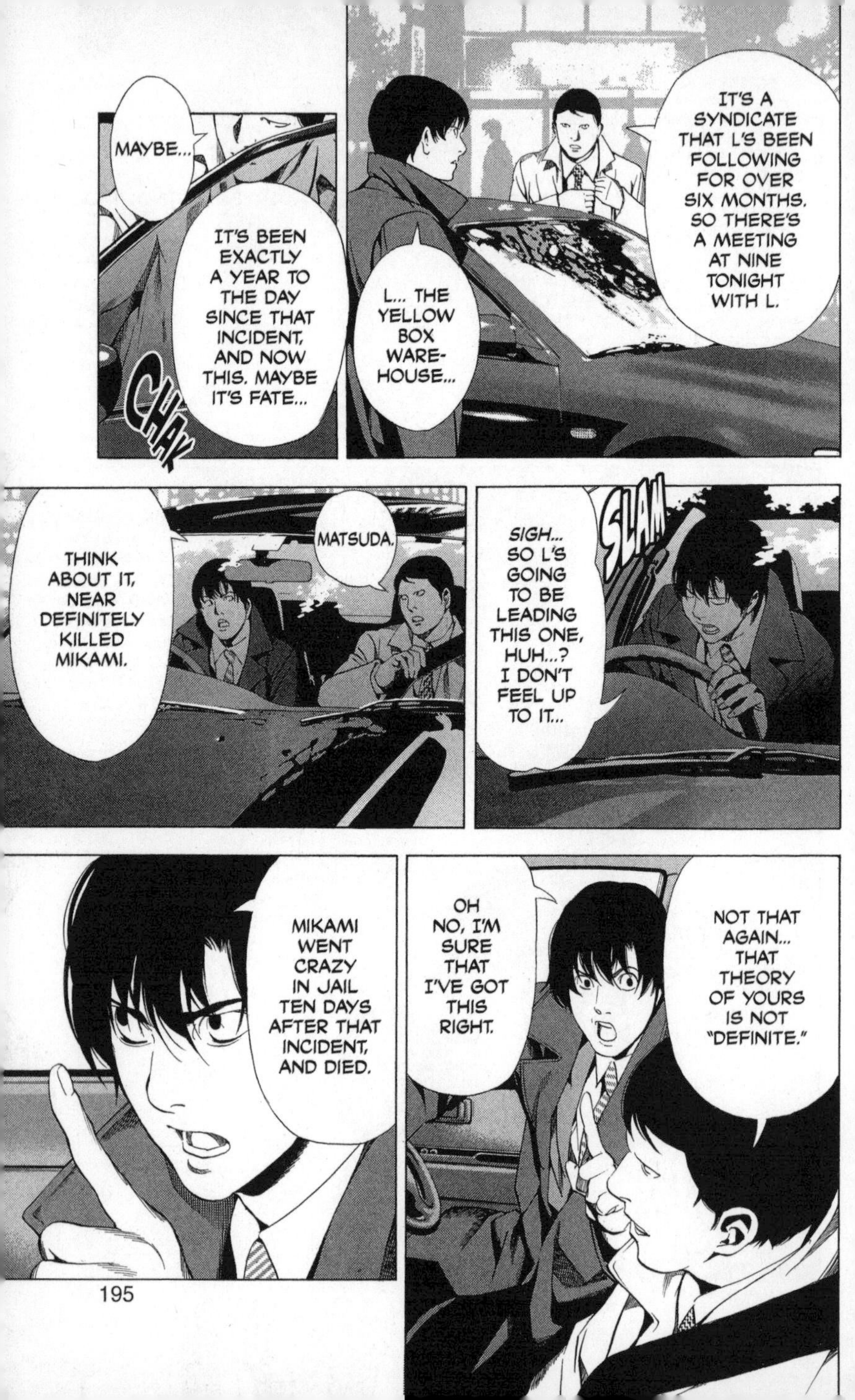
IT'S A SYNDICATE THAT L'S BEEN FOLLOWING FOR OVER SIX MONTHS. SO THERE'S A MEETING AT NINE TONIGHT WITH L.
L... THE YELLOW BOX WARE-HOUSE...
MAYBE...
IT'S BEEN EXACTLY A YEAR TO THE DAY SINCE THAT INCIDENT, AND NOW THIS. MAYBE IT'S FATE...
CHAK
SLAM
SIGH... SO L'S GOING TO BE LEADING THIS ONE, HUH...? I DON'T FEEL UP TO IT...
MATSUDA.
THINK ABOUT IT, NEAR DEFINITELY KILLED MIKAMI.
NOT THAT AGAIN... THAT THEORY OF YOURS IS NOT "DEFINITE."
OH NO, I'M SURE THAT I'VE GOT THIS RIGHT.
MIKAMI WENT CRAZY IN JAIL TEN DAYS AFTER THAT INCIDENT, AND DIED.

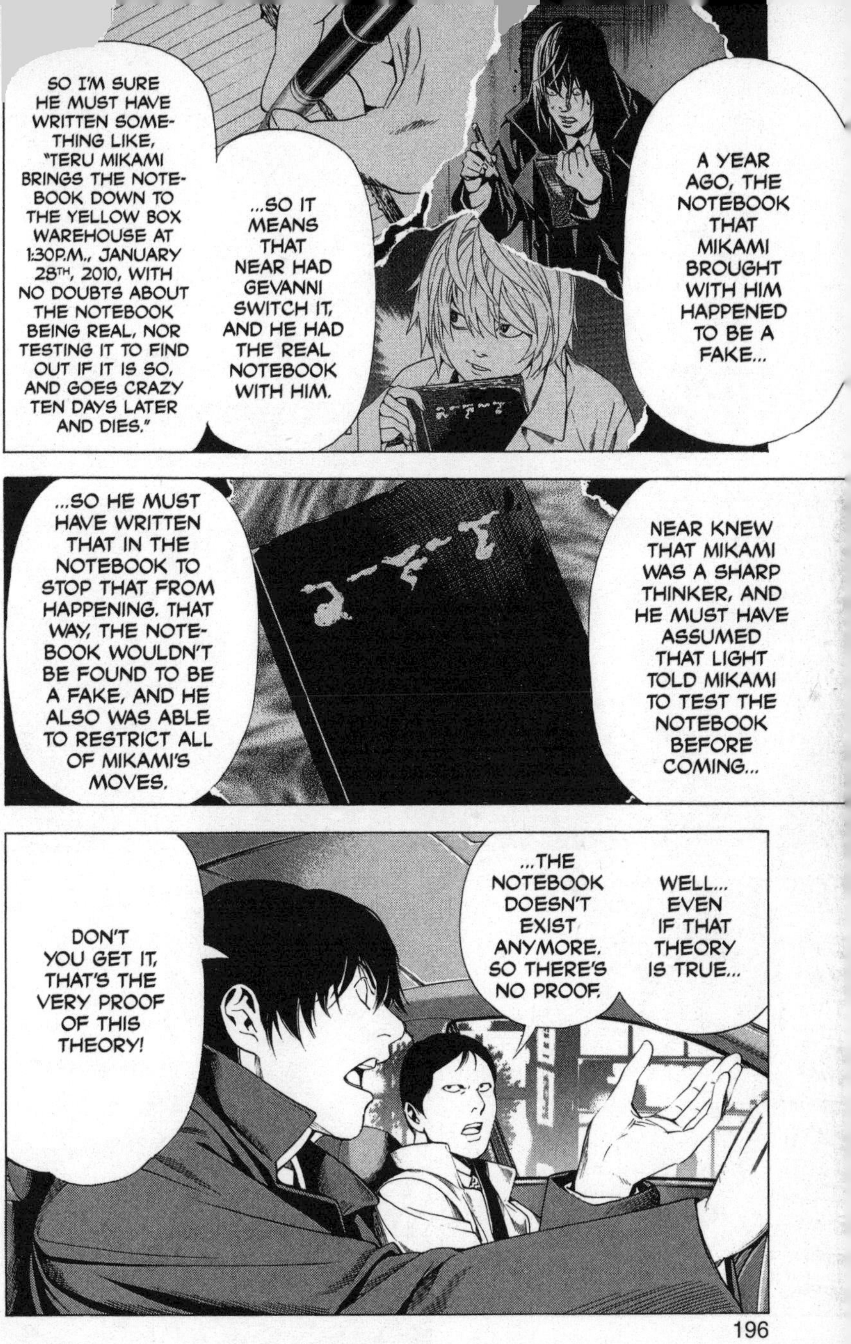
A YEAR AGO, THE NOTEBOOK THAT MIKAMI BROUGHT WITH HIM HAPPENED TO BE A FAKE...
...SO IT MEANS THAT NEAR HAD GEVANNI SWITCH IT, AND HE HAD THE REAL NOTEBOOK WITH HIM.
SO I'M SURE HE MUST HAVE WRITTEN SOME-THING LIKE, "TERU MIKAMI BRINGS THE NOTE-BOOK DOWN TO THE YELLOW BOX WAREHOUSE AT 1:30P.M., JANUARY 28TH, 2010, WITH NO DOUBTS ABOUT THE NOTEBOOK BEING REAL, NOR TESTING IT TO FIND OUT IF IT IS SO, AND GOES CRAZY TEN DAYS LATER AND DIES."
NEAR KNEW THAT MIKAMI WAS A SHARP THINKER, AND HE MUST HAVE ASSUMED THAT LIGHT TOLD MIKAMI TO TEST THE NOTEBOOK BEFORE COMING...
...SO HE MUST HAVE WRITTEN THAT IN THE NOTEBOOK TO STOP THAT FROM HAPPENING. THAT WAY, THE NOTE-BOOK WOULDN'T BE FOUND TO BE A FAKE, AND HE ALSO WAS ABLE TO RESTRICT ALL OF MIKAMI'S MOVES.
WELL... EVEN IF THAT THEORY IS TRUE...
...THE NOTEBOOK DOESN'T EXIST ANYMORE. SO THERE'S NO PROOF.
DON'T YOU GET IT, THAT'S THE VERY PROOF OF THIS THEORY!

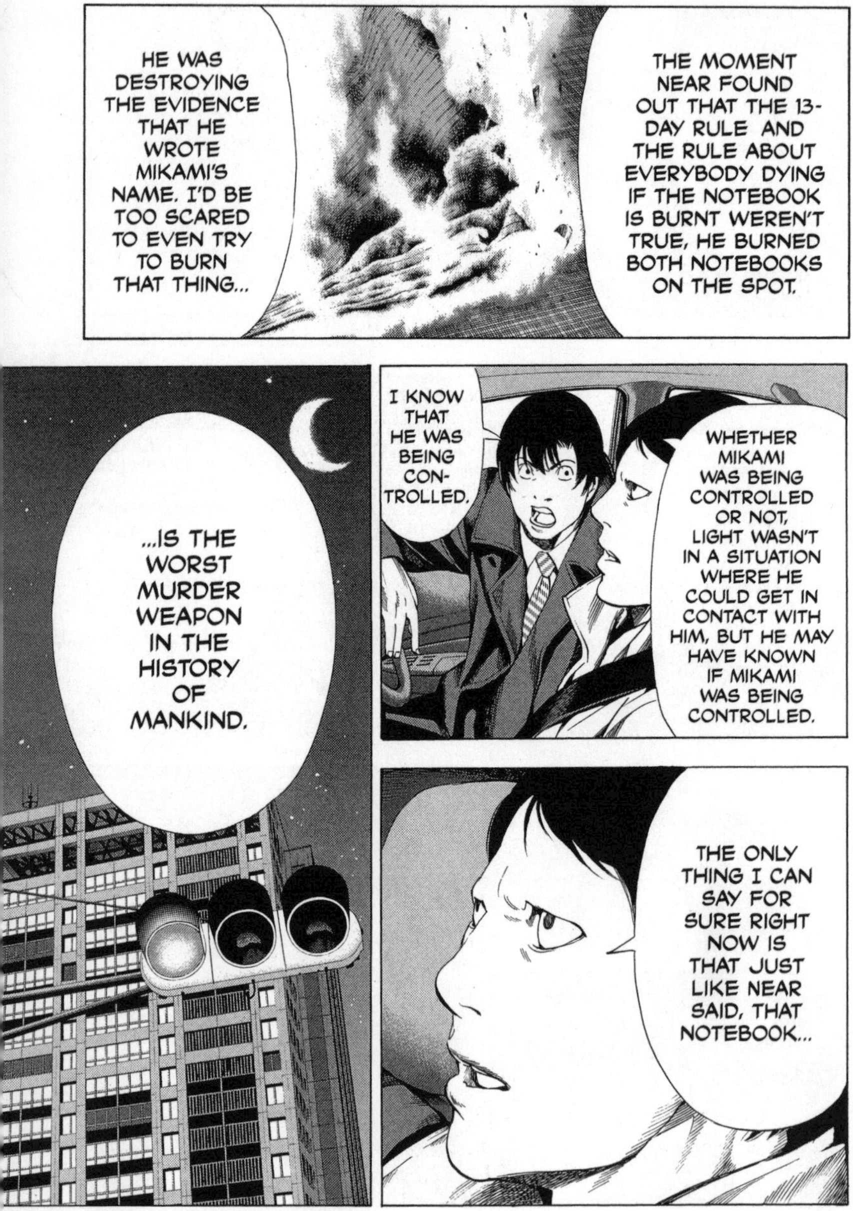
THE MOMENT NEAR FOUND OUT THAT THE 13-DAY RULE AND THE RULE ABOUT EVERYBODY DYING IF THE NOTEBOOK IS BURNT WEREN'T TRUE, HE BURNED BOTH NOTEBOOKS ON THE SPOT.
HE WAS DESTROYING THE EVIDENCE THAT HE WROTE MIKAMI'S NAME. I'D BE TOO SCARED TO EVEN TRY TO BURN THAT THING...
WHETHER MIKAMI WAS BEING CONTROLLED OR NOT, LIGHT WASN'T IN A SITUATION WHERE HE COULD GET IN CONTACT WITH HIM, BUT HE MAY HAVE KNOWN IF MIKAMI WAS BEING CONTROLLED.
I KNOW THAT HE WAS BEING CON-TROLLED.
THE ONLY THING I CAN SAY FOR SURE RIGHT NOW IS THAT JUST LIKE NEAR SAID, THAT NOTEBOOK...
...IS THE WORST MURDER WEAPON IN THE HISTORY OF MANKIND.

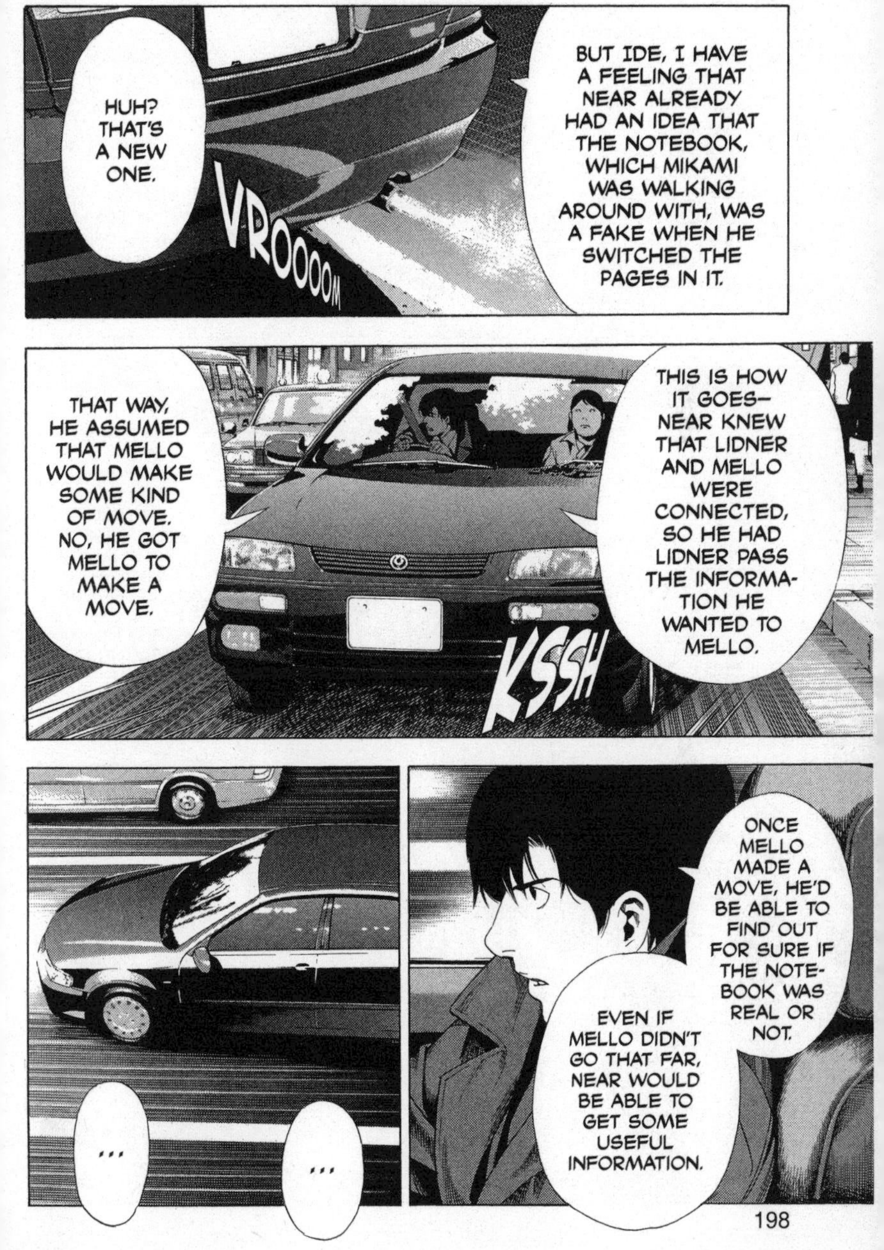
BUT IDE, I HAVE A FEELING THAT NEAR ALREADY HAD AN IDEA THAT THE NOTEBOOK, WHICH MIKAMI WAS WALKING AROUND WITH, WAS A FAKE WHEN HE SWITCHED THE PAGES IN IT.
HUH? THAT'S A NEW ONE.
VROOOOM
THIS IS HOW IT GOES—NEAR KNEW THAT LIDNER AND MELLO WERE CONNECTED, SO HE HAD LIDNER PASS THE INFORMATION HE WANTED TO MELLO.
THAT WAY, HE ASSUMED THAT MELLO WOULD MAKE SOME KIND OF MOVE. NO, HE GOT MELLO TO MAKE A MOVE.
KSSH
ONCE MELLO MADE A MOVE, HE'D BE ABLE TO FIND OUT FOR SURE IF THE NOTEBOOK WAS REAL OR NOT.
EVEN IF MELLO DIDN'T GO THAT FAR, NEAR WOULD BE ABLE TO GET SOME USEFUL INFORMATION.
...
...

READ THIS WAY

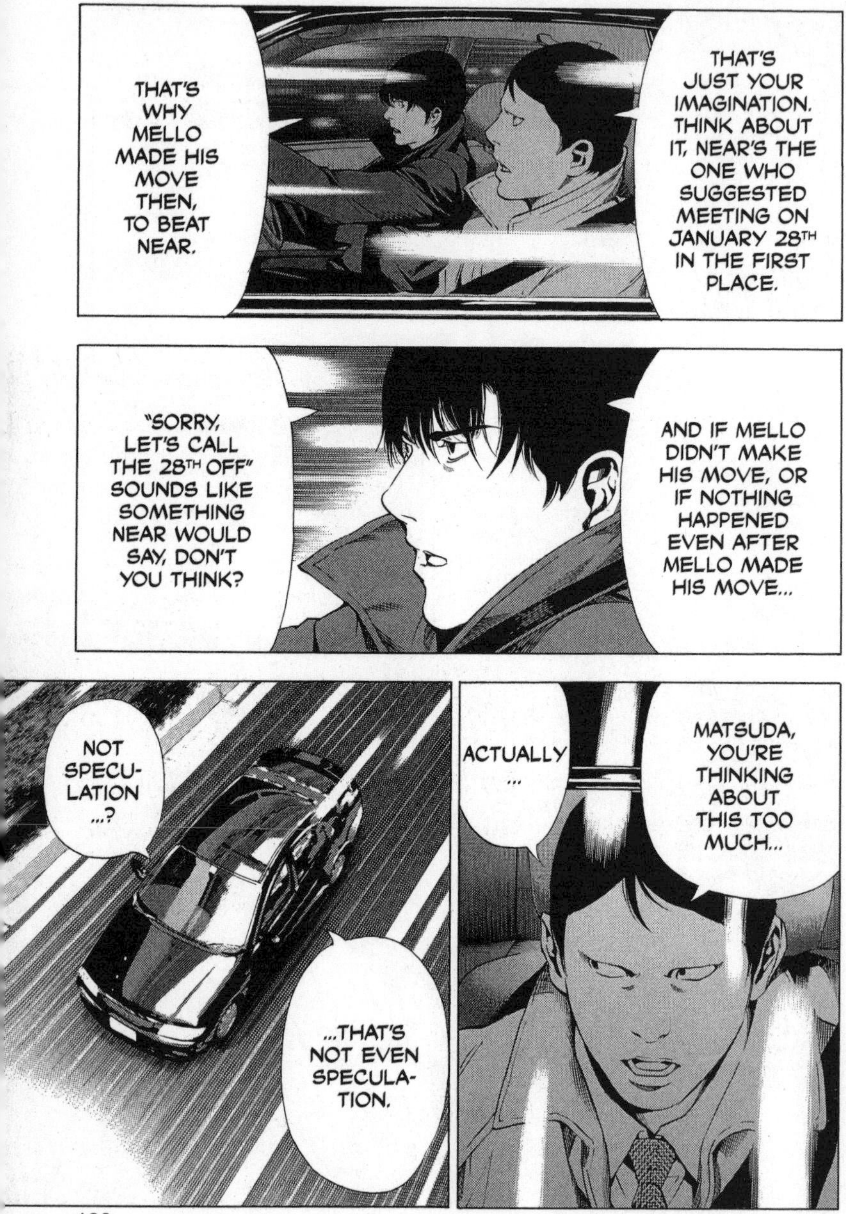
THAT'S JUST YOUR IMAGINATION. THINK ABOUT IT, NEAR'S THE ONE WHO SUGGESTED MEETING ON JANUARY 28TH IN THE FIRST PLACE.
THAT'S WHY MELLO MADE HIS MOVE THEN, TO BEAT NEAR.
AND IF MELLO DIDN'T MAKE HIS MOVE, OR IF NOTHING HAPPENED EVEN AFTER MELLO MADE HIS MOVE...
"SORRY, LET'S CALL THE 28TH OFF" SOUNDS LIKE SOMETHING NEAR WOULD SAY, DON'T YOU THINK?
MATSUDA, YOU'RE THINKING ABOUT THIS TOO MUCH...
ACTUALLY ...
NOT SPECULATION ...?
...THAT'S NOT EVEN SPECULATION.

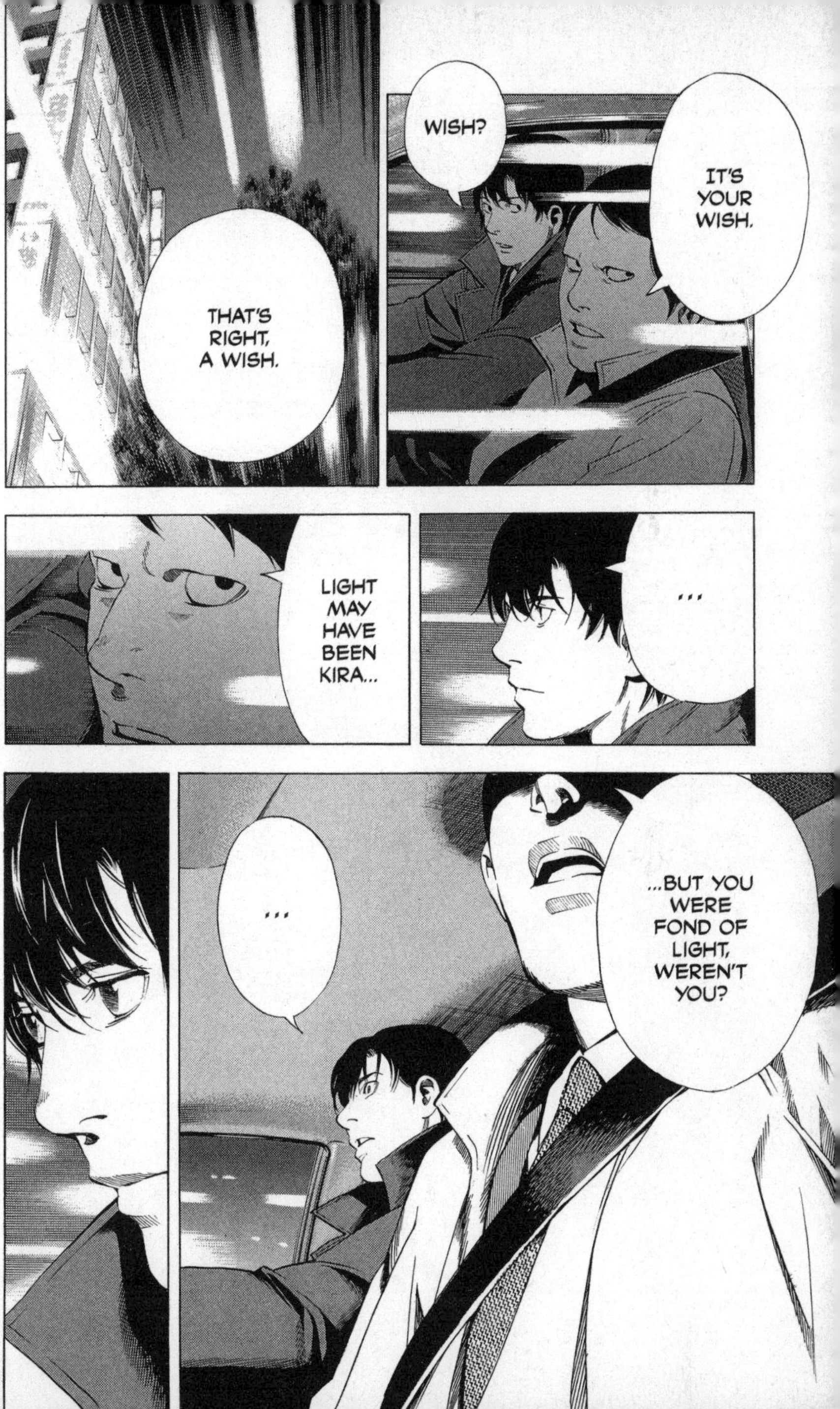
IT'S YOUR WISH.
WISH?
THAT'S RIGHT, A WISH.
...
LIGHT MAY HAVE BEEN KIRA...
...BUT YOU WERE FOND OF LIGHT, WEREN'T YOU?
...

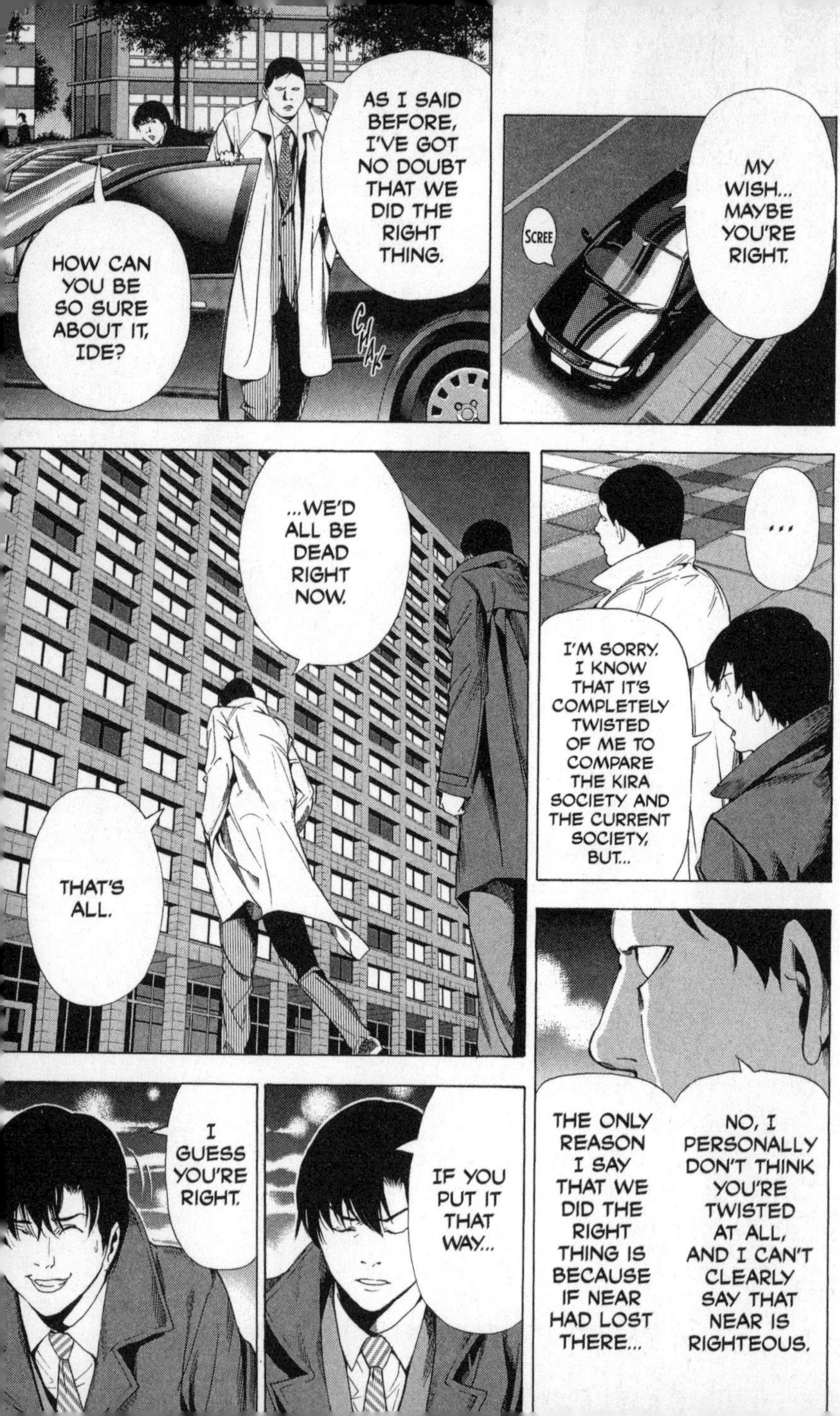
MY WISH... MAYBE YOU'RE RIGHT.
SCREE
AS I SAID BEFORE, I'VE GOT NO DOUBT THAT WE DID THE RIGHT THING.
HOW CAN YOU BE SO SURE ABOUT IT, IDE?
CHAK
...
I'M SORRY. I KNOW THAT IT'S COMPLETELY TWISTED OF ME TO COMPARE THE KIRA SOCIETY AND THE CURRENT SOCIETY, BUT...
NO, I PERSONALLY DON'T THINK YOU'RE TWISTED AT ALL, AND I CAN'T CLEARLY SAY THAT NEAR IS RIGHTEOUS.
THE ONLY REASON I SAY THAT WE DID THE RIGHT THING IS BECAUSE IF NEAR HAD LOST THERE...
...WE'D ALL BE DEAD RIGHT NOW.
THAT'S ALL.
IF YOU PUT IT THAT WAY...
I GUESS YOU'RE RIGHT.

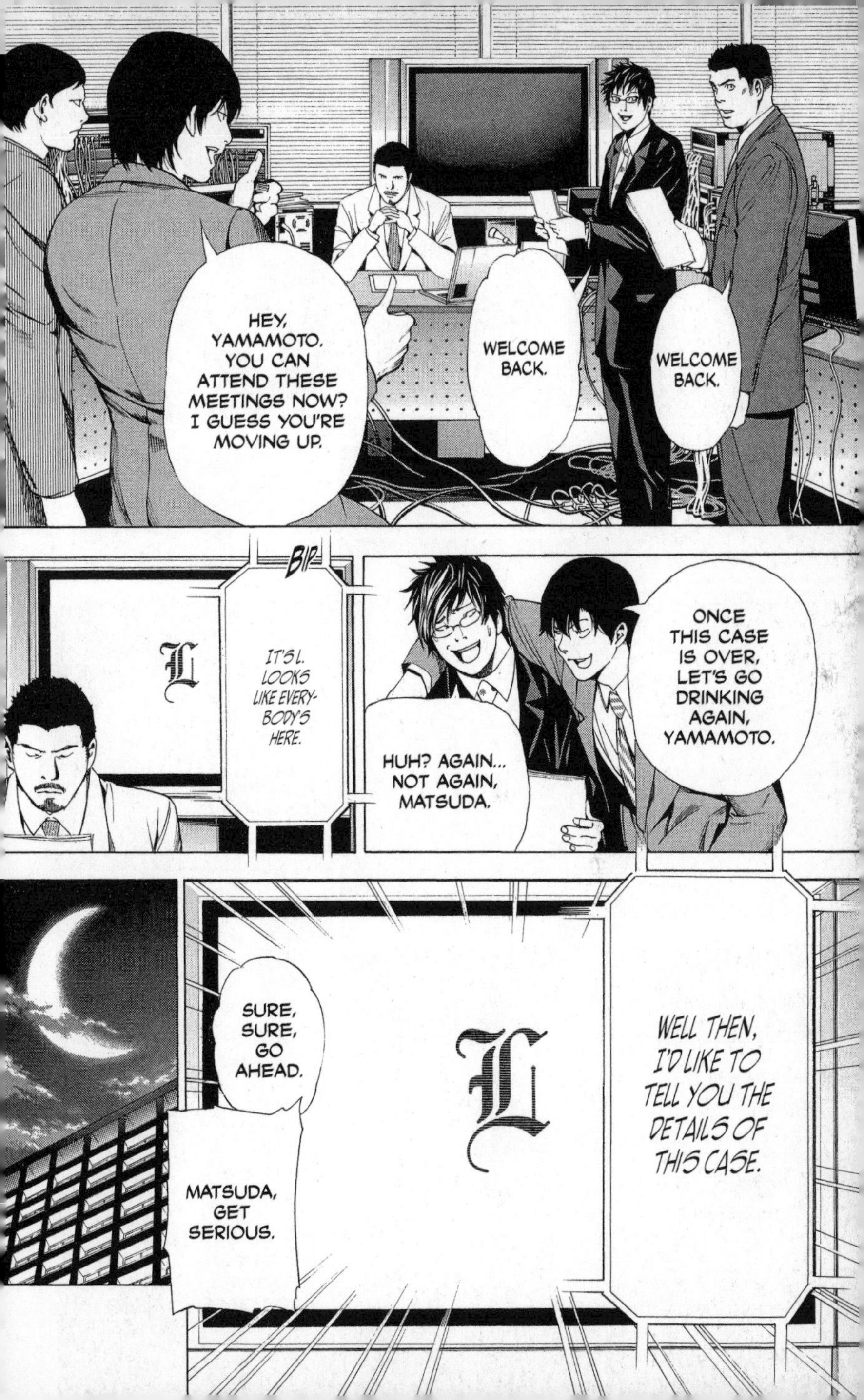
WELCOME BACK.
WELCOME BACK.
HEY, YAMAMOTO. YOU CAN ATTEND THESE MEETINGS NOW? I GUESS YOU'RE MOVING UP.
ONCE THIS CASE IS OVER, LET'S GO DRINKING AGAIN, YAMAMOTO.
HUH? AGAIN... NOT AGAIN, MATSUDA.
BIP
IT'S L. LOOKS LIKE EVERY-BODY'S HERE.
L
WELL THEN, I'D LIKE TO TELL YOU THE DETAILS OF THIS CASE.
L
SURE, SURE, GO AHEAD.
MATSUDA, GET SERIOUS.

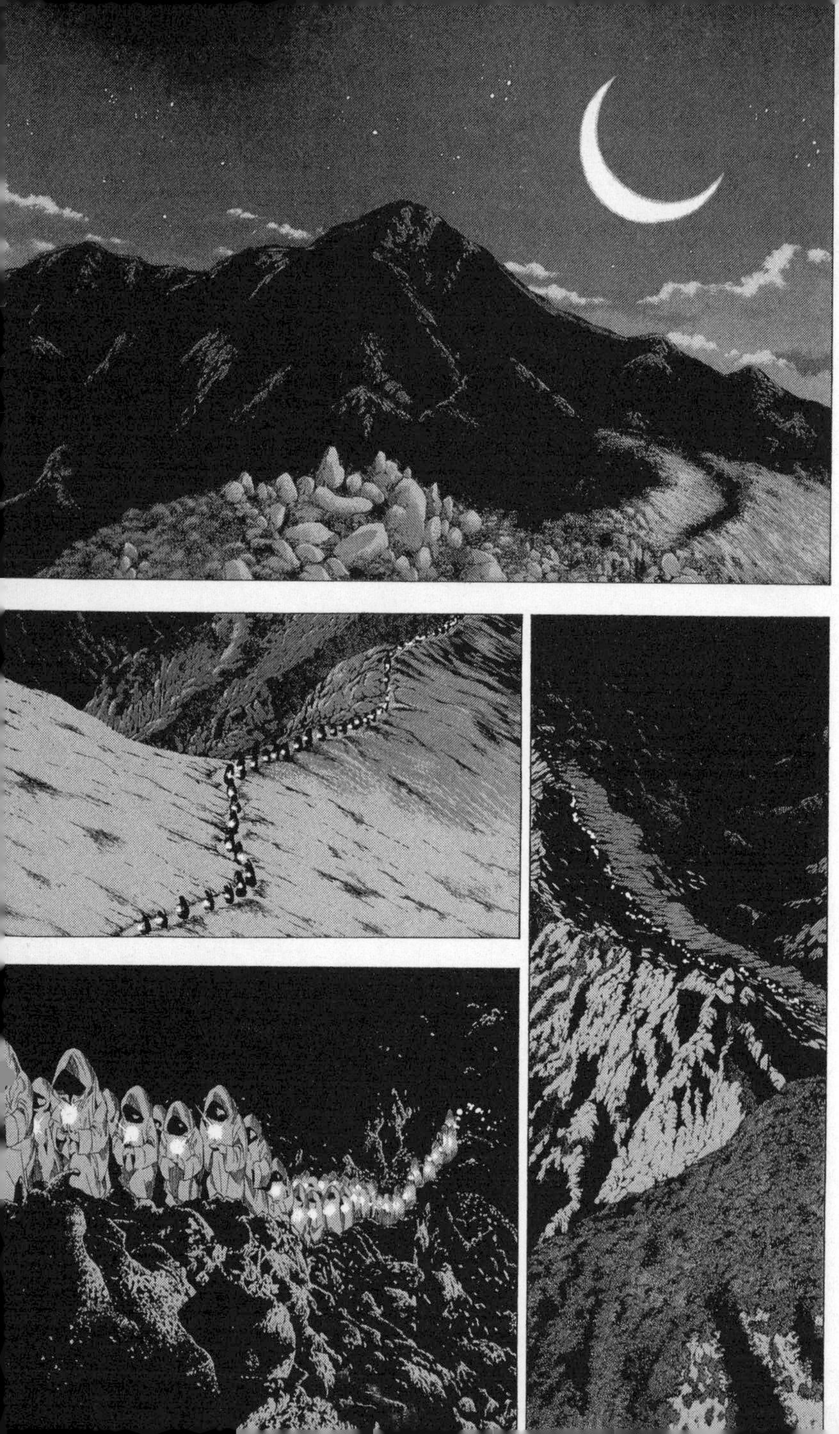

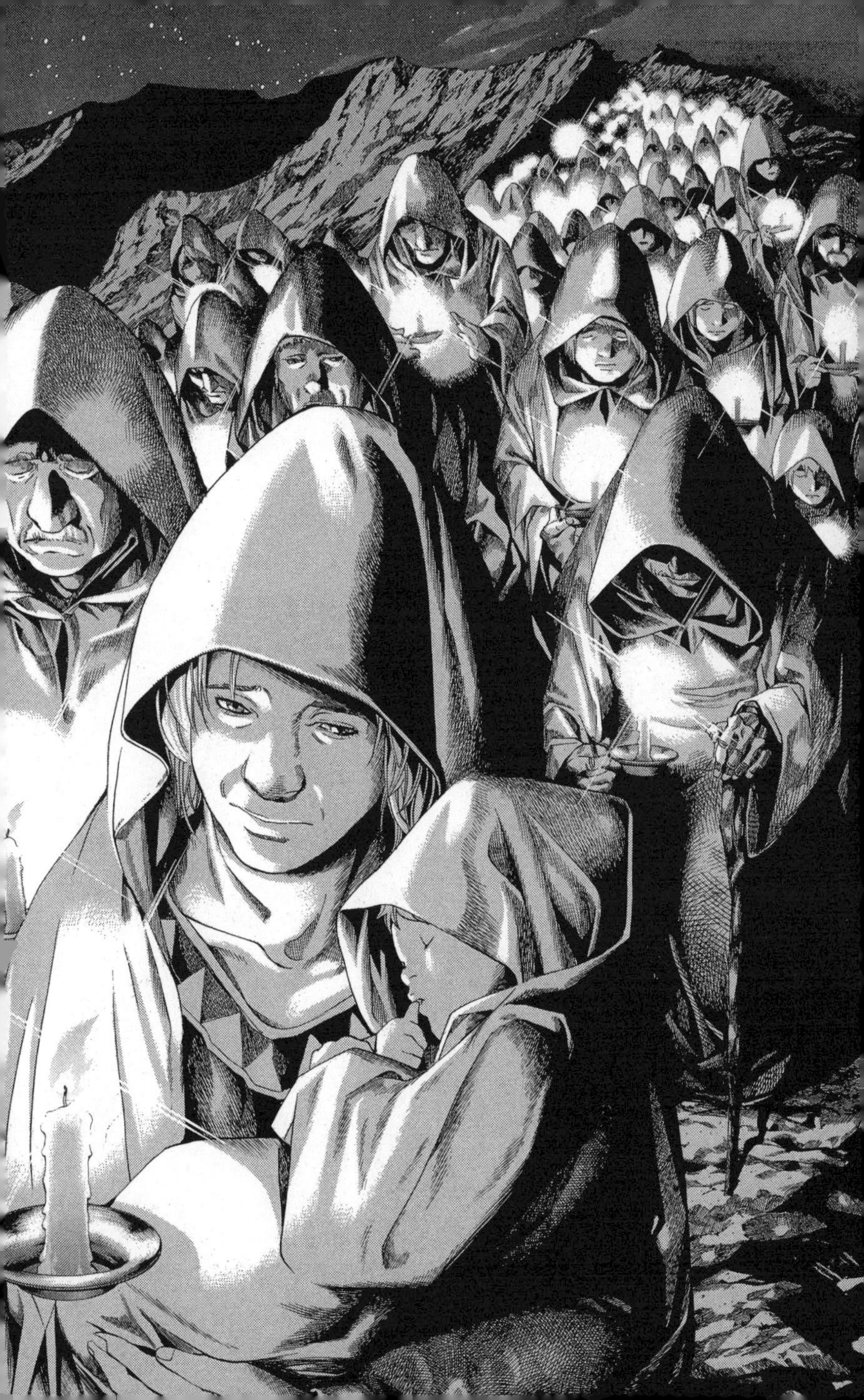

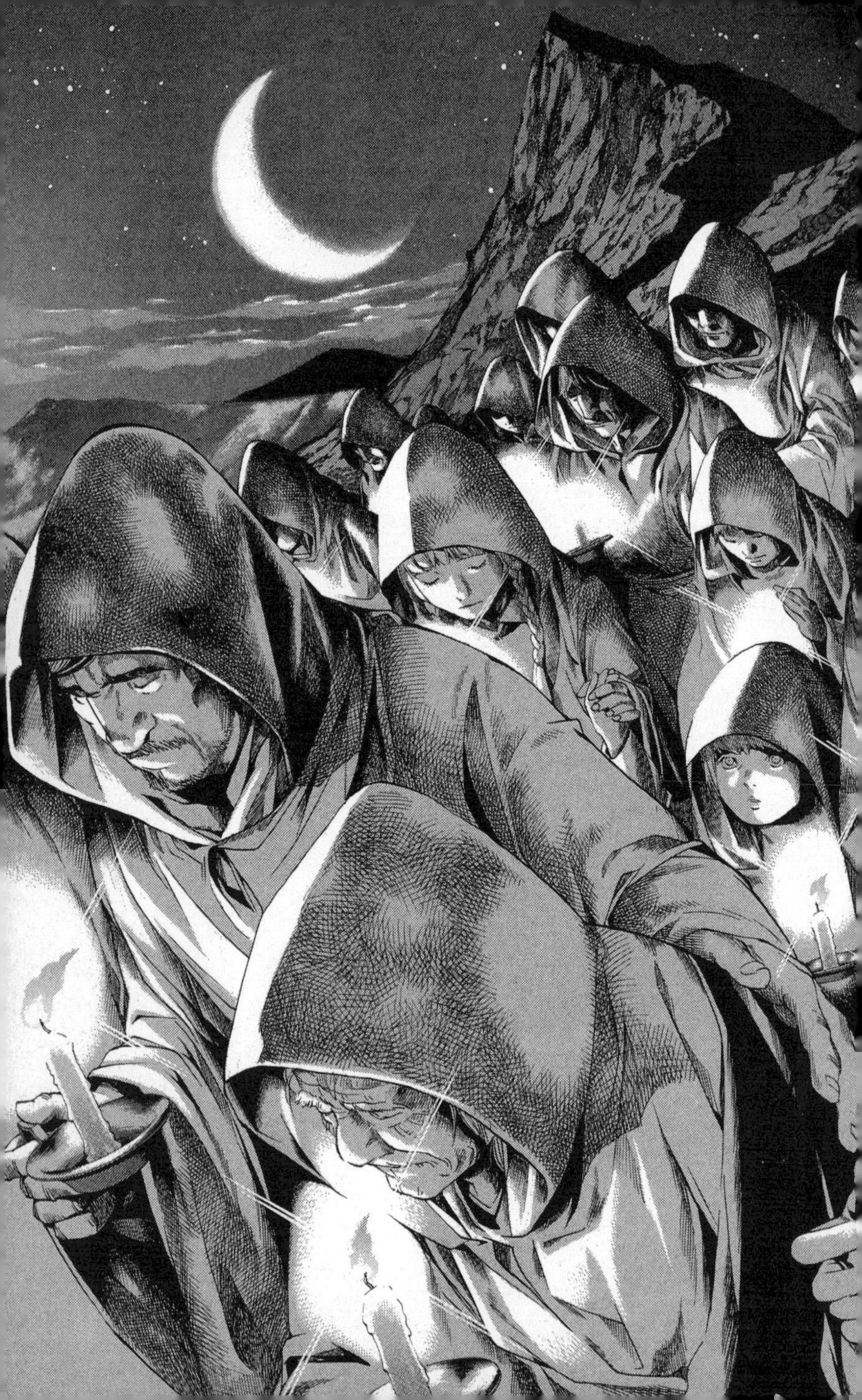

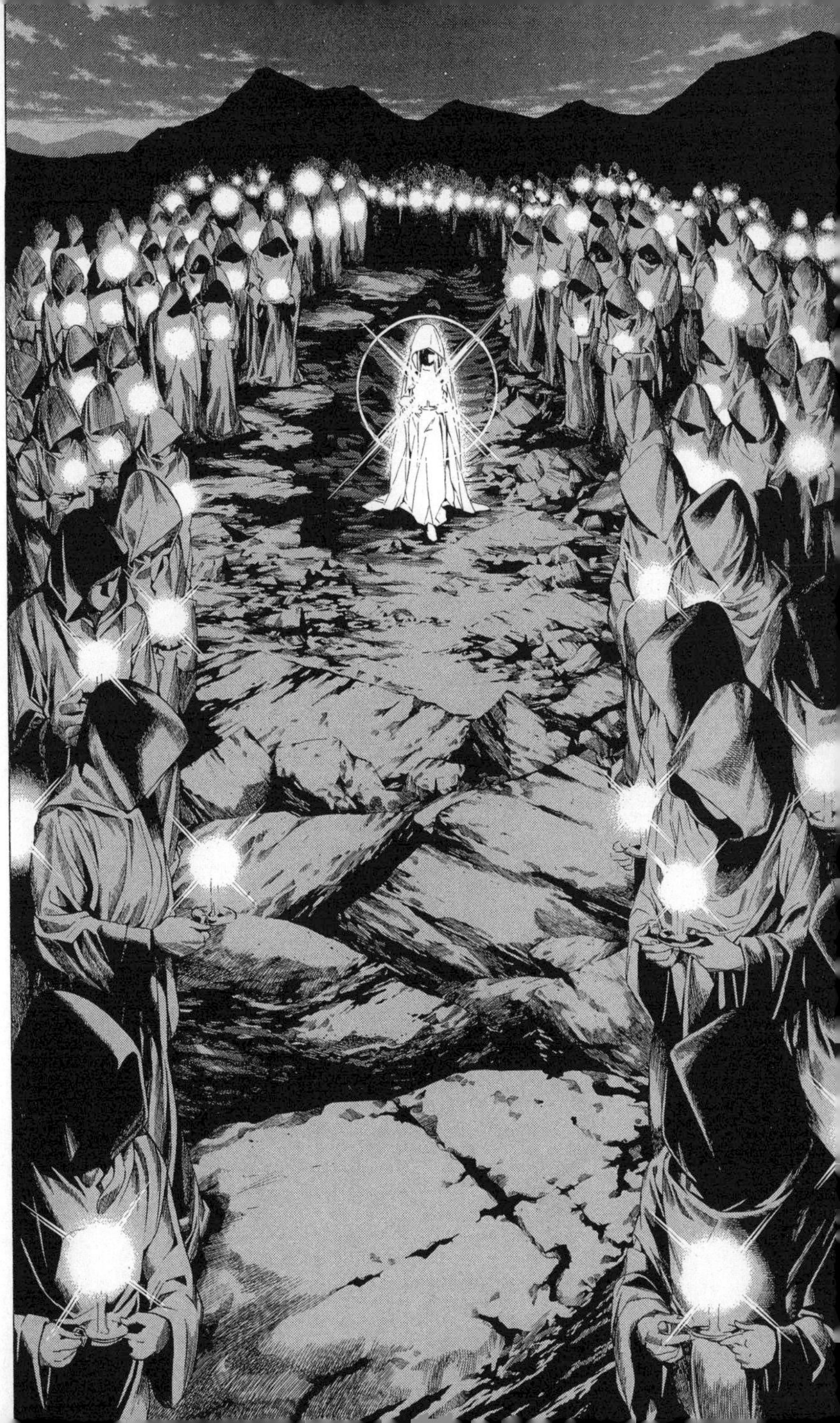

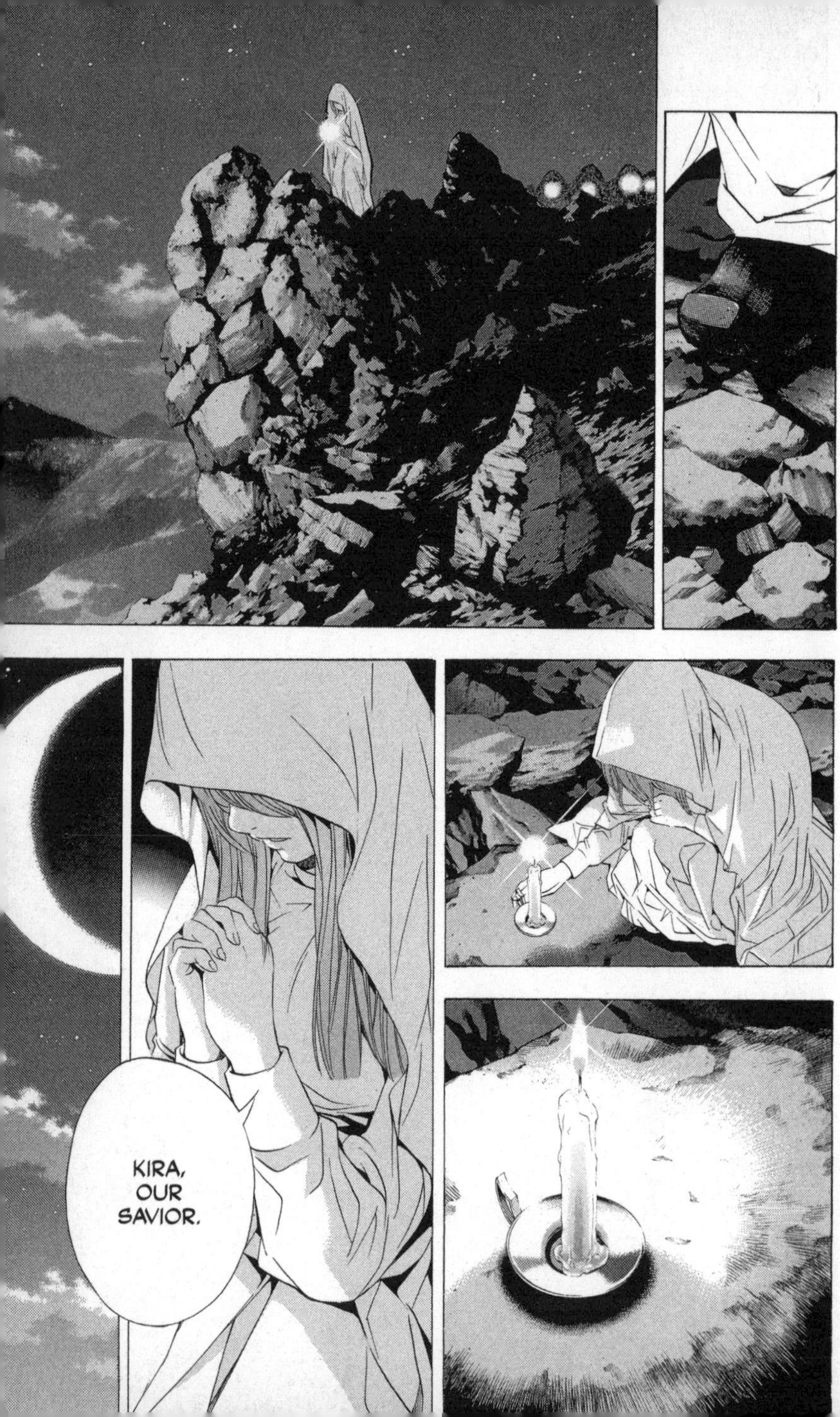
KIRA, OUR SAVIOR.

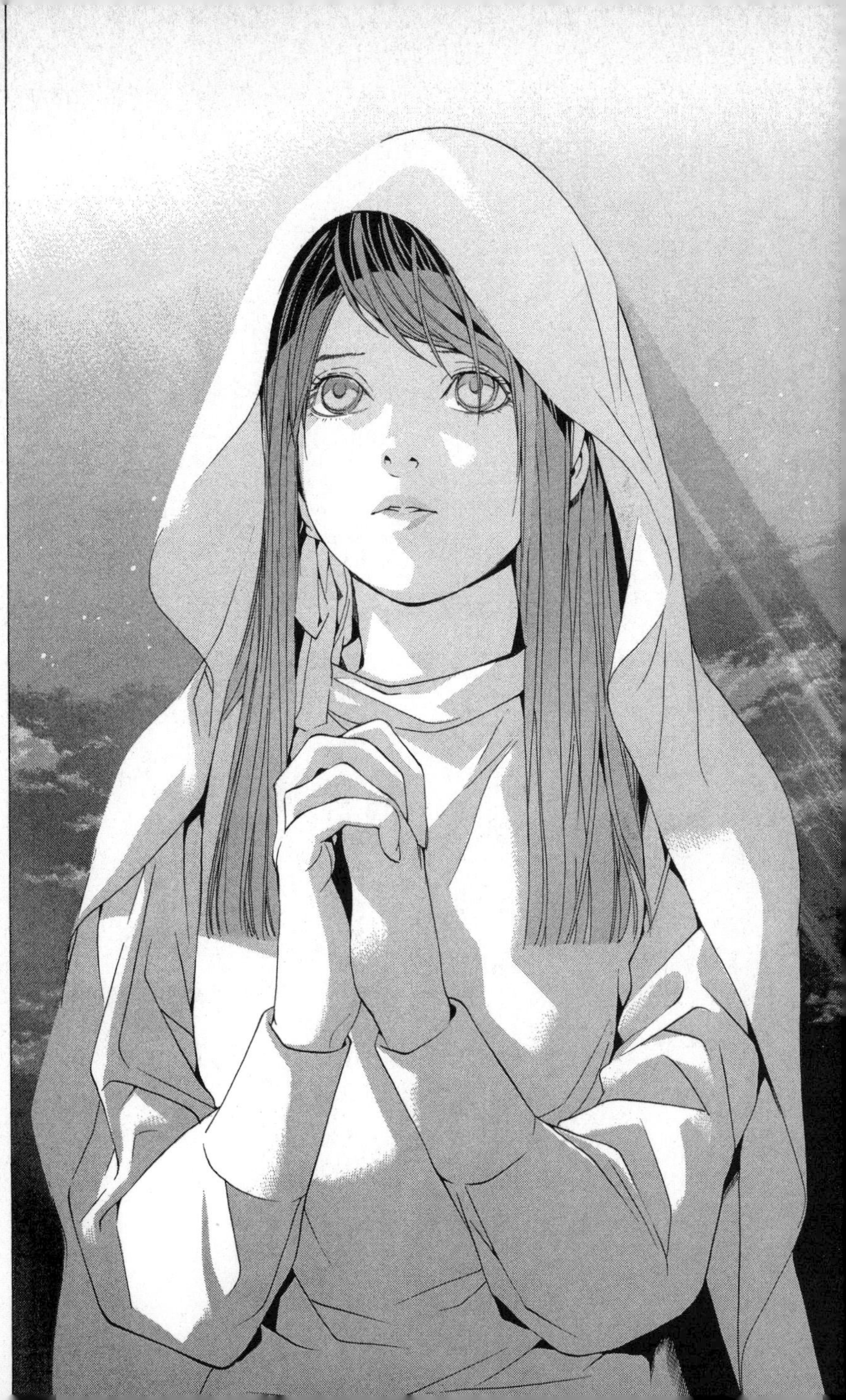

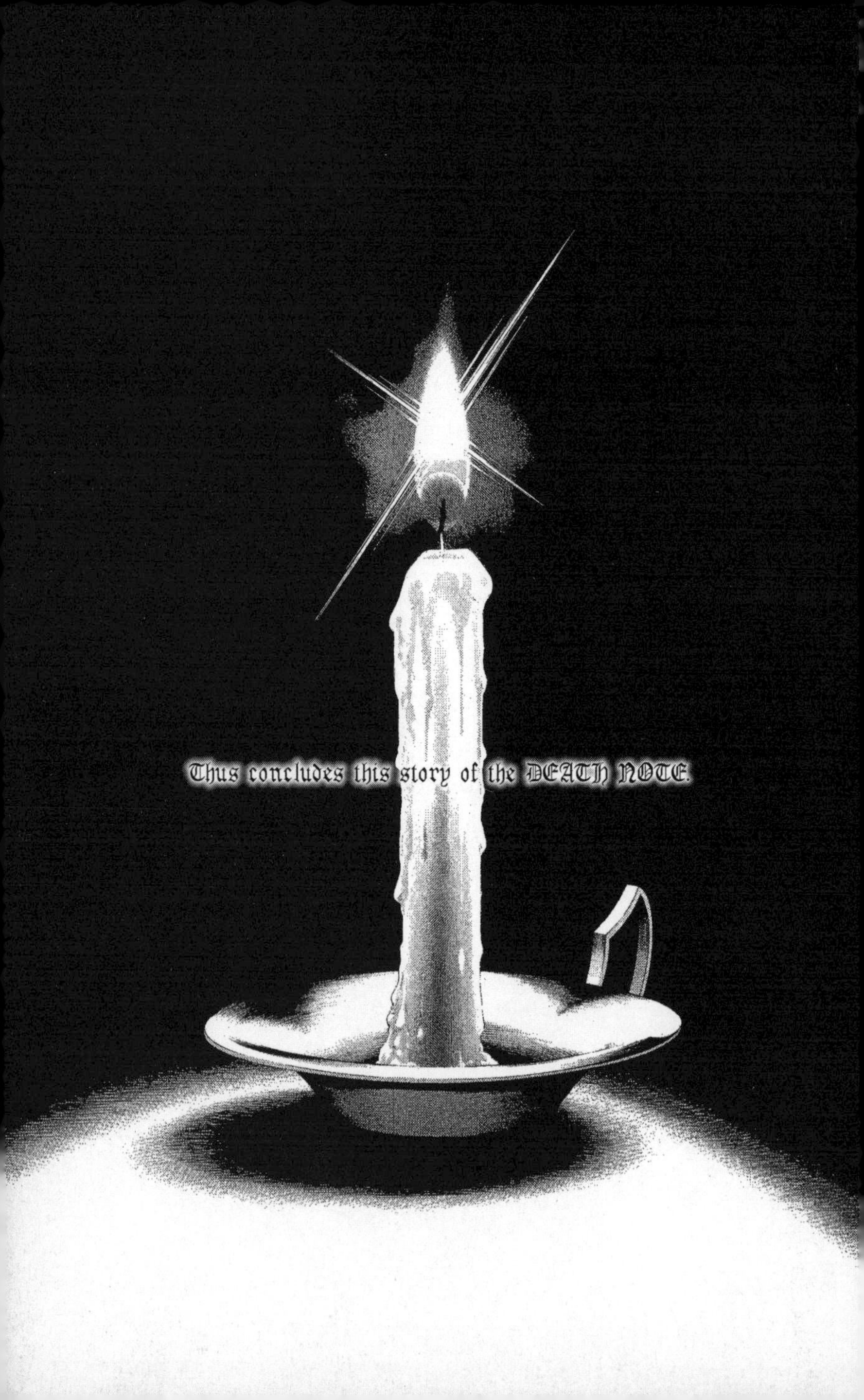
Thus concludes this story of the DEATH NOTE.

▣ Once dead, they can never come back to life.

死んだ者は、生き返らない。

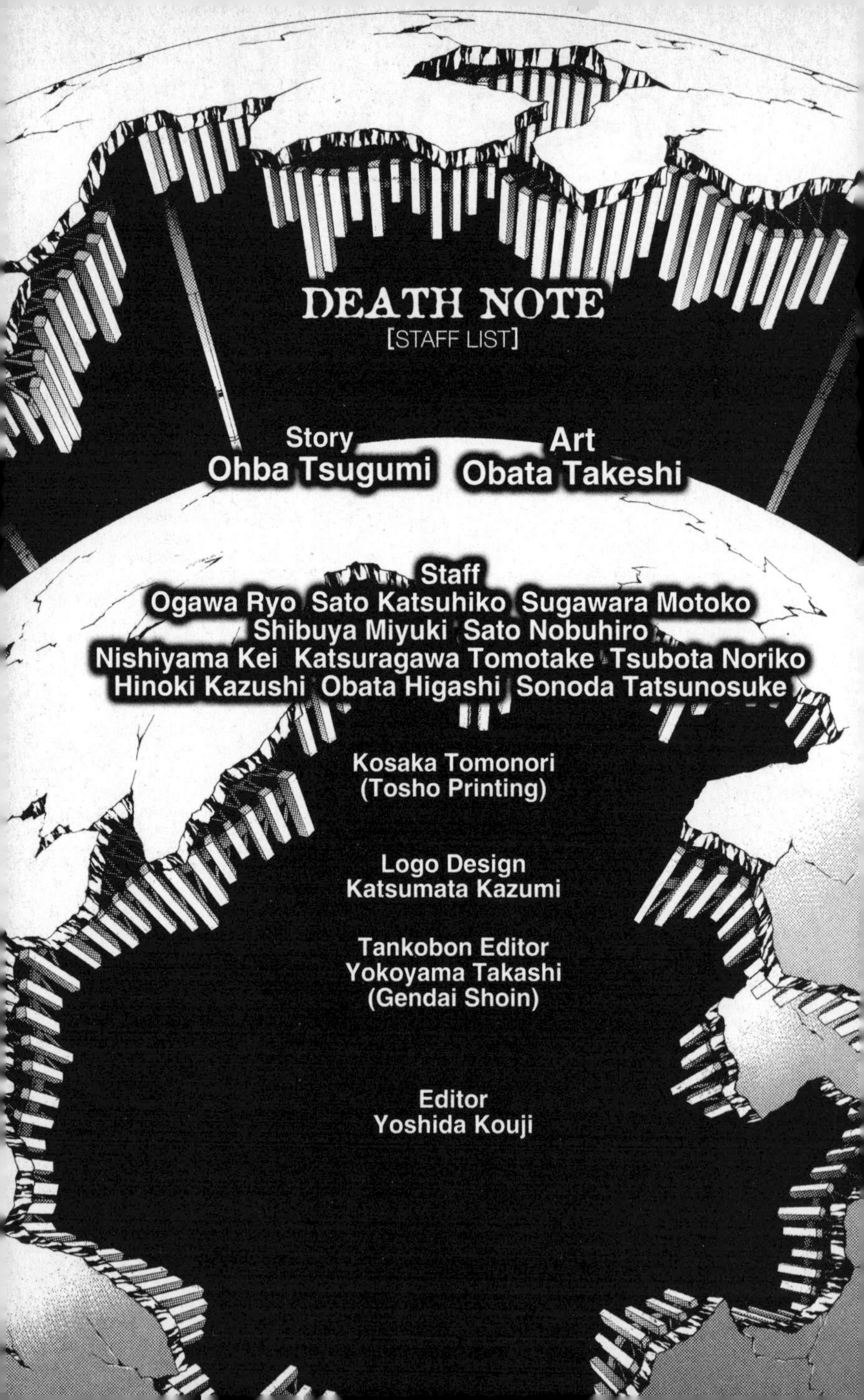

DEATH NOTE

[STAFF LIST]

Story
Ohba Tsugumi

Art
Obata Takeshi

Staff
Ogawa Ryo Sato Katsuhiko Sugawara Motoko
Shibuya Miyuki Sato Nobuhiro
Nishiyama Kei Katsuragawa Tomotake Tsubota Noriko
Hinoki Kazushi Obata Higashi Sonoda Tatsunosuke

Kosaka Tomonori
(Tosho Printing)

Logo Design
Katsumata Kazumi

Tankobon Editor
Yokoyama Takashi
(Gendai Shoin)

Editor
Yoshida Kouji

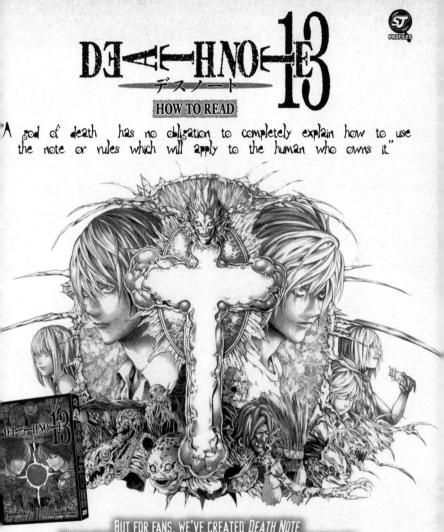

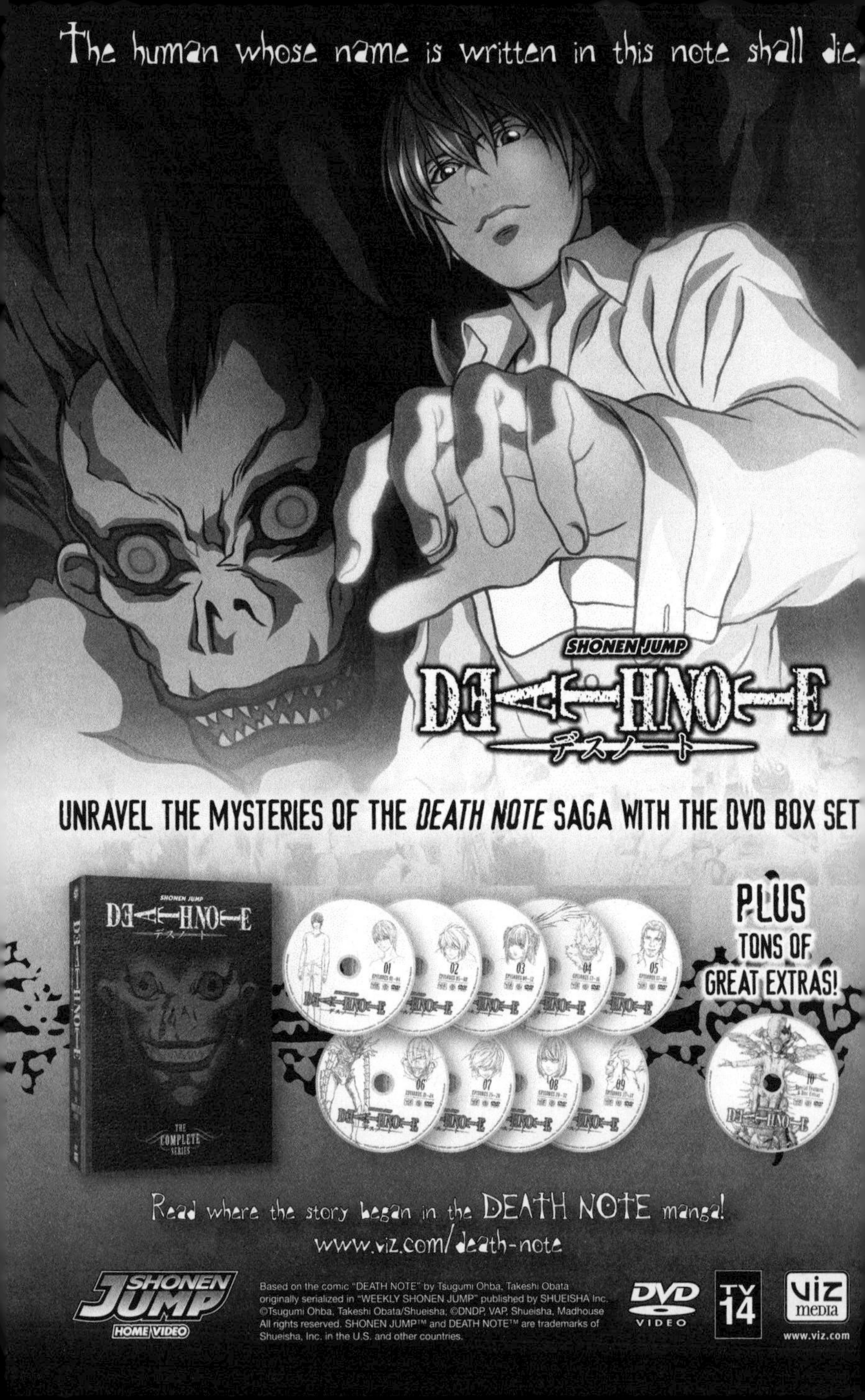
The human whose name is written in this note shall die.
SHONEN JUMP
DEATH NOTE
デスノート
UNRAVEL THE MYSTERIES OF THE DEATH NOTE SAGA WITH THE DVD BOX SET
SHONEN JUMP
DEATH NOTE
デスノート
THE COMPLETE SERIES
PLUS
TONS OF
GREAT EXTRAS!
Read where the story began in the DEATH NOTE manga!
www.viz.com/death-note
SHONEN JUMP HOME VIDEO
Based on the comic "DEATH NOTE" by Tsugumi Ohba, Takeshi Obata
originally serialized in "WEEKLY SHONEN JUMP" published by SHUEISHA Inc.
©Tsugumi Ohba, Takeshi Obata/Shueisha, ©DNDP, VAP, Shueisha, Madhouse
All rights reserved. SHONEN JUMP™ and DEATH NOTE™ are trademarks of
Shueisha, Inc. in the U.S. and other countries.
DVD VIDEO
TV 14
VIZ media
www.viz.com

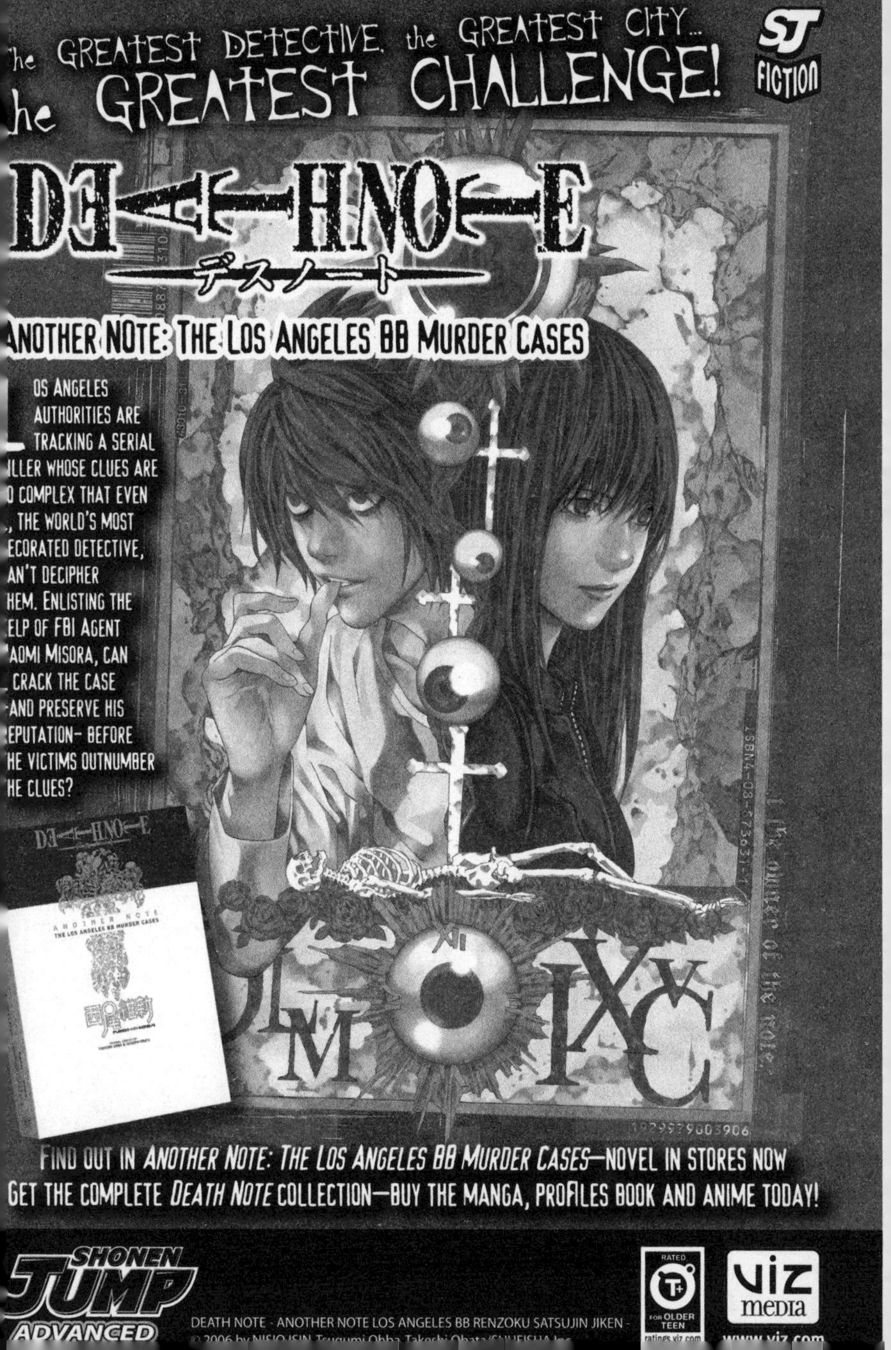
he GREATEST DETECTIVE, the GREATEST CITY...
he GREATEST CHALLENGE!
SJ FICTION
DEATH NOTE
デスノート
ANOTHER NOTE: THE LOS ANGELES BB MURDER CASES
OS ANGELES AUTHORITIES ARE TRACKING A SERIAL ILLER WHOSE CLUES ARE O COMPLEX THAT EVEN , THE WORLD'S MOST ECORATED DETECTIVE, AN'T DECIPHER HEM. ENLISTING THE ELP OF FBI AGENT AOMI MISORA, CAN CRACK THE CASE AND PRESERVE HIS EPUTATION- BEFORE HE VICTIMS OUTNUMBER HE CLUES?
ANOTHER NOTE
THE LOS ANGELES BB MURDER CASES
FIND OUT IN ANOTHER NOTE: THE LOS ANGELES BB MURDER CASES—NOVEL IN STORES NOW
GET THE COMPLETE DEATH NOTE COLLECTION—BUY THE MANGA, PROFILES BOOK AND ANIME TODAY!
SHONEN JUMP ADVANCED
DEATH NOTE - ANOTHER NOTE LOS ANGELES BB RENZOKU SATSUJIN JIKEN -
© 2006 by NISIO ISIN, Tsugumi Ohba, Takeshi Obata/SHUEISHA Inc.
RATED T+ FOR OLDER TEEN
ratings.viz.com
VIZ media
www.viz.com

The World's Greatest Manga
Now available on your iPad

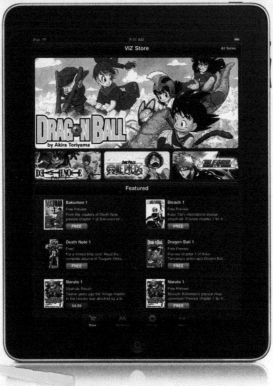

Full of FREE previews and tons of new manga for you to explore

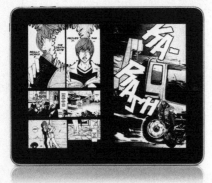

From legendary manga like *Dragon Ball* to *Bakuman。* the newest series from the creators of *Death Note*, the best manga in the world is now available on the iPad through the official VIZ Manga app.

- **Free App**
- **New content weekly**
- **Free chapter 1 previews**

You're Reading in the Wrong Direction!!

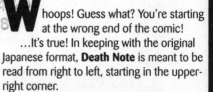

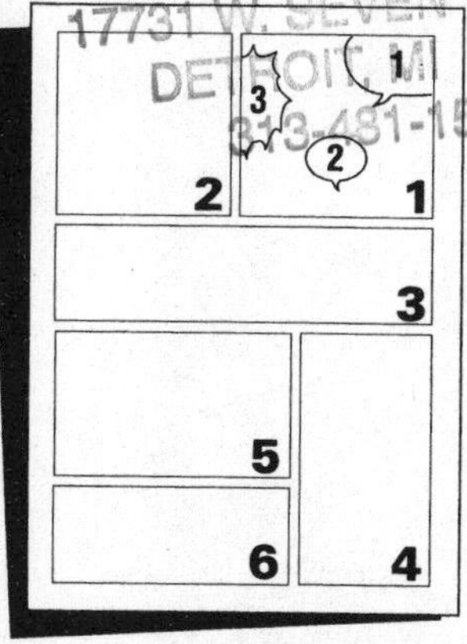

Whoops! Guess what? You're starting at the wrong end of the comic!

…It's true! In keeping with the original Japanese format, **Death Note** is meant to be read from right to left, starting in the upper-right corner.

Unlike English, which is read from left to right, Japanese is read from right to left, meaning that action, sound effects and word-balloon order are completely reversed… something which can make readers unfamiliar with Japanese feel pretty backwards themselves. For this reason, manga or Japanese comics published in the U.S. in English have sometimes been published "flopped"—that is, printed in exact reverse order, as though seen from the other side of a mirror.

By flopping pages, U.S. publishers can avoid confusing readers, but the compromise is not without its downside. For one thing, a character in a flopped manga series who once wore in the original Japanese version a T-shirt emblazoned with "M A Y" (as in "the merry month of") now wears one which reads "Y A M"! Additionally, many manga creators in Japan are themselves unhappy with the process, as some feel the mirror-imaging of their art alters their original intentions.

We are proud to bring you Tsugumi Ohba & Takeshi Obata's **Death Note** in the original unflopped format. For now, though, turn to the other side of the book and let the quest begin…!

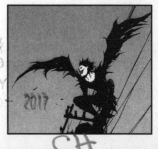

–Editor

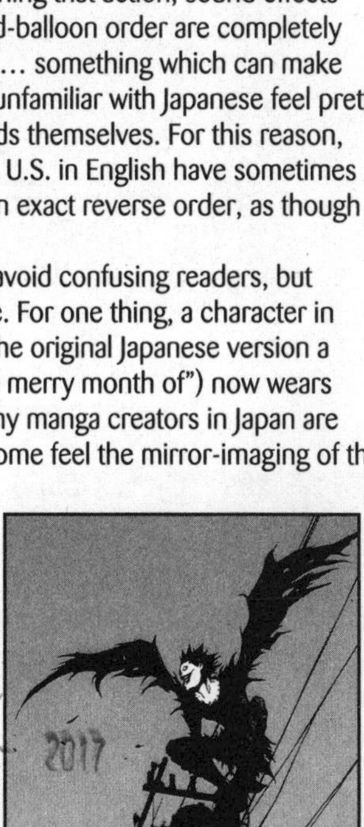